CHINA
BRIEFING
2000

Society

www.asiasociety.org

The Asia Society is a nonprofit, nonpartisan public education organization dedicated to increasing American understanding of Asia and broadening the dialogue between Americans and Asians. Through its programs in policy and business, the fine and performing arts, and elementary and secondary education, the Society reaches audiences across the United States and works closely with colleagues in Asia.

The views expressed in this publication are those of the individual contributors.

CHINA BRIEFING
2000

The Continuing Transformation

Tyrene White
Editor

Published in cooperation with the Asia Society
Mai Shaikhanuar-Cota, Series Editor

An East Gate Book

M.E.Sharpe
Armonk, New York
London, England

An East Gate Book

Library of Congress ISSN: 0740-8005
ISBN 0-7656-0612-7 (c)
ISBN 0-7656-0613-5 (p)

BM (c)   10   9   8   7   6   5   4   3   2
BM (p)   10   9   8   7   6   5   4   3   2

Contents

Preface

The twentieth century opened and closed with Chinese attacks on U.S. diplomatic offices in Beijing. These oddly symmetrical events serve as unsettling bookends to a century during which China has literally risen up and become engaged in the international community—and how the world, and particularly the United States, has responded to that engagement. At the start of the century China was a reluctant international actor. By the end of the century, China is a force with which the world must reckon.

This volume of *China Briefing 2000: The Continuing Transformation* examines China at the turn of the twentieth century. The topics discussed are extensive and cover the period 1997–99, coming right to the cusp of the twenty-first century. Many of the chapters were completed over the summer of 1999 and anticipate developments in the Sino-American relationship, particularly the agreement between the United States and China on terms for China's entry into the World Trade Organization. Invariably the significance of this event is hard to measure without the benefit of time. Throughout the book, the authors provide valuable insights into understanding China at the end of this century. They provide cogent and penetrating explorations of China's economy, political environment, growing consumer culture, society, international relations, and gender relations. As a result, the reader will be rewarded with new and personal insights into many of the topics addressed in this book.

Our deepest appreciation goes to Tyrene White, editor of this volume. She conceived of the general outline of the book and selected chapter authors. Each chapter author is to be commended for accepting the challenge of drawing conclusions about the last century of Chinese history and for attempting to peer into the future. We appreciate the efforts of the editor and the authors who worked hard to complete the volume in the very short time they were given to do so. As always, the content of the chapters and views expressed therein are the responsibility of the authors and do not necessarily reflect the view of the Asia Society.

The Society also thanks Patricia Farr, Peter Smith, and Rayne Madison who assisted in the production of this book. We also thank our colleagues at M.E. Sharpe, notably Doug Merwin, Diana McDermott, Angela Piliouras, and Patricia Loo, who continue to support our country briefing series. At the Society we would like to thank Robert W. Radtke and Michelle Caswell for their assistance, and Mai Shaikhanuar-Cota, who worked tirelessly to ensure continuity between this edition of *China Briefing* and those that have come before.

Nicholas Platt
President
Asia Society

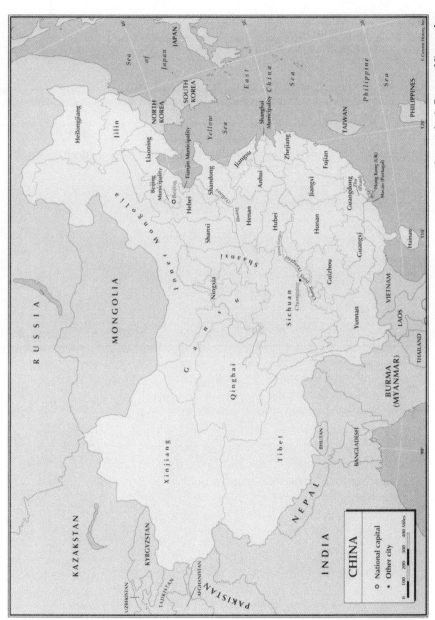

CHINA BRIEFING
2000

Introduction

Tyrene White

In the autumn of 1999, as much of the world was gearing up for grand celebrations to mark the end of the century and the millennium, in China the party was over. It had been held on October 1, in honor of the fiftieth anniversary of the founding of the People's Republic. On that date, and following the example of Mao Zedong exactly fifty years earlier, Chinese Communist Party (CCP) general secretary Jiang Zemin stood in front of the Gate of Heavenly Peace in Tiananmen Square to deliver the national address. On this historic occasion, Jiang reveled in all the traditional symbols of power and authority, even donning a Mao-style tunic as he and other leaders presided over the spectacular military parade down Chang'an Avenue.

This meticulously orchestrated and choreographed anniversary event, like all such anniversary celebrations, sought to recapture the memory of a historic moment (in this case, one that was still a living memory for many Chinese) and draw political strength from it. More important, however, it also sought to emphasize the accomplishments of the moment and the prospects for the future. The attempt to accomplish both of these tasks simultaneously laid bare the immense contradictions that define China today. For example, the anniversary celebration was organized like a Mao-era mass campaign, with CCP mobilization meetings to coordinate, plan, and execute every aspect of the celebration. Yet this campaign's organizers had faxes, cellular phones, pagers, and e-mail to assist their coordination efforts, which would have been unthinkable even fifteen years ago. Similarly, no campaign would be complete without its official slogans, and this time the CCP offered a list of fifty official slogans, one for each year of the People's Republic. Unlike in the past, however, the admonition to "rely on the working class wholeheartedly" came in only at number nineteen on the list, after "rule the country by law" (number fifteen) and before "improve socialist culture and ethics" (number twenty-five). And no parade would be complete without a contingent of old revolutionaries, but in a surreal twist of history, this time around they were joined by brigades of fashion models and private entrepreneurs.[1]

It is never easy turning fifty, of course, and it is especially hard for revolutions to turn fifty. The youthful revolutionary fervor is gone, the adolescent turbulence and rebellion have subsided (leaving behind their deep emotional scars), and all that is left, as Jiang Zemin pointed out in his October 1 speech, is the "hard work" of building a modern China and the "hardship" that goes along with it.[2] By Jiang's calculus, China is now only halfway through that process; it has another fifty years to go before reaching the "glorious destination" of socialist modernization.[3]

But what about "modernization by the year 2000," the grand slogan first of Premier Zhou Enlai and then of Deng Xiaoping? It will no doubt be the centerpiece of China's millennial celebrations, with figures and charts and graphs and the entire statistical apparatus mobilized to show just how far China has come in five decades. Yet one senses somehow that the old slogan has become obsolete, a quaint idea now buried under the astonishing and unanticipated economic successes of the past fifteen years, and under the bewildering realization that the most difficult trials may still lie ahead.

Age fifty is a time for reflection, and to that end, this special edition of *China Briefing* reflects on where China stood at century's end, midstream in its process of continuing transformation. To assess that, the contributors were asked to consider the present in light of the past (whether the span be twenty, fifty, or one hundred years), to look for patterns of continuity as well as change, and to illuminate the questions so hotly debated at century's end: Can the Chinese regime survive in the face of the enormous challenges it faces? Will the profound social changes under way in China lay the foundations for greater democracy? What will be the fate of the Chinese Communist Party as it attempts to facilitate political change over time? Will it be given the time, or will a restless society rebel against its strictures? Will a militarily stronger

---

1. Mark O'Neill, "Mass Parade Gears Up for Anniversary," *South China Morning Post*, August 14, 1999.

2. Xinhua News Service for Hong Kong, "Hardship Will Bring Development" (text of President Jiang Zemin's October 1 speech), *South China Morning Post*, October 1, 1999.

3. Ibid.

China threaten peace in East Asia, or will China be a bulwark of stability in the region? Can China and Taiwan find a peaceful way to resolve their fifty-year conflict over sovereignty? Are the United States and China on a collision course, or can they master the domestic and international pressures that so often conspire to keep them at cross-purposes?

That these questions were so hotly debated at the end of the twentieth century was itself an indicator of just how far China had traveled over the last two decades and how important China was perceived to be as a rising power. But answers were not easy to come by, as the following essays attest. Rather than clear answers, what emerges in the chapters to follow is four themes around which the questions and the commentary seem to circle.

The first of these themes is the intense contestation of ideas within China. China's intellectuals, like those of a century ago, are engaged in a rich and productive debate over the meaning of the past, the impact of the present reform-era policies, and the choices that lie ahead. One hundred years ago, much of the debate revolved around the question of whether reform or revolution was the best path to redemption from foreign influence and revival to greatness. Eighty years later, in the aftermath of foreign invasion, civil war, revolution, socialist transformation, and then "cultural revolution," the terms of debate had understandably changed, and reformist thought had new power. As Joseph Fewsmith points out in the opening essay, however, the intellectual struggle to come to terms with the radical "leftism" of the Cultural Revolution (1966–76), to eliminate its lingering influences, and to promote the enlightenment project of the May Fourth tradition had been spent by the early 1990s, rendered obsolete by the profound changes that had occurred during the 1980s. In the wake of Deng Xiaoping's famous "southern tour" of 1992, which inaugurated a new and accelerated wave of reform, intellectual skepticism and concern were turned toward the reform process itself, and toward the troubling consequences of the process. Thus began a new wave of intellectual criticism, a wave joined, as Cheng Li discusses, by a younger generation of scholars, intellectuals, experts, and officials who enjoy more autonomy than their predecessors, are subjected to less censorship, and have the technical advantages of e-mail and the Internet. As important as their debates over the reform process are, Li argues, more important still may be the increasingly dynamic and pluralistic character of the debates and the participants. Where ideas can be more fully and openly contested, Li argues, pluralistic politics may have the chance to grow.

A second theme to emerge from these essays concerns the dilemmas of institutional reform and institution building. To a large extent, China's entire twentieth-century history has been shadowed by the heavy burden of constructing workable and effective institutions capable of meeting the needs of state and society, and in the 1990s there was no rest for the weary. Barry Naughton reminds us that China came to the end of the century only part way through two profound transformations. The first, the transition from a rural to an urban society, has moved more rapidly in the past two decades but has its roots in the early decades of the twentieth century. The second, the transition from a socialist planned economy to a market economy, is of more recent vintage, but that process too was accelerated in the 1990s. Through it all, Naughton argues, China's reform process has been "institutionally conservative." Institutions have been adapted on an "as-needed" basis, and change has been incremental. While the weaknesses of this strategy have received widespread attention, Naughton reminds us that it also has its virtues in that it gives the system a certain resiliency in the face of failures and setbacks. As a result, China manages to muddle through, repeatedly avoiding the disasters that observers have predicted as virtually inevitable.

Jonathan Unger develops a similar argument to explain how there can be so much prosperity and so much discontent in China's countryside at the same time. He argues that China's failure to change much in the structure of governance in the countryside at the same time that it has fundamentally transformed the structure of economic power has opened up room for the growth of local networks of bureaucratic power, privilege, and corruption. The means by which this is accomplished and its consequences vary for rich and poor villages, but the result has been a dramatic increase in the number of rural protests in the late 1990s. Paradoxically, however, this weakness of rural governance may also be a source of strength, insofar as these protests are generally directed toward local governments, not the central government. Indeed, Unger notes that villagers often appeal to the central state for protection from the predations of local officials, and as long as villagers need Beijing's help, they are unlikely to pose a serious threat to the regime. Here too, then, the Chinese state may be muddling through with its strategy of "institutional conservatism."

A third theme that emerges in these essays is that of rapid social change, and along with it, changing notions of individual and collective identity. Yan Yunxiang, for example, focuses on the impact and changing nature of consumerism in the late 1990s and argues that it is fast becoming an alternative ideology as individuals come to believe in the idea and practice of consumption, as they aspire to consume at ever higher levels, and as they come to define their social status in terms of what they are able to purchase and consume. He suggests that this growing presumption of quality service and goods and the freedom to choose among them, conditions that pertain in a buyer's market, may translate into political change as citizens transfer that knowledge into the political arena by demanding a higher quality of public goods and services.

Yet the power of choice has its negative consequences as well, as my own essay shows. In the 1990s, a rise in disposable income, combined with the widespread availability of fetal ultrasound technology capable of determining the sex of a fetus, led to a marked increase in sex-selective abortion, so much so that officials had become publicly alarmed by the end of the decade. For many (and not just those in the countryside), it seemed that having a son was as much a measure of status and identity as was having a coveted consumer item. Of course, the former was a far more weighty concern than the latter, since in Chinese culture a son is required in order to maintain the ancestral family line. Both decisions, however, and the opportunities to make them, were by-products of the thoroughgoing commercialization of all types of transactions in the last years of the twentieth century.

While individuals struggled with changing patterns of choice and self-definition, the nation continued to struggle with its collective identity and its place in the world. Fewsmith, drawing on the work of philosopher Li Zehou, reminds us that China's self-definition and its national identity have been persistently complicated by the tension between the cultural goal of "enlightenment," which entails a cultural critique of China, and the goal of "national salvation," which has often evoked nativistic and even xenophobic responses to the threat posed by the power and ideas of the West. In the 1980s, with the critique of Cultural Revolution "leftism" in ascendancy, intellectuals rejected nativism for a more cosmopolitan stance that looked favorably on the United States and the West. By the 1990s, rapid change in China and in the world raised new and more complex questions about what was "good" for China. Deng-era reform was now open to criticism, as were the global economic order, the hegemonic power and specific policies of the United States, and the entire enlightenment tradition. The result was an attempt to transcend the old nationalist categories of nativism and cosmopolitanism in favor of a more sophisticated approach that Fewsmith calls "cynical realism."

Both Fewsmith and Yan find a connection between the transformation of nationalism in the 1990s and the intensified process of commercialization that took off after 1992. Fewsmith shows how growing commercialization fueled a popular debate over how best to express one's nationalism, as more rarefied forms of intellectual discourse on the topic gave way to mass publishing of books such as *China Can Say No* and *China Should Not Be 'Mr. No.'*[4] Yan focuses on the erosion of consumer-based nationalism as domestic and global economic change has altered the meaning and implications of buying foreign goods. If nativism in the early twentieth century was sometimes expressed through boycotts of foreign goods, Yan suggests that this will be a declining feature of nationalism in the years ahead.

Susan Brownell picks up on these issues by exploring the deeper structure of popular Chinese nationalism and its links to official and intellectual nationalism. Brownell points our attention to the crucial role of gender in establishing a national identity; she argues that nations "have a gender relative to other nations, states have a gender," and those "conducting affairs of state are influenced by gender in ways we are just now beginning to understand." Beginning with an examination of how Chinese imperial and republican authorities sought to define themselves vis-à-vis the world and their own near peripheries (for example, the borderlands and the minorities on the outskirts of the empire), Brownell argues that China's twentieth-century nationalism has from its beginnings been bound up with a gender ideology that has viewed women as weak and in need of protection and strengthening (through the end of foot binding and the promotion of sports). Feelings

---

4. Song Qiang, Zhang Zangzang, and Qiao Bian, *Zhongguo keyi shuobu* (China can say no) (Beijing: Zhonghua gongshang lianhe chubanshe, 1996); and Shen Jiru, *Zhongguo bu dang 'bu xiansheng'* (China should not be 'Mr. No') (Beijing: Jinri Zhongguo chubanshe, 1998).

of male impotence to prevent incursions by the West and Japan, therefore, were often channeled into rage over the violation of women. In this way, the suffering of weak and self-sacrificing Chinese women could be used to stoke a male discourse on the weakness of the masculine-defined nation. Brownell traces this pattern into the present by focusing on two critical events in 1999—the nationalist response to the United States' accidental bombing of the Chinese embassy in Belgrade, and the World Cup championship soccer game between the United States and China. In both, she finds that nationalist discourse is built upon familiar gendered themes. In the case of the embassy bombing, for example, she notes the overwhelmingly male composition of the protesting crowds and the intense media focus on a father's grief for his lost daughter and his motherless granddaughter. This enduring nationalist theme of woman as victim and male as protector (in this case an impotent and ineffectual protector) translates into an outward view of the aggressor as hyperpotent and dangerous. In the aftermath of the sex scandal of 1998, it was exceptionally easy to cast President Bill Clinton in that predatory role.

A fourth and final theme is the echoing of the past across the landscape of the present, particularly in the arena of international affairs. The past several years have brought powerful reminders of how the legacy of imperial aggression, civil war, and the Cold War live on in the present, and in particular of how this legacy continues to dog U.S.-China and China-Taiwan relations. If 1997 marked a high note for China with the return of Hong Kong to Chinese sovereignty after a century and a half of British colonial rule, as the century came to an end the majority of the notes appeared to be low ones. As Nancy Bernkopf Tucker discusses, Taiwan forged ahead in its strategy of stretching the linguistic and policy limits of a "one China" policy, undeterred by Chinese threats and a show of force in 1996 and 1999. Meanwhile, U.S.-China relations took a roller-coaster run, as the predictable array of conflicts—most favored nation trade status, China's entry into the World Trade Organization, the security of Taiwan, human rights abuses, and military weapons sales—were upstaged by the even bigger allegations hurled at each other of nuclear weapons espionage by China and calculated attack on Chinese citizens (in the Belgrade embassy) by the United States.

As each side flung accusations at the other in the spring of 1999, it made some observers wonder whether the oft-predicted "coming conflict with China" had arrived sooner than expected.[5] As Bruce Cumings points out, however, it was remarkable how quickly the spring and summer of discontent in 1999 faded away, as the Cox Report on Chinese espionage was filed away by Congress and as China's senior leaders came back from their August meetings at the Beidaihe resort refreshed and prepared to forgive the United States' trespasses. Noting that the frequent oscillations in the China-U.S. mood have become dizzying of late, Cumings nevertheless emphasizes the logic of this movement back toward friendly cooperation: China has far more to lose than to gain from a rupture in China-U.S. relations.

Still, what the future holds remains a point of sharp debate, and the two essays by Tucker and Cumings provide a valuable gateway into that ongoing discussion. Whereas Tucker concludes that, despite common ties and interests, confrontation between the United States and China is "almost inevitable" given Washington's power in the world and Chinese aspirations, Cumings takes a different view. Noting that China has historically been careful to limit its expansion and "constrain its choice of means," quick to recognize the "ultimate weakness of a power that only expresses itself militarily," and far more cooperative with the United States on international security issues than most observers give it credit for, Cumings suggests that confrontation, if it comes, is more likely to grow out of U.S. *mis*calculation than Chinese calculation. In light of that, he counsels the United States toward greater self-knowledge as the key to handling its affairs with China.

One final thought, as a fresh century begins. In different ways, all of the authors in this volume salute the creativity, resilience, courage, and ingenuity that the Chinese people—on the mainland, in Taiwan, and in Hong Kong—have shown in the face of the upheavals, hardships, and disasters of the past one hundred years. I would like to join them in that salute. If the nineteenth century was marked by imperial decline, and the twentieth by revolution and transformation, let the twenty-first be marked by a prolonged era of peace, stability, and prosperity. The Chinese people would benefit greatly from such an era, and so would we all.

5. See Richard Bernstein and Ross Munro, *The Coming Conflict with China* (New York: Knopf, 1997).

Historical Echoes and Chinese Politics: Can China Leave the Twentieth Century Behind?

Joseph Fewsmith

As the twentieth century wound to a close in China, it was impossible not to be struck by two somewhat contradictory thoughts. One was that the echoes of the major political anniversaries of the past century still ring with unnerving clarity, suggesting just how relevant the issues of the late nineteenth and early twentieth centuries remain at the turn of another century. The other was that the social and political changes that are underfoot are so dramatic and fundamental that China really is moving into a new era in which those echoes will finally grow fainter. Which of these impressions becomes the more accurate depends much on the course of the next ten years or so.

There seem to be nothing but anniversaries these days in China. The hundredth anniversary of the "Hundred Day" reform—the radical reform movement championed by Kang Youwei and Liang Qichao in the closing days of the Qing dynasty—fell in 1998, and Beijing University, which was founded in the course of that movement and became the symbol of political liberalism in modern China, marked its centenary in a grand but contested ceremony. At the same time, 1998 marked the twentieth anniversary of the Third Plenary Session of the Eleventh Central Committee, at which Deng Xiaoping decisively launched China on the course of reform, thus leading everyone to discuss even more fervently the successes and failures of the past two decades.

The following year, 1999, was perhaps even more portentous. It marked the eightieth anniversary of the May Fourth Movement, the iconoclastic cultural and nationalistic movement that gave birth simultaneously to liberalism and communism. The fiftieth anniversary of the founding of the People's Republic of China was celebrated with elaborate ceremonies and a well-orchestrated military parade on October 1, 1999. Most sensitive of all, 1999 also marked the tenth anniversary of the Tiananmen demonstrations and their suppression, an event that cuts the reform period neatly in half and has generated continuing controversies about the meaning of reform and the course China should follow in the future.

Finally, the year 2000 marks the hundredth anniversary of the Boxer Rebellion, the xenophobic peasant movement whose magic was believed to protect its adherents from bullets. This anniversary has taken on new saliency as demonstrations and armed outbursts pock the countryside, and as the Falun Gong (Buddhist Law Society) movement, which combines traditional *qigong* exercises with a potent spiritual message, has attracted millions of adherents and most famously mobilized ten thousand people to sit in sudden and silent protest outside Zhongnanhai on April 25, 1999, before the government tried to suppress it (not completely successfully) in a virulent and widespread crackdown that started in July.

These anniversaries resonate with the present because they raise issues of continuing importance: China's relationship with the West (politically, economically, and culturally); the simultaneous desire for wealth and power and social fairness; popular political expression and participation; and the relationship of the present to the past, which is to say the value of the revolution. Moreover, the meanings of these anniversaries remain contested; indeed, it is precisely because they are contested that they continue to have such salience. In fact, one way to try to comprehend the state of Chinese society at the turn of the century is to contrast the way these anniversaries echo today with the way they did just a decade ago. Doing so underscores how very different the China of the 1990s is from the China of the 1980s.

A decade ago, prior to Tiananmen, intellectuals almost universally keyed on the upcoming seventieth anniversary of the May Fourth Movement to push the themes of intellectual freedom and democratization further. The West, particularly the United States, was viewed as a model, or at least as a useful embodiment of ideals that could be evoked to propel reform forward. The fortieth anniversary of the founding of the PRC, in contrast, was something few intellectuals were in a mood to celebrate; the phrase from the Confucian *Analects* saying that "at forty one should not have doubts" (*sishi er buhuo*) could not but be cited with irony. Cosmologist Fang Lizhi wrote off the history of the PRC as "forty years of failure";[1] others may have demurred from such an extreme judgment, but not by much.

These concerns and doubts reflected the experience of intellectuals and were broadly shared by other sectors of society. Coming out of the Cultural Revolution, intellectuals were obsessed by a desire to understand where the revolution had gone wrong and by a profound wish to prevent anything resembling the Cultural Revolution from ever happening again. Intellectuals placed the blame squarely on "leftism." The enormous excesses of the Chinese revolution—from the "socialist transformation" of the mid-1950s to the anti-rightist movement of 1957, the Great Leap Forward of 1958–60, and finally the Cultural Revolution of 1966–76—were attributed to a "leftism" that accepted uncritically a (contradictory) mix of Stalinist economic planning and Maoist mobilization, that rejected the importance of rationality and hence of intellectuals, that emphasized the "class nature" of human beings to the detriment of their humanity, and that turned the nation inward, rejecting the importance of learning from the West. These trends were also encompassed by the term "feudalism," a word of opprobrium that had nothing to do with its meaning for the economic and political history of the West or even its traditional meaning of local self-rule in China, but instead connoted everything negative that had been attributed to Chinese traditional society through the long course of China's revolution, including patriarchalism, authoritarianism, bureaucratism, anti-intellectualism, and fanaticism. As China's revolution had increasingly criticized capitalism, trying desperately in the course of the Cultural Revolution to "cut off the tail of capitalism" and to criticize the "bourgeois right," feudalism had flourished. "Leftism" was thus rooted in "feudalism," and the task of intellectuals and reform-minded Party people was to expunge these evils and thus set China on a course toward "modernity."

Given this basic, if somewhat oversimplified, diagnosis of what was wrong with China, it was natural that intellectuals turned to the May Fourth tradition for inspiration and moral sustenance. The May Fourth tradition had always contained contradictory elements: a radical critique of traditional Chinese culture and the demand to learn from the West and to introduce science and democracy were combined with

---

1. Fang Lizhi, "China's Despair and China's Hope," *New York Review of Books,* February 2, 1989, reprinted in Fang Lizhi, *Bringing Down the Great Wall* (New York: Alfred A. Knopf, 1991), pp. 250–57.

a nationalism that rejected cosmopolitanism in favor of nativism. Chinese Academy of Social Sciences (CASS) Philosophy Institute scholar Li Zehou articulated for his generation of 1980s scholars the need to disentangle the "liberal" elements of the May Fourth tradition, those that emphasized "enlightenment," from those that were caught up in nationalistic efforts to "save the nation." Every time the cultural critique seemed to offer hope of introducing new enlightenment values into Chinese culture, Li argued, it was overwhelmed by nationalism ("national salvation") as China faced one crisis after another.[2] Now, in the 1980s, it was finally time to take up the task of enlightenment and carry it through to fruition.

This enlightenment project dominated intellectual discourse in the 1980s. Whether it was discussions of "alienation" in socialism,[3] efforts to bring an end to lifelong tenure and create a rational civil service,[4] policy proposals to marketize the Chinese economy,[5] translations of Western thinkers,[6] nascent writings about human rights and democracy,[7] or "reconceptualizations" of capitalism and socialism to emphasize their similarities, the task was to expunge "leftism" from Chinese social, economic, and political life. This focus on the dangers of leftism and feudalism assigned a lofty position to the West, particularly the United States. The United States took on an aura of modernity that provided a mirror opposite of the leftism that intellectuals sought to root out. Western culture provided fuel for ongoing critiques of

---

2. Li Zehou, *Zhongguo xiandai sixiangshi lun* (History of contemporary Chinese thought) (Beijing: Dongfang chubanshe, 1987). Vera Schwarcz's masterful study *The Chinese Enlightenment: Intellectuals and the Legacy of the May Fourth Movement of 1919* (Berkeley: University of California Press, 1986) builds on some of Li's insights.

3. Wang Ruoshui's *Wei rendao zhuyi bianhu* (In defense of humanism) (Beijing: Sanlian chubanshe, 1986) is the classic work in this regard.

4. Yan Jiaqi was one of the first and best-known advocates of instituting a civil-service system. See Yan Jiaqi, *Toward a Democratic China: The Intellectual Biography of Yan Jiaqi*, trans. David S. K. Hong and Denis C. Mair (Honolulu: University of Hawaii Press, 1992).

5. Wu Jinglian was probably the best-known of the early advocates, but there were many others. See Joseph Fewsmith, *Dilemmas of Reform in China: Political Conflict and Economic Debates* (Armonk, NY: M.E. Sharpe, 1994).

6. Gan Yang edited a famous series of translations under the general title *Culture: China and the World*. See Chen Fong-ching and Jin Guantao, *From Youthful Manuscripts to River Elegy: The Chinese Popular Cultural Movement and Political Transformation, 1979–1989* (Hong Kong: Chinese University Press, 1997), pp. 159–85.

7. Su Shaozhi was an early and consistent advocate of democratization. See Su Shaozhi, ed., *Marxism in China* (Nottingham: Russell Press, 1983). See also Su's memoirs, *Shinian fengyu: Wengehou de dalu lilunjie* (Ten years of storms: The mainland's theoretical circles after the Cultural Revolution) (Taibei: Shibao chuban gongsi, 1996).

Chinese culture, thus continuing the May Fourth rejection of traditional values, while Western economic and political systems served as foils against which to criticize the planned economy and authoritarian political system of China. If discussions of the United States and other Western countries in the 1980s were superficial, it was because the point was not to understand how those systems actually worked but to provide a fulcrum from which faults in the Chinese system could be criticized. However superficial these discussions may have been, their participants clearly saw themselves as lying within the May Fourth enlightenment tradition and providing a cosmopolitanism that helped support the political relationship being forged with the West as well as reformers within the Party.

A decade later, the May Fourth legacy appears badly tattered. The liberal tradition of the May Fourth period has been ignored and suppressed many times since 1919, as Li Zehou points out, because revolution or foreign war seemed more pressing. But never in the seven decades since then had intellectuals themselves come to see the May Fourth tradition as outdated or irrelevant to their concerns. That changed in the 1990s, and the turn away from the enlightenment project of the May Fourth Movement marks a major, one is tempted to say fundamental, change in the way many intellectuals view China and its place in the world.

The change in the intellectual atmosphere in China can be dated fairly precisely to the 1992–93 period. It was in 1992 that Deng Xiaoping made his famous journey to the south of China to reinvigorate his reform program.[8] Deng was highly successful not only in changing the political atmosphere but also in setting off a major upsurge in economic activity (bolstered by a loose monetary policy) and, more important, a critical structural shift in the economy as the private sector finally emerged as a major factor in its own right and as foreign investment expanded greatly.[9] These changes, which have generally received high praise in the Western press, have been greeted by

---

8. Suisheng Zhao, "Deng Xiaoping's Southern Tour: Elite Politics in Post-Tiananmen China," *Asian Survey*, vol. 33, no. 8 (August 1993), pp. 739–56.

9. Figures on the size of China's private economy are notoriously hard to pin down, but the official figures give a sense of the explosion of such activity in the wake of Deng's trip to the south. In 1992 there were 139,633 registered private enterprises selling 9.1 billion yuan of goods; the following year there were 237,919 private enterprises with sales of 68.1 billion yuan. See Li Peilin, ed., *Zhongguo xinshiqi jieji jiceng baogao* (Report on classes and strata in China's new period) (Shenyang: Liaoning renmin chubanshe, 1995), p. 225.

greater skepticism in China because they have challenged vested interests, have created new vested interests, and have been accompanied by a host of social problems: rapidly rising intra- and interregional income inequalities, corruption on a scale that would have been unimaginable in 1989 (when students took to the streets to protest corruption), a massive stripping of state-owned assets as officials have taken advantage of their positions to preside over a large-scale de facto privatization, a large increase in the number of migrant workers looking for employment outside their native areas, increases in crime and other social-order problems, and a growing unemployment problem as hard-pressed state-owned factories finally began to move to reduce the size of their labor forces.

In short, in the eyes of many intellectuals, the *problematique* of China had shifted dramatically from the need to push reform forward by criticizing leftism and feudalism to the need to deal with the effects of reform. For these intellectuals, the left was no longer a problem; it was a spent force that had little, if any, practical effect on China. Marketization was likewise no longer a problem; it had succeeded, perhaps too well. And opening to the outside world, that counterpart to Dengist domestic reforms, had also succeeded. Not only was China opened to the outside world, but it found itself inextricably linked to a new global order that was not necessarily benevolent—as the Asian financial crisis demonstrated forcefully and brutally. Such concerns led many intellectuals to become quite critical of the effects of reform in China and of the global order China was trying to join. This was a wholly different set of concerns from that which had dominated the intellectual agenda in the 1980s.[10]

Ironically, these intellectuals were far more familiar with the West and with the intellectual trends of the West than were those who had dominated intellectual discourse in the 1980s. Many of them had studied extensively in the West before either returning to take up prestigious positions within China or staying in the West in university teaching positions. Indeed, this internationalization of intellectual discourse distinguished the 1990s from the 1980s. In the first decade of reform, Chinese intellectuals generally resided in China and discussed issues

---

10. Perhaps the best summation of the changed intellectual atmosphere and concerns of these intellectuals is Wang Hui, "Dangdai Zhongguo de sixiang zhuangkuang yu xiandaixing wenti" (Contemporary Chinese thought and the problem of modernity), *Tianya* (Frontier/Haikou) (September 1997), pp. 133–50.

with other intellectuals in China; by the 1990s, particularly with the spread of the Internet, the conversation had become truly global, encompassing not only intellectuals in China and those who were studying or working in the West but also non-PRC Chinese intellectuals from Taiwan, Hong Kong, and elsewhere.

What this new, sophisticated, and international group of intellectuals latched onto as they focused on a new set of social problems was a variety of perspectives that are generally referred to as "critical methodologies" in the West: postmodernism, postcolonialism, deconstructionism, critical legal studies, analytic Marxism, world systems theory, and so forth.[11] Such methodologies were highly critical of capitalism and globalization and were determined to "unmask" the various power relations that were said to be hidden behind "hegemonic" rhetoric. Although such critiques are widespread within U.S. and European academe, they have remarkably little impact on public policy, standing as academic critiques of a very dominant capitalist order.[12]

In China, however, their position is quite different and hence highly controversial. First, instead of representing minority critiques of a dominant trend, critical methodologies have arguably become the mainstream of intellectual discourse in China. Second, although advocates of critical methodologies in China argue that they want to transcend such dualities (usually said to be a legacy of Cold War thinking) as East/West, tradition/modernity, and capitalist/socialist, their very focus on these dualities tends to accentuate their importance. For instance, Chinese scholars following in Edward Said's footsteps to unmask the relationship between "Orientalist" rhetoric and the power interests of the United States invariably end up not transcending the East/West duality but emphasizing the need for a nativist response to a Western "hegemonic" discourse.[13]

Third, it is difficult for followers of critical methodologies to escape from nationalist modes of discourse, and indeed many seek to

---

11. A large number of books and articles have been published from various critical perspectives. See, for instance, Wang Hui and Yu Guoliang, eds., *90 niandai de 'houxue' lunzheng* (Post-ism in the nineties) (Hong Kong: Chinese University Press, 1998); and Cui Zhiyuan, *Di'erci sixiang jiefang* (The second thought liberation) (Hong Kong: Oxford University Press, 1997).

12. Areas in which such critiques have had a visible impact are those of gender and race.

13. See Zhang Kuan, "Wenhua xinzhimin de keneng" (The possibility of cultural neocolonialism), *Tianya* (April 1996).

adopt such rhetoric either because they are concerned with the way they see China being absorbed into an international capitalist order in which it has little say or because they share a sense of frustration with (largely) U.S. rhetoric and policies in the post–Cold War era. In this sense, those who promote critical methodologies ironically adopt a nationalistic attitude that is far from the orientation of those using parallel methodologies in the West. Those opposed to critical methodologies criticize, sometimes in extremely harsh terms, those who adopt them for becoming, in their view, spokespersons for the government, while those who adopt critical methodologies state with equal validity that they are highly critical of the government and its policies.[14]

To point to such harsh polemics is to suggest another feature of the 1990s landscape that is different from that of the 1980s or arguably even earlier. Although there have been some notably harsh polemics throughout the twentieth century, intellectuals in China have generally shared a sense that they were one group. This sense was particularly strong in the 1980s, as intellectuals had endured a common fate during the Cultural Revolution and generally shared a desire to move China as far away from that period as possible. By the 1990s, however, the traditional world of Chinese intellectuals had largely vanished. Some had moved into the government and its think tanks as specialists and technocrats, others had retreated into academia to pursue specialized research, and still others had responded to the rapidly growing commercialization of culture by writing popular literature and the like. Indeed, one of the most interesting intellectual debates of the 1990s, and arguably the only one that was truly indigenous, was about the loss of the "humanistic spirit" (*renwen jingshen*) among intellectuals.[15] It was a debate that reflected the growing marginalization of intellectuals in the face of commercialization. In short, by the end of the 1990s, it was difficult to speak of China's intellectuals as a coherent social stratum or as the "conscience" of Chinese society, their traditional role.

Critical methodologies, as just mentioned, have an affinity with nationalism, even if they are inherently critical of the government and the course of reform as well. Nationalism is hardly new in China; it has in fact been the leitmotif of twentieth-century China. Chinese intellec-

---

14. See, for instance, the critical essays contained in Wang and Yu, eds., *90 niandai de 'houxue' lunzheng*.

15. Wang Xiaoming, ed., *Renwen jingshen xunsi lu* (Reflections on the humanistic spirit) (Shanghai: Wenhui chubanshe, 1996).

tuals were just as nationalistic in the 1980s as they were in the 1990s, but in the earlier decade their nationalism took a more cosmopolitan approach, seeking a path to wealth and power through learning from the West.[16] As noted above, this learning from the West simultaneously served the purposes of criticizing "leftism" and "feudalism" and promoting reform. As intellectuals have become more critical of reform, they have simultaneously become more critical of the neoclassical economics and political liberalism that have been offered up as models for China's reform. There has been a new desire in the 1990s to forge a uniquely Chinese path to reform, and this desire to explore a "native" approach to reform that conforms with Chinese culture and tradition necessarily entails an emphasis on asserting Chinese identity.

This assertion of Chinese identity, however, has mingled with other feelings of suspicion directed primarily against the United States that are an outcome of the specific atmosphere that has prevailed in U.S.-China relations since Tiananmen. The sea change in public opinion came in the 1992–93 period when President Clinton, trying to bridge the gap between his campaign rhetoric and the realities of international relations, extended China's most-favored nation status conditionally. This flawed decision, later reversed, was followed by other gaffes that reflected a sensitivity to certain opinion groups in the United States and an insensitivity to opinion in China. Such decisions included the opposition to China's bid to host the summer Olympics in the year 2000 and the forceful inspection of a Chinese ship, the *Yin He*, believed to be transporting chemicals that could be used in the manufacture of chemical weapons to Iran.

One of the most interesting aspects of Chinese intellectuals' response to these and similar incidents is the widespread and deep-seated assumption that the United States was taking such measures in a well-calculated effort to "contain" China. Whereas few officials or scholars in the United States could identify a clear-cut "China policy" in the early Clinton administration, much less one that was implemented consistently, Chinese intellectuals could explain in detail how various measures were all clear expressions of a U.S. "national interest" in keeping China down. This new intellectual focus on "interests"

---

16. Joseph Fewsmith and Stanley Rosen, "The Domestic Context of Chinese Foreign Policy: Does 'Public Opinion' Matter?" in David M. Lampton, *The Making of Chinese Foreign and Security Policy in the Era of Reform: 1978–2000* (Stanford University Press, forthcoming).

speaks volumes about the intellectual atmosphere in contemporary China. Intellectuals have been twice disillusioned regarding idealism, first by the Cultural Revolution, which turned into a nightmare, and second by the liberalism of the 1980s, which ended in political disaster. Particularly in the atmosphere of commercialism that has prevailed in recent years, any talk of idealism seems out of place. In some ways, the blunt discussions of "national interest" are a refreshing change from the ideological stridency of the past, but they reflect not so much realism as it is conceived by Western students of international relations as out-and-out cynicism. Since ideological pretensions have been unmasked in China, so the logic seems to go, it is inconceivable that a nation such as the United States would not be a careful calculator of its national interests.

This "cynical realism" was deeply reflected in Chinese reactions to the war in Kosovo and especially to the tragic bombing of the Chinese embassy in Belgrade. Even before the bombing, there were elaborate scenarios set out to explain how the NATO action in Kosovo reflected U.S. national interests. These generally focused on the shift in NATO's mission statement to reflect an expanded, "out-of-area" role and explained the conflict in Kosovo as simply a first step in the U.S. plan to dominate the world. Following the bombing incident, the explanations became even more fanciful and far-fetched.[17] Chinese critics were deaf to explanations that suggested that the United States and other nations were in fact concerned with human rights and that the military action with respect to Kosovo largely reflected idealism (whether misguided or not).

Not only has the nature of nationalism changed in China in the course of the 1990s, but its base has also widened substantially. The broadening of nationalist appeals is part and parcel of the decline of "elite" culture and the consequent "flattening out" of public discourse. The widening of intellectual discourse started in the 1980s, but it is the commercialization of culture in the1990s that has reshaped the public arena. The market for Wang Shuo's anti-establishment "hooligan" literature reflected a new populist culture and a new social mood. Wang,

---

17. For instance, Wang Jian, an economist with the State Planning Commission, posted an article on the *Jianchuan zhishi* Web site on June 2 arguing that the United States bombed the Chinese embassy to keep the war going because it wanted to maintain the value of the U.S. dollar vis-à-vis the euro.

18. Jianying Zha, *China Pop* (New York: Free Press, 1995).

who is not college educated, flouted the conventions of Chinese litera-ture and showed no deference to his better-educated colleagues. Another turning point was the popularity of *Yearnings (Kewang)*,[18] a soap opera featuring stock characters but written in part by respected writers Zheng Wanlong and Wang Shuo (who were quickly accused of selling out). The show attracted a huge audience and marked a turning point in the commercialization of culture. As Li Xiaoming, the chief scriptwriter, put it, "If you're a television writer, and you know that the majority of your Chinese audience had to save up for years to buy a TV set, then you'd better come to terms with them."[19]

Popular nationalism then emerged on the scene in 1994 with the publication of Wang Shan's book, *Looking at China through a Third Eye*.[20] This was a highly critical look at the state of Chinese society and the impact of the reforms as well as a bold statement of nationalism. Two years later, the better-known *China Can Say No* was published and became an instant best-seller.[21] A whole series of similar books soon appeared, cashing in on the market that *China Can Say No* had pioneered.[22] Indeed, one of the hallmarks of the new era of the 1990s was the way in which official books had to compete more with non-official books to influence public opinion. Thus, books such as *Heart-to-Heart Talks with the General Secretary* and *China Should Not Be 'Mr. No'* (discussed below) appeared on the market to oppose the upsurge of nationalism.[23] These books were soon followed by others touting the U.S.-China "constructive strategic partnership" as Jiang Zemin and Clinton exchanged summits.

This expansion of the public realm, which was due both to secular

---

19. Zha, *China Pop*, p. 38.

20. Luo yi ning ge'er (pseud.), *Disanzhi yanjing kan Zhongguo* (Looking at China through a third eye), trans. Wang Shan (Taiyuan: Shanxi Publishing House, 1994). See also Joseph Fewsmith, "Review of *Disanzhi yanjing kan Zhongguo*," *Journal of Contemporary China*, no. 7 (fall 1994), pp. 100–4.

21. Song Qiang, Zhang Zangzang, and Qiao Bian, *Zhongguo keyi shuobu* (China can say no) (Beijing: Zhonghua gongshang lianhe chubanshe, 1996).

22. The authors of *China Can Say No* were the first to exploit their own success with a quick sequel called *Zhongguo haishi neng shuo bu* (China can still say no) (Hong Kong: Ming bao, 1996). Imitations quickly followed. See, in particular, Li Xiguang and Liu Kang, *Yaomo Zhongguo de beihou* (Behind the demonization of China) (Beijing: Zhongguo she-hui kexue chubanshe, 1996).

23. Weng Jieming et al., eds., *Yu Zongshuji tanxin* (Heart-to-heart talks with the gener-al secretary) (Beijing: Zhongguo shehui kexue chubanshe, 1996); and Shen Jiru, *Zhongguo bu dang 'bu xiansheng'* (China should not be 'Mr. No') (Beijing: Jinri Zhongguo chuban-she, 1998).

changes in Chinese society and to the government's recognition that the sort of heavy-handed ideological campaign it had pursued following Tiananmen was counterproductive, begins to make more explicable the public reaction to the bombing of the Chinese embassy in Belgrade. However, one must also factor in the frustrations that are evident in Chinese society.

Political Implications of Socioeconomic Change

The very different intellectual atmosphere in China, as well as the fractionalization of intellectuals and their very different relationship with the state, is one of the profound changes that have taken place in state-society relations over recent years. Although these changes have their roots in the early years of reform, they have accelerated in recent years as the marketization, internationalization, and diversification of the Chinese economy have accelerated. Whereas through much of the 1980s most social groups gained from reform, as the 1990s progressed, there were increasingly obvious differences between "winners" and "losers." And as more people joined the ranks of the losers, or at least the relative losers, there were widely felt implications for politics. Put simply, the very different socioeconomic environment that has emerged in recent years not only fuels the tensions that erupt in worker and farmer protests but also generates the critical attitude many intellectuals have adopted in recent years and undermines Party discipline as well as the confidence that many Party members and social elites have in the future of the Party, which in turn stimulates the corruption, illegal transfer of wealth abroad, and cynicism that are themselves so much a part of the problem that China's political elite faces. Management of this complex and rapidly changing sociopolitical environment presents a formidable political challenge, arguably one greater than that faced by Mao or Deng, and inevitably leads to sharply differing political views within the elite.

The single most important change in Chinese society has been the emergence of a class of *nouveaux riches*. In the mid-1980s, there was fevered talk in the Chinese press, which turned out to be exaggerated, of the emergence of "ten thousand-yuan households" (*wanyuanhu*)— almost unimaginable in a period when the average rural resident earned only about 350 yuan per year. A decade or so later, the reality was that there were at least one million households with annual incomes exceeding one million yuan. This was an enormous change with profound social, psychological, and political implications. In many ways, of course, this was a long overdue and healthy change seemingly marking the appearance of a middle class, albeit one that was still quite small in terms of China's population, even if one considered only its urban population. Nevertheless, the new middle class, including the much more prosperous *nouveaux riches*, drove the new consumerism of the 1990s, changing the nature and role of culture in Chinese society by commercializing it and diversifying it.

In part, this new middle class marked the internationalization of the Chinese economy; by the mid-1990s, there were some hundred thousand joint-venture enterprises employing perhaps eighteen million people, and most of them paid salaries that far exceeded those of state-owned enterprises (SOEs). Enterprise managers who formed joint ventures or jumped into the international economy sometimes made very large incomes indeed. The new middle class also marked an important structural change in the Chinese economy as the "knowledge economy" boomed; new high-tech firms sprouted up everywhere. As knowledge became a commodity, some intellectuals, whose incomes had lagged behind in the 1980s, found that their skills were valuable and began enjoying a comfortable lifestyle. Whereas previously their only choice had been to join a university or government research organ, now intellectuals could hang out their own shingles as consultants. Such people developed a stake in the system, and as they did so radicalism waned. Other intellectuals, it should be noted, did not do as well, and were profoundly discomforted by the fact that income, not intellectual prowess, had become the measure of success.

The seamy side of this story is that those who did the best in this new economy—and some did very well indeed—almost always seemed to have strong political connections. Sometimes they were bureaucrats who had tired of the office routine and jumped into the sea of business but retained their connections to colleagues who could offer all-important approvals or access to scarce resources. Sometimes they were family members of officials still in office. Sometimes they were enterprise heads who used their positions to siphon off large amounts of state-owned assets to private firms that they controlled directly or indirectly. Often they were the offspring of high cadres who used their family connections to amass large sums of money. In other words, corruption—massive corruption—was a major part of the story of income redistribution in the 1990s.

A recent study calls this *nouveau riche* group the "never-left-out class" (*bu luokong jieji*) because every time Chinese society has entered a new round of adjustment in which resources are reallocated, this group has benefited the most. The same study argues that this group possesses "comprehensive" (*zongtixing*) capital resources, meaning that it is able to mobilize its multidimensional economic and political contacts to monopolize the best opportunities.[24] This is the same group of people that economic journalist He Qinglian described in her 1998 best-seller when she argued that through the "marketization of politics," officials or those with close relations with officials have directed millions of dollars' worth of assets into private hands, bringing about a form of "primitive socialist accumulation" that rivals anything Marx and Engels observed about "primitive capitalist accumulation." The result, He argued, has been income inequality surpassing that in either Japan or the United States (keeping in mind that China had a much more equal distribution of income than either of those countries less than a decade ago), the rise of secret societies, and mass resentment. China, she argues, seems to be heading not toward liberal democracy and capitalism but toward a "government and mafia alliance" (see Cheng Li's chapter in this volume).[25]

The losers in this process are, at least in a relative sense, urban workers, particularly those in smaller cities and towns, who are thrown out of work, furloughed (*xiagang*), not paid for months at a time, or simply made anxious about their prospects. According to official figures, 3.1 percent of the urban workforce—some 5.7 million workers—were registered as unemployed at year-end 1998, and an additional 8.9 million workers were furloughed,[26] giving a total unemployment rate of about 8 percent. Unofficial estimates suggest an unemployment rate that is considerably higher.[27] To be a worker in a state-owned enterprise

---

24. "Zhongguo shehui jiegou zhuanxing de zhongjinqi qushi yu yinhuan" (Trends and hidden shoals in the transformation of China's social structure in the near and mid-term) *Zhanlue yu guanli* (Strategy and Management/Beijing), no. 5 (1998), pp. 1–17.

25. He Qinglian, *Xiandaihua de xianjing* (Pitfalls of modernization) (Beijing: Jinri Zhongguo chubanshe, 1998). See Liu Binyan and Perry Link, "A Great Leap Backward?" *New York Review of Books*, October 8, 1998, pp. 19–23; and Ming Xia, "From Comraderie to the Cash Nexus: Economic Reforms, Social Stratification, and Their Political Consequences in China," *Journal of Contemporary China*, no. 21 (July 1999), pp. 345–58.

26. Ma Hong and Wang Mengkui, eds., *1998–1999 Zhongguo jingji xingshi yu zhanwang* (China's economic situation and outlook, 1998–1999) (Beijing: Zhongguo fazhan chubanshe, 1999), p. 162.

27. "Zhongguo shehui jiegou zhuanxing de zhongjinqi qushi yu yinhuan" (p. 11) cites

used to be an honored and secure position in society, but today it is relatively less well paid and much less secure, making many workers resentful. There is also an economic impact as workers, worried about their futures, hoard their savings, exerting a deflationary pressure on the economy. Ironically, the "tiger" of savings that economists had long worried would come leaping out of its cage to drive up inflation now cannot even be lured out!

Rural agricultural workers have also lost out, at least in a relative sense. Rural incomes have not increased as quickly in recent years, and local exactions appear not to have abated despite repeated directives from Beijing. Potentially more destabilizing, there remain some 150 million agricultural workers who are grossly underemployed and should shift out of agriculture. But there is no apparent outlet for their services. In the 1980s and 1990s, over 100 million farmers were able to shift out of agriculture by finding jobs in the township and village enterprises (TVEs) that were springing up. By the late 1990s, however, TVEs were undergoing their own readjustment, and many were encountering the same sort of problems that SOEs had previously faced—debts that had been contracted through political relationships and now could not be paid back.[28]

The large numbers of urban and rural people who have been relative losers over the past decade of reform (in contrast to the 1980s when they did relatively well) provide a base of discontent that fuels a constant stream of protest that threatens social order. In a passage worth quoting at length, the authors of the study referred to above write:

> Along with the proliferation of labor disputes, hired workers in many urban and rural enterprises, in an attempt to vent their dissatisfaction with the system, have taken to all sorts of destructive measures, such as burning down factories, sabotaging machinery, and even personal damage to managerial personnel. Such incidents have already become fairly commonplace in the economically developed areas in Southern China. In addition, there are all sorts of focused social movements and actions, such as demonstrations, presentations of petitions and appeals, and labor strikes. Incidences of such petitions and strikes, in which workers in enterprises in large and medium-sized cities raise slogans demanding that their basic livelihood be protected and assured, have become increasingly

a study by CASS researcher Feng Lanrui that estimates that unemployment in "cities and towns" will peak at around 21.4 percent during the Ninth Five-Year Plan period (1996–2000), meaning that some 153 million people would be jobless. Unfortunately, the citation for Feng's study is not given, so the basis for these calculations cannot be checked.

28. Ma and Wang, eds., *1998–1999 Zhongguo jingji xingshi yu zhanwang*, pp. 25–26.

numerous. Although such information and news is almost never reported in the newspapers—out of consideration for "social stability"—it is already an "open secret."[29]

It is precisely such discontent that provides a potential basis for large-scale social protest and explains why sects—such as the Falun Gong—frighten the leadership so much.

The existence of widespread, if unorganized, discontent explains the leadership's concern with providing jobs. Generating sufficient numbers of jobs in a country in which the workforce grows by more than eight million a year is never easy. Rapid economic growth is critical for creating the necessary jobs: each additional percentage point of growth accounts for about 1.2 million jobs, so growth rates have been at the top of the government agenda. So far, growth has managed to keep the government ahead of the curve—unemployment is up but not unmanageable, and both urban and rural incomes have continued to increase—but the margin for error is not great. Given widespread resentment of corruption and income inequality, the potential for social unrest is real.

The profound socioeconomic changes of recent years offer both hope and concern. On the one hand, the growing wealth of a significant number of mostly urban residents, even if much of that wealth has been acquired in a less than pristine manner, could pave the way for the emergence of a genuine middle class, something that China has never had in its more than two thousand years of history. Such a development would have profound, and profoundly positive, implications for Chinese culture, society, and politics. At the moment, Chinese society falls well short of such a development, but nevertheless, there is emerging a group of people who have a real stake in the stability of Chinese society, who are outside of (if well connected with) the political system and positioned to make demands on that system, and who may well discover (however belatedly) an interest in law and property rights. Moreover, as Shanghai historian and social critic Xiao Gongqin points out, the diversification that has taken place in Chinese society over recent years means that most problems are localized. Workers and farmers raise demands specific to their own circumstances, and the prospects for societywide social movements are correspondingly reduced.[30] Such optimistic scenarios, however, require a period of con-

---

29. "Zhongguo shehui jiegou zhuanxing de zhongjinqi qushi yu yinhuan," p. 13.
30. Xiao Gongqin, "Zhongguo shehui ge jieji de zhengzhi taishi yu qianjing zhanwang"

tinued high-speed economic growth. Unfortunately, the prospects for that are uncertain at best. Should there be a major slowdown in economic growth, to say nothing of a crisis similar to those experienced by many other Asian nations in recent years, the potential for social violence is high.

On the other hand, if this *nouveau riche* group, as the study cited above suggests, squeezes out an emerging middle class and forms the sort of corrupt relationship with the political elite that has long plagued Latin American politics, then the prospects for social and political stability, not to mention democratization, are much less.

There are many indications that China's top leadership is aware of and intensely concerned about these socioeconomic problems and their political implications. The repeated crackdowns on corruption and the efforts to get the military out of business and to stop (or at least significantly slow) smuggling and the illegal remittance of funds abroad reflect this awareness.[31] So too do the ideological campaigns that seem so incomprehensible to Westerners, not to mention many of those forced to take part in them. One of the few tools the Party has to fight social and political disintegration is to force Party members to study official documents and to write self-examinations in an effort to bolster compliance, but the "three stresses" (*sanjiang*) campaign that Beijing has carried out since early 1999 seems to have created as much resentment among those forced to participate as it has compliance. Campaigns may buy the Party some time, but they are not an effective way to build institutions.

Politics in an Era of Domestic Change and Globalization

When one turns to the more specifically political aspects of contemporary China, it is apparent that there are important shifts under way both as generational change forces new adaptations and as the very changed intellectual and socioeconomic environment in which the government operates presents challenges to which the government must learn to respond with greater rapidity and flexibility if it is to survive.

The single greatest change in the political system in recent years

---

(The political attitudes of the various strata in China's society, and their prospects for the future), *Zhanlue yu guanli* (Strategy and Management/Beijing), no. 5 (October 1998), pp. 36–43.

31. Joseph Fewsmith, "China in 1998: Tacking to Stay the Course," *Asian Survey*, vol. 39, no. 1 (January/February 1999), pp. 99–113.

has been the passing of the revolutionary generation and the emergence of a new, better-trained, but less authoritative generation. Although there remain veteran revolutionaries who continue to constrain the top leadership in various ways, Deng Xiaoping's death in February 1997—which followed the deaths of other senior leaders such as Chen Yun (April 1995), Li Xiannian (June 1992), and Hu Qiaomu (September 1992)—really brought about the demise of the first generation of Chinese Communist Party (CCP) leadership and of revolutionary legitimacy as well. Deng liked to refer to himself as the "core" of the "second generation" of leadership in order to distinguish himself from the discredited leadership and policies of Mao Zedong. But Deng, born in 1904, was merely a decade younger than Mao and had participated in all the great revolutionary struggles, including most significantly the Long March. It was a generation that felt assured both of its right to rule and of its ability to do so. By and large, these claims were accepted by younger people in the Party and by society at large.

No such natural legitimacy accrues to Jiang Zemin and his colleagues. In part because neither his nor the Party's legitimacy is assured in the way Deng's was, Jiang is intensely conscious of ideology. He understands that both the coherence of the Party and the legitimacy of the government depend significantly on articulating a rationale for their continued rule. Reflecting on the challenge he faced, Jiang reportedly once said that Mao Zedong's generation had the theory of revolutionary socialism and Deng Xiaoping's generation had the theory of building socialism with Chinese characteristics, but the third generation (that is, Jiang Zemin's generation) had not yet put its ideological stamp on politics.[32] The absence of such an ideological stamp reflected both the very different state-society relationship Jiang faced and the more particular problem of establishing Jiang's legitimacy vis-à-vis his colleagues. In terms of the party-state's relationship to society, Jiang had (and has) the unenviable task of trying to build an institutionalized, regularized relationship. In a sense, Mao and Deng had the easy jobs: Mao centralized, and Deng decentralized. Neither built viable institutions regulating the central government's relationship either with local levels of government or with the broader society. That task falls to Jiang.

---

32. Joseph Fewsmith, "Jockeying for Position in the Post-Deng Era," *Current History*, vol. 94, no. 593 (September 1995), pp. 252–58.

In terms of the narrower political question of establishing his authority vis-à-vis his colleagues, Jiang had the task of replacing leaders of his own generation and older who felt, with some legitimacy, that they were as well qualified as Jiang and thus were reluctant to take orders from him with a younger group who would, he hoped, be more compliant. This was a process that Jiang undertook in several steps, first defeating a challenge from military leader Yang Shangkun in 1992, then elevating protégés at the Central Committee's Fourth Plenum in 1994, and then significantly rejuvenating the Central Committee at the Fifteenth Party Congress in 1997. Yet Jiang has never believed that simply replacing people is sufficient either to ensure his own control or to maintain the Party's control over society. The explosion of corruption and smuggling as well as the fusion of party and business, not only in the Party but also in the military, was testimony to the erosion of party discipline and the loss of faith not only in any ruling ideology but perhaps in the future of the Party as well.[33] That is why Jiang places so much emphasis on ideology and party discipline.

If legitimacy has been Jiang's number one problem, coping with the very rapidly changing socioeconomic conditions outlined above has ranked a close second. There were at least two aspects of this problem. One was that as Chinese society and economy diversified and as the Party lost much of its ability to command allegiance, the role of interests became conspicuously greater. Although there continued to be problems with those who objected to reforms on ideological grounds, the influence of the "Old Left"—the ideologically more orthodox wing of the Party identified with senior ideologue Hu Qiaomu before his death and former propaganda head Deng Liqun—waned after 1992 and nearly evaporated after 1997.[34] Its place, however, was taken by a variety of interests—regional, local, ministerial, and sectoral—that seemed to defend their turf more vigorously and more directly than

---

33. Joseph Fewsmith, "Reaction, Resurgence, and Succession: Chinese Politics since Tiananmen," in *The Politics of China: The Eras of Mao and Deng,* ed. Roderick MacFarquhar, 2nd ed. (Cambridge: Cambridge University Press, 1997), pp. 472–531.

34. The term "Old Left" generally refers to a group of older CCP cadres who remain wedded to more orthodox understandings of Marxism-Leninism and worried about the impact of trends, such as the growth of private business and new interpretations of ideology, that undermine the traditional social and ideological bases of Party rule. In addition to the Old Left, there are many people with nationalistic or conservative ideas who are not particularly identified with the Old Left but who constitute a Party constituency that is threatened by the changes that are taking place, both domestically and internationally. This pressure must be taken seriously by Jiang Zemin and other top Party leaders.

before. Moreover, a strong sense of nationalism has taken the place on the ideological spectrum once occupied by the Old Left.

Second, the hard nut of SOE reform, which was inextricably bound up with the increasingly severe problems in the fiscal system, presented an increasing drag on the economy as well as on state resources. Although the size of the state-owned economy shrank from some 75 percent of GNP at the beginning of the reforms to less than 35 percent by 1995, it continues to dominate some sectors of the economy, particularly heavy industry. Because these are important sectors of the economy and because their reform (or lack thereof) has strong implications for the viability of the banking sector, SOE reform is something that simply cannot be avoided. Moreover, half measures have arguably made the situation worse, not better.[35]

Both the "interest group" nature of contemporary Chinese politics and the severity of sectoral problems in the economy are closely related to China's role in the international economy, particularly to its probable entry into the World Trade Organization (WTO). Exports are essential for shoring up the economy, but entry into the WTO would present formidable competitive challenges to many industries.

The conflicting demands on the political system are reflected both in the composition of the top leadership and in the group of people Jiang has gathered around him to advise on policy. Within the top leadership, there are conservative figures, headed by former premier Li Peng (now head of the National People's Congress), who have extensive ties throughout the government bureaucracy and with Party elders. There are also bold reformers, personified by the current premier Zhu Rongji, who understand the need to bring about a rapid and dramatic restructuring of the economy. Within Jiang's own entourage, there is likewise a diversity of people, reflecting Jiang's need to keep in close touch with different constituencies in the Party. There are, for instance, conservative officials such as Teng Wensheng, Deng Liqun's protégé, who heads the Policy Research Office of the Central Committee, and Ding Guan'gen, the conservative head of the Propaganda Department, who Jiang continues to employ despite his being widely disliked within the Party, not to mention among intellectuals. At the same time, there are more "liberal" advisors, such as former Shanghai mayor and

35. Edward Steinfeld, *Forging Reform in China* (New York: Cambridge University Press, 1998), pp. 13–22; and Nicholas Lardy, *China's Unfinished Economic Reform* (Washington, D.C.: Brookings Institution Press, 1998).

all-around political mentor Wang Daohan, who has played a critical role in helping Jiang navigate the hidden shoals of elite politics, has shaped much of Jiang's approach to foreign affairs, and has been invaluable as a liaison with the intellectual community. There is also Liu Ji, Jiang's close friend from Shanghai who served as vice president of the Chinese Academy of Social Sciences (CASS) from 1993 to 1997 and has continued to play a very active if much lower profile role since leaving CASS. In between, there are a number of people who have worked to further Jiang's interests bureaucratically. The most important of these is Zeng Qinghong, who served as head of the Central Committee's General Office from 1993 to 1998 and then moved over to head the important Organization Department. Zeng was promoted to alternate member of the Politburo at the Fifteenth Party Congress in 1997 and may well one day emerge as leader of China in his own right.[36]

This effort to pull together, or at least accommodate, divergent views and interests within the Party has been reflected in Jiang's political stewardship over the past several years, particularly since he began to come into his own following the Fourth Plenum in late 1994. In general, what Jiang has done has been to steal a page from Deng Xiaoping's book of political strategy by trying to carve out a "middle course" that encompasses a fairly wide spectrum of opinion within the Party but nevertheless isolates both ideological hard-liners and "bourgeois liberals."[37]

If one looks back to 1995, one can see the ideologically conservative side of Jiang on display. Coming out of the Fourth Plenum the previous fall, and meeting the challenge raised by the Old Left in the first of a series of "ten-thousand-character manifestos" (*wanyanshu*), Jiang stressed ideological orthodoxy by calling for "talking politics" (*jiang zhengzhi*).[38] This was, perhaps, a natural outcome of the Fourth Plenum, which had taken "party building" as its theme, and of Jiang's

---

36. This paragraph draws on Gao Xin, *Jiang Zemin de muliao* (Jiang Zemin's counselors) (Hong Kong: Mirror Books, 1996).

37. On Deng's middle course, see Tang Tsou, "Political Change and Reform: The Middle Course," in *The Cultural Revolution and Post-Mao Reforms*, ed. Tang Tsou (Chicago: University of Chicago Press, 1986), pp. 219–58.

38. The "ten-thousand-character manifestos" were a series of conservative ideological statements circulated informally but widely between 1995 and early 1997 that challenged the direction of reform. Although they represented a rear-guard action by the Party's more ideologically orthodox wing, they presented a real problem for Jiang at the time. See Shi Liaozi, ed., *Beijing dixia 'wanyanshu'* (Beijing's underground ten thousand–character manifestos) (Hong Kong: Mirror Books, 1997).

overall efforts to secure his own authority in the face of obvious challenges from both the left and the right. By late 1995 and early 1996, one sees Jiang trying to define his program in somewhat more positive terms by giving a series of internal speeches distinguishing Marxism from anti-Marxism in seven areas, including socialist democracy versus Western parliamentary democracy, developing a diverse economy with a predominant public sector versus privatization, and studying what is advanced in the West versus fawning on the West. As such distinctions suggest, Jiang was reaching for a formula that would permit him to move pragmatically beyond the ideological strictures of the Old Left without leaving him open to the charges of being "lax" on "bourgeois liberalization" that had toppled his two immediate predecessors, Hu Yaobang and Zhao Ziyang.

The most systematic effort to define a middle course and respond to the criticisms of the left came when Xing Bensi, vice president of the Central Party School, published a long article in the *People's Daily*. Apparently angered by the silence with which the *People's Daily* greeted his speeches—a silence apparently induced by the inability of top leaders to agree on how to respond—Jiang arranged for the publication of Xing's article.

In trying to define what constituted "real" Marxism (and thus refute the Old Left that positioned itself as the defender of the faith), Xing argued that a lot had changed since the birth of Marx 150 years before. Xing argued that there are parts of Marxism that contain universal truth and are still applicable, parts that need to be supplemented, and parts that are "completely unsuitable for use, which should not be continued or upheld in the present day."[39] Thus, Xing stated, "The criterion for determining the border dividing Marxism and anti-Marxism has to rest on developed Marxism; in present day China the 'only correct' criterion for distinguishing Marxism and anti-Marxism is the 'theory of socialism with Chinese characteristics established by Deng Xiaoping'"—most importantly upholding the "one center [economic construction] and two basic points [the four cardinal principles and emancipating the mind]." Xing thus juxtaposed "Deng Xiaoping theory" against leftist thought and referred explicitly to the first ten-thousand-character manifesto when he criticized those who declared that reform had created a "new bourgeoisie."

---

39. Xing Bensi, "Jianchi Makesi zhuyi bu dongyao" (Uphold Marxism without wavering), *Renmin ribao* (People's Daily), June 6, 1996, p. 9.

At the same time, Xing defined a "right" that was just as anti-Marxist as the left. Xing cited several manifestations of rightism, including "privatization" and revisionist interpretations of Chinese history that implied that China had taken the wrong road in pursuing the revolutionary path and that it was now necessary to say "farewell to revolution." This was a reference to a well-known book of the same title by prominent philosopher Li Zehou and leading literary critic Liu Zaifu, both of whom were then living in the United States.[40] The criticism of their book appears to have been a useful bit of political artifice. Although *Farewell to Revolution* does raise uncomfortable legitimacy issues, its primary function in Xing's piece appears to have been to provide a "right" to complement the "left" and thus define a "middle course" for Jiang. It may also have been chosen as a symbol of rightist thinking to warn liberal thinkers to hold their peace as Jiang turned his primary attention to warding off the left.[41]

Another sign of Jiang's effort to distinguish his own political program from those of the left and right was the publication, in late 1996, of *Heart-to-Heart Talks with the General Secretary*. This book brought together fourteen young scholars, mostly based at CASS, to flesh out the contents of the speech Jiang had made on twelve major problems confronting China at the Fifth Plenum the previous year. Part of the intent of the book was to counter the rising tide of nationalism and to point the way to adopting the shareholding system for SOEs, which would be made official the following year at the Fifteenth Party Congress. What was most eye-catching about the volume was the preface and endorsement by Liu Ji, vice president of CASS and close friend of Jiang Zemin. *Heart-to-Heart Talks with the General Secretary* anticipated the publication of a new series of books, called *Contemporary China's Problems* (Dangdai Zhongguo wenti), under the sponsorship of Liu Ji that would eventually include more than twenty titles.

Following Deng's death in February 1997, Jiang began to move with remarkable self-confidence. In his eulogy at Deng's funeral, Jiang quoted Deng as saying when he returned to power in the late 1970s that there are two possible attitudes: "One is to act as a bureaucrat, the other

---

40. Li Zehou and Liu Zaifu, *Gaobie geming: Huiwang ershi shiji Zhongguo* (Farewell to revolution: Reviewing twentieth-century China) (Hong Kong: Cosmos Books, 1996).

41. Shen Hongpei, "Ershi shijimo gongchan zhuyi dalunzhan" (The great debate over communism at the end of the twentieth century), *Beijing dixia 'wanyanshu,'* p. 9.

is to work."[42] It seemed a risky quotation for Jiang to cite, given his reputation for caution. In retrospect, however, it seems that Jiang was using Deng to make a personal declaration, namely, that he was determined to "work," too. Indeed, he did, for by the time of Deng's death, Jiang had the Fifteenth Party Congress clearly in mind. Within a month of Deng's death, a draft of Jiang's report to the Fifteenth Party Congress, which would make important revisions to the Party's understanding of "socialist ownership," was circulated for comment.

Although economic liberals welcomed Jiang's report, ideological conservatives hated it. Rather than again tacking to the left, as he had many times in the past, Jiang went to the Central Party School in late May to give the most important political speech of his career. In a thinly veiled jab at the left, Jiang declared that "there is no way out if we study Marxism in isolation and separate and set it against vivid development in real life." In the unpublicized portion of the speech, Jiang went further, explicitly criticizing the left and laying out his rationale for reform of the ownership structure. Deng had raised the slogan "Guard against the right, but guard primarily against the left" in his 1992 trip to the south, but it had been largely dropped from the official media (except for inclusion in formal Party resolutions) following the Fourteenth Party Congress later that year. Now Jiang was reviving it and identifying himself with Deng's reforms. For a leader often criticized as bland, cautious, and technocratic, Jiang was beginning to reveal a boldness previously visible only in his deft maneuvers against political enemies.

The relaxation of the political atmosphere that was associated with the discussions leading up to and following the Fifteenth Party Congress brought about what is sometimes called the "Beijing spring," a period of limited opening up of public discussion that actually started the previous fall. This limited opening can perhaps be traced to the letter that Beijing University economics professor Shang Dewen sent to the Central Committee in August 1997, the first of three such missives. Shang argued that economic reform could not go further without an opening of the political system. In October, a month after the party congress, Fang Jue, a reform-minded official in the southeastern province of Fujian, distributed a statement calling for political reform.[43] In

---

42. Xinhua, February 25, 1997.

43. Fang Jue, "China Needs a New Transformation: Program Proposals of the Democratic Faction," *China Rights Forum*, spring 1998. This discussion draws on my arti-

December, Hu Jiwei, the crusading former editor-in-chief of the *People's Daily*, published a series of articles calling for political reform in a major Hong Kong daily.[44] In January, the economics journal *Reform* carried an article advocating political reform written by Li Shenzhi, the highly respected former head of the Institute of American Studies at the CASS,who had been removed in the wake of Tiananmen.[45] In March, the little-known journal *Methods (Fangfa)*, carried several articles calling for political reform.[46] And in May, a rapidly edited book called *Beijing University's Tradition and Modern China* took advantage of the approaching centennial anniversary of Beijing University to emphasize the liberal tradition in China. A preface by Li Shenzhi noted that liberalism is not native to China but that since its introduction into China through Beijing University, liberalism has struck roots and become a part of China's tradition.[47]

The most controversial book of the spring was *Crossed Swords (Jiaofeng)*. Written by two journalists at the *People's Daily*, the book starts by tracing the history of the emergence of the Dengist reforms—particularly the opening up of intellectual freedom—against the opposition of Mao's successor, Hua Guofeng. *Crossed Swords* goes on to link this early period of relaxation to the heated debates surrounding Deng Xiaoping's trip to the south in 1992. Finally, and most controversially, the book details the sharp political debates of 1995–97. These debates pitted those who wanted to advance reform further against those leftist ideologues who continued to oppose the marketization,

---

cle, "Jiang Zemin Takes Command," *Current History*, vol. 97, no. 620 (September 1998), pp. 250–56.

44. Hu Jiwei, "If the Party Is Correct, Bad Things Can Be Turned into Good Things; If the Party Is Wrong, Good Things Can Be Turned into Bad Things," *Hsin Pao*, December 29, 1997, trans. in *FBIS-CHI-97-363* (December 30, 1997); Hu Jiwei, "Despotic Dictatorship Lingers On—Notes on Studying the Political Report of the 15th Party Congress," *Hsin Pao*, December 30, 1997, trans. in *FBIS-CHI-97-364* (January 1, 1998); and Hu Jiwei, "Given a Good Central Committee, We Will Have a Good Party; Given a Good Party, We Will Have a Good State—Notes on Studying the Political Report of the 15th Party Congress," *Hsin Pao*, December 31, 1997, trans. in *FBIS-CHI-97-365* (January 2, 1998).

45. Li Shenzhi, "Cong genbenshang shenhua gaige de sixiang" (Fundamentally deepening thinking about reform) *Jiefang wenxuan (1978–1998)* (Beijing: Jingji ribao chubanshe, 1998).

46. See *Fangfa* (Methods/Beijing) (March 1998), pp. 4–15.

47. Li Shenzhi, "Hongyang Beida de ziyou zhuyi chuantong" (Extol the liberal tradition of Beijing University), preface to *Beida chuantong yu jindai Zhongguo* (Beijing University's tradition and modern China), ed. Liu Junning (Beijing: Zhongguo renshi chubanshe, 1998), pp. 1–5.

and especially the privatization, of the Chinese economy, as well as China's continued integration into the world economy and the progressive abandonment of Marxism. Ignoring certain historical realities—particularly that much of Deng's animus in his 1992 trip was directed against Jiang Zemin, who was then seen as lukewarm at best toward reform—the book portrays Jiang as inheriting and pushing forward the "emancipation of the mind" begun in 1978.[48] Picking up on Jiang's report to the Fifteenth Party Congress and Li Peng's remarks at the same time, the book calls the current opening China's "third emancipation of the mind."

Crossed Swords was even more controversial than other works published during the Beijing spring because it was included in Liu Ji's series, *Contemporary China's Problems*, mentioned above. Despite Liu Ji's close relationship with Jiang Zemin, it seems that the publication of *Crossed Swords* was part of the ongoing conduct of the "court politics" surrounding the Party leader, thus reflecting the inevitable conflicts among the diverse group of people Jiang had brought together under his wing. For instance, Wang Renzhi, the former head of the Propaganda Department who was forced to step down following Deng's trip to the south and take up the position of Party secretary of CASS, took a very negative view of the publication of *Heart-to-Heart Talks with the General Secretary* and quarreled on more than one occasion with Liu Ji. This may well have influenced Liu's willingness to allow the publication of *Crossed Swords*. In any event, it was clear that the publication of *Crossed Swords* did set off a political maelstrom. Ding Guan'gen, the conservative head of the Propaganda Department, quickly condemned the book. Wang Renzhi was predictably outraged, as was conservative elder Song Ping. On the liberal side, Party elder Wan Li had an unusual meeting with the authors in which he defended the book. Nevertheless, leftists, who were angered by the wholesale criticism of them in *Crossed Swords*, organized a meeting in April to criticize the book, to which they invited Communist ideologues from Russia (provoking liberals to mock the event as a gathering of the "Communist International"). Eventually, the editors of the conservative journal *Zhongliu*, which had published some of the "ten-thousand-character manifestos," took the authors of *Crossed Swords* to court,

---

48. Ling Zhijun and Ma Licheng, *Jiaofeng: Dangdai Zhongguo disanci sixiang jiefang shilu* (Crossed Swords: The third thought liberation campaign in contemporary China) (Beijing: Jinri Zhongguo chubanshe, 1998).

charging copyright violation. The court eventually dismissed the charges, but not until after some dramatic political theater.[49]

Jiang's limited movement to the "right" reflected an interesting intersection of domestic and foreign policy. On the domestic front, in view of the very difficult problems facing the economy, Jiang had clearly decided to distance himself from Li Peng's more cautious approach to economic reform and had decided to endorse Zhu Rongji's bold moves to restructure the government, the economy, and the relationship between the two. Major reform measures simply require a more open political atmosphere in China. At the same time, the political relaxation on the domestic front was related to a broad-ranging effort to repair relations with the United States. The nationalist mood that had welled up in the wake of the *Yin He* incident and particularly following Taiwan president Lee Teng-hui's visit to the United States hampered both domestic reform and the stability of China's international environment, which was seen as essential to continued economic reform and development, which in turn depended on both stable export markets and a large amount of investment from abroad.

Indeed, the evidence strongly suggests that as Jiang was coming into power, his strategy was to ease China's international relations so as to create a better environment for domestic reform and to support a major restructuring of the economy (including making the necessary ideological revisions) while nevertheless sounding certain conservative ideological themes both to shore up support among the conservative wing of the Party and to try to reinforce Party discipline. Thus, in early 1995, Jiang tried to ease relations across the Taiwan Strait, only to have the policy blow up in his face as Lee Teng-hui traveled to the United States and made highly provocative comments while visiting his alma mater, Cornell University. The crisis that soon unfolded in the Strait, however, ironically provided a new opportunity to relax international tensions as both the United States and China worked to back away from the abyss.

Part of this effort consisted of quasi-official initiatives to depict the United States in a more favorable light. That there was a need to do so says much about the public resentment that had built up against the United States in the mid-1990s and about the role that public opinion was beginning to play, even in the formulation of foreign policy.

49. "Zhongliu Loses Lawsuit against 'Jiaofeng,'" *Ming Pao*, April 23, 1999, p. B15, trans. in *FBIS-CHI-1999-0423* (April 23, 1999).

Perhaps the most important of these initiatives was the publication of *China Should Not Be 'Mr. No'* by Shen Jiru, a senior researcher with CASS's Institute of World Economics and Politics. Part of Liu Ji's *Contemporary China's Problems* book series, *China Will Not Be 'Mr. No'* joined the longstanding debate about the causes of the collapse of the Soviet Union. Shen argued that it had been the steadfast refusal of the Soviet leaders to cooperate with other countries and open their country up (which earned Soviet foreign minister Andrei Gromyko the nickname of "Mr. No") that had brought about its demise. In opposition to conservatives' argument that it was reform that led to collapse, Shen argued that it was the *lack* of reform that had brought about the failure of socialism in the Soviet Union and Eastern Europe.[50]

Jiang's strategy reflected at least in part the growing recognition in Beijing, particularly in the wake of the Asian financial crisis, that China's fate was bound up with joining the world, not with resisting global trends. Thus, Jiang stated in March 1998, "We have to gain a complete and correct understanding of the issue of economic 'globalization' and properly deal with it. Economic globalization is an objective trend of world economic development, from which none can escape and in which everyone has to participate."[51] It was this recognition that lay behind the exchange of summits between Jiang and President Clinton in October 1997 and June 1998. It also lay behind the far-ranging reforms announced at the Fifteenth Party Congress in September 1997 and the First Session of the Ninth National People's Congress in March 1998 (when a major restructuring of the government was announced), as well as the sweeping efforts made to join the WTO in 1999. Overall, Jiang was remarkably successful in combining this recognition with domestic politics in the first year following Deng's death; he would not be so lucky in 1999.

A Politically Sensitive Year

By late 1998, it was already apparent that the last year of the century was shaping up to be one of extraordinary political sensitivity—but no one could have predicted the bizarre twists that would occur. The Asian financial crisis, which had seemed at first to have bypassed China, began to bite as exports became more difficult and foreign investment

50. Shen, *Zhongguo bu dang 'bu xiansheng.'*
51. *Renmin ribao*, March 9, 1998, p. 1.

began to fall. The slowed economy, accompanied by a fall in the consumer index, made the ongoing economic restructuring even more politically sensitive as more than the expected number of workers lost their jobs or could not find employment in the first place. Reports of violence in the countryside, as described in Jonathan Unger's chapter in this volume, suggested the volatile situation there.

It was under these conditions that the Chinese leadership faced the most politically sensitive season in a decade, which would include the fortieth anniversary of the Tibetan revolt (March 10), the eightieth anniversary of the May Fourth Movement, the tenth anniversary of Hu Yaobang's death (April 15), the tenth anniversary of Tiananmen (June 4), and, finally, the fiftieth anniversary of the founding of the PRC (October 1). The leadership was clearly already thinking about this series of anniversaries: one of the construction projects that was to be completed before October 1 was a renovation of Tiananmen Square, which somehow required the square to be surrounded by a solid fence for some seven months between December and July, denying the public space to potential demonstrators. Caution was clearly the order of the day as Jiang and others focused on orchestrating a grand birthday party for the PRC.

As carefully as the leadership planned, events would conspire to make 1999 a less than successful year. Neither foreign relations nor the domestic situation fell into place, raising new questions about the ability of the regime to provide a political "soft landing."

Jiang Zemin's November 1998 summit meeting in Japan provided an intimation of what was to come. This trip was intended as the capstone of a successful year of diplomacy. The exchange of summits with the United States and Jiang's trip to Russia just prior to his Japanese sojourn had seemingly repaired or improved all of China's great power relations. The trip to Japan would display Jiang's diplomatic prowess by showing that he could promote good relations on terms favorable to China. But Jiang overreached. Japan had offered a full apology for its history of aggression in Korea to Kim Dae-Jung, and Jiang thought he could extract a similar statement. He also wanted to push Japan on the Taiwan issue, asking that it repeat the "Three No's" that President Clinton had offered during his trip to China. The trip was new foreign minister Tang Jiaxuan's first big test. A diplomat trained as a Japan specialist, Tang might have been expected to orchestrate a smooth visit, but domestic pressures in China made it difficult to pull off. The results were disappointing. Jiang gave his hosts a long lecture on history,[52] and a prepared joint communiqué was left unsigned. Japanese public opinion was alienated by Jiang's seemingly rude behavior, and Jiang returned home not in triumph but to new doubts about his diplomatic skills.

More unexpected, and more serious, than Jiang's diplomatic dust-up in Japan was the downturn in U.S.-China relations. The exchange of summits had created a significantly better atmosphere, but this goodwill quickly dissipated as old problems returned and new ones came up. The human rights issue, seemingly tempered by the summit meetings, suddenly returned to plague the relationship as China moved to jail a number of dissidents trying to form a new political party. The arrest and sentencing to long jail terms of Xu Wenli, Wang Youcai, and other China Democratic Party activists in December 1998 was merely the prelude to further arrests and sentencings the following year. Critics quickly charged China with blatant hypocrisy: it signed the UN Covenant on Political and Civil Rights in October and then rounded up dissidents in December.

These new outcries came at a time when charges of campaign finance violations involving the United States were once again heating up. Stories of Chinese contributions had first been raised in the winter of 1997–98 but had died down after the Thompson hearings failed to produce any solid evidence. In May 1999, however, the charges acquired new life as Democratic fund-raiser Johnny Chung finally testified before Congress. According to Chung, Ji Shengde, head of China's military intelligence, had given him $300,000 toward support of President Clinton's presidential campaign—only $35,000 of which was actually passed to the Democrats.[53]

The most explosive charges, however, came from the committee headed by Christopher Cox, which alleged that the Chinese government had systematically stolen the United States' most advanced nuclear weapons designs. The release of the declassified version of the

---

52. Jiang Zemin, "Take a Warning from History and Usher in the Future," Xinhua, November 28, 1998, trans. in *FBIS-CHI-98-333*.

53. David Johnson, "Committee Told of Beijing Cash for Democrats," *New York Times*, May 12, 1999, p. A1; and Ann Scott Tyson, "Tale of Deep Pockets and Diplomacy," *Christian Science Monitor*, May 17, 1999, p. 1. Ji was later reassigned. See Henry Chu and Jim Mann, "Chinese Reassign Intelligence Chief Implicated in Fund Raising Scandal," *Los Angeles Times*, July 3, 1999, p. A4.

report in March created a new upsurge of anti-Chinese sentiment—despite the fact that the report was so hedged with suppositions that most weapons experts distrusted its conclusions, or at least the farthest-reaching of its conclusions, doubting that the Chinese had acquired anywhere near as much as the Cox report intimated or that they had put it into production.[54] Chinese American scientist Wen Ho Lee was removed from his job at Los Alamos laboratory, but it was months before he was eventually indicted—and then on security violations rather than espionage charges.

Against this background, the United States began to bomb Yugoslavia on March 24. Frustrated by its failure to persuade Yugoslav president Slobodan Milosevic to sign a compromise agreement at Ramboulait and by its repeated failure to cow him with threats, NATO embarked on a course of military action intended to force an end to systematic human rights violations in Kosovo. The United States and its NATO allies clearly saw going through the United Nations as fruitless, whereas the Chinese leadership just as clearly saw the failure to do so as a gross violation of international law. There was certainly much hypocrisy in the position of the Chinese leaders—they consistently ignored Serbian violations of human rights and made no effort to bring about a viable solution in the United Nations—but the willingness of NATO to simply ignore the United Nations raised China's worst fears about U.S. intentions.

It was in this poisonous atmosphere that Premier Zhu Rongji arrived in the United States on April 6 to discuss China's accession to the WTO. With his unique ability to combine humor and intelligence, Zhu almost single-handedly turned back the wave of anti-Chinese sentiment that had grown up in the preceding months. Making sweeping concessions, Zhu made clear that China wanted to join the WTO and the world. This was a leadership that understood the importance of trade and the inevitability of globalization.

Then, as if to prove that history really does progress without rhyme or reason, mistakes started happening. The first was made by President Clinton. Presented with an opportunity to top off the years he had devoted to improving U.S.-China relations (after notably contributing to their decline during his first two years in office), the president flinched. Once again the trees blinded him to the forest. Trent Lott, in

54. Patrick E. Tyler, "Who's Afraid of China," *New York Times Magazine*, August 1, 1999, pp. 46–49.

stating his unalloyed opposition to China's entry into the WTO, left no doubt in the president's mind that China policy would be a divisive domestic issue.[55] At the same time, Secretary of the Treasury Robert Rubin, perhaps not adequately briefed on the total package, voiced doubts over the banking and securities portions of the agreement. So the president, perhaps feeling that a yet better deal could be done, sided with the doubters over the advice of his national security advisor Sandy Berger and Secretary of State Madeleine Albright.

Zhu returned to Beijing on April 21 to accusations that he had given up too much, but before Zhu had a chance to overcome the naysayers, the domestic atmosphere in China was transformed once again. In spite of having prepared for months for the possibility of demonstrations in the spring, the leadership was caught completely unawares on April 25 when ten thousand members of the Falun Gong—many of them elderly—appeared suddenly and without warning outside of Zhongnanhai, the leadership compound. There were no speeches or protests; the crowd simply sat and meditated, directing their *qi* (inner spirit) at the CCP leadership.

Zhu Rongji, the "passionate premier" as some in Beijing call him, sent people to the gate of Zhongnanhai to ask what was going on. In response, five members of the Falun Gong were deputed to talk to Zhu in Zhongnanhai. What must have been more disturbing than anything said was the rank of the representatives. At least three of the five were reportedly very high-ranking, albeit retired, officials, including one retired major general who had worked in the military intelligence section of the People's Liberation Army's General Staff Department.[56]

Jiang Zemin was clearly disturbed by the demonstration. Sometime after midnight, he reportedly took pen in hand and wrote a letter to his colleagues in the Politburo Standing Committee. Saying that he could not sleep because of the day's events, he wondered how such a large demonstration could have occurred without any warning from any central department. His concerns could only have been compounded when he received a long letter from Li Qihua, former head of the 301 hospital (the top military hospital that serves the leadership). Li said that Marxism-Leninism could explain many things

---

55. Paul Blustein and Steven Mufson, "Clinton Urges China Foes Not to Stoke a New Cold War," *Washington Post*, April 8, 1999, p. A2.

56. Author's interviews; John Pomfret, "China Sect Penetrated Military and Police; Security Infiltration Spurred Crackdown," *Washington Post*, August 7, 1999, p. A15.

about the natural world but that there were many things beyond the natural world that it could not explain. The teachings of the Falun Gong filled this void and should not be seen as incompatible with Marxism-Leninism. Jiang Zemin reportedly wrote him a long letter criticizing his views. Li was then visited by two high-ranking officials and subsequently wrote a two-page self-criticism recanting his views.[57]

The subsequent crackdown on the Falun Gong, including arrests, detentions, study sessions, and a very wide-ranging and harsh propaganda campaign, has evoked new concerns abroad with human rights issues. No doubt the campaign has been, as all such campaigns are, harsher and more ham-handed than necessary, but the government's crackdown draws more on a two-thousand-year tradition of political autocracy than it does on Marxism-Leninism or communist dictatorship—just as the Falun Gong itself draws on a long millenarian tradition of combining martial arts with spiritual mysticism. What obviously disturbed Jiang Zemin and other leaders most was the extent of the Falun Gong's organization, its obvious ability to mobilize people quickly, and its deep penetration into the military and security ranks, which potentially diluted the Party's ability to control those important pillars of rule.[58] Jiang thus reacted just as China's imperial governments had acted before him; the risk was that the crackdown would further politicize the Falun Gong or similar movements, just as imperial crackdowns had provoked rebellion from the White Lotus, Taiping, and other sects.[59]

Domestic politics and international relations came crashing together dramatically and unexpectedly early on the morning of May 8 (Beijing time) when five laser-guided U.S. bombs slammed into the Chinese embassy in Belgrade, killing three and injuring twenty. The Chinese leadership was stunned and confused. It spent three days in an intense round of meetings, reflecting both the weakness of China's crisis-management system and the array of conflicting opinions that existed at high levels. It is clear that domestic considerations were the highest

---

57. Author's interviews; "Resolutely Support the Party Central Committee's Policy Decision, and Forever Listen to and Follow the Party, *Jiefangjun Bao*, July 30, 1999, trans. in *FBIS-CHI-1999-0823* (August 24,1999); and Seth Faison, "Ex-General, Member of Banned Sect, Confesses 'Mistakes,' China Says," *New York Times*, July 31, 1999, p. A5.

58. John Pomfret, "China Sect Penetrated Military and Police."

59. Daniel L. Overmyer, *Folk Buddhist Religion: Dissenting Sects in Imperial China* (Cambridge: Harvard University Press, 1976).

priority. The depth of public anger was real and should not be under-estimated. Talk of "mistakes" was quickly dismissed by most of the public; not only had the bombs clearly been targeted to hit the building, but also the people believed that U.S. intelligence could not make a mistake of that magnitude. And the event seemed to fit into a pattern of U.S. efforts to hold China down: everything from human rights concerns to the Cox report to U.S. support for Taiwan seemed to reflect hostility toward China. Understanding the need for a public release of anger, the leadership quickly yielded to students determined to march on the U.S. embassy. The government provided buses to bring the students to the embassy area; directed them to march past the ambassador's residence, the embassy, and the visa section; allowed them to throw stones, bricks, and ink bottles; and then bused them back to their campuses. It was a way of channeling genuine public anger and preventing the alternative, namely, that students would take to the streets outside Zhongnanhai if they perceived the Chinese government as being "weak."

Despite this public show of anger, the Chinese leadership quickly came to two basic conclusions: first, whatever the reason for the bombing, it did not reflect policy at the highest levels of the U.S. government, and second, U.S.-China relations were too important to be sacrificed to the emotions of the moment. Trade and a stable international environment were essential for China's continued economic development, and domestic stability was impossible without economic development.

This basic understanding hardly meant that the Chinese government was unified. Hard-liners quickly spun out scenarios that "proved" that the bombing was deliberate and, more important, that the United States was engaged in a long-term strategy to "contain" China.[60] The military quickly demanded more money to counter the perceived strategic threat. Even sophisticated and open-minded intellectuals viewed international trends in ominous terms. The focal point for much of this anger and frustration was Zhu Rongji. Conservatives had cautioned against Zhu's going to the United States in the first place (because of the Kosovo situation) and were particularly angered when it was revealed (by the U.S. trade representative office's unilateral posting on

---

60. Zhang Wenmu, "Kesuowo zhanzheng yu Zhongguo xinshiji anquan zhanlue" (The Kosovo war and China's security strategy in the new century), *Zhanlue yu guanli* (June 1999), pp. 1–10.

the Internet) that he had made sweeping concessions in order to win WTO entry.

Zhu was abused mercilessly by public opinion and criticized within the government. Articles on the Internet as well as student demonstrators labeled him a "traitor" (*maiguozei*). At the same time, some old cadres were known to mutter that the government's readiness to accept globalization was like Wang Jingwei's willingness to serve as head of Japan's puppet government in occupied China during World War II. Others have called Zhu's compromises in Washington the "new twenty-one demands selling out the country"—a reference to Japan's infamous demands of 1915 that sought to reduce China to a near colony.[61]

By the time the Party retreated in late July for its annual conclave at the seaside resort of Beidaihe, Chinese politics had taken on a more conservative tone. Backing away from the limited liberalization of the "Beijing spring," Jiang had directed Party cadres to put their thoughts in order through a rectification campaign known as the "three stresses." Then, in response to Falun Gong activities, Jiang ordered the detention or arrest of numerous leaders as well as special study sessions for Party members who were also members of the Falun Gong. Still adhering to a middle course, Jiang was nevertheless closer in 1999 to the ideological conservative that he had been in the earlier years of his stewardship than to the more open-minded leader he had seemed in 1997–98.

Neither Jiang's efforts to bolster his own and the Party's authority through study campaigns nor his efforts to prevent social unrest by cracking down on democracy activists suggested a retreat to the old days. Jiang and the Party recognize the need to move forward with economic reform, as the Fourth Plenary Session of the Fifteenth Central Committee in September 1999 demonstrated. Nevertheless, the Party seems reluctant to endorse the far-reaching measures needed. Following a series of speeches on the reform of state-owned enterprises over the spring and summer, the Party endorsed a plan to move economic reform forward by further "corporatization" of SOEs. But further introduction of the shareholding system is not likely to revive the state sector unless hard-budget constraints can be enforced. And the intermingling of enterprise Party committees with the managerial boards of enterprises—which Jiang called for—seems designed more

---

61. Joseph Fewsmith, "The Impact of the Kosovo Conflict on China's Political Leaders and Prospects for WTO Accession," *NBR Briefing*, no. 6 (July 1999).

to make sure the "never-left-out class" never gets left out than to enforce market-conforming behavior.[62] The unstable social and political environment undoubtedly makes the Party reluctant to take more decisive measures, while the failure to implement more fundamental reforms, including political reforms, breeds further instability.

Conclusion

There is a "presentness" in the historical anniversaries that fell in the last years of the twentieth century not only because China is a country with a deep historical consciousness and not even because it is a country obsessed with its modern history but particularly because the unfolding of its reforms over a twenty-year period, during which both the domestic and international situations have changed dramatically, has allowed for a continual reflection on the meaning of history, on the roads taken and not taken, and on the choices for the future. The major issues that have roiled China's political waters over the past few years—China's relations with the United States, Japan, and Taiwan; the enormous socioeconomic changes brought about by the growth of the nonstate sector and the continuing problems in the state-run sector; and the problem of maintaining political control in the face of generational change, rising interest-group politics, an orgy of corruption, and a loss of political faith—all raise profound issues that are embedded in Chinese history, either the history of the revolution or the history of reform. This is why the intellectual debates outlined at the beginning of this article and explored in Cheng Li's chapter are of such importance and have taken on such a harsh tone.

During the decade of the 1980s, reformers could dismantle much of what Mao had built without fear of going "too far." However, with the student demonstrations of 1989, the poles around which debate had centered in the 1980s—reformers versus conservatives—were joined by a third possibility: political collapse and social disorder. The 1989

---

62. See "Zhongguo gongchandang di shiwuju zhongyang weiyuanhui di sici quanti huiyi gongbao" (Communiqué of the fourth plenary session of the Fifteenth Central Committee of the CCP), Xinhua, September 22, 1999. According to the communiqué, the plenum adopted the "Decision on Issues Related to State-Owned Enterprise Reforms and Development," the text of which was not available at the time this chapter was written. A pretty good idea of the content can be gathered from Jiang Zemin's long speech, "Strengthen Confidence, Deepen Reform, Create a New Situation in Development of State-Owned Enterprises," Xinhua, August 12, 1999, trans. in *FBIS-CHI-1999-0817* (August 18, 1999).

crisis provoked not only a political reaction but also, especially in light of the experience of Eastern Europe and the Soviet Union, a profound and sometimes painful intellectual reflection. Widespread concerns over "stability" were soon joined by new frustration over the corruption that accompanied marketization, especially the explosion of profiteering that occurred in the wake of Deng Xiaoping's trip to the south. If reformers in the 1980s, whether in policy-making circles or among the intelligentsia, had wanted to introduce "capitalism" (then more delicately called "market forces") to shake off the heavy hand of a bureaucratized ministerial economy, to create millions of new jobs, and to pursue China's comparative advantage internationally, China seemed to have too much capitalism by the mid-1990s—particularly the raw sort associated with Dickens' novels and Engels' early writings.

Does one continue to introduce more capitalism to right the wrongs of the capitalism that has already been introduced? And if one does, is there anything left to the revolution that cost China millions of lives and untold hardship? Is there anything of value in China's revolutionary legacy or was it all a mistake? These are some of the painful questions that lurk behind the very changed intellectual atmosphere of the 1990s, but they also affect, however indirectly, the political leadership as it tries to secure the loyalty, or at least the compliance, of the citizenry and to shore up its own legitimacy.

The political difficulties of dealing with the diverse problems of China at the turn of the century are formidable. The optimism of the 1980s that reform could easily rectify the problems of the past if only "leftism" and "feudalism" could be eradicated has faded. Economic development, diversification, and decentralization have created interests that erode compliance, while ideology has lost the attraction it once had. Nationalism has emerged as the ridgepole supporting the Party's claim to rule, but it is also a double-edged sword. Nationalism not only distinguishes China from a world its leadership knows China must join but also presents a powerful, populist critique of the leadership. Nationalism is inherently critical of the "never-left-out class" that has gorged itself at public expense for the last decade and more, and it demands that the political system open up to accommodate the "true" representatives of the people. The leadership senses a need to open up (hence the "Beijing spring" of 1998), but it also fears the challenges that come with doing so.

Both the pressures that Beijing faces and the problems of postrevolutionary succession have forced the leadership to look, albeit tentatively and uncertainly, to institutions—including tax reform, local elections, institutionalized retirement, property-rights reform, law, and the National People's Congress—to shore up the center's control, to allow different voices to be heard, and to regularize the relationship between state and society. Such changes, accompanying the far-reaching socio-economic changes outlined above, could lead to broad, though by no means instantaneous, changes in the conduct of politics. But institution building has come late to China. Not only have socioeconomic changes eroded much of the basis for institutional compliance at local levels, but the CCP itself seems conflicted about the desire for institutions. As institutions start to come into being, there are inevitably challenges to the CCP's control over power, and the Party responds with campaigns designed to shore up Party discipline—which inevitably undermine the institutions that are necessary for fundamental political change.

The answer to the question raised in the title of this chapter—can China leave the twentieth century behind?—depends on whether Jiang Zemin and other leaders of the CCP can deal with the various international and domestic political problems they face in ways that can absorb, channel, and institutionalize the socioeconomic changes that have taken place in recent years rather than yield to the pressures of interests that seek protection in the face of domestic and international competition, back down in the face of corruption that threatens to undermine all notions of law and order, and stifle all voices calling for change. Such changes would not revivify the CCP, at least in the traditional sense (whether or not the Party survives), but rather would change the zero-sum conception of political contestation that has so dominated and distorted twentieth-century politics.[63] The alternatives, as China enters the new century, are to allow the growth of pluralism and institutionalization or to replay much of the tragic history of the past century.

---

63. See Tang Tsou's observation that Chinese politics have been dominated by a conception that political power is "monistic and indivisible." Zou Dang (Tsou Tang), *Ershi shiji Zhongguo zhengzhi: cong hongguan lishi yu weiguan xingdong jiaodu kan* (Twentieth century Chinese politics: Viewed from the perspective of macro history and micro actions) (Hong Kong: Oxford University Press, 1994), p. 244.

The Chinese Economy:
Fifty Years into the Transformation

Barry Naughton

During the late 1990s, China's leaders have built on the achievements of two decades of economic reform, and the economy has taken new steps forward in industrialization and technological upgrading. The activity of recent years can readily be seen as a continuation of long-standing trends, as it has advanced both reform and modernization. Yet recent measures also represent some of the most difficult—and the most contested—steps in the long and ongoing transformation process. And after many years in which the external environment was extremely favorable to China's economic objectives, recent economic trends in Asia and elsewhere have heaped problems onto China's already difficult economic transition. As a result, China approaches the turn of the millennium with more than a little extra uncertainty.

The challenges facing contemporary economic policy go well beyond the immediate problems of weak market demand and fragile financial institutions. Both technical and political obstacles may obstruct smooth economic development. China faces all the technical problems of creating a range of market institutions and managing the transition to a full market economy. The initial transition—away from a planned economy and toward a rudimentary market economy—has been achieved with remarkable success. But today, China faces a new set of challenges that are increasingly similar to those of other middle-income developing countries that are trying to reform and open their economies. Compared with past decades, the problems are actually more familiar, and the experiences of other countries are more available and more relevant. Nonetheless, there are no simple answers. Liberalization in developing countries often fails, owing to unsound institutions or misguided sequencing of liberalization measures, and China has no obvious model for future development nor roadmap to avoid pitfalls.

Liberalization, whether it succeeds or fails, is often accompanied by political or economic crisis. Economic changes often miscarry because important elements of institutional reform are obstructed or distorted by political opposition. As for China, it has been said that reform in the 1980s was change "without losers," in which most social groups gained and almost nobody was made worse off in absolute terms.[1] While this was true of the 1980s, it is emphatically not the case in the late 1990s. The further stages of state-owned enterprise (SOE) reform and the subjection of labor to market forces have created a clear class of losers, most apparent in the large number of SOE workers laid off since 1993. If any stage of China's economic transition is likely to provoke mass discontent, this is it. In one sense, China is simply pushing forward with its heretofore successful program of reform and modernization. In another sense, today's policy environment demands new measures that are more difficult and more dangerous than any in recent memory.

The Continuities of Change and China's Diversity Today

China has enormous geographical diversity, and it encompasses an enormous range of technologies and economic models as well. In vast stretches of rural China, peasants struggle on the margins of subsistence with primitive agriculture, while in Guangdong and Beijing a modern information economy takes root. Primitive machine shops powered by coal-fueled boilers coexist with e-commerce and ingenious software solutions. Bureaucratic public ownership struggles on, but it must compete both with hardworking petty capitalists and with slick finance specialists trained in the latest techniques at Western business schools. China contains incredible economic diversity that encompasses material conditions, type of activity, and variety of economic system. The diversity is due not only to China's vast size but also to two incomplete transitions. First, China is in the middle of the protracted transformation from a rural to an urban society, in the midst of the processes of modernization and industrialization. Second, China is still completing its transition away from bureaucratic socialism and

---

1. Lawrence Lau, Yingyi Qian, and Gerard Roland, "Reform without Losers: An Interpretation of China's Dual-Track Approach to Transition," *Journal of Political Economy*, forthcoming.

toward a market economy. Both these transitions are far from complete, and so China today carries with it parts of the traditional, the socialist, the modern, and the market, all mixed up in a jumble of mind-boggling complexity.

The year 1999 is the fiftieth anniversary of the founding of the People's Republic of China. While 1949 is certainly a political milestone, it also represents an important economic turning point. The Chinese economic "takeoff"—that is, the unambiguous transition from a traditional rural economy toward a modern urban economy—dates from the period immediately after the founding of the People's Republic. Within two or three years, China had begun its race to industrialize. In the fifty years since, apart from a few years of profound crisis, China has been pouring material resources and human effort into the building of a modern industrial economy. While the policy model has fluctuated, the developmental effort has been constant. Both the half-finished industrialization process and the fluctuating and inconsistent development-policy model contribute to China's contemporary diversity.

Industrialization would have occurred without the Communist Party, but it would have displayed different patterns under different systemic conditions. Everything about the postwar experience of East Asia shows that China would be undergoing rapid modernization today under virtually any conceivable political scenario. Indeed, the seeds of industrialization had clearly been sown during the 1920s and 1930s, and many now argue that the early sprouts of industrialization show that the Chinese soil was fertile. But the early 1950s were nonetheless a turning point. The sprouts of industrialization in the 1920s and 1930s, though vigorous enough, were only a few seedlings in the vast expanse of China. There is no evidence that China "as a whole" was being transformed by these tiny transplants. In addition, whatever progress was made during the 1920s and 1930s came to a halt during the subsequent decade-plus of war and civil war. So the simple statement remains true: China before 1949 had not embarked on economic transformation on a massive scale, whereas China after 1950 has never ceased a process of massive economic transformation.[2] Moreover, during the 1950s, China created a set of social and economic institutions,

---

2. Thomas Rawski, *Economic Growth in Prewar China.* Berkeley: University of California Press, 1989. For a long-term perspective on Chinese growth, see Angus Maddison, *Chinese Economic Performance in the Long Run* (Paris: OECD Development Centre, 1998).

patterned on the Soviet model, that persist and remain influential today, despite the multiple, massive intervening changes.

China's fifty-year-long, still-incomplete process of economic modernization corresponds roughly to what England went through between about 1820 and, say, 1930, or what Japan went through between about 1890 and 1965. The long perspective is essential, because it is so natural to see China's post-1978 economic reform as the antithesis of the pre-1978 planned economy. While the reform in many respects is antithetical to the planned economy, the long-term developmental process also synthesizes different elements from each successive phase. Socialism brought mass literacy, improved public health, and the beginnings of a heavy industrial base. Reform brought an explosion of entrepreneurship and China's entry into the information age, along with much else. Economic transformation has gone on for fifty years and has another twenty years or so to run. At the current pace of transformation, around 2020, the transition from rural to urban will be basically complete. By that time, most of the workers leaving agriculture will already have left, and growth of the modern labor force will slow sharply.[3] China will then face the challenges of a mature modern, predominantly urban, middle-income economy.

The Transition Process in Perspective

China's strategy of "growing out of the plan" involved gradually introducing elements of the market economy into the overall framework of the socialist economy. The result was what I have described elsewhere as a "Swiss-cheese economy," in which market-oriented entrepreneurs rushed into pockets in the old government-run economy. Initially, those entrepreneurs primarily took over vacant positions in the economy, producing goods and services that the state-run economy either did not provide at all or else provided at such low levels of efficiency and service that entrepreneurs could easily replace them and earn supernormal profits. Later, reformist policymakers began systematically opening up new areas in which entrepreneurial individuals and new styles of organization could operate. Finally, the state economy became more like a sponge, floating in the sea of a market economy. As if to confirm

---

3. Assuming current demographic patterns persist. See Barry Naughton, "China's Emergence and Future as a Trading Nation," *Brookings Papers on Economic Activity*, 1996:2, pp. 281–83.

this metaphor, Chinese refer to individuals as "leaping into the sea" (*xia hai*) when they abandon state-sector employment for the private sector.[4]

It is crucial that the entrepreneurship described in the previous paragraph was not limited to private businesses and individuals. Reformers created a "dual track" system that encouraged existing SOEs, collectives, government organizations, and research and educational institutions to play a major role in the market. For about a decade, these organizations operated both under a plan and in the market: once their plans were fulfilled, they had the incentives and the ability to operate in the market, at market prices. All these organizations—and behind them, local governments—were given incentives to engage in entrepreneurial and market-oriented activity. The results were sometimes comic, as when units of the People's Liberation Army set up firing ranges where foreign tourists could fire automatic weapons for a fee; sometimes tragic, as when pharmaceutical companies sold adulterated and dangerous medicines; and sometimes corrupt, as when officials used their government positions to divert parts of new revenue streams into their own pockets and bank accounts abroad. But more important, in the big picture, this approach caused a movement toward the market that was exceptionally broad based. In the end, it succeeded in moving China to a market economy.

Underpinning the dual-track transition was a broad program of administrative decentralization. Central leaders delegated authority to local governments and created fiscal systems that allowed local officials to retain the bulk of locally generated revenues. Township and village enterprise (TVE) growth took off both because TVEs had real economic advantages (cheap labor and great institutional flexibility) and because local government officials had a strong financial interest in fostering their local TVEs. Authority over foreign trade and investment was delegated to the southern provinces of Guangdong and Fujian, which cooperated with capitalist businesses in Hong Kong and Taiwan to expand both trade and investment dramatically. In an unprecedented manner, the central government surrendered control over authority and resources (*fangquan rangli*), primarily to local gov-

---

4. Barry Naughton, *Growing Out of the Plan: Chinese Economic Reform, 1978–1993* (Cambridge: Cambridge University Press, 1995); and "China's Transition in Economic Perspective," in *The Paradox of China's Post-Mao Reforms*, ed. Merle Goldman and Roderick MacFarquhar (Cambridge: Harvard University Press, 1999), pp. 30–44.

ernments and SOEs. Decentralization was always controversial and led to a dramatic erosion of central government resources. But at the same time, decentralization was a way of adapting the hierarchical bureaucracy to the new challenges and tasks of the market economy. By adjusting authority and incentives, top government and Communist Party leaders were able to keep the chain of command relevant and avoid a Soviet-style collapse.

The survival of the administrative hierarchy brings into sharp focus another important aspect of China's reform process. China's reforms have been *institutionally conservative*. That is, they have proceeded as if it were expensive and risky to create new institutions and organizations. If an existing organization can be adapted to perform a new function, that is preferred to creating a new organization. In a related fashion, if it has not been absolutely necessary to restructure a given sphere of the economy, it probably has not been restructured: if it is not badly broken, it probably has not been fixed. This approach has had both shortcomings and benefits. The shortcomings include that China's economy is weakly institutionalized. New laws and regulations and new organizations have less influence than one would sometimes prefer. Old ways of doing business persist. Transparent rules have not generally replaced tacitly understood and agreed ways of doing things. Power and influence get handed down in a way that makes it possible for old elites—and their children— to claim a share of new economic resources. Some of the dramatic and very rapid productivity gains that come when a new player enters the game and significantly changes the rules have been forgone.

The benefits stem from the fact that it may indeed be less expensive and less risky to adapt old, rather than create new, organizations and institutions. The process of adapting old institutions may be slower and might even fail more often, but the consequences of failure are much less dire. Incremental adaptation followed by failure can usually be rectified by retreat. After reformulation, the way is open to renewed advance. During 1984, China's leaders adopted an extremely broad-based, comprehensive reform program, but the program failed because essential institutional components were not in place in time. As a result, major problems occurred in macroeconomic stability, foreign trade, and agricultural-product marketization. But reformers were able to pull back in time, prevent a Soviet-style economic collapse, and reformulate a more incremental program. Despite problems, that incremental program went ahead, and it became the dual-track system described above. Institutional conservatism means that legal protections are weak but also that traditional understandings about the rights and obligations of stakeholders take on some of the functions that would be performed by explicit legal regulation in another society. For example, it is often said that property rights in China are "vague," but that is not really true. Property rights in China are complex and the control of those rights is divided among numerous stakeholders, but those stakeholders usually have a pretty good idea of what property rights are, including the limitations on unencumbered exercise of ownership rights. Those shared expectations are possible because they are rooted in a shared history and shaped by a kind of de facto case law. Individuals understand the broad principles underlying property rights, even though it would be difficult for any individual to articulate precisely what the rules are.[5]

Institutional conservatism is visible both in the countryside and in the cities. In the countryside, despite the return to family farming, the land remains publicly owned. In most villages, landholdings are adjusted periodically (although not frequently) to account for demographic changes. In areas where successful TVEs developed in the 1970s and 1980s, powerful township and village governments continue to play an active and intrusive role in economic life.[6] In the cities, one of the most striking features of the 1980s reform period was the survival of the work-unit (*danwei*) system of permanent employment and workplace-centered benefits. The *danwei* system outlived the planned economy, which it was originally created to serve. Indeed, between 1978 and 1992, the number of employees of state manufacturing enterprises actually increased by almost half, from twenty-four million to thirty-five million. Moreover, during that time, state employees retained a virtually ironclad employment guarantee, and benefits provided through the *danwei*, particularly enterprise-supplied housing, actually increased.[7] Some aspects of life were surprisingly unaffected by the broad changes of the 1980s.

---

5. For a formal model, see D. David Li, "A Theory of Ambiguous Property Rights in Transition Economies: The Case of the Chinese Non-State Sector." *Journal of Comparative Economics*, 23(1), August 1996, pp. 1–19.

6. James Kai-sing Kung and Shouying Liu, "Farmers' Preferences Regarding Ownership and Land Tenure in Post-Mao China: Unexpected Evidence from Eight Counties," *The China Journal*, No. 38 (July 1997), pp. 33–63; Scott Rozelle and Guo Li, "Village Leaders and Land Rights Formation in China," *American Economics Review*, May 1998.

7. Xiaobo Lu and Elizabeth Perry, eds., *Danwei: The Changing Chinese Workplace in*

Perhaps because of the constant adaptation of institutions, the system has an enormous capacity to "muddle through." Despite tremendous social and economic problems, commentators who have predicted disaster—in the form of national bankruptcy, unchecked inflationary spirals, fragmentation into regional economies, or financial panic—have so far been consistently wrong. Long-run performance has been consistently better than short-term problems and challenges seem to suggest it should be. This must reflect some kind of systemic resilience that lies beneath the surface and underpins sustained and robust growth. We should bear this resilience in mind when we consider the formidable problems that confront the Chinese economy today.

The End of an Era of Reform

By early 1994, the Chinese economy had basically completed the reform agenda of the 1980s. Economic activity had been opened up. Markets had been introduced, and the economy had "grown out of the plan." Moreover, the Party Congress in 1993 committed the leadership to a "socialist market economy," clearing away the ideological obstacles to further marketization. Following this congress, a number of reforms were adopted that created basic rules regarding the regulation of activity and the establishment of new institutions. The most important of these were the fiscal and foreign-exchange reforms. The fiscal reform gave the government budget a more reliable revenue base by instituting a broad-based value-added tax and established uniform (and lower) tax rates for most types of activity and for all ownership systems. The foreign-exchange reform devalued and unified the currency, setting the stage for an export boom and a liberalization of the foreign-exchange regime. Within a few years, the currency was made convertible on the current account (that is, money could be traded in association with legitimate exchange of goods and services). The economy was booming, foreign investment was flooding in, and the process of economic transformation was accelerating.

However, at this stage, a number of fundamental institutions of the old economy remained in place. These were the institutions that had seemed to be performing reasonably well in the transitional environment and had not been directly confronted. Perhaps they served the interests of the top leadership, or perhaps they were institutions that

---

Historical and Comparative Perspective (Armonk, NY: M.E. Sharpe, 1997).

had significant political support, such that an attack on them would seem politically risky. Under the regime of institutional conservatism, these institutions were left untouched. But under the intensified marketization following 1993, economic forces began to reveal the costs and shortcomings of these institutions, which had been obscured before. Gradually, after 1993, policymakers resolved to tackle the reform of these most recalcitrant institutions.

We can identify four institutions—or institutional rigidities—from the former system that still significantly affected the economy as of the mid-1990s. The four were interrelated and mutually supporting, and they had survived because *politically* these were the hardest institutional features of the system to change. They were

- the institutionalized division between urban and rural residents;
- the organization of urban workers into all-encompassing work units, or *danwei*;
- the monopoly over bank credit by the state banking system, and the use of the banks to direct credit to the state-owned enterprise system; and
- protection of the domestic market against competition from imports.

Each of these institutional features had originally been an integral part of the planned economic system. The urban-rural division was created as part of the drive to organize the entire population into social units that could be directly controlled, and the formation of two separate systems—rural collective farms and urban work units—was a consequence of the need to extract low-price produce from farmers. The urban work unit was the basic organizational "cell" in the city; it ensured political control and provided an economical delivery vehicle for social benefits. Government control over bank credit was initially a subsidiary part of the planned economy, a minor offshoot of government control over the entire investment process. Import protection, finally, was essential to maintaining the separate socialist price system and thus the profitability of state enterprises, on which the government depended for revenue. These institutions had thus supported the system by which government commands had displaced the market as the predominant form of resource allocation.

By the 1990s, with the market having become the dominant form of resource allocation, these institutional features no longer shared a fundamental organic link with the planned economy nor with each other. Instead, they were united by a new political link. All four institutions had persisted because they were useful in protecting the economic position of important parts of the government's constituency, namely, government cadres and urban workers. Functionaries and managers within the Communist system (that is, *ganbu*, or cadres) benefited from access to subsidized credit and from their positions of influence within the sheltered urban *danwei* system. The urban-rural divide served to shield urban workers from competition from their far more numerous country cousins, and the *danwei* delivered to urban workers a fairly rich menu of social benefits—including health care, housing, and retirement—to which rural residents had little access. In turn, the subsidized credits and import protection allowed the government to continue to shield and prop up urban *danwei*, even when those units were no longer in a position to survive increasingly fierce competition.

These institutions were the fundamental instruments that allowed the government to protect these relatively privileged groups from the vicissitudes of economic competition despite the growth of market forces. Concerned with protecting its core constituencies, and worried about the consequences of angry, disgruntled workers concentrated in the largest and most sensitive cities, the government was understandably slow to dismantle these institutional features. But as a renewed and intensified round of market reforms rippled through the economy after 1993, it became increasingly difficult to sustain these features of the old economy. The playing field had become increasingly level, and so the cost of institutional distortions was becoming more obvious. At the same time, it was no longer the case that all urban dwellers were beneficiaries of these institutions. Highly skilled and educated workers did not need these protections and increasingly were able to parlay their skills into higher incomes in nonstate businesses. Finally, it was becoming clear that in order for China to move up to the next level of productivity and international competitiveness, it would have to permit the creation of a new generation of more dynamic, creative companies, and that this would only happen in an institutional environment that was overall more fluid and competitive. Economic policy began to shift in ways that seemed increasingly targeted on these traditional institutional rigidities.

The Zhu Rongji Policy Regime

Since mid-1993, Chinese economic policy has been strongly marked by the dominant influence of the current premier, Zhu Rongji. Zhu's power has experienced ups and downs, and there has occasionally been friction between Zhu and top leader Jiang Zemin (the general secretary of the Communist Party). Nevertheless, since 1993 Zhu Rongji has been the principal architect of economic policy and has shaped the details of important economic decisions in an extremely hands-on fashion. As a result, economic policy consistently shows evidence of Zhu Rongji's philosophy and personality. One of the most important outcomes of Zhu's policy package has been the movement toward a more open play of market forces in each of the four areas described above. But in none of the four areas has the process been completed, nor in any of the areas has it thus far been unambiguously successful.

Zhu's administration has been marked by a strong desire to reassert the interests of the central government over the interests of local cadres and interest groups. Zhu's recentralization of resources has been moderately successful. A good indicator is the size of total government revenues as a share of GDP. This number declined steadily throughout the 1980s reform era, dropping from 35 percent in 1978 to only 11.5 percent in 1995, its lowest point. Since 1995, it has increased slightly in each subsequent year, and it surpassed 13 percent in 1998. This may seem to be a small change, but it is significant: A longstanding trend has been reversed, and in any economy, control of a single percent of total GDP is an important matter.[8] Zhu has therefore in an important sense reversed the direction of China's reforms. Decentralization has been replaced by recentralization, though of course on different terms. Recentralization is not a reversal of market-oriented reforms but rather a reassertion of the necessary role of the central government in the new market-oriented environment. Decentralization facilitated the introduction of the market; now that the market is established, recentralization is necessary to enable the government to carry out its essential regulatory functions and provide public goods, social services, and some redistribution.

It is impossible for the central government to increase its take and

---

8. Data have been adjusted from those supplied in the Chinese Statistical Yearbook, various years, and *Zhongguo Tongji Zhaiyao 1999* (China Statistical Abstract 1999) (Beijing: Zhongguo tongji, 1999), pp. 11, 55, 67.

for local officials and SOEs to maintain all their protections at the same time. The only way to perform that feat would be to raise taxes across the board and squeeze the entrepreneurial, market-oriented elements of the economy, that is, to roll back reforms. Instead, the Zhu Rongji administration has attempted to combine recentralization with a steady chipping away of the institutional barriers that hold back the economy and shelter specific interest groups. The result has been significant change with respect to each of the four institutional rigidities described earlier.

Rural-to-urban migration grew rapidly in the mid-1990s, and the economic position of rural migrants changed substantially. By the best estimates, the number of long-term economic migrants in cities increased to over forty million by 1996 before leveling off. Rural migrants still face discrimination in the cities as well as a kind of second-class citizenship. Lack of an urban residence permit is not the overwhelming barrier it once was, but it still hampers efforts to establish long-term residence in the city. Migrants do not qualify for most urban social benefits, have trouble getting their children into school, and are forced into a high-cost, low-quality segment of the housing market. But the barriers that kept most rural migrants out of many sectors of the urban job market are crumbling. Rural migrants play a large role in the informal sector, selling goods and working on construction projects, but they now also work in urban factories in large numbers (especially textile mills and foreign-invested light manufactures). Rural migrants compete with urban residents in the low-skill segments of the economy. The result has been a substantial increase in incomes accruing to rural households and increased competitive pressure on the incomes of urban households.[9] In this respect, the economy has become more open and more similar to those of other developing countries.

Increased rural-to-urban migration is one element of a new economic environment that has had a huge impact on state-owned enterprises and on the entire *danwei* system that surrounds the SOEs. Competition has been increasing rapidly in the manufacturing arena—a consequence of the continued development of domestic private enter-

9. Dorothy J. Solinger, *Contesting Citizenship in Urban China: Peasant Migrants, the State, and the Logic of the Market* (Berkeley: University of California Press, 1999); Beijing University Chinese Economics Research Center, Urban Labor Market Research Group, "Shanghai: Stratification and Integration of Urban and Rural Workers," *Gaige* 1998:4, pp. 99–110.

prises and TVEs and of the increased presence of foreign-invested firms active in the Chinese market. In addition, SOEs suffered greatly as changes in the financial system (described below) curtailed their access to easy bank credit as well. SOEs found themselves caught between the increasing pressures of the product market and of the financial side of the business, just as SOE workers were facing the beginnings of labor-market competition from rural migrants. Under these conditions, economic pressure accumulated on the *danwei* system, and eventually it cracked. Increasingly, SOEs found themselves exposed to market forces without any mechanisms available to shelter them. Hammered by macroeconomic austerity policies, market-oriented reforms of the banking system, and heightened competition from TVEs, private firms, and foreign companies, the state-owned enterprise system began to crumble in the mid-1990s.

The most dramatic evidence of change was the abrupt collapse of the permanent employment system. SOE workers began to be laid off in massive numbers beginning in 1994. Authorities avoided recording a significant increase in registered unemployment by creating a new category of laid-off (*xiagang*) workers who retained ties to their former work units. The number of laid-off workers grew rapidly, and these workers were gradually weaned from their formal links to their units and transferred to euphemistically labeled "reemployment centers" in major cities. Effective unemployment increased rapidly, from under 6 million in 1993 to about 15 million at the end of 1998 (this number includes registered unemployed plus estimates of the number of laid-off workers who had not found formal employment). In parallel fashion, the number of workers in state-owned manufacturing enterprises plummeted. From the peak in 1992 of just over 35 million, the number of state manufacturing workers began to decline. In 1998, statisticians stopped reporting laid-off workers as state employees, and the number of manufacturing workers plummeted to only 18.8 million at year's end. Publicly owned commerce declined rapidly as well, as did urban collective firms of most kinds. Former public-enterprise workers have gone into the new private sector (sometimes through privatization of a formerly public enterprise), into retirement, and into enterprises of "other" ownership forms (new joint-stock and foreign-invested firms). But so far, the largest destination of laid-off public workers has been unemployment.[10]

---

10. Employment data from *Zhongguo Tongji Zhaiyao 1999*, p. 35. Explanation of

Changes in the banking system have been an important part of the overall change in economic conditions. Since mid-1993, Zhu Rongji has exercised direct personal control over the banking system and has used this authority to make banks more authoritative and independent of local officials and state enterprises. In the past, local bank branches had no choice but to take commands from local government and party officials, making loans to local state-owned enterprises regardless of profitability because of political pressures to prop up employment or develop local showcase projects. Zhu reorganized the banking system to reduce the control of local bank branches by provincial Communist Party personnel. The commercial banks remained state owned but were given increased authority to say no to SOEs and their local government patrons. In order to free the commercial banks to operate truly on commercial principles—but still allow the central government to direct some lending toward priority or politically favored projects—new "policy banks" were established to take over government-mandated lending.

State-bank bargaining power was also substantially increased by official tight-money policies put in place during 1993 to control inflation. A side benefit of tough macroeconomic policy, it was hoped, was that it would give the banks backbone, allowing them to stand up to local interest groups and decline to make loans that did not make good business sense. The results of banking reform have been mixed, but tough macroeconomic policy definitely succeeded in curbing inflation. From its peak of 24 percent in 1994, inflation as measured by the consumer price index declined to only 2.8 percent in 1997 and then drifted into negative territory during 1998. Macroeconomic austerity also reduced growth, but not in catastrophic fashion. GDP growth in 1997 was 8.5 percent (down from the unsustainable peak of 14 percent in 1992), and official 1998 growth was 7.8 percent, although it is widely recognized that the official figure was inflated in that year. Growth was slowed by the impact of the Asian financial crisis, which erupted in 1997 and compounded the effect of a slowdown already under way

---

unemployment and laid-off worker data is provided in Mo Rong, *Jiuye: Zhongguo de shiji nanti* (Employment: China's problem of the century) (Beijing: Jingji Kexue, 1998), pp. 20, 28–29; and Yang Yiyong, "China's Unemployment Problem: Current Conditions, Trends, and Appropriate Measures," in *1998 Nian Zhongguo jingji xingshi fenxi yu yuce: Jingji lanpi shu* (1998 China's economic conditions, analysis and projections: Economic Blue Book), ed. Liu Guoguang, Wang Luolin, and Li Jingwen (Beijing: Shehui kexue wenxian, 1997).

because of domestic macroeconomic policies. Tough macroeconomic policies, external recession, and slower domestic growth presented a much less favorable environment for China's businesses at the end of the 1990s than had existed at any previous time in the reform era.

A final major area of economic policy reform is the foreign-trade regime. Foreign trade experienced some major successes through the mid-1990s. Exchange rates were unified and realigned, exports soared, and a flood of incoming foreign investment began to transform the productive capacity of the Chinese economy significantly. However, there were substantial limits to this process as well. In essence, the apparent openness of the Chinese economy was less than it appeared to be, because the openness was circumscribed within a particular trading regime and a specific geographical area. Chinese policymakers in the late 1980s through mid-1990s created a dualistic trade regime. Exporters, and especially foreign-invested enterprises, were given very liberal access to world markets. Through provisions permitting "export processing," exporters were allowed to bring imports into the country duty-free and with few administrative obstacles, as long as the imports were associated with export production. In addition, generous tax breaks allowed exporters and foreign firms to enjoy substantial fiscal benefits. This liberal regime permitted the free transmission of world price relations into the export-oriented sector, allowed China to take advantage of its low-price and relatively skilled labor, and fostered rapid growth. Moreover, in the core areas of this trading regime, Guangdong and Fujian provinces, local officials worked hard to ensure that the rules were interpreted in the most liberal and flexible way possible. Aided by Hong Kong and Taiwan businesses, these provinces boomed.

But the explosive development of an export-oriented economy in Guangdong and Fujian was accompanied by much less progress in the general trading regime. Tariffs were reduced, but they remained relatively high. More important, ordinary trade imports—those not related to export processing—continued to be allowed only to registered foreign-trade corporations (FTCs). Until 1998, all these FTCs were state owned. Although several thousand FTCs nominally have export and import rights, each FTC can only import specific product categories that it is authorized to handle. In practice, a hundred large FTCs dominate many types of ordinary trade imports. Moreover, all FTCs must understand that their ability to import is contingent on their being perceived as good citizens by the Ministry of Foreign Trade. These restrictions create a kind of nontariff restraint on imports, and they are important because only ordinary trade imports can be sold directly on the Chinese market, to arm's length customers. Foreign businesses cannot import commodities into China and then market them directly, so import protection remains substantial.[11]

One result of this dual system was that foreign firms were privileged in some respects (favorable tax treatment gave them competitive advantages in the domestic market for goods they produced in China, and they had easy access to export markets) but penalized in other respects (they were prevented from marketing imported products directly to Chinese buyers). This discriminatory treatment was inconsistent with the direction of Chinese reform overall as well as with the spirit of membership in the World Trade Organization (WTO).[12] Beginning in 1996, Chinese policymakers declared their intention to reduce the disparities between these two trade regimes by liberalizing the ordinary trade system while scaling back tax breaks and granting non-discriminatory "national treatment" to foreign firms. Gradual progress in this direction was begun but ran into difficulties because of the Asian financial crisis. Suddenly, in 1999, Premier Zhu Rongji arrived in Washington, D.C., with a dramatic breakthrough offer for WTO membership. After years of glacial progress, Zhu offered a stunning series of market-opening measures, including eliminating the system of registered FTCs, agreeing to import agricultural goods, and providing access to markets for telecommunications services. Although it was not immediately accepted in Washington, the offer clearly represented a dramatic, bold, and hugely positive initiative for the Chinese economy.

Thus, under Zhu Rongji, movement on economic reform has extended into the most sensitive areas, the areas that had been forbidden zones until recently. By advancing policies that would reduce restrictions on population mobility, labor markets, and foreign trade and at the same time reducing patronage and subsidization through the state banking system, Zhu is pushing for a vastly more open and competitive economic environment. Moreover, in clear distinction from

---

11. Naughton, "China's Emergence and Future as a Trading Nation," pp. 298–308.

12. Wenguo Cai, Murray G. Smith, and Xu Xianquan, eds., *China and the World Trade Organization: Requirements, Realities, and Resolution* (Ottawa: Centre for Trade Policy and Law, 1996); Frederick M. Abbott, ed., *China in the World Trading System: Defining the Principles of Engagement* (Cambridge, MA: Kluwer Law International, 1998).

earlier reforms, these are policies that create obvious losers. Many urban workers, many SOEs, and many local government officials can expect to see their absolute and relative standards of living decline as a result of these changes.

Current Policy Dilemmas

Having launched a bold set of policy initiatives, Premier Zhu Rongji, as of mid-1999, found himself in the midst of a sea of difficulties. Initially, it was the Asian financial crisis that disrupted progress on reform. During 1998, the economy slowed more than anticipated, and concerns about unemployment grew rapidly. The problem was not so much the rise in layoffs, which had been anticipated. The problem rather was that in the context of economic slowdown, far fewer laid-off workers were finding new work than had been hoped. Workers losing privileges and earning less than before are likely to be angry; workers entirely idle have both anger and time on their hands to express their anger. Concern about the treatment of laid-off workers led, during 1998, to an accelerated effort to incorporate them into "employment projects" that provided make-work or other alternate employment. Despite numerous official expressions of concern about unemployment, the pace at which workers are being laid off has not slowed substantially.

The economic slowdown also had an impact on other aspects of liberalization. With the slowing of urban job growth—and increased competition from laid-off urban workers—rural migrants became less enthusiastic about pulling up stakes and moving to the city. The pace of rural-to-urban migration, and thus the pace of overall economic restructuring, clearly slowed after 1997. The desire to spark economic growth also led Zhu to relax his macroeconomic austerity programs somewhat. A hastily assembled program of government infrastructure investment was rolled out in 1998, giving banks an excuse to fund an array of central- and local-government-sponsored projects. Although the expansion of bank credit was limited to infrastructure-construction projects (and not channeled to bail out production enterprises), there was inevitably some relaxation of the nascent credit culture that had been designed to shore up the independence of the banking system. Finally, the Asian financial crisis eroded China's bargaining power vis-à-vis foreign investors. It became increasingly difficult to scale back preferential treatment when foreign investors were being actively courted by all Asian economies. Meanwhile, import protections were actually increased, as China feared a surge of imports from nearby cheap-currency countries, such as Korea. Slow growth checked progress on all the institutional reforms described above.

Moreover, the obstacles to deeper institutional reform do not lie solely in short-run economic conditions. Serious technical issues remain to be resolved. This is perhaps most obvious in reform of the financial system, which many observers have identified as the weakest link in China's current economic system.[13] After years of rapidly growing lending to SOEs, China's state banks now hold huge portfolios of nonperforming loans, variously estimated at up to 25 percent of GDP. In a technical sense, the banks are probably bankrupt, and if depositors decided that their funds were in jeopardy, a massive bank run could create financial panic. Recognizing the magnitude of the problem, the government began in 1999 to address it. It began the process of establishing "Asset Management Corporations" (AMCs) for each of the major state banks; these are charged with purchasing nonperforming loans from the banks, restructuring the companies as well as possible, and realizing as much as possible of the underlying value of the assets.

This is a recognized approach that in theory can resolve the problem of bad loans: the AMCs are in some respects patterned after the Resolution Trust that cleaned up after the savings and loan debacle in the United States in the 1980s. The bad loans are essentially the responsibility of the government, which owns the banks and owned the enterprises to which the loans were made. The AMCs will initially issue bonds to finance their purchase of loans, but these loans are guaranteed by the Ministry of Finance and will inevitably end up being paid off by the government. This is acceptable because the government has relatively low levels of public debt and can assume responsibility for the bonds. The government is in the process of authorizing the issuance of government-guaranteed bonds in an amount exceeding one trillion yuan, over 12 percent of GDP. Thus, in practice, the government is recapitalizing the banks with a massive injection of public money. The government also implicitly guarantees bank deposits, and there has never been a default of a state-owned bank in China.

---

13. Nicholas Lardy, *China's Unfinished Economic Revolution.* Washington, DC: The Brookings Institution, 1998; Baizhu Chen, J. Kimball Dietrich and Yi Feng, eds., *Financial Market Reform in China: Progress, Problems, and Prospects* (Boulder, CO: Westview, 1999).

Nonetheless, the practical problems involved in the follow-through of this program are immense. Without a well-developed legal system, it will be difficult for the AMCs to track down loans and recover assets that are currently underperforming or have been siphoned off for private purposes. Moreover, while important improvements are under way in the internal monitoring and rewarding of bank employees, the kind of misguided bank-lending decision making that created massive bad debt in the first place is still going on. If bank loan officers are simply forgiven for all the bad loans made in the past, what force will discipline them to start making only good loans from today onward? Clearly, loan officers will anticipate further bailouts and will continue to make bad loans to influential officials, enterprises, and their own personal cronies. Creating new incentives is obviously key, but the most effective way to create new incentives is to introduce competition and market forces. However, the introduction of competition in the area of finance might well trigger a flight of funds out of the state banking system and set off the very crisis policymakers wish to avoid. There is no easy solution.

In 1999, a further set of bizarre events obstructed progress of the reform agenda. The U.S. failure to accept China's WTO offer, followed by the U.S. bombing of the Chinese embassy in Belgrade, created a crisis of economic diplomacy. In the atmosphere of intense suspicion with which China viewed the embassy bombing, further WTO negotiations were put on hold. Moreover, Zhu Rongji's WTO offer became much more vulnerable to attack by domestic interest groups. As we have seen, Zhu's current policies create a formidable potential coalition of losers: heads of state-owned industrial empires fearful of losing their protection against foreign competition; laid-off state workers; and local officials angry at the loss of access to banking and fiscal resources. These groups have real incentives to block further reforms. Despite the apparent surge in domestic opposition, the two sides eventually managed to return to the bargaining table, and on November 15, 1999, signed an agreement. This bilateral agreement is the key step in China's eventual accession to WTO membership, but a number of additional hurdles remained as of year-end. Bilateral agreements with other WTO members (crucially with the European Union) were still pending, and the U.S. Congress had to pass related legislation normalizing China's trade status. China's WTO membership seemed assured, but it was uncertain whether it could be achieved during 2000.

Thus, as of the end of the century, economic reform and transformation are running into substantial difficulties. With a weakened Premier Zhu Rongji, forceful economic initiatives were few and far between during 1999 (with the exception of the bank-recapitalization program). A key party meeting in September 1999 seems to have done little to break down the prevailing sense of hesitation and sclerosis. To a certain extent, these difficulties are the intrinsic result of the stage of economic reform to which China has now graduated. To a certain extent, they are the result of a series of unfortunate external accidents: the Asian financial crisis; U.S. domestic politics; and the Belgrade embassy bombing. And to a certain extent, they reflect the continuing reality of Chinese economic development: massive challenges, constantly recurring dilemmas, and huge liabilities of poverty, overpopulation, and environmental degradation. It is only because China also has enormous reserves of human ingenuity and resourcefulness that it can have any hope of surmounting the difficulties facing it.

The Future

In the final analysis, China will continue with its program of economic transformation because there is simply no alternative. This is already apparent in the personal position and status of Zhu Rongji. Despite the many enemies Zhu has made, he is likely to retain his stature until the end of his term. Ultimately, this is because other policymakers in China recognize that the economic problems are formidable, and they have little confidence in their own ability to manage those problems better than Zhu. Thus, while Zhu is easy to attack, he is difficult to replace.

More broadly, there is no feasible position to which to retreat. The problems of SOEs, the banking system, and urban-rural relations simply need to be addressed now. Marketization has progressed far enough to reveal the flaws and costs of the institutions inherited from the planned economy. In terms of foreign trade, China could certainly opt to retain a protected domestic economy and a degree of divergence from the world economy. China does not need to expand exports in order to sustain economic growth: it can be an economy unto itself. But such a policy will condemn China to long-term second-class status in the world. China can have a reasonably prosperous, healthy economy behind protective barriers. But it can have no chance of reaching world frontiers in high-technology businesses without a much higher degree of openness than it now possesses. And ultimately, without competitive technology, China cannot be a world-class economy or a world-class power. Based on the persistence of the developmental effort over the past fifty years in China, it appears that such an outcome is not one that successful Chinese leaders are likely to accept.

Another important factor indicating continuing efforts at economic transformation is that China today has a demographic window of opportunity. China's population is exceptionally young and has an extremely low dependency rate. Sixty-eight percent of the population is between the ages of fifteen and sixty-four, about ten percentage points higher than in most comparable middle-income countries. Moreover, the average age of the working population is quite young, below thirty. The basic reason for this unusual age structure is that the elderly population is small—because China has so recently emerged from abject poverty—and the child population is also small—because of China's rigorous birth control policy. The result is an exceptionally active, flexible, and adaptable population, because it is a young population. If there is any populace that can accept the dramatic changes and challenges associated with the final stages of economic reform, this is it.

China's young population and rapid labor-force growth through the 1980s and early 1990s have helped keep the economy growing rapidly. Constant reinvigoration of institutions because of the entry of new young workers may have facilitated institutional adaptations as well. But these demographic factors will not continue indefinitely. The age structure of the population is already beginning to change. Dependency rates will actually continue to fall until about 2010, because now smaller numbers of young adults are reaching childbearing age and having even fewer children. But the proportion of aged is beginning to increase. After about 2015, it will begin to increase rapidly. Then overall dependency rates will begin to increase again.

Future changes in dependency will coincide with other demographic changes. Already, the growth of the labor force is slowing down. Simultaneously, massive conversion from agricultural to non-agricultural jobs has begun to draw down the stock of excess labor in the countryside. Given continued economic growth, these processes will all converge around 2015. Labor-force growth will decline almost to zero as the number of retirements becomes as large as that of new labor-market entries. Given another twenty years of rural-to-urban migration, the agricultural labor force will already have declined sufficiently that its proportion in the total work force will be similar to that of other medium-income countries. Aging, slowing labor-force growth, and slowing labor-force restructuring will all coincide after about 2015.[14] After that time, the pace of change in China is likely to slow considerably. Until that time, we are in the midst of a process of transformation that will likely produce continuous rapid change and many surprises. It is a process that still has another twenty years to run.

China can no longer count on an extremely benevolent external environment to support its domestic changes. The East Asian economies have so far been recovering from the Asian crisis with remarkable speed, and it may well be that the crisis is over. But it is impossible to have confidence that Japan has resolved its economic problems, and the fortunes of the Japanese economy dominate the future prospects of the rest of East Asia. Institutional fragility is still apparent throughout East Asia, most obviously in Indonesia. Thus, China will not necessarily experience the same boost from vigorous growth in the neighborhood that has been common in the past twenty years. On another dimension, many influential people in the United States, and especially in the U.S. Congress, seem to have lost confidence that the successful development of China will be a boon to the United States. The gulf of misunderstanding separating Washington and Beijing has rarely been wider than it is today. This is unfortunate, for there can be little doubt that a China that resolves its problems and develops to a higher economic level is greatly in the interest of the United States, just as a China that fails to resolve its problems and collapses in disorder is a grave threat to world security. In the first case, China would contribute to the world the products of its vast reservoir of human ingenuity, large new markets, and important new innovations; in the latter case, China would deplete the world's resources for crisis management. Much depends on the ability of the Chinese to resolve their problems and contribute the products of their vigorous young population to the rest of the world. We can gain some reassurance from examining the record of the last fifty years, which is one of continuous problems but also of resilience and progress, and a sustained trajectory of development and growth.

---

14. This scenario is based on unpublished projections of the Chinese population from the U.S. Bureau of the Census, International Data Base. I am indebted to Loraine West, Christina Harbaugh, and Judith Banister for providing the data and taking the time to explain details of the methodology used in the projections.

Power, Patronage, and Protest in Rural China

Jonathan Unger

The Chinese countryside at the turn of the millennium presents observers with a perplexing puzzle. On the one side, significant increases in agricultural production have been recorded. In the most recent available statistics, the output of grain, for instance, stood 55 percent higher than when Mao died in 1976,[1] while rural industrial production has leaped eightfold during the past decade alone.[2] Yet in the face of these gains, evidence has mounted of increasingly open disgruntlement among villagers in many parts of the countryside, and word has sporadically leaked abroad of violent incidents of protest in the rural hinterlands. Why this widespread discontent?

It will be seen in this chapter that one major reason is the failure of China's rural political system to adapt successfully to the post-Mao era. When farming was decollectivized in the early 1980s and villagers returned to tilling family farms, the Chinese government largely retained the framework for governing rural China that had been established by the Chinese Communist Party during the 1950s and 1960s. This had been designed under Mao as a top-down structure to enforce central control. But today power has become more decentralized under the post-Mao regime, and it will be seen how the Mao-era apparatchiki have transformed themselves into local satraps who make use of their strategic position between state and society to develop new bases for their own power and prosperity. It will be seen, too, that this is occurring in very different ways in the rich and poor regions of China. Finally, the chapter will examine why and how the central government

---

1. For the 1976 data, see *China Statistical Yearbook 1988* (Beijing: State Statistical Bureau, 1988), p. 212; for the 1997 data, see *China Statistical Yearbook 1998*, p. 386.

2. *Zhongguo xiangzhen qiye nianjian 1998* (1998 rural enterprise yearbook of China) (Beijing: Zhongguo nongye chubanshe, 1998), p. 6.

is attempting to counteract the tactics of grassroots officials by making them more accountable through a new system of village elections.

But crucial to any understanding of these shifts in the countryside is the essential fact that, until this new electoral effort began, surprisingly little in the *structure* of rural government had been transformed since the period of Mao's rule. It is therefore necessary first to examine briefly the shape of rural political life under Mao.

The Rural Scene in Mao's Day

When the Chinese system of communes was consolidated in the 1960s, a hierarchy of administrative levels was established to ensure that the central party's writ penetrated all parts of the countryside. Within every village of a commune, the lowest level at which the farmers were organized was the "production team," each of which comprised a hamlet or village neighborhood and contained some fifteen to sixty households. The team owned blocks of agricultural land, and its member households worked the land together and shared in the proceeds. To encourage the farmers to accept their team head's leadership in their daily work, the head was normally either elected to his position from within the team or informally selected by consensus, on the basis of his knowledge of agriculture and personal leadership skills. To this extent, the teams were democratic—which had no parallel in any other part of the Chinese political system.

However, the teams were dominated by the next-higher level in the chain of command of party rule that reached from Beijing into each and every village. Sitting atop the production teams, each large village (or in the absence of sizable villages, each cluster of small neighboring hamlets) was designated a "brigade." This was the lowest level at which a Communist Party branch operated, and the branch's party secretary was empowered to supervise the workings of the village government and the production teams. Although each village had a brigade head, deputy brigade heads, and other official posts, these were supposed to take second place to the party branch and its party secretary. To keep the party secretary of each brigade attuned to the wishes of the party, he (few party secretaries were women) was always selected by higher levels of the party.

Above the village and its party branch sat the commune government. A commune consisted of a small rural market town and the dozen or so agricultural villages that surrounded it. The commune

administration sometimes owned and operated some small rural factories and perhaps a few orchards, ran the local secondary school, and
sometimes established a rudimentary hospital. But the commune
served most essentially in the role of a political watchdog: it served as
the seat of a local party machine that kept a close watch on the villages
within its jurisdiction and relayed the state's policies and commands to
the village party secretaries. The commune and its party secretary were
needed as a "bridge" between the rural community and the central
state. This was because the rural county, which constituted the next
higher level in the chain of political command, normally contained
upward of a hundred villages, too large a number to be supervised
directly by the government organs in the county capital.

The higher in the rural administration an official sat, the more he
or she found it personally worthwhile to abide by the party-state's
demands, even when these conflicted with the local populace's interests. For one thing, the officials at the commune and county levels,
unlike the village-level brigade leadership, did not necessarily feel attached to the rural district where they were stationed. In fact, the commune heads normally were rotated from one commune to another
rather than allowed to serve in their own native commune district, just
as the county's leaders were rotated in from elsewhere. (This was very
much in keeping with the longstanding practices of the Chinese emperors, who had sent officials to rule counties and regions of which
they were not natives so as to circumvent the dangers of localist loyalties and connections.) And if we can intuit anything from the policies
that these county and commune officials sometimes pushed, it would
seem that their jobs were not jeopardized by crop failures in the villages or stagnating peasant living standards as long as Beijing's
demands were met. Rural bureaucrats who were eager for promotions
or anxious to keep their posts obediently looked to see what Beijing's
wishes might be. Whenever the Chinese Communist Party Central
Committee in Beijing issued a set of directives, or even indirectly indicated its preferences, far-flung counties and villages shifted in the
same direction at the same time as if, to use the Chinese term for this
phenomenon, there had been a "single stroke of the knife."

A consequence of this top-down responsiveness was that even the
question of which crops to produce in which fields sometimes was not
left to the good sense and experience of the team heads and farmers.
If need be, compliance to the party's diktat was enforced through

political threats: team leaders or members who balked could be accused of resisting the revolution. In a political system wracked by periodic "struggle" campaigns and the uncertainty and fear that these aroused, such a threat was effective. When I first began conducting interviews with Chinese from rural areas in the 1970s, during the commune era, the interviewees saw the strength of China's central authorities as overwhelming and irresistible.[3]

While the uncertainty and fear generated by the recurring bouts of campaign fever strengthened upper-level controls over the lower levels and a cowed populace, some of these campaigns were also turned by Mao against the local officialdom itself, to keep officials in line. A massive campaign of this type, the Four Cleanups campaign, shook the countryside during the first half of the 1960s; it was orchestrated by so-called work teams of higher-level officials who took over villages for the duration of the campaign.[4] This campaign was followed shortly by the Cultural Revolution upsurge of 1966–68, during which villagers were given a freer rein. In both campaigns, local officials who had abused their positions and engaged in corruption were pulled up short, as ordinary people responded to the calls from China's top leaders to level accusations. Such campaigns served, intermittently, as the main buttress against corruption in a system that had few other safeguards. But for the most part, political campaigns tightened controls on the rural populace rather than loosened them, demanding even greater conformity from the populace than in ordinary times. By targeting both ordinary people and officials, the campaigns in China served a role not dissimilar to the centralizing function filled by the secret police in Stalin's Soviet Union.

This Maoist system could not persist over the long term, however. Year after exhausting year of periodic campaigns and irrational, unchecked interference from above in agricultural practices led by the 1970s to stagnating rural living standards.[5] Irritated and frustrated,

---

3. Almost all of this interviewing during the 1970s with respondents from the countryside was conducted from Hong Kong. From the 1980s onward, such interviewing could be conducted from within China, and I was able to confirm what I had earlier been told.

4. This is described in Richard Madsen, *Morality and Power in a Chinese Village* (Berkeley: University of California Press, 1984), chap. 3; and in Anita Chan, Richard Madsen, and Jonathan Unger, *Chen Village under Mao and Deng* (Berkeley: University of California Press, 1992), chaps. 1–3.

5. David Zweig, *Agrarian Radicalism in China, 1968–1978* (Cambridge: Harvard University Press, 1989).

many farmers began to slack off in their work. In a downward spiral, by the mid-1970s the collective agriculture of a great many villages was operating with ever decreasing effectiveness. Faced with this, after Mao died in 1976, his successors, under the emerging leadership of Deng Xiaoping, began to contemplate a dramatic break with the past.

Rural China under Deng Xiaoping and Jiang Zemin

Over a four-year period between 1979 and 1983, a decollectivization drive swept through rural communities in much the same way as previous campaigns had: in a "single stroke of the knife," almost all villages across China ended up adopting exactly the same system of family farming.[6] Under these egalitarian Deng-era reforms, the production-team land and the team animals were divided among the households free of charge, normally on a per capita basis.

Up to the present day, however, the families remain harnessed to quotas of agricultural produce, most often grain, that must be sold to the state at below-market prices. Under Mao, each production team as a whole was responsible for meeting such quotas. When the land was distributed to households during the 1980s, the teams divided these quota deliveries among the individual families by attaching a quota to each plot of distributed land. This crop-quota system continues to impinge upon the living standards of a great many farmers. This is especially the case in the poorer parts of China, which depend most heavily upon grain production. It will be seen in later pages how this has become one of the factors that translate today into growing disgruntlement with local officials.

In one very important respect, though, decollectivization was the final act of a passing era. Even though most of the political structure remained in place, with the return to family farming in the early 1980s rural officials lost control over the daily work of the peasantry. As one interviewee observed, "If those so-called cadres tell us to do something today we don't always carry it out. We farmers are practical: if we don't depend upon earning collective work-points that you control, why listen so much to you?" In short, one of the beneficial conse-

---

6. See Jonathan Unger, "The De-Collectivization of the Chinese Countryside: A Survey of Twenty-eight Villages," *Pacific Affairs*, vol. 58, no. 4 (winter 1985–86), pp. 585–606. A different interpretation is provided in Daniel Kelliher, *Peasant Power in China* (New Haven: Yale University Press, 1992).

quences of decollectivization was that the arbitrary power of the state and rural officials to exact cowed compliance from the peasantry was weakened.

A second beneficial change was the near abandonment by the government of political campaigns as mechanisms of top-down control. The state would no longer be so intrusive, with the single exception of family planning. Beijing under Deng Xiaoping's guidance was intent upon giving a politically exhausted populace the sense that they had greater regularity and security in their lives. In practically all respects, this has meant a much more relaxed stance by Beijing toward the grassroots of rural China. In this milieu, villagers have turned back toward traditional anchors—reconstructing lineage halls and local temples, giving ancestral altars pride of place again in their homes, and once again participating in lavish ceremonies to mark weddings, funerals, and the other key events in the life cycle.

The party-state simultaneously enacted steps to reduce the party's primacy over all aspects of rural administration. There was now to be a "separation of party and government" (*dang zheng fenkai*) to allow local government functions to operate more routinely.[7] As a symbol of this, the politically laden titles "commune" and "brigade" were abolished, and these levels of government reverted to the prerevolution titles of "township" (*xiang*) and "administrative village" (*xingzheng cun*). But to a certain extent this can be considered a case of old wine in new bottles, consisting as it did of new official titles and new declarations of intent while the actual content of the rural political structure remained largely intact. In most localities, the party secretary remains a very powerful figure, often more so than the local government head, and continues to play a direct role in setting policy. In addition, village officials still often operate in an authoritarian style reminiscent of earlier times, to the extent that villagers, a quarter century after Mao's death, frequently continue to refer to the village government as the "brigade."

Another form of continuity lies in the rotations of county-level and township-level leaders, in a system similar to what had prevailed under Mao and, before that, in imperial times. The consequences are similar, too: such officials do not feel any particular attachment to the populace

---

7. The at-times-unexpected consequences during the first decade of decollectivization of this and other administrative reforms are discussed in Tyrene White, "Political Reform and Rural Government," in *Chinese Society on the Eve of Tiananmen*, ed. Deborah Davis and Ezra F. Vogel (Cambridge: Harvard University Press, 1990).

of the districts they command. Many of them today put energy during their tenures into showy projects to impress visiting officials. They pour money into launching impressive-looking new economic projects and into erecting taller public buildings and widening and prettifying streets in the county capitals and township market towns, in the knowledge that promotions depend upon making a splash. Within a few more years they have departed, leaving behind debts that must be paid out of future local revenues. Such a scenario is surprisingly common today, particularly in the richer districts, but is found even in relatively poor areas. It is the modern variant of the dam-building and backyard steel-making campaigns so vigorously pursued in Mao's day by promotion-seeking county and commune officials.

In a departure from previous practices, however, starting in the early 1980s the central government's more relaxed posture toward rural society was paralleled by its approach to rural officials. Among other things, anticorruption campaigns that targeted local officials for public exposure and purge were no longer unleashed. Calling off such campaigns was, in one respect, all to the good, in that it moved China away from a politics of unpredictability, fear, and arbitrary retribution. But the national government appears tacitly to have had a separate motive also in mind. Abandoning its major technique for combating corruption meant it could buy the rural officials' cooperation for economic reforms—by allowing them to benefit illicitly from those reforms.

As expected, local officials have taken advantage of the central state's pullback to favor their own private interests and those of their favorites. Sometimes this takes the form of outright corruption, such as the siphoning off of publicly owned assets into their own pockets. But an alternative and even more common means to augment their own incomes—and their authority—is to establish patronage relationships with villagers. In doing so, the officials can bank upon the fact that even after decollectivization, they retain at least some administrative leverage over the rural population. The latter remains dependent upon the goodwill of village and higher-level rural cadres to get access to fertilizers, credit, new housing sites, and licenses to engage in business. Chinese peasants frequently need to resort to currying the favor of local officials through gifts, quiet offers of money, and shows of deference.[8]

---

8. See Jean Oi, "Communism and Clientelism: Rural Politics in China," *World Politics*, vol. 37, no. 2 (January 1985), pp. 238–66.

Previously, under the communes, the range of potential patrons was greatly restricted. Because only a small group of grassroots officials controlled all of a village's economic and political affairs, all patronage flowed through them. Now a more pluralistic structure of patronage has developed. For different sorts of favors, peasants can go to different patrons. For example, peasants who hope to get regular preferential access to special fertilizers or bank loans develop *guanxi* (personal connections) and personal favors-trading with various marketing-bureau personnel or bank staff. Procurements and loans no longer need to be funneled through a single set of village cadres. This growth of diffuse patron-client networks provides the peasants with considerably greater freedom to maneuver, and in some districts their autonomous building of patronage links has eroded the former rigid structure of rural power.

This is true only to a certain extent, though. In some districts, the officials as a group have developed new ways to extend their powers of patronage and to assert a new form of dominance. But the wherewithal to do so varies dramatically across localities. Under Mao, when central policy was enforced far more strongly, there was a sameness to rural circumstances across China: the very same government programs were pursued throughout the great bulk of the villages, everywhere using the very same mechanisms of control. Today, in contrast, different villages and townships follow very different drumbeats.

The Industrializing Rural Districts

Under Deng, local rural governments were granted the leeway to take greater initiative to develop their localities economically in diverse ways. Especially in the coastal regions and in districts near the cities, they have been able to take advantage of this. As the Mao-era political machinery atrophied, the rural officials in those regions have been able to establish new bases for their authority and power by developing industry.

Under Mao, they had received mixed signals from above. On the one side, they were encouraged to start local factories, but on the other, they were denied access to most kinds of industrial inputs, which were largely reserved for China's state-owned enterprises. They also were usually forbidden to erect factories that produced goods that competed with the lumbering state-owned industrial sector. Under Deng, these restrictions gradually disappeared, and the countryside was given the go-ahead to take advantage of its lower administrative and labor costs. A huge surge in rural industrialization ensued, starting in the 1980s and accelerating in the 1990s.[9] For most of the past two decades, the rural industrial sector has been the fastest-growing portion of the most rapidly developing nation on earth.

Much of the new rural industry is owned by township governments. Through this industrialization, some of the townships that are in striking distance of coastal and urban markets have developed their own substantial sources of revenue and their own large constituencies of workers. Officials in such townships have used the budget surpluses and their control over hiring to develop a homegrown political base. To cement local support, they have spread largesse in the form of public-welfare benefits, in particular through schools and health clinics. Whereas under Mao they had to rely upon coercive political campaigns to sustain their authority, which at the same time reduced them to serving largely as instruments of the state, the wealthy township administrations now are in a financial position not only to assert their own authority locally but also to use their budgetary independence to attain greater autonomy from the pressures of higher-level bureaucracy. He who pays the piper calls the tune.

At the same time, the township government today gains from the fact that the market town, the seat of its administration, has taken on greater importance in the lives of the local populace. Before the revolution, peasants frequently gathered in the town on market days to buy and sell. But during the period of collective agriculture, there was little need to visit the town. Agricultural produce was sold directly to the state in bulk by the production teams, and the state also became the farmers' main provider of consumer goods, often through rationing. Free markets often were shut down, and lateral trade between villages was all but cut off. The "intermediate world" beyond the village—the local marketing district—shrank in importance to the peasants, while their own village and production-team community as well as the central state and its policies became increasingly significant to them.

That "intermediate world" has reemerged today in their lives. In the 1980s, farmers again became responsible for marketing most of

---

9. The fixed assets of the rural enterprises increased at a phenomenal rate of 27 percent per annum in the five-year period between 1985 and 1990 and then at an even more sizzling rate of 37 percent per year between 1990 and 1995. Jean Oi, *Rural China Takes Off* (Berkeley: University of California Press, 1999), p. 82.

their own produce (they even are required to carry their own quota grain into town), and they must purchase their own inputs in town as well. They now congregate in the market town at frequent intervals, make social contacts there with people from other villages within the township, and through this have come to identify more closely with the territory of the township. In sum, decollectivization and the increased scope of commercialization during the past two decades have significantly increased the salience to farmers of the township—and the higher the level of commercialization and industrialization in a given township, the more this is the case.

The village government has similarly been restrengthened markedly in those villages that own profitable factories. In such villages, the leaders have sometimes created mini–welfare states based on the revenues. Some have also established a high level of control over villagers dependent upon them for largesse. One example among many is a Sichuan village in which village-government-owned factories have been flourishing since the 1980s. The system of patronage there has created a situation in which clusters of families who are related to the officials through kinship or friendship occupy the village's economic and social upper crust, and the village's other families make up a resentful but powerless and dependent lower stratum.[10]

There are also village governments that are more even-handed in their largesse and have built up broad-based loyal constituencies within their villages. Local leaders in such cases may feel emboldened to resist township policies that run counter to their village's interests. In other cases, in contrast, village leaders have squandered their base of support within their village but can get away with local abuses of power because they are protected by their immediate superiors in the township and county. As the central state has pulled back, independent networks have arisen of local officials who scratch each other's backs and cover up for, and enrich, each other. To both the central government and the local populace, this has proven a worrisome development.

The tensions and disappointments of the last decade of Mao's rule left as its heritage an atmosphere of cynicism and opportunism among

10. Gregory Ruf, *Cadres and Kin: Making a Socialist Village in West China, 1921–1991* (Stanford: Stanford University Press, 1998); also see his "Managing Interests: Collective Property Rights and Village Enterprise in Rural Sichuan," in *Property Rights and Economic Reform in China*, ed. Jean Oi and Andrew Walder (Stanford: Stanford University Press, 1999). This information is also based on personal correspondence with Ruf.

many of the county, township, and village officials. Over the years, in many parts of rural China, this has translated into officials living well at public expense. This can be seen in well-off and impoverished districts alike. County and township officials in particular tend to exhibit a palpable desire for perks, be it expensive cars that are put at their disposal or lavish meals and entertainment that are billed to their government budgets. They help each other's kith and kin to obtain good public-sector employment or to win local government contracts. It is partly a matter of private favors trading and partly that each rural level of government—village, township, and county—finds that it pays off in terms of its own governmental interests to ingratiate itself with officials in the levels above and below it. This cooperation extends to policy matters, in which the different levels of rural government often work together informally to protect local interests and to bend central-government programs to their own liking. To a slight extent, these various types of bureaucratic behavior and linkages had been true, too, of Mao's time. But they were constricted then by the harsh, unpredictable nature of upper-level party rule, which was intent upon retaining a whip hand over the connivances of lower-level officialdom. That hand has largely been stilled.

As the self-interested bonds strengthen between officials occupying the different rural levels of government, the local political scene in many districts has been turned on its head. During the period of Mao-era collectives, village officials could not ignore central-government directives and orders but instead could attempt much more readily to side-step or resist commands that originated only at the commune level, knowing that the commune administration, when acting on its own, was the weakest level in the party-state's chain of command. Interviewees during the Maoist period observed that a commune generally held few economic assets of its own, had no natural constituencies that its leadership could turn to for support, and had to depend upon the borrowed power of the state to get its way. Today the opposite situation sometimes prevails, in which village cadres find themselves tied to the programs of the township (formerly commune) officialdom through compacts of mutual interest and mutual support, while they feel less pressure to conform to the preferences of the faraway central state. As will be seen most clearly when we examine the poorer districts, these cadres can ride roughshod over the local populace today, no longer on behalf of the party-state but rather to serve their own ends. Mao-era central tyranny enforced by locals was supplanted in some parts of the countryside during the 1980s by local tyranny indulged by the center.

The lowest level of local rural organization, the production team, collapsed throughout China as a locus of activity when the agricultural fields were distributed to the households to farm. The teams continue to exist today only in the sense that they remain the de jure owners of the land. Each year they divide among their member households the proceeds, if any, from fish-pond rentals and the ground rents of industrial sites. But they no longer count as part of the political equation in villages, as the team heads no longer oversee or represent anyone. Although the teams were not able to adequately protect the interests of the peasantry under the collectives, their effective disappearance as a meaningful institution leaves the farmers even more disorganized and vulnerable in the face of local officialdom.

Taking advantage of this, officials sometimes overplay their hand, leading to violent outbursts. One scheme that has been reported many times in the Chinese press occurs when officials at the township level, sometimes with the assistance of village officials, connive to rob farmers of valuable land. The officials first decree that stretches of local farmland must be sold at a low price for the inauguration of an "industrial development zone"; this land is then handed over at that price to semi-private "development companies" that the officials themselves establish and largely own; and the land is immediately resold at a very high profit for use as industrial sites. Throughout the past decade, Chinese newspapers have reported on farmer riots in several provinces in reaction to this form of corrupt land expropriation.

Such outbursts, and also nonviolent forms of protest (to be discussed later in the chapter), appear to be on the increase in the more rapidly developing parts of the countryside. One reason is that the effectiveness of patronage systems is beginning to erode. For one thing, the enterprises that are owned by rural governments no longer can provide as many jobs to local people as in the past. In the 1980s, the wages provided to local workers were higher than what they could earn in the fields. Gaining access to such coveted jobs cemented the fortunate workers' loyalty. The local factories enjoyed local protectionism against competing goods from outside, and with monopoly profits they could afford to be generous to the local workforce. But that local protectionism has largely broken down over the years as the national economy continues to marketize. To remain profitable, the local factories need to be competitive in their labor costs, and so increasingly they have turned to hiring people from the poorest parts of China at low wages. In some districts, only the supervisory jobs in industry remain in local hands, and the local authorities are left with far fewer patronage jobs to dispense.

In many of these same townships, the patronage networks have been further weakened because lucrative livelihoods outside of agriculture have emerged that are beyond the control of the officials. In particular, the latter part of the 1980s witnessed the rise of private enterprises, and this trend has accelerated in the 1990s. In fact, during much of the 1990s, rural private industry has developed at a faster rate than the collective (township- and village-owned) enterprises. As a result, by the close of 1997, according to official statistics, the value of production of private industry in the countryside reached 300 billion yuan, almost as large as the total production value of China's rural collective industry (360 billion yuan), and the total profits of the private sector already stood higher than those of the collective sector.[11] Sometimes these private businesses are tied to the officials, but increasingly they are not. The proprietors are becoming an increasingly independent, affluent, and influential constituency on the local scene, a counterweight to the unilateral power of officialdom.[12] These several trends provide political and social "space" for the expression of protest.

The Poorer Districts

The parts of the countryside in which villagers have a deeper cause for discontent are the nonindustrialized, less affluent districts. They have little reason there to be grateful to rural officials and, as will be seen, considerably more reason to be resentful. It comes as no surprise that the great bulk of rural protests have arisen in these poorer parts of China.

For one thing, the villagers who depend entirely upon agriculture for a livelihood have not shared in China's boom times. Initially, in the

---

11. *Zhongguo xiangzhen qiye nianjian 1998*, p. 107.

12. Such rural areas are discussed in Yia-Ling Liu, "Reform from Below: The Private Economy and Local Politics in the Rural Industrialization of Wenzhou," *The China Quarterly*, no. 130 (June 1992), pp. 53–64; and in Jonathan Unger and Anita Chan, "Inheritors of the Boom: Private Enterprise and the Role of Local Government in a Rural South China Township," *The China Journal*, no. 42 (July 1999), pp. 45–74.

first half of the 1980s, the central government increased the prices paid for farm produce, but during most of the years since 1985 the prices have not kept up with inflation, farm incomes have stagnated, and in some areas they have even dropped.

The low profits from agriculture have been more than a cause for peasant disgruntlement: in the nonindustrialized rural areas, this pinch on household earnings has also jeopardized the capacity of local governments to raise tax revenues from households. Under the Mao-era collectives, such exactions were quietly siphoned off from each production team's pool of postharvest income before the remainder of the proceeds were divided among the village households as wages. The farmers thus were not even fully aware of the taxes. Today, in contrast, village officials must seek tax funds openly from independent farmers, going from household to household to collect them, and these are households that are already struggling economically.

In some of these poorer districts, village leaders do not have the willpower or capacity to coerce the farmers to pay up. Chinese government publications refer to these as "paralyzed villages." In some of these, so few funds are collected that village medical care and schooling are no longer available. In one village in Yunnan province that I visited in the late 1980s, a site without a drinkable water supply, funds had been raised by the village in the early 1970s, under the Mao-era collectives, to install a system of pipes leading from a spring a mile away. More recently the pipes have begun to leak badly, but the village government can no longer raise enough money from households to fix the pipes, and the farmers once again must laboriously haul buckets of drinking water from the spring by shoulder pole.[13]

Officials at the county and township levels, however, still normally push to have their own tax revenues collected in full. They not only have legitimate government outlays to cover but also often want a share of the bureaucratic perks available in better-off locales, including the fleets of cars, the wining and dining, and the relatives slotted into public-sector jobs in a bloated bureaucracy. To accomplish these ends, they resort to coercion to extract funds from villagers.

Their performance thus differs markedly from that of officials in the rich industrialized rural districts. Whereas local officials in the lat-

13. This and similar villages are discussed in Jonathan Unger and Jean Xiong, "Life in the Chinese Hinterlands under the Rural Economic Reforms," *Bulletin of Concerned Asian Scholars*, vol. 22, no. 2 (April 1990), esp. pp. 13–14.

ter districts advance their own interests by keeping local household taxes low and by setting aside enterprise profits to create mini-welfare states, in the poor districts the county and township officials frequently find it in their interest to engage in predatory behavior. They concoct an imposing array of local fees, taxes, and fines—say, for reforestation, for owning radios or motorcycles or bicycles, policing, road building, population planning, slaughtering household animals for personal consumption, you name it. A survey of one thousand peasant households in twenty counties of Sichuan province, undertaken by the provincial government, disclosed that the average household's burden had increased from 64 separate fees and local taxes in 1985 to 107 in 1991.[14] Since then, the situation has, if anything, worsened. A national party journal reported in 1998 that recently "these three categories of burdens (fees and taxes, quota apportionments, and fines) have increased markedly, and the amount of the increase has far outstripped the farmers' gains in cash income."[15]

During the 1990s, the central government began increasing the amount of low-priced quota deliveries demanded on a number of crops, including cotton, silk cocoons, and even grain, and provincial and local authorities could not resist getting into the act. Some localities have added their own extra share of quotas, and in some other districts the county or township government, as monopolist middleman, has gone so far as to force farmers to hand in their entire crop (tobacco is a good example) at prices far below those of the free market.[16] The local government then sells these extra deliveries at a high market price.

Township and village cadres alienate their neighbors by collecting the extra revenues and crop deliveries, and so they have good reason to resist doing so—unless driven by pressures and inducements from above. Since the Mao-era political levers over cadres through campaigns and control through party committees no longer are effective, the county and township elicit the cooperation of lower-level rural officials today by setting job-performance quotas each year. This tech-

---

14. "Peasant Unrest in Szechwan and Mainland China's Rural Problems," *Issues and Studies*, vol. 29, no. 6 (July 1993), p. 130.

15. *Qiushi* (Seek Facts), no. 3, 1998, pp. 46–49. Also see Mobo Gao, *Gao Village: Rural Life in Modern China* (Honolulu: University of Hawaii Press, 1999), esp. pp. 186–96.

16. An extraordinary picture of how this operates in several poor counties is provided in Yali Peng, "The Politics of Tobacco: Relations between Farmers and Local Governments in China's Southwest," *The China Journal*, no. 36 (July 1996), pp. 67–82.

nique is a carryover from Maoist times, but with a twist. Officials today are rewarded monetarily, as well as through promotions, for fulfillment and overfulfillment of their assignments' quotas, and they are penalized monetarily if they do not meet their quotas. One consequence of this mechanism is that "charts of targets and progress towards those targets are ubiquitous features of township meeting rooms, offices and bulletin boards."[17] The most stringent example of such target setting is in the area of birth control, where level by bureaucratic level, pressures are imposed upon cadres to enforce central decrees by meeting fixed birth quotas. The other type of assignment that most often receives this type of priority, with rewards and penalties attached, is, not surprisingly, the collection of taxes, locally levied fees, and quotas of agricultural products.[18]

In some impoverished villages, the officials themselves have so little incentive to stay in office that they prefer to ignore higher levels. In such cases, the revenues simply do not get collected or, more often, county and township officials periodically raid the village with police officers in tow. One way or another, then, even in very poor villages, money usually gets squeezed out of households.

The central government is well aware of this, and a bit worried, especially since the tax and fee burdens sporadically spark protests in these poor regions. The response of the government has been to decree an upper limit on local taxes and fees: cumulatively, they cannot exceed 5 percent of the average income in a village. This is an unrealistically low figure, since even minimal public services and local government expenses normally cost more than that amount. This is especially true in poor areas, where that "5 percent" benchmark represents a smaller absolute amount of money than elsewhere. This may be a

---

17. Scott Rozelle, "Decision-Making in China's Rural Economy: The Linkages between Village Leaders and Farm Households," The China Quarterly, no. 137 (March 1994), p. 114. Incentives for the managers of publicly owned rural enterprises operate in a similar fashion of targets and quotas. On this, see Jean Oi, "Fiscal Reform and the Economic Foundations of Local State Corporatism in China," World Politics, vol. 45, no. 1 (October 1992), p. 114.

18. See Kevin J. O'Brien and Lianjiang Li, "Selective Policy Implementation in Rural China," Comparative Politics, vol. 31, no. 2 (January 1999), pp. 167–86. The pressures on grassroots cadres are also frequently discussed in the Chinese news media; as one example, "When funds are collected from the peasants, every penny must come from door-to-door collections by village and hamlet cadres. Some locales give them time limits to make their collections. If any amount is still uncollected at the end of this period, the cadres are penalized or their salaries are withheld." Liaowang (Outlook Weekly, Beijing), issue 14, 1998, p. 38, trans. in Inside China Mainland, June 1998, p. 61.

moot point, however, since the 5 percent limit does not usually seem to be adhered to. Local officials either ignore the central government's decree or rewrite local statistics to show far higher average incomes than actually exist, so as to claim falsely that they are sticking within the government's 5 percent limit.

Peasant Protests

As the impositions upon peasants have grown, they have reacted violently in some places. Between January and July 1998 alone, a total of 3,200 incidents of collective protests were sufficiently serious to be recorded at the national level, and more than 420 of these involved conflicts in which rural government buildings were surrounded by angry crowds. During that half-year period, casualties were officially reported as topping 7,400, including more than 1,200 cadres and police wounded.[19]

In their demonstrations against local officialdom, farmers regularly point to the central government regulation about the 5 percent tax maximum. It is a handle they can use in order to place the local officials on the defensive: they, the farmers, legally are in the right, and the local cadres are in the wrong. In fact, the largest peasant protest movement thus far recorded, in Renshou County, Sichuan province, was sparked when a villager confronted cadres with the 5 percent rule, refused to pay anything beyond this, posted the national regulation so that others would know about it, and rallied other farmers to his cause.[20] (After the protest movement was crushed, the villager ultimately went to prison for having instigated a public disturbance.)

Rural governments, as in the above case, often try to conceal information about central policies from the peasants.[21] But it is obvious that channels of information no longer can be tightly or effectively controlled by local authorities. Literacy is too widespread today, and villagers no longer are confined to their own small localities but go out in large numbers to the cities to work, where they mingle and exchange

---

19. *Dongxiang* (Trends, Hong Kong), October 1998, pp. 11–12.

20. *BBC Summary of World Broadcasts: Asia Pacific*, May 3, 1993 (FE/1678-B2/1).

21. "Why is it," a national newspaper asked, "that in some locales peasants who post newspapers carrying central government policies on rural bulletin boards are accused of 'disturbing public order'?" *Zhongguo qingnian bao* (China Youth Daily), December 10, 1998, p. 5, quoted in *Inside China Mainland*, March 1999, p. 61.

information with migrant workers from other parts of the country-side.[22]

Armed with such information, by far the greatest number of farmers' protests today are entirely within the letter of the law. They include signature petitions, appeals to courts of law, approaches to national newspapers and magazines, and delegations of peasants traveling to seek out high-level officials to lodge direct complaints.[23] Most of these peaceful protests—and also many of the violent ones—involve implicit or explicit appeals to the central government against local policies, even when central policies are in part the reason for disgruntlement.[24] Farmers who in Maoist times lacked protection *from* the central state feel today that they lack protection *by* the central state, and they want more of an assertion of central power in order to enforce central edicts.

For this very reason, the rural unrest, no matter how severe it may become, does not appear to pose any imminent danger to the central government. The disgruntlement, after all, is not aimed against the government; and the protests are localized and isolated from each other.

Beijing, for its part, is increasingly willing today to promote the viewpoint among disgruntled peasants that errant local cadres are to blame for their plight, painting itself as a good, caring government. National leaders see the sense of posing as allies and protectors of the farmers, just as the farmers see the sense of appealing to the central authorities in hopes of playing them off against the local officialdom. In point of fact, already by the mid-1980s, after the reforms to decollectivize the countryside had been accomplished with the local offi-

---

22. Elisabeth Croll, *From Heaven to Earth: Images and Experiences of Development in China* (London: Routledge, 1994), chap. 5.

23. See, for example, Kevin J. O'Brien, "Rightful Resistance," *World Politics*, vol. 49 (October 1996), pp. 31–55.

24. Even when the main complaint of farmers involves heavy centrally imposed crop-quota burdens, local cadres more safely get blamed. A researcher in rural Xinjiang province who found precisely that situation observed that "Many times I was told [by farmers], 'the policies issued at the top are good, but they are not implemented as they should be.'" Ildiko Beller-Hann, "The Peasant Condition in Xinjiang," *Journal of Peasant Studies*, vol. 25, no. 1 (October 1997), p. 103. Chinese farmers throughout much of history have had a reservoir of such faith in distant rulers. In an interesting article, Lucien Bianco points to parallels in European history: "Criticizing the local authorities by appealing to the decisions of the Politburo is the reappearance, within a Communist regime, of older beliefs deeply held by the subjects of all absolutist regimes: the King of France (or the Tsar of Russia) is thought to be betrayed by his servants." Lucien Bianco, "The Weapons of the Weak: A Critical View," *China Perspectives*, no. 22 (March–April 1999), p. 8.

cials' acquiescence, the central government no longer saw as much need to placate the rural cadres. As the years passed, Beijing instead expressed increasing concern that the independent back-scratching networks of local officials impeded central authority, and the national news media was regularly encouraged to publish exposés about local officials' impositions upon the peasantry. It was within this context that the 5 percent rule was decreed and that provisions were written into the 1993 Law on Agriculture stating that farmers could legally "refuse" (*jujue*) to pay the excessive, unauthorized fees and taxes.[25]

The Inauguration of Grassroots Elections

Reformers in Beijing are willing to go beyond these measures. They have urged the creation, at the village level, of an institutionalized check on cadres' power. Beginning in the mid-1980s and extending into the 1990s, they have argued that villagers would be more willing to abide by national-level taxes and quotas and birth-control policies if they were given an organized voice to overturn the grassroots abuses.[26] In 1987 the reformers in Beijing were able to push through an official regulation calling for the establishment of "village representative assemblies" (that is, grassroots legislatures that were supposed to monitor the village cadres). It was subsequently directed, more importantly, that not just these representative bodies but also the body of village officials—the so-called villagers committee—should be elected by village residents, and it was decided, even more importantly, that the village heads themselves should be elected for three-year terms of office through multicandidate elections.[27]

These were major political reforms, especially since the Communist Party tradition is, by its very essence, antidemocratic. The Marxist-Leninist belief system had always stressed that the party leadership held a special mission to push history forward through its supe-

---

25. Thomas P. Bernstein, "Farmer Discontent and Regime Responses," in *The Paradox of China's Post-Mao Reforms*, ed. Merle Goldman and Roderick MacFarquhar (Cambridge: Harvard University Press, 1999), p. 214.

26. See, for example, Daniel Kelliher, "The Chinese Debate over Village Self-Government," *The China Journal*, no. 37 (January 1997), pp. 63–86.

27. On the origins and operations of these several types of village elections, see Kevin O'Brien, "Implementing Political Reform in China's Villages," *Australian Journal of Chinese Affairs*, no. 32 (July 1994); Susan V. Lawrence, "Democracy, Chinese Style," in the same journal issue; and Lianjiang Li and Kevin O'Brien, "The Struggle over Village Elections," in *The Paradox of China's Post-Mao Reforms*, pp. 129–44.

rior knowledge of Marxism and its commitment to the revolution, and that the party stood far in advance of the at times "feudal" ideas held by ordinary people. To select a local government by majority vote, as in "bourgeois democracy," would only reflect the average, unprogressive, unenlightened views of the people. Today, the party does not hold to that Marxist ideology any longer in reality, but it still firmly believes in its unilateral right to power—now at the helm of a "developmental state." The very notion of multicandidate elections goes against the grain of the party's long-entrenched aversion to democratic processes.

The Communist Party is not alone in its distrust of democracy. Even the bulk of China's university students and intellectuals, who normally are portrayed in the West as pro-democracy, do not believe in a one-person-one-vote universal franchise. They share in an urban antipathy and disdain for the countryside, afraid that the peasants are ill-equipped to vote and would be prone to support demagogues.[28]

It is ironic, then, that the peasantry is the only group in China allowed to select local leaders in multicandidate secret ballots. But it perhaps is even more ironic that urban dwellers should have disdain for the farmers' capacity to participate in such elections. The farmers, after all, are the only portion of China's population who have had experience in local democracy, since they were allowed under Mao to select their own production-team leadership. Now, in the 1990s, with the production teams hollowed out and rendered irrelevant by decollectivization, they were again to choose their grassroots leaders, raised one degree to the village level.

To issue directives in Beijing is one thing, but to actually carry them through in the provinces and localities is another, and it is not known how many of China's 930,000 villages have experienced genuine elections in which the residents get to nominate the candidates. For one thing, many of the incumbent officeholders in villages understandably did not see the electoral reforms to be in their own best interests, nor did many of the provincial, county, and township bureaucrats. In most parts of the countryside, all of these levels of officials were slow to implement village elections. Indeed, Guangdong, the last hold-

---

28. At Tiananmen in 1989, when they called for democracy, what they meant by the word was "freedom": freedom of the press, of assembly, and of association, and an impartial independent court system. They wanted the government to take into account a wider range of voices, with a widening of the decision-making elite to include them as an educated constituency.

out among China's provinces, did not begin to require any elections for villager committees until 1999.

In many other parts of China, even when elections are held, local officials often conspire to keep the new representative bodies toothless. In some villages, the deputy village head, for instance, serves as the head of the village representative assembly even though the assembly is supposed to oversee him and his superior, while in a large number of other villages the assembly is rarely called into session. In a great many places, thus, they remain ineffective or inactive or serve as a tool of the village leadership. In yet other villages, the new direct elections for village officials are dominated by the township administrators or by the village incumbents, and potential rivals for office are not allowed to run on one pretext or another. And even when elections are fairly held, in some villages the selections are dominated by members of the largest lineage group, which only reinforces longstanding patterns of favoritism and intravillage antagonism.

Perhaps most important of all, in only some of the villages do direct multicandidate elections take place to select the village leaders. In many other villages, the residents are just provided with a list of six or seven candidates from among whom five are to be selected to serve as the village's officials. Thus the residents' influence over the composition of the village leadership is effectively minimized—their choice confined to the essentially negative role of vetoing one or two disliked candidates.

Nonetheless, in many of China's villages, corrupt cadres have been ousted through such elections, and in the best of cases entirely fair full-scale elections have been held. In some of these latter villages, the popularly elected village representative assemblies have even gained a say in supervising the village budget.[29] Given all this, reports from China suggest that in an increasing number of rural districts the electoral reforms are serving their purpose, which is to assuage peasant disgruntlement by restoring a sense of legitimacy to village government.

In all of these elections, whether they be for village assemblies or for village leadership posts, no political parties are allowed, nor slates of candidates with common platforms, nor any overarching electoral organizations transcending the village. Elections are allowed in vil-

---

29. Anne F. Thurston, *Muddling toward Democracy: Political Change in Grassroots China* (Washington, D.C.: United States Institute of Peace, 1998).

lages, rather than in cities, precisely because the villages are atomized. China's top party leadership appears to hold to the premise that if elections can be restricted to a local level and isolated from the all-important structure of party rule, they cannot provide the seeds for any organized challenge to higher-level party rule.

The problem the party faces, however, is that the example set by the village-level elections is contagious. Already, some reformist provincial, prefectural, and county leaders have been willing to go beyond Beijing. They can observe that in many villages the present sets of elections are not sufficient to restore legitimacy to village governments. The most important village figure under the Chinese political system even today, after all, is often not the village head but the village party secretary, who is still insulated from popular opinion. The village elections may be of little importance when the party secretary retains control over village enterprises and the village's purse strings and his power trumps that of the village head and villager committee.[30]

Thus, despite Leninist antipathy to allowing non-party members to elect party leaders, the logic of the village-level electoral reforms has led to a further step, starting in rural Shanxi province, with elections for village party secretary.[31] Other provinces have picked up the cue. By late 1999, direct elections for village secretaries and village party committees were being conducted throughout a section of Shandong province containing 6,500 villages.[32] Despite the discomfiture of the party organization in Beijing, democracy is creeping into previously taboo areas.

The electoral process is also creeping upward out of the villages. The level of rural administration that most alienates many farmers in the less prosperous parts of China is the township: it appears to them to be the source of most of the local fees and fines. Village-level elections cannot assuage peasant discontent against township leaders; so if the process of electing officials at the lower level proves successful in restoring farmers' goodwill, why not attempt elections for rural town-

30. Jean Oi, "Economic Development, Stability and Democratic Village Self-governance," in *China Review 1996*, ed. Maurice Brosseau, Suzanne Pepper, and Tsang Shu-ki (Hong Kong: Chinese University Press, 1996), p. 136.

31. Lianjiang Li, "The Two-Ballot System in Shanxi Province: Subjecting Village Party Secretaries to a Popular Vote," *The China Journal*, no. 42 (July 1999), pp. 103–18.

32. *Nongmin ribao* (Farmer's Daily), December 11, 1999.

ship leaders? Even some of the top leaders in Beijing are enticed by such a notion. Jiang Zemin, China's Communist Party secretary and president, himself tentatively endorsed the idea in 1997,[33] although the measure has not yet been officially approved. However, with support from reformist officials and mass-media outlets in Beijing, in league with reformist regional officials, efforts have begun in selected areas to set the stage gradually for this next shift. Thus, bucking the official policy in Beijing, prefectural officials in Sichuan province successfully conducted elections for a rural township chief in late 1998 and garnered widespread favorable publicity among reformers elsewhere.[34] Within months, a township in Guangdong had followed suit.[35]

We may be witnessing the initial building blocks for the emergence of higher-level democracy in China. If village and township elections can be conducted, and if rural party secretaries are not immune from elections, then pressures and demands can begin to grow from within the ranks of political reformers for elections to be initiated to resolve the problem of unpopular and unresponsive county governments.

These should *not* be interpreted as bottom-up initiatives by the villagers themselves; they are not in a position to play any precedent-setting part in the initiation of new electoral reforms. There is a mistaken belief among some people outside China regarding this, just as there exists a similar mistaken belief that the farmers were able to take the initiative into their own hands to decollectivize in the early 1980s. But still, elections are quietly being instituted at levels above the village, through the connivance of political reformers in the upper echelons of government, officials in the Ministry of Civil Affairs (the government organization that is supposed to organize and oversee elections),[36] and middle-ranking officials out in the regions.

In short, democracy by stealth, strategically engineered first in rural districts at a distance from Beijing and creeping upward level by

33. Tyrene White, "Village Elections: Democracy from the Bottom Up?" *Current History*, vol. 97, no. 620 (September 1998), pp. 263–67.

34. See, for example, "China Praises Sichuan Election: Television Report Calls Vote Key Step toward Rural Reform," *Washington Post*, February 27, 1999, p. A12.

35. A report on this election is contained in *Zhongguo shehui kexue jikan* (Chinese social science quarterly), no. 26 (summer 1999), pp. 27–30.

36. For an interesting study of the successful gradualist strategy by reformers in the Ministry of Civil Affairs to overcome resistance to the earlier spread of village-level elections, see Tianjian Shi, "Village Committee Elections in China," *World Politics*, vol. 51, no. 3 (April 1999), esp. pp. 396–410.

rural level, seems to be under way. The structure of rural governance, which has largely stood unchanged since the end of Mao's era, is beginning to crack. If present trends continue, the Chinese polity may, gradually, change immeasurably.

The Shape of Society:
The Changing Demography of
Development

Tyrene White

Just over two hundred years ago, in 1798, the Reverend Thomas Robert Malthus published the first edition of his classic work, *An Essay on the Principle of Population.*[1] In it he argued that population growth had a constant tendency to outstrip food supplies, and he counseled policy changes in Britain that would discourage excessive childbearing, especially among the poor. Two centuries later, and fifty years into the reign of the Chinese Communist Party (CCP), one might reasonably ask whether Malthus should rank just below Mao Zedong and Karl Marx on the list of those whose ideas had the greatest impact on China in the twentieth century. For it was China's fate in the twentieth century to be racked by Malthusian questions. How to feed, clothe, house, and employ the people; how to provide them with education, health care, and social security; how to alleviate poverty and backwardness; how to control the movement of the people and the rate of urbanization—these core questions were a constant part of the landscape for China's leaders. How the Chinese Communist regime responded to these questions left an indelible mark on Chinese society, giving it a shape that must now be managed by the leaders of the twenty-first century.

Despite the enormous changes of the past fifty years, the basic questions the leaders confront will remain the same over the next hundred years. As China's population continues to grow from its 1999 level of 1.25 billion to a peak of 1.5 or 1.6 billion by midcentury, how to feed and employ the population will remain the fundamental chal-

---

1. Thomas Malthus, *An Essay on the Principle of Population* (London: Penguin Books, 1982).

lenge. But that challenge must now be met under twenty-first-century conditions (global and local) and in the face of new and rising expectations for achieving the "good life" promised by the market economy, even as the old expectations of socialist entitlements—especially the guarantee of gainful employment—fade slowly at best. It must also be met at a time when the state's own twentieth-century interventions have engendered demographic changes that pose new and formidable challenges.

The purpose of this chapter is to examine several of those challenges. After briefly reviewing the demographic picture that the CCP inherited in 1949 and how the state's economic and population policies under Mao and Deng reshaped Chinese society, I then consider three major consequences of these changes—population aging, urbanization and internal migration, and skewed sex ratios—and the challenges they will pose to the policy makers of the future. I conclude by considering two wild cards in China's demographic equation: the possible impact of an AIDS epidemic, and the emergent phenomenon, after twenty years of the one-child policy, of a society increasingly divided by the answer to the question, "Do you have any siblings?"

The Demography of Development under Mao and Deng

Fifty years ago, when the CCP came to power, China had experienced two centuries of rapid population growth. The expansion of arable land sown to agriculture, the introduction of new food crops, and the improvement of agricultural techniques had all contributed to a tripling of the population between 1750 and 1950. Despite the extra casualties of war and revolution between 1937 and 1949, general improvements in basic health and nutrition were also contributing to an increase in the average life span and a slow decline in rates of mortality, including infant mortality.

These trends were accelerated dramatically by the improvements made in public hygiene, food distribution, diet and nutrition, and civil order after 1949. By 1957, China's crude death rate and infant mortality rate were only about half of what they had been in 1949, and average life expectancy had increased from about forty to fifty years. With the exception of the Great Leap Forward period (1958–60), when China experienced a catastrophic man-made famine that caused thirty to forty million excess deaths, these trends continued through the

1960s. Between 1957 and 1970, China's crude death rate was halved again.[2]

Fertility, meanwhile, remained high. Urban fertility rates did not begin a sustained decline until after 1964, and rural fertility remained high until the early 1970s. As a result, China's total population soared from about 540 million in 1949 to about 830 million in 1970. In other words, China gained during this period a number of people greater than the entire population of the United States in 1998 (270 million). And though fertility levels began to decline precipitously after 1970, demographic momentum meant that the total population continued to grow, right up to the present. The very large cohorts of young people born in the 1950s, 1960s, and 1970s still had to move through their childbearing years. Even though they had fewer children on average than the generation that came before them, total population size continued to increase.

It is this demographic momentum that has propelled China's population to its current 1.25 billion, an increase of 400 million from its 1970 level. This increase has occurred despite the onset in 1970 of one of the fastest and most precipitous fertility declines ever recorded, a decline brought about by aggressive state intervention to promote contraceptive use and the implementation of a strict state program to limit childbearing. In the 1970s, the state promoted a two-child limit. In the 1980s, the limit was tightened to one child per couple (with some exceptions).

Why the long delay in promoting birth control? In large part, this was because birth control and antinatalism were so closely linked to the ideas of Malthus. In 1949, Malthus was for the CCP what he had been for Karl Marx—a contemptible spokesman for the propertied classes whose prescription for alleviating poverty was to advise the poor to have fewer babies and the rich to cut back their charity. By that time, Malthus's original thinking was being adapted and updated by contemporary demographers who saw population growth as the primary obstacle to economic development in the postcolonial developing world. When U.S. officials picked up on this Malthusian pessimism and predicted that China's vast population would pose an insuperable

---

2. These and other data on China's demographic transition can be found in Judith Banister, *China's Changing Population* (Stanford: Stanford University Press, 1987). See also Alice Goldstein and Wang Feng, *China: The Many Facets of Demographic Change* (Boulder, CO: Westview Press, 1996).

obstacle to the CCP's development plans, the reaction from China was harsh and swift. Such views were condemned as bourgeois and rejected as the ravings of imperialists. China took the optimistic socialist view, which assumed that capitalism, not population growth, was responsible for poverty and backwardness. Mao declared China's population to be its greatest asset, and for a time, a pronatalist policy was adopted.

In 1954, however, China's leaders were confronted with the results of the first national census, which estimated the population at approximately 540 million. Some urged immediate efforts to encourage family planning and fewer children, while others, including Mao, rejected such proposals as misguided and unnecessary.[3] Over the next fifteen years, therefore, China experienced rapid population growth—the combined result of declining rates of infant mortality, increased life expectancy, and high, stable rates of fertility. So large and steady was the population increase that China's food production made little headway on a per capita basis. Instead, production gains were eaten up by extra mouths. China's agricultural policies were not resulting in the levels of production necessary to offset these population gains and still provide satisfactory increases in food consumption across the board. Rapid population growth also strained the regime's ability to house and employ the population and to control the growth of cities. Per capita housing space stagnated for thirty years, and factories and other workplaces grew more inefficient as employment rolls were padded with excess laborers. Cities swelled from the combined results of planned and unplanned growth, forcing the Mao regime to impose strict limits on internal migration, limits that were enforced with the help of a national system of household registration that tied people to their official places of residence.

In the early 1970s, therefore, Premier Zhou Enlai responded to this dilemma by turning his attention to population control. He oversaw the implementation of a nationwide birth-planning program, one in which provinces and localities added population targets to their economic production goals. Though cloaked in socialist thought, its logic was ruthlessly Malthusian: in order to modernize rapidly, China first had to

---

3. For more on the early debate over China's population control policy, see Tyrene White, "The Origins of China's Birth Planning Policy," in *Engendering China: Women, Culture, and the State,* ed. Christina K. Gilmartin, Gail Hershatter, Lisa Rofel, and Tyrene White (Cambridge and London: Harvard University Press, 1994), pp. 250–78.

control population growth and population size. Population control became the linchpin for the entire modernization effort. Births had to be state planned and allocated, according to the needs of the economy and society as a whole. China became the international poster child for neo-Malthusianism.

This was an embarrassing position for China to find itself in. Like many other developing countries, in the early 1970s China publicly denounced U.S. efforts to link poverty to overpopulation, encourage population control, and tie economic aid packages to the creation of family-planning programs. At the 1974 United Nations Conference on Population and Development, held in Bucharest, Romania, China joined a loud protest against such views organized by many developing-world countries and reiterated the Marxist position linking poverty to capitalist exploitation and class conflict. Back home, meanwhile, fertility rates began to plummet as the new strict population control regime began to take hold. A mass campaign was launched urging couples to marry later, to limit their children to two (urban) or three (rural), and to space their children more widely. To make that possible, contraceptives were made available free of charge, and party officials were pressed to meet local population plan targets as if they were economic planning targets—which they now were. This policy was distinguished from its nonsocialist counterpart by the argument that reproduction, like production, should be planned according to the needs of the socialist state. Birth planning (*jihua shengyu*), it was argued, had nothing in common with the bourgeois notion of family planning (*jiating jieyu*) or with Malthusian pessimism. In a more practical vein, the policy was justified on grounds of maternal and infant health, just as the abortive efforts to introduce birth control in the 1950s and 1960s had been. Women who gave birth to fewer children, it was argued, had more time to invest in raising the "quality" of their children and more time left over to serve the revolution.

As the program gained strength, birth limits were formalized, and by the late 1970s, urban residents were already being urged to have only one child and being penalized for having more than two. In rural areas, implementation was more variable, but by the mid-1970s, peasants in some areas were losing collective support for a fourth or higher-order child or were being fined and penalized. With the death of Mao Zedong in 1976 and the subsequent political defeat of the remaining Cultural Revolution radicals, however, China began to embrace openly the neo-Malthusianism it had been practicing for several years. The abolition of poverty and the achievement of modernization were now said to be predicated on strict population control, and in 1979, a one-child policy was announced, complete with economic rewards for those who complied and financial penalties, political intimidation, or coercion for those who resisted. Within a few years, compliance was nearly universal in the cities. In rural areas, however, intense resistance to the idea of not bearing a son to carry on the ancestral line, combined with the value of male labor power—both in the present (as income) and in the future (as old-age support)—led the regime to modify its policy in the early 1980s. Those whose first child was a girl could try again, with several years' spacing, for a boy. Those who had a boy first, however, were to stop with one child. Either way, rural childbearing was also strictly limited, and the percentage of annual births that were third and higher order began to decline.

If strict population control spanned the Mao and Deng eras, other policies with demographic implications underwent a major overhaul in the Deng era. The reforms implemented after 1978 were designed to achieve modernization and improve material welfare as rapidly as possible, following an evolving "plan and market" formula that came to be known as "socialism with Chinese characteristics." This formula allowed for the reemergence, after long hibernation, of private entre-preneurship, giving the unemployed, the underemployed, and new graduates the chance to pursue more gainful and lucrative employment opportunities than had been available in the past, or merely to dream of leaving the village. With the gradual lifting of restrictions on popu-lation movement, a necessity to fuel the new "commodity economy," that dream became a growing reality. Peasants began to flock to cities to participate in urban markets for temporary labor, and urbanites began to move more freely in pursuit of work, education, or leisure. The result was a process of rapid urbanization and an unprecedented degree of population mobility.

Whatever the gains may have been from these reform-era policies, however, their side effects have been serious and will affect Chinese society throughout the twenty-first century. Rapid fertility decline in the 1970s and low fertility in the 1980s and 1990s have produced new worries about demographic aging, as ever larger cohorts of elderly and middle-aged people begin to move through or toward retirement age. The influx of large numbers of migrants into urban areas has strained city infrastructures and provoked a backlash against the "floating population." The one-child policy and the availability of ultrasound technology have joined to produce skewed sex ratios, as couples try to fine-tune the composition of their families by taking measures to eliminate female fetuses or infant girls (in rare cases through infanticide, and far more often through infant abandonment or sex-selective abortion) so as to assure that they have a son. Below I examine these three phenomena and their implications for Chinese society in the twenty-first century.

Population Aging

Demographers often use a pyramidal chart to represent the population distribution of a developing society that has not yet completed a demographic transition. The population distribution resembles a pyramid for two reasons. First, the elderly, who sit at the top of the pyramid, constitute a very small proportion of the population, since life expectancy remains relatively short and mortality rates for those beyond the age of 50 remain high. Second, the young, who form the base of the pyramid, make up a very large percentage of the population, because fertility rates remain high even as infant and child mortality begin to decline. Many children are born, and many survive. Those under the age of 30 may thus constitute as much as one-half to two-thirds of the total population.[4] As life span increases, however, and fertility drops to a very low level, the population pyramid for a nation begins to take on a columnlike form, representing a more even distribution of the population across age categories. Because more people are surviving longer, the elderly population grows as a proportion of the total, and the working-age population shrinks as a percentage of the total. The result is an increasing dependency ratio (that is, the ratio of the number of dependents, whether old or young, to the total number of working adults).

The challenges of an aging society are raising alarms all across the developed world, where it is expected that 30–35 percent of the population will be over age 60 by the year 2030, and 6 percent will be over the age of 80.[5] So great has been the increase in this over-74 age group

---

4. For an excellent introduction to population issues and demography, see Joseph A. McFalls, Jr., "Population: A Lively Introduction," *Population Bulletin*, vol. 53, no. 3 (September 1998).

5. These trends were explored in a special survey section called "The Economics of Ageing" in the *Economist*, January 27, 1996, pp. 5–10.

that demographers now refer to them as the "old-old," as opposed to the "young-old" between the ages of 65 and 74. Not only does this increased survivorship among the elderly raise new questions about how to maintain social security systems established in a very different demographic era, but when combined with the low birthrate it also provokes concerns about how a dwindling adult labor force can absorb the public tax burden that will be needed to sustain the safety net while simultaneously shouldering the growing private burden of care for both the young and the old. In the United States, for example, where those over the age of 75 are expected to make up fully half of its elderly population by 2030, these demographic trends have provoked an intense debate over how to provide social security benefits to the huge cohort of soon-to-be-retiring "baby boomers" without bankrupting the benefit system or placing too steep a tax burden on the smaller generations following.[6]

If the socioeconomic challenges of population aging will be hard to meet in the developed world, they will be far more formidable in China, which will be pressed on both ends of the demographic spectrum. Although China retains at present a pyramidal demographic structure, it is now entering an era of accelerated population aging. Rapid fertility decline after 1970 and increased longevity have combined to produce a rapid increase in the percentage of the population over age 60, but that trend is occurring even as the percentage of the population under age 15 remains extremely large. The 14-and-under age cohort made up 26 percent of the total population in mid-1998, compared with a peak of 40 percent in 1964 and with 34 percent in 1982. This decline, which is the direct result of China's strict population control, also signals a declining child dependency ratio, with about forty-nine children for every hundred working-age adults (ages 15–64).[7] Twenty-six percent of 1.25 billion, however, still translates into 325 million young dependents, a figure that exceeds by nearly 50 million the entire population of western and northern Europe.

---

6. On the figures for the United States, see Judith Treas, "Older Americans in the 1990s and Beyond," *Population Bulletin*, vol. 50, no. 2 (May 1995). On the debate over how to manage the retirement system, see, for example, Peter G. Peterson, "Will America Grow Up Before It Grows Old?" *Atlantic Monthly* (May 1996), pp. 55–86.

7. See table 2-7, "Population Age Composition and Dependency Ratio by Region," in Population and Employment Section of the State Statistical Bureau, *Zhongguo renkou tongji nianjian* (China Population Statistics Yearbook, 1998) (Beijing: Zhongguo renkou tongji chubanshe, 1998).

At the same time, population aging is expected to accelerate rapidly over the next several decades. Whereas retirees (defined in China as women aged 55 and over and men aged 60 and over) constituted about 8–9 percent of the population between 1953 and 1982, in 1990 that figure jumped to 10.3 percent. By 1996, the proportion of the population over age 65 reached nearly 7 percent, and it is expected to rise rapidly to 11 percent in 2005 and 20 percent in 2040.[8] As the proportion of the elderly rises, its composition will begin to shift toward the old-old, though not nearly as rapidly as in the developed world. In 1982, the proportion of the elderly population aged 80 and over was 6.6 percent, in 1990 it was 7.9 percent, and by 1995 it had risen to 8.6 percent.[9]

What do these numbers mean for the twenty-first century? They mean that China's elderly population will climb from around 90 million in 2000 to 290 million in 2040, or to about 20 percent of the predicted total population of 1.5 billion. With an inadequate system of retirement pensions in urban areas and little coverage at all in rural areas, China's working-age population, though large and robust at present, will increasingly be caught in a double vise. It will have to provide for child care and elder care, and do so without benefit of a reliable system of pensions or health care insurance, during a time of great flux in domestic economic institutions and policies.

The dimensions of the problem, and its importance to China's future, have produced a flurry of attention over the past several years, with articles on the topic betraying the existence of an immense anxiety over how China will cope with near-term retirement needs, to say nothing of long-term needs. Whatever the virtues of the Deng-era reforms, they destroyed the modest semblance of collective social security that rural China had enjoyed under the commune system. Those in the rural population who enjoy retirement benefits or health care (and they are few and far between) do so only because they have

---

8. Hu Ying, "China Will Have How Many People by the Middle of the Next Century," *Zhongguo Guoqing Guoli* (China's National Condition and Power), no. 64 (April 28, 1998), pp. 25–26, trans. in *Foreign Broadcast Information Service, Daily Report—China* (hereafter *FBIS-China*), July 23, 1998.

9. Yang Erzhang, "Wo guo laonian renkou zengzhang xunsu" (The rapid increase in our country's elderly population), *China Population Statistics Yearbook, 1998* (Beijing: Zhongguo renkou tongji chubanshe, 1998), p. 447; and Yang Rizhang, "China's Aged Population Grows Quickly," *Zhongguo tongji* (China Statistics), no. 190 (November 17, 1990), pp. 17–18, trans. in *FBIS-China*, March 11, 1998.

the good fortune to live in a prosperous village or be employed by a wealthy enterprise. The reforms have also put great strain on an inadequate and outdated system of benefits for employees of state-owned enterprises (SOEs). This system, first established in the 1950s, provided basic pension and disability coverage to most SOE employees. For a time, while the numbers of retirees remained relatively small and the cost of living strictly controlled, the system was able to function adequately, within its limited means. By the late 1980s, however, that began to change. Enterprises were now faced with a growing pool of retirees, just as the Deng-era economic reforms began to press them for greater profitability and efficiency in enterprise operations. To shore up the pension system and compensate for the partial withdrawal of state subsidies, workers were asked to pay more into their pension and health plans, with the contribution formula as well as the level of benefits varying across enterprises and sectors. According to one report, workers pay anywhere from 15 to 30 percent of their wages into pension funds, while enterprise contributions and payouts to retirees vary dramatically from place to place and region to region.[10]

Beyond the deficiencies within the system lies the problem of the growing number of urban workers not covered by the system. As of 1998, only 78 percent of China's 87.5 million enterprise employees and 24.5 million retirees were covered by the pension system.[11] And only a small percentage of workers employed outside the SOE sector enjoyed any sort of retirement or health care benefits. Many of those who should have been covered, moreover, were not receiving pensions. According to one report, more than three million retirees had been affected by enterprise defaults by early 1998.[12]

To deal with this looming crisis, the state began in the 1990s to lay the groundwork for a new national pension system. In the meantime, however, the door has been opened to commercial insurance and other nontraditional forms of insurance funding. In the countryside, for example, the Chinese Family Planning Association has implemented a system of health and pension insurance for those complying with childbearing limits, as well as life and property insurance for family-

---

10. Zhang Jianping, "China's Social Security System—Its Predicaments and Breakthroughs," *Jingji ribao* (Economic Daily), August 5, 1998, p. 4, trans. in *FBIS-China*, August 24, 1998.

11. Ibid.

12. See the untitled article by Fan Haijian in *Zhongguo shuiwu bao* (China Taxation Journal), September 4, 1998, p. 2, trans. in *FBIS-China*, October 1, 1998.

planning workers. Benefits are guaranteed through a system of contributions by enrollees, central and local governments, and township enterprises. In January 1998, forty-five million were enrolled in the CFPA plan, which oversaw a fund of four billion yuan.[13] Since that translated into an average of only about ninety yuan per member, however, it is clear how far the regime must go to even begin to solve the social security problem in the countryside, where the large majority of twenty-first-century retirees will be located.

The state insists that it will soon put into place a more comprehensive pension and retirement support system, but it is difficult to see how it can do so given the scale of the problem and the constraints on its resources. Yet the family, which has been the traditional source of old-age support, is undergoing rapid change, even in the countryside. Whether the family as an institution can weather the pressures that will accumulate over the next fifty years may make all the difference in how China copes with its senior dependents.

Urbanization and Internal Migration

In 1949, less than 10 percent of China's population was classified as urban. By 1978, after thirty years of the People's Republic, that proportion had increased only to 18 percent, a remarkably slow rate of growth given China's overall rate of population growth. Urbanization was kept under strict control after the 1950s through a household registration system that was used, among other things, to monitor all population movement closely. Under this system, every household was given a *hukou*, or residency status, that labeled its members permanently as either rural or urban, depending on the status of their place of abode. An urban *hukou* was a coveted prize for villagers, while those in smaller provincial towns and cities longed for a Shanghai or Beijing *hukou*. With the exception of short periods of disruption—as during the Great Leap Forward, when famine and its aftermath led to a breakdown in the control system, or during the Cultural Revolution, when young Red Guards were given permission to travel freely—travel within China was tightly controlled and limited primarily to official business. One could neither purchase a train ticket to a city nor get food or lodging upon arrival without the requisite travel permits and food coupons.

---

13. Zhu Baoxia, "Family Planners Build Insurance for Rural Areas," *China Daily*, January 3, 1998.

A food-ration ticket from one's hometown was useless in another location, since each urban area had its own ration coupons. And last, all visitors staying for more than three days were required to register with the authorities at the work unit or neighborhood being visited. Public security officials kept very careful track of the arrival and departure of all nonresidents.

The reforms implemented under Deng Xiaoping began to speed up the pace of urbanization, however. In anticipation of that development and of the likelihood that millions of underemployed rural laborers would leave the village at their very first opportunity and head for the major metropolitan areas, the new development policy placed special emphasis on the development of county seats and rural towns (*zhen*) and townships (*xiang*). This program of rural industrialization and urbanization was consistent with the overall goals of the regime, and it was the only viable option for coping with the enormous pent-up demand for access to urban life and opportunities. By concentrating on localized urbanization and the reclassification of localities (and *hukou* within those localities) to reflect the changing character of the workforce and the local economy, policy makers hoped to diminish migration pressures on large cities of five hundred thousand or more. As a result of this policy, by 1992 more than 27 percent of the population was officially classified as urban, and by 1998 that figure had risen to nearly 30 percent. Thus, while China's urban population rose by about 4 million a year during the first thirty years of the People's Republic, it increased at a rate of 10 million a year between 1978 and 1998, to 380 million. With fertility rates at much lower levels in these last two decades than in the previous three, it is clear that much of this increase was accomplished through the addition of new migrants to the urban population and through the creation of new urban areas.

This increase in the urban population strained the patience of city dwellers who struggled daily with housing shortages, transportation bottlenecks, and inadequate services, and the problem was vastly compounded by the influx of temporary migrants from all points around the country. This transient "floating population" (*liudong renkou*), which was estimated at as much as one hundred million by the late 1990s, began pouring into cities in the mid-1980s in search of seasonal or semipermanent work. The early destinations of choice were the major metropolitan areas of Beijing, Shanghai, and especially Guangzhou, where at first thousands and then millions flocked during the Chinese New Year holiday (a fallow period for agriculture) in search of temporary jobs. These periodic floods of temporary migrants, many of whom moved in and out quickly, soon evolved into a steadier stream of population flow, as migrants began to discover that the temporary shelters they erected for themselves would be tolerated (at least for a time) by local authorities.

As with all population migrations, this massive population movement soon began to take on certain patterns as early migrants sent for relatives and became magnets for other migrants from their home regions. Analyses of data based on the 1990 national census, for example, showed that the large majority of migrants were young (under age thirty), of rural origin, and male. As Delia Davin has pointed out, however, female migrants made up a larger proportion of the total than one might expect—43 percent of all migrants in 1990. Among migrants to major cities, men greatly outnumbered women, but among migrants within the countryside (from one rural area to another), women outnumbered men.[14]

As these gender figures suggest, not all of the migration was rural to urban, and not all of it was interprovincial. On the contrary, much of it was "local." In 1988, only 20 percent of migrants left their home provinces for other destinations, and nearly 44 percent migrated from one rural area to another in the same county. The remaining 36 percent migrated to another location in the same province. Only two years later, however, a significant change began to occur. Migrants across provincial lines grew to 36 percent of the total by 1990, while migrants within the same county declined to 31 percent.[15] Similarly, a study of migration patterns in Sichuan province conducted by the Ministry of Agriculture in 1994 found that, of the ten million transients in the province, nearly 52 percent migrated to other provinces, with the coastal areas and cities preferred destinations.[16] And more recently, senior demographer Gu Shengzu claimed that fully three-quarters of China's transients had moved from rural to urban areas, suggesting that rural-to-rural migration declined rapidly in the 1990s compared with

---

14. Delia Davin, *Internal Migration in Contemporary China* (New York: St. Martin's Press, 1999), pp. 29–30.

15. Ibid., p. 34.

16. Zhao Guangrong, "On the Application of 'The Three Theories' in Governing the Floating Population," *Renkou yu jingji* (Population and Economics), no. 2 (March 25, 1997), pp. 45–49.

the 1980s.[17] As the numbers of these migrants grew, so did urban anxiety and resentment. These "squatters" were blamed for all of the emerging urban ills, including clogged transportation, rising crime, deteriorating sanitation, displacement of urban workers from jobs, and excessive childbearing. Early migrants became conduits for others from their regions of origin, resulting in the growth of enclave "villages" that developed their own miniature bureaucracies and leadership structures to organize and provide services for the community of migrants. The most famous such settlement, Beijing's Zhejiang Village, had drawn twelve thousand migrants by 1986, and by the late 1990s that number had increased eightfold.[18] To gain some measure of control over this burgeoning population, central and local governments worked to create a system of temporary registration. First introduced in 1985, the new regulations required each migrant to register with the public security bureau, providing proof of identity and paying a registration fee. To qualify, the migrant had to be sixteen years of age. The temporary registration card generally expired after six months or a year, forcing the migrant to return for renewal. Migrants were expected to produce their registration cards on demand, and employers were expected to require registration cards of all temporary laborers that they hired. Guangzhou, for example, was home to 3.7 million registered migrants by 1997.[19]

Although sound in theory, in practice the system was more of a monitoring device than a control device, and not a very good monitoring device at that. In the early years of this system, most migrants did not go through the registration formalities, and most employers did not demand registration cards as a condition of employment. As anxieties about the size of the migrant populations grew, therefore, those who had not properly registered became prime targets during periodic regime campaigns to round up "illegal migrants" and deport them. In some cases, a campaign was launched out of security concerns, as in 1989 after the Tiananmen Square crackdown. In other cases, as in Beijing in the summers of 1990 and 1999, the motive was a desire to spruce up and secure cities for special events such as the Asian Games

---

17. Gu Shengzu, "The General Line of Thinking on Countermeasures to Manage the Floating Population in Urban Areas," *Zhongguo renkou bao* (China Population Newspaper), April 20, 1998, p. 3.

18. Davin, *Internal Migration*, pp. 108–10.

19. Matthew Miller, "Migration Feeds Unemployment Fears As Flood-Hit Provinces See Exodus," *South China Morning Post*, November 10, 1998.

and the fiftieth anniversary celebration of the founding of the People's Republic.[20]

This constant and relatively ineffective rearguard action to contain the growth of migrant communities, combined with growing concerns about urban unrest in the wake of rising unemployment, led to renewed efforts in the late 1990s to manage the flow of transients. In 1997, a national leading group for managing the floating population was established, with the hope of coordinating the efforts of different cities to control such phenomena as illegally rented housing and failure to register. The group also concentrated on the question of how to provide needed services for transients, including schooling for an estimated 20 million children to be found among the migrants.[21] Of primary concern to cities, however, was the problem of containment—how to limit the number of transients present at any one time. In Beijing, for example, the permanent population of more than 10 million was bloated with an additional 3.3 million transients by 1995, prompting a decision to limit the migrant population to 3 million. This figure was subsequently revised downward to 1.8 million.[22]

Such measures may well have some modest effect on controlling the number of migrants, but there is good reason to be skeptical. The size and scale of the population movements in China today are unprecedented, the numbers staggering. China's 100 million migrants already constitute a country within a country, a roving population so large that only the populations of the twelve most populous nations in the world exceed its size. And though the migration is contained within national boundaries, if it were transposed into the European context, the migration flows would crisscross Europe from Spain to Russia. Overlapping and intersecting this migrant population are China's 160 million surplus rural laborers; their number will grow in the years ahead, even as urban unemployment worsens and the population continues to climb toward its expected peak of 1.5 billion. How any local

---

20. An AFP report on September 8, 1999, claimed that sixteen thousand migrant workers had been expelled from Beijing in preparation for the fiftieth-anniversary celebrations on October 1, 1999. "AFP: Beijing Expels Migrant Workers Prior to Anniversary," in *FBIS-China*, September 8, 1999.

21. Untitled Xinhua Domestic Service report by Wang Leiming, December 29, 1997, in *FBIS-China*, January 4, 1998.

22. Xinhua Domestic Service (in English), "Regulations to Govern Beijing Transients," June 20, 1995, in *FBIS-China*, June 20, 1995. Jasper Becker, "Beijing Plans to Expel More Than Million Migrant Workers," *South China Morning Post*, November 1, 1998.

government could contain population movements of this size without benefit of the instruments available to nations—monitored border crossings, armed border patrols, and immigration bureaucracies backed by strict laws—is hard to imagine.

Sex Ratio Imbalance

The challenges of population aging and of urbanization and migration, great as they are, are inevitable parts of the transition to a modern industrial society. In contrast, the third demographic challenge China faces—an increasingly and unnaturally skewed sex ratio—is neither inevitable nor usual, and it may ultimately prove to be the most troublesome and consequential of the three.

In human populations, the ratio at birth of males to females is usually about 105 to 100. Because males tend to die in larger numbers than do females on their way to adulthood, the excess number of infant males assures an adequate supply of adult males as mates for the females. In 1995, a national 1-percent sample survey conducted in China reported a sex ratio at birth of 117.4 boys for every 100 girls, up from 116 in 1992, 113.8 in 1989, 111.2 in 1985, and 107.2 in 1982. By 1997, the sex ratio reported in China's annual population yearbook for ages four and under was 120 males for every 100 females.[23] This relentless trend left no further doubt about the reality and seriousness of the skew toward males in late twentieth-century China, though the trend had been denied persistently through the 1980s. It was only left to debate the causes and the solutions, while avoiding raising the state's deep complicity in the creation of the problem.

Despite the CCP's massive and prolonged effort to justify its claim to control childbearing by emphasizing the public and social costs of child rearing and insisting that population growth is an impediment to modernization, the party has been unable to overcome the influence of traditional patriarchal culture, which places great weight on producing a son. In this culture, family loyalty and filial obligation, not socialist ethics, are at the center of the childbearing calculus. Because only a son can continue the ancestral line, perform ancestral rites, and provide economic security for parents, the duty to produce a son and male heir supersedes any duty to the motherland. Not only does a son tend to

---

23. See table 1-2 in the *China Population Statistics Yearbook, 1998* (Beijing: Zhongguo renkou tongji chubanshe, 1998), p. 4.

earn more income, but he also brings a bride into the household to help care for her parents-in-law and raise the children. Not only does a daughter traditionally earn less, but she also marries out of the village and is obliged to shift her investments and loyalties toward her husband's family. To have no son, then, is to be vulnerable in every way.

What was true for rural families over the past decades remains true today. Despite rapid changes in rural China in the 1980s and 1990s, the sonless remain vulnerable. The abandonment of collective agriculture and welfare and the privileging of men in the process of distributing collective goods (such as land, contracts, and equipment) has reinforced the importance of a son for prosperity and security. And as the tight CCP control of the collective era gave way to a new rural world of money, markets, corruption, and clans, the weak became subject to the predations and bullying of the strong. In this climate, having a son was perceived to be one of the most important things a family could do to avoid the miserable fate of being among the weak.

It was in recognition of these rural realities—that income, status, and security flowed from having sons, not daughters—that led the state in 1984 to modify its one-child policy in the countryside. After three difficult years of attempting to enforce a one-child limit and prevent all third or higher-order births, and after an extreme and ill-advised sterilization campaign in 1983, the state decided to "open a small hole" in its policy to allow rural couples who gave birth to a girl to try again for a son (after a four- or five-year waiting period). It took this step in the wake of mounting evidence of female infanticide and growing fears of rural instability. Although justified as a pragmatic and humane concession to rural realities, this concession came at the expense of an ideological education campaign repudiating what authorities called the "feudal" idea that a male (traditionally called a "big happiness") was superior to a female (a "little happiness") and insisting on the equal value of boys and girls. Rather than continue to press forward on this ground, the state effectively conceded the issue by modifying rural policy to allow single-daughter households (*dunü hu*) to try again—for a boy. The state did not condone the cultural preference for males and continued to insist on the equal value of women, but it did concede the economic and social realities that made sons more valuable.

Although the intent of the 1984 policy change was merely to legitimize what was already the de facto rural policy in many areas (namely, a two-child norm in the countryside), its effect was to reinforce gender prejudices.[24] Rural women were thus caught between the pressures family-planning workers placed on them to have only one child and the pressures brought to bear by their families. This push-pull was further complicated by their own internalization of rural norms that linked their worth and value to their ability to produce a son. The state and its family-planning representatives might heap praise on a woman for having a single daughter, but in the real world of the village she could be subject to a lifetime of pity, social ridicule, and blame, much of it heaped upon her by other rural women who had themselves endured such pressures.

After 1979, when the one-child policy began to take effect, some women (or other members of a woman's family) sought to extricate themselves from this dilemma by resorting to female infanticide, often accomplished through drowning. Appalled by the reappearance of a practice associated with the prerevolutionary past, family-planning workers and government officials quickly began a campaign to condemn these acts as immoral and criminal. The revision of state policy to allow *dunü hu* to have a second child was designed to address this problem, but as noted above, it may have done little more than confirm rural prejudices. The number of reported cases did seem to dwindle after the mid-1980s, but the scattered and sporadic nature of the published data on female infanticide prevents an accurate assessment. What is clear, however, is that as the 1980s progressed into the 1990s, many found a more convenient way to assure having a son. They began to turn in ever larger numbers to fetal ultrasound technology, which made it possible for a pregnant woman to discover the sex of the fetus.[25]

When the history of China's twentieth-century demography is written, it may turn out that the introduction and growing utilization of widely accessible ultrasound technology ranks second only to China's strict birth control program in its demographic impact on Chinese society. China produced its first ultrasound B machine in 1979, and by 1982, mass production had begun. Thirteen thousand machines were in

24. Susan Greenhalgh and Jiali Li, "Engendering Reproductive Policy and Practice in Peasant China: For a Feminist Demography of Reproduction," *Signs: Journal of Women in Culture and Society*, no. 20 (Spring 1995), pp. 601–41.

25. This discussion draws on material in my article, "Domination, Resistance, and Accommodation in China's One-Child Campaign," in Elizabeth Perry and Mark Selden, eds., *Societal Resistance in Contemporary China* (London: Routledge, 2000).

use by 1987, or roughly six machines for each county. By the early 1990s, all county hospitals and clinics and most township clinics and family-planning stations had ultrasound equipment capable of fetal sex determination.[26]

Despite attempts by the state to outlaw the use of ultrasound technology to determine the sex of a fetus, easy access to the technology, combined with the lure of lucrative bribes and consultation fees, made ultrasound use vastly popular. This was especially true in rapidly developing county towns and rural townships, where prosperity and proximity made ultrasound diagnosis possible and where modest degrees of upward mobility had done nothing to undermine the cultural prejudice and practical logic that favored male offspring. Young couples raised as peasants in villages but now employed in township factories and living in township seats may have been far more willing than their peers a decade earlier to have only two children. If the first were a girl, however, it remained vital to many that the second be a boy. They may have been modern in their preference for a small family in order to hold onto their newfound prosperity, but when it came to desiring a son, tradition and contemporary social realities conspired. Because township and village cadres tacitly agreed with them, couples could often count on them to look the other way when they made their payoff to the medical technician. The cadres, after all, would much prefer to see couples resort to induced abortion of females to guarantee having a son rather than have a second daughter and be tempted to try again, as many two-daughter households did. If a couple kept trying for a son, the local birth plan was threatened. If a couple used available technology to guarantee the birth of a son, the couple was happy and the cadres' problem was solved.

For several years, state family-planning officials and some Chinese demographers denied any significant problem with the sex ratio at birth, attributing much of the growing statistical distortion to the underreporting of female births as couples sought to evade family-planning controls and local cadres sought to avoid evidence of failing to meet their birth control targets. As the sex ratio at birth began to rise

---

26. Su Ping, "Wo guo chusheng yinger xingbie wenti tanlun" (Investigation into the question of our country's birth and infant sex ratio), *Renkou yanjiu* (Population Research), no. 1 (January 1993); and Mu Guangsong, "Jinnian lai Zhongguo chusheng xingbie bi shanggao pian gao xianxiangde lilun jieshi" (A theoretical explanation of the elevation and deviation in recent years of the sex ratio at birth), *Renkou yu jingji* (Population and Economics), vol. 88, no. 1 (January 25, 1995), pp. 48–51.

steeply in the 1990s, however, there was no avoiding the truth: sex-selective abortion was being utilized on a wide scale to help couples personally engineer the sex of their offspring. And the sex in greatest demand, of course, was male. Some of this increase was evident in first births, but sex ratios in second and higher-order births reflected a very strong male bias. By 1989, for example, the sex ratio for second-order births was 120.9; for third- and fourth-order births, it was 124.6 and 131.7, respectively.[27]

Some of the deficit in females can indeed be accounted for by the underreporting of female births, as Chinese authorities and demographers have long claimed. Underreporting is suggested both by surveys of rural areas that reveal "hidden" births not reported in official statistical reports and by the lessening of the sex ratio imbalance of school-age children compared with that of children aged four and under.

Chinese demographer Zeng Yi, along with several colleagues, argued in the early 1990s that such underreporting accounted for anywhere from 43 to 75 percent of the skew in the sex ratio at birth.[28] However, since incentives and pressures to undercount all unplanned births have been relatively constant over the past decade, underreporting alone cannot explain the steady rise in the sex ratio at birth.[29] By the late 1990s, therefore, more candid assessments focused on the role of sex-selective abortion. Jie Zhenming, writing in one of China's premier demography journals in 1998, concluded that the main reason for skewed sex ratios in some areas of China was sex-selective abortion and that female infanticide by drowning remained "a commonplace action" in more backward areas.[30] Similarly, a 1997 report in the popular news journal *Renmin luntan* (People's Forum) stated flatly that

---

27. These figures are reported in Zeng Yi, Tu Ping, Gu Baochang, Xu Yi, Li Bohua, and Li Yongping, "Causes and Implications of the Recent Increase in the Reported Sex Ratio at Birth in China," *Population and Development Review*, vol. 19, no. 2 (June 1993), pp. 283–302.

28. Ibid.; see also Gao Lin, Liu Xiaolan, and Xia Ping, "Beijing shi renkou chusheng xingbiebi fenxi" (An analysis of the sex ratio at birth in Beijing), *Renkou yanjiu* (Population Research), no. 21 (September 1997), pp. 25–33.

29. One cannot rule out an increase in underreporting, of course, given the difficulties of getting an accurate count of rural births across the countryside. Repeated efforts to outlaw ultrasound screening for sex selection, however, such as the ban instituted by Shandong province in January 1999, suggest a growing conviction within China that the sex ratio imbalance is real and rising. See "Shandong Province Bans Ultrasound Screening," CND-Global, December 30, 1998, at www.cnd.org/CND-Global/.

30. Jie Zhenming, "Why Do People Emphasize Male Children over Female?" *Renkou yu jingji* (Population and Economics), no. 109 (July 25, 1998), pp. 56–61.

sex-selective abortion had become "the number one factor in the strangulation of female fetuses and the creation of the imbalance in the male-female ratio."[31]

Although they acknowledge the prominent role of sex-selective abortion in producing China's skewed sex ratios, these reports nevertheless treat it as a rural phenomenon, avoiding any discussion of the increasingly urban and national character of the problem. Jie Zhenming, for example, draws on conversations with rural women in various regions to illustrate the mentality that leads to sex-selective abortion. The question the author puts to them, "Why must peasants always have sons?" sets the boundaries of the inquiry and prompts the respondents to contrast their situation with that of city folk. One woman prefaces her answer with "We are not the same as in the city," and another with "The country and big cities are not the same."[32] They go on to cite the usual rural concerns of losing daughters to marriage, old-age support, and continuing the family line. In this fashion, gender bias and sex-selective abortion are associated with rural backwardness, and enlightened thinking with urban modernity and its influence on the countryside. Rural women from the prosperous and highly commercialized Sunan region of Jiangsu province, for example, are juxtaposed with those above to illustrate the impact of urbanization and economic development on women's preferences for the sex of their child.

This relentless attempt to associate sex-selective abortion with the "feudal mentality" of the countryside, however, can no longer obscure the reality that those who desire a son sufficiently to take the steps of fetal sex determination and sex-selective abortion are by no means confined to the countryside. The results of a 1995 sample survey revealed how serious the problem had become even in urban areas. Beijing, for example, registered an overall sex ratio at birth of 122.6 and a ratio of 148.8 for second and higher-parity births. This high sex ratio at birth placed Beijing on a par with such provinces as Jiangsu (125.1), Henan (128.0), Guangdong (125.2), and Shaanxi (125.4). Tianjin also came in high, with an overall sex ratio at birth of 110.6 and a ratio of 142.9 for second and higher-parity births.[33] All of these localities, even the major metropolitan areas, include both urban and rural

31. Wang Qiangzhuang, "China's Population: Imbalance of Gender Proportion," *Renmin luntan* (People's Forum), no. 11 (November 8, 1997), pp. 50–51.

32. Jie Zhenming, "Why Do People Emphasize Male Children over Female?"

33. Gao, Liu, and Xia, "An Analysis of the Sex Ratio at Birth in Beijing," p. 27.

regions, of course, and it may well be that people with rural residencies and origins more frequently opt for sex-selective abortion. Nevertheless, the fact that sex ratios in the very cosmopolitan and prosperous regions of Beijing and Guangdong are on a par with those of the very rural and much poorer areas of Henan and Shaanxi suggests that "rural backwardness" explains far less than is usually assumed.

A 1997 study of Beijing's sex ratio statistics confirmed the growing trend toward skewed sex ratios in the nonrural population. The study used data from the national 1-percent sample survey of 1995 to examine in great detail Beijing's sex ratio status. The authors found that high sex ratios occurred at all educational levels and across all occupational categories. For example, among those in the sample with one child, the sex ratio ranged from a high of 134 for those with elementary school education to 119 for those with post-secondary school education, suggesting that gender bias varied incrementally across educational levels but was serious at every level. Similarly, the study's authors found that sex ratios were skewed across nearly all occupational categories but were slightly higher among workers and the unemployed than among those employed in agriculture. And perhaps most important, they found that among those with household registrations in Beijing municipality, sex ratios were seriously skewed for both those holding urban and those with rural registrations. The 1995 sex ratio at birth for rural Beijingers (the population living in the rural areas surrounding the city and within its municipal boundaries) was reported to be 126.1, and the ratio for urban residents was 118.1.[34]

In light of the trends reported elsewhere in East Asia, these figures should come as no surprise. South Korea, Taiwan, and India have all registered increases in the male to female sex ratio as ultrasound technology has become widely available.[35] Outside of China, the problem is most severe in South Korea, where the sex ratio at birth in 1993 was

---

34. Ibid., pp. 29–30. It should be noted that the total number of births in this sample was only 1,950, a relatively small sample size from which to draw broad conclusions about sex ratio trends. Nevertheless, what is striking about Jie's analysis is that there is not one single category in any of his tables in which girls outnumber boys. In a small but balanced sample, one might expect odd fluctuations to occur in both directions, with girls occasionally outnumbering boys.

35. On skewed sex ratios elsewhere in Asia, see Chai Bin Park and Nam-Hoon Cho, "Consequences of Son Preference in a Low-Fertility Society: Imbalance of the Sex Ratio at Birth in Korea," *Population and Development Review*, vol. 21, no. 1 (March 1995), pp. 59–84; also Monica Das Gupta and P.N. Mari Bhat, "Fertility Decline and Increased Manifestation of Sex Bias in India," *Population Studies*, no. 51 (1997), pp. 307–15; and

116. This figure, which is roughly equivalent to the Chinese case, demonstrates clearly that the problem is not limited to China, not merely the result of the one-child policy, and not something that can be explained away (as the CCP has sought to do) as a product of rural backwardness. Rather, it is a cultural and structural problem that is likely to worsen with time. Already, Chinese reports are raising fears of an "army of bachelors," and projections suggest a shortage of roughly ten million women by 2020. As Nicholas Eberstadt has noted, such gender imbalances are traditionally solved by men drawing their wives from a younger age cohort. With fertility low and declining, however, these younger cohorts of potential brides will be smaller than the cohorts that preceded them.[36] As a result, looking to younger women to meet the demand for brides will not solve the bride shortage. Instead, it will produce a ripple effect, forcing the problem farther downstream into younger cohorts of men, who may be even more constrained.

What will be the consequences for young Chinese women? The speculation on this point is just beginning, but opinion will likely be divided. Some adhere to a market theory, believing that a shortage of women will of necessity increase their value and bargaining power relative to men. Others, however, suspect the worst, assuming that the combination of unchanging male appetites and a shortage of women will lead to an increase in crimes against women, particularly the abduction and sale of women as wives or prostitutes. What both perspectives overlook is the poignancy of this type of speculation, and the way in which both perspectives cast women in the passive role of being helped or hurt coincidentally, as a result of the unintended consequences of current policy.

What is certain, however, is that the situation will be complicated by two further trends that principally affect infant girls—abandonment and international adoption. Civil-affairs officials, who have primary responsibility for social welfare, estimate that about 160,000 children were abandoned annually in the early 1990s, the vast majority of whom were girls. As Kay Johnson has argued, however, this figure likely underestimates the size of the problem, since many abandoned girls never enter state institutions such as those managed by the civil-

---

Nicholas Eberstadt, "Asia Tomorrow, Gray and Male," *National Interest*, no. 53 (fall 1998), pp. 56–65.

36. Nicholas Eberstadt, "Mis-Planned Parenthood: The Unintended Consequences of China's One-Child Policy," *AEI Articles* (1999), available on the Web site of the American Enterprise Institute.

affairs bureaucracy.[37] With strict controls on domestic adoption loosened only in 1998, allowing couples over thirty years old with one child to adopt a second child, hundreds of thousands (and perhaps millions) of young girls are still growing up in state orphanages, and a small but rising number of them are being adopted internationally. In the United States, for example, approximately 13,000 children from China (nearly all female) were adopted between 1995 and 1998, up from less than 1,500 between 1990 and 1994 and from only about 100 between 1984 and 1989. Under ordinary demographic circumstances, this out-migration by adoption would be statistically insignificant. If the numbers of adoptions continue to rise, however (and, for the girls' sake, one must hope that they do), this will drain even more young females out of Chinese society over the next twenty-five years, while millions more grow up as wards of the state without benefit of the support and love of a family unit.

What is also certain is that the long-term consequences of current trends, whatever they prove to be, will only reveal themselves with time. They *will* reveal themselves, however, since there is now no way to change the gender mix of this turn-of-the-century generation. The challenge for China will be to prevent its continuation into yet another generation by overcoming the great political inertia the regime has exhibited on this issue. Despite the rhetoric, gender bias seems to be regarded by policymakers as a sort of unfortunate but inevitable problem that they have little power to influence. Yet this is the same regime that has worked so single-handedly and determinedly over the past thirty years to reduce fertility and control population growth. If it can achieve that world-historic feat, surely it has the means, if it has the will, to shrink the market for sex-selective abortion and more effectively address the problem of gender bias.

New Demographic Frontiers in the Twenty-First Century

At the same time that China struggles to cope with the issues of population aging, sex ratio imbalance, and internal migration, it also faces two new and unconventional demographic challenges. The first is the

---

37. Kay Johnson, "The Politics of the Revival of Infant Abandonment in China, with Special Reference to Hunan," *Population and Development Review*, vol. 22, no. 1 (March 1996), pp. 77–98.

AIDS epidemic, which began to ravage Asian societies in the 1990s, forcing Chinese authorities toward a more frank appraisal of the number of HIV/AIDS cases nationwide. Between 1985 and 1997, China officially reported a cumulative total of only 281 AIDS cases to the World Health Organization (WHO), but growing consultation with the WHO led to a shift of public stance by 1998. Chinese officials admitted that the number of HIV/AIDS cases had probably reached 300,000 and was expected to climb rapidly to more than 1 million by 2000, with the vast majority of those infected being males between 20 and 40 years of age.[38]

Predictably, China responded to this public-health threat by drafting a comprehensive twelve-year plan (1998–2010) to control the spread of the disease, including a target of no more than 1.5 million cases by 2010.[39] More important, it took steps to better regulate the blood supply, much of which had not been subject to proper HIV screening. These belated measures, however, may not be sufficient to prevent a much larger epidemic from erupting. Either way—as a result of the campaign to prevent the spread of AIDS, or as a result of the treatment of millions of infected patients—the AIDS epidemic will inevitably drain resources away from competing needs, particularly those of the elderly.

A second wild card for the future is what I call the demographic "sibling gap." As a result of the uneven implementation and enforcement of the one-child policy over the past two decades, China's urban homes, schools, and workplaces are now being filled with a youthful generation that is almost uniformly without siblings. These urban products of the one-child policy, who in their youth were dubbed by Chinese observers "little emperors" (both because of their privileged position as only children and because China's new prosperity was being showered down upon them), are now heading for young adulthood in ever larger numbers. As they do, they are beginning to change the demographic and family landscape. For now, they are unique simply because they so uniformly lack brothers or sisters. Twenty-five years from now, they will be unique for their lack of nieces and

---

38. Yuan He, "China Announces Long-Term Year 2010 AIDS Control Program," Xinhua News Service (Hong Kong), November 30, 1998, in *FBIS-China*, December 8, 1998. For the annual number of officially reported cases, see the World Health Organization, "Epidemiological Fact Sheet on HIV/AIDS and Sexually Transmitted Diseases: China," p. 6.

39. Yuan He, "China Announces Long-Term Year 2010 AIDS Control Program."

nephews, since they have no siblings to produce them. In turn, their children will lack the typical childhood universe of aunts, uncles, and cousins.

China's rural population, in contrast, has produced what we might call a "sibling generation"—that is, a generation coming of age marked by the traditional presence of brothers and sisters. To be sure, this generation has fewer sisters and brothers on average than the one that preceded it, but one-child policy notwithstanding, most teenagers and young adults in rural China still have at least one sibling, and about a third of them have two or more. This rural generation, then, will carry forward for Chinese society as a whole the more traditional, complex set of family bonds and relationships that results from multi-child families.

What this will mean for China in the century ahead is impossible to say, since it is an unprecedented demographic phenomenon. Perhaps it will mean very little. China's one-child policy makes provision for couples who are both only children to have a second child, and Guangdong province recently passed legislation giving this provision legal standing.[40] Whether many in this generation will make use of that provision is unclear, however. It is hard to predict how the one-child policy and the pervasive rhetoric about China's overpopulation will affect childbearing preferences among the young. Historically, fertility that slides to a very low level generally stays at a very low level, and so it is not clear that China's forced march to low fertility can readily be reversed. The sibling gap, then, a product of China's confident demographic engineering of the twentieth century, may prove resistant to retrofitting. The young childbearing-age couples of the early twenty-first century will live with the results of that engineering, and their views about it are likely to be shaped by their own experiences. Urbanites, who tend to blame overpopulation on the peasantry, already resent the "profligacy" of rural families and of the floating migrants they call "guerrilla birth corps" because of their violations of birth limits. Many peasants, by contrast, cling to their traditional childbearing preferences (at least the preferences for a son and for more than one child), yet they aspire to the living standards of

40. Pamela Pun, "Guangdong Legislature Relaxes One-Child Policy," *Hong Kong Standard*, February 22, 1999, p. 6, in *FBIS-China*, February 22, 1999. See also "'Special Dispatch': One-Child Policy Remains Unchanged for the Time Being," *Ming Bao* (Hong Kong), June 22, 1999, p. A19, in *FBIS-China*, June 23, 1999.

prosperous, urban one-child families and resent their own second-class social status.

How will these resentments express themselves in the years ahead? The answer surely depends on the social context in which the question is asked and answered, and that is where the traditional demographic issues discussed above will be significant. Rural-born adults are far more likely to have siblings, nieces, and nephews to help them with their elderly parents and their child-rearing obligations than are urban-born only children, but the urban-born will rely heavily on the tax contributions of the far more numerous rural-born workers to fund social security and health care plans. The rural-born might come to see this as an unfair burden, particularly if the social security system is not extended fully to the rural population. Similarly, rural-born males are far more likely to have sisters, at a time when brides will be in short supply. Although this phenomenon may give some women of rural origin an unprecedented opportunity for upward mobility as they marry into urban households, it may also be a source of tension and resentment between urban and rural males, as rural males lose out not only to other rural males (those who are more prosperous and better educated, perhaps) but also to urban males who are obliged to take the undesirable step of marrying "down" to the countryside rather than "up" the urban social ladder.

Whether or not such tensions erupt in the twenty-first century, the generation coming of age at the turn of the millennium is a generation divided along a new type of urban-rural fault line. Whatever the repercussions of such a divide, let us hope that the state will not be foolish enough to try to solve them by further demographic engineering. That approach, born under Mao, perfected under Deng, and implemented at great human and social cost over the past thirty years, would be best left behind as a relic of the twentieth century.

Promises and Pitfalls of Reform: New Thinking in Post-Deng China

Cheng Li

The late premier Zhou Enlai and a Westerner reportedly had a conversation about European history. When asked what he thought of the French Revolution, Zhou replied, "It is still too early to tell."

The evaluation of historical events always requires great caution, as the above anecdote suggests. The public's initial reaction to a major transformation in a given society can be in sharp contrast to later opinions. This is particularly true for those who study twentieth-century China. Each remarkable event—the 1911 Revolution, the Nationalist reign, the Communist triumph, the Great Leap Forward, and the Cultural Revolution—first aroused great hope and then caused immense despair in millions of people in the country. A crucial question for China now is whether or not the two-decade-long reform (*gaige*) follows the same pattern—moving from promises to pitfalls.

Indeed, nothing seems to be more dramatic and more bewildering than the recent shift in public sentiment and intellectual discourse regarding China's reform. The unequivocal praise of the reform voiced by both government leaders and public intellectuals during the 1980s has been replaced by more critical appraisal on the part of the Chinese intellectual community in the past few years. Three interrelated debates on the economic, political, and social implications of the reform are taking place in China today. They raise three crucial questions: (1) Do China's current economic problems reflect the necessary process of "growing pains" or the symptoms of "deepening pitfalls"? (2) Is the reform leading to a new political regime characterized by a "capitalization of power," which means the convergence of economic

I would like to thank Sally Carman, John Farranto, and Tyrene White for their very helpful comments on an earlier version of this chapter.

wealth and political power" or is it moving China toward a "pluralist system"? and (3) Does the earthshaking socioeconomic transformation mean "moral decay" or the "renaissance of individuality" in Chinese society?

Arguably, controversies have surrounded the reform process since its beginning in 1978, but the current debates were largely triggered by a recently published book entitled *China's Pitfall* (hereafter *Pitfall*). Written in 1998 by He Qinglian, a previously obscure economist in her early forties, this economics book for general readers launched probably the most provocative criticism of the reform to date. The book was a great success, and the author became a celebrity in contemporary Chinese studies overnight, both in China and abroad. Approximately 170,000 legal copies of the book were printed in Beijing and Hong Kong.[1] The total number of copies in circulation, including at least eight pirate editions, could be as high as 3 million.[2] The author was frequently interviewed on national television programs in China, including Chinese Central Television's (CCTV's) prime-time news program, "30-Minute Economic News" (*Jingji banxiaoshi*). Abroad, she appeared on the BBC, CNN, and other international media. A review of her book was published as the lead essay in an issue of the *New York Review of Books*.[3]

He Qinglian is certainly not alone in addressing the pitfalls and problems of the reform. In fact, she represents a new generation of public intellectuals in China. These new thinkers are as fascinating in their collective identities as in the sharp views and ideas that they convey to the public. The new generation of critics is marked by at least four distinctive characteristics. First, a large number of them can be identified as members of the Cultural Revolution generation. They were born in the 1950s, grew up during the Cultural Revolution, received college education in the early years of the reform era, and have now become a formidable political and intellectual force in the

---

1. He Qinglian, *Zhongguo de xianjing* (China's pitfall) (Hong Kong: Mingjing chubanshe, 1998). A slightly different version of the book was published in the People's Republic of China, entitled *Xiandaihua de xianjing: Dangdai Zhongguo de jingji shehui wenti* (Pitfalls of modernization: Economic and social problems of contemporary China) (Beijing: Jinri Zhongguo chubanshe, 1998).

2. Susan V. Lawrence, "Celebrity Critic," *Far Eastern Economic Review*, October 22, 1998, p. 13.

3. Liu Binyan and Perry Link, "A Great Leap Backward?" *New York Review of Books*, vol. 45, no. 15 (October 8, 1998).

country. Since the mid-1990s, many members of this generation have openly debated various important aspects of the reform. Some bold critics of government policies have gone far beyond both those who criticized the Cultural Revolution when Mao died and those who called for democracy in the spring of 1989.

Second, participants in the ongoing intellectual discourse on China's reform come from various professional backgrounds and diverse political spectra. Many teach at universities, and some others work as freelance writers. Market reform has made public intellectuals more independent because they are no longer necessarily employed by the state. They can work in the private sector, be sponsored by non-governmental research foundations, or even be self-employed. Meanwhile, some outspoken critics of reform policies actually work in major think tanks for the Chinese government or for "mouthpieces of the Chinese Communist Party" (CCP), such as the *People's Daily*. These public intellectuals within the establishment seem to have more autonomy now than ever before.

Third, an important contributing factor to the discourse is the rapid development of the Internet during the past few years. As a result, new ideas and arguments often spread very quickly. For example, He Qinglian's thought-provoking views were placed in an electronic magazine even before her book was published.[4] In addition, the Internet has closely connected overseas sinologists, especially those Chinese natives who study or teach abroad, with their counterparts in China.

And finally, although critics differ sharply in their assessments of the current status of the reform, the issue has never been one of pro-reform versus antireform but has rather involved the priorities, purposes, promises, and pitfalls of the reform. In her interview with a correspondent from the *People's Daily*, He Qinglian said that students of China should not use dichotomous adjectives such as "forward" and "backward," "right" and "wrong," or "success" and "failure" to refer to the reform.[5] In He's view, these simplistic terms can only prevent people from understanding the complexity of the reform; moreover, those who participate in the current intellectual discourse cannot be divided

---

4. He Qinglian, "Zhongguo dangdai de ziben yuanshi jilei" (Private capital accumulation in contemporary China), *Zhongguo yu shijie* (China and the world, on-line electronic magazine), December 1997.

5. Li Hui and Ying Hong, *Shiji zhiwen: Laizi zhishijie de shengyin* (The question of the century: Voices from the intellectual community) (Zhengzhou: Daxiang chubanshe, 1999), p. 205.

into two contending ideological camps. Critics are more interested in specific socioeconomic issues than in political ideologies or economic theories.

The above observation challenges a common problem in Western studies of China's reform—the dichotomous and dogmatic way of thinking among some foreign observers. They tend to identify Chinese leaders (as well as public intellectuals) as either reformers or hardliners. Since the Chinese regime is communist, any opposition to that system, such as the 1989 Tiananmen movement, is unquestionably considered democratic. Similarly, China's path to economic development is seen as a choice between socialism and capitalism, between "planning" and "market." Perry Link, the coauthor of the review of *Pitfall* published in the *New York Review of Books*, recently explained his "enlightenment" after reviewing the book. In Link's words, He Qinglian's book made him realize that "dichotomous categorization" (*liangtou moshi*) was inherently wrong in analyzing China's reform.[6] The possible scenarios for China consist not just of two choices—a conservative ideology, an authoritarian political system, and a planned economy on the one hand, and an open civil society with a market economy on the other hand. There is at least a third possibility, one that He Qinglian calls "marketization of power," which would lead to a country run by corrupt bureaucratic capitalists.

To a certain extent, this third possibility has already become a reality in some postcommunist regimes in which economic transition has led not to the expansion of the middle class and prosperity in society but rather to a kind of gangsterism. This phenomenon echoes the description offered by George Soros in his best-selling book, *The Crisis of Global Capitalism*, which was immediately translated into Chinese after it was published in 1998. Having witnessed the Russian economic crisis, Soros came to realize that the "collapse of a closed society does not lead automatically to the establishment of an open society; on the contrary, it may lead to the breakdown of authority and the disintegration of society. A weak state may be as much of a threat to an open society as an authoritarian state."[7]

China's top leaders have clearly been worried about possible loss of control. Probably because of these worries, current technocratic

---

6. *Shijie zhoukan* (World Journal Weekly), March 14, 1999, pp. 31–32.
7. George Soros, *The Crisis of Global Capitalism: Open Society Endangered* (New York: Public Affairs Press, 1998), pp. 69–70.

leaders seem to be more willing to admit problems and mistakes, more enthusiastic about policy advice and suggestions from think tanks, and more tolerant of criticism from public intellectuals in the country than were their predecessors in Mao's and Deng's generations of leaders.

The current intellectual discourse certainly reflects the paradoxical situation that China confronts at present. After two decades of remarkable socioeconomic changes, the reform is at a crossroads. Many solutions to the old problems of socialism have themselves turned into new problems, and the undesirable side effects of the rush to Chinese-style capitalism have become acute. When the reform began in 1978, it clearly had the mandate of the Chinese people. Turning away from the emphasis on revolutionary campaigns against "class enemies" and the ideological indoctrination of the Mao era, Deng Xiaoping and his associates stressed economic development and social stability. The switch from a planned economy to a more market-oriented economy and from autarky to an open door policy brought thrilling economic prosperity. Between 1979 and 1997, the growth rate of China's gross domestic product (GDP) was 9.8 percent annually, about three times greater than the world's average growth rate. During the same period, a total of 170 million people were lifted out of poverty. China's foreign trade increased from $20 billion to $325 billion. Total bank savings of Chinese citizens increased from 21 billion yuan to 4,628 billion yuan, a 220-fold increase.[8] As some China watchers have observed, never before in history had so many people made so much economic progress in a single generation.

This rosy picture of the great success of the reform, although it is not just an illusion, has been increasingly challenged by a gloomy reality—the dark side of the swift socioeconomic transformation. The glaringly lit skyscrapers of Shanghai and Shenzhen mask the barren soil in Guizhou and Gansu. The emergence of the "entrepreneurial class" hides the reality of merciless exploitation in sweatshops throughout the country. The development of township and village enterprises (TVEs) has been achieved at the expense of environmental degradation of China's precious rural land. During the past few years, the growth in China's GDP has slowed. The decline in consumer spending has been even more evident. Some of this decline is due to the Asian financial crisis, but much of it is due to a growing sense of

---

8. The data in this discussion are based on *Renmin ribao*, September 24, 1998, p. 1; and *Financial Times* (London), China Survey supplement, November 16, 1998, p. 6.

insecurity. The absence of a social safety net and the increasing cost of major living expenses such as urban housing, children's education, and medical care for the elderly have made the public very nervous.

If these problems are not serious enough, the high unemployment rate and rampant official corruption have surely put those who uncritically sing the praises of the reform to the test. A leading think tank for the Chinese government recently reported that unemployment has risen to its highest level since the founding of the People's Republic of China (PRC) in 1949.[9] Official corruption is much worse today than during the 1989 Tiananmen crisis, when ethical government was one of the main demands of students and the general public. Corruption has become such a serious problem that China's top leaders have depicted corruption as a "cancer within" and a "life and death" issue for the CCP and the state. The Chinese regime seems to sit atop a volcano of mass social disturbance, much as its Nationalist and imperial predecessors did earlier in the century.

Of course, it would be premature for anyone to announce the failure of China's reform. Reform, by definition, is a movement that attempts to institute improved socioeconomic and political conditions through peaceful means. It takes time, and its results cannot be measured by a single anniversary date, such as those for the 1911 and the 1949 revolutions. Even its most vocal critics thus acknowledge the necessity of the reform process and the important role it must play in China's long-term quest for development.

What makes this moment in the reform process truly extraordinary, and this emerging generation of public intellectuals particularly remarkable, is the fact that problems and pitfalls are so frequently and fervently debated in today's China. This fact alone may be one of the most promising aspects of the reform. The debate itself and the nature of the participants thus deserve further scrutiny, for the course of the reform and China's fate in the twenty-first century will be closely linked to this dynamic new thinking in post-Deng China.

New Critics and New Thinking

Most public intellectuals who are currently active in the discourse about the reform did not emerge until the mid-1990s. This is under-

---

9. Hu Angang, *Zhongguo fazhan qianjing* (Prospects of China's development) (Hangzhou: Zhejiang renmin chubanshe, 1999), pp. 35–36.

standable for a number of reasons. First, the crackdown on the 1989 Tiananmen movement led to years of severe control over intellectual and political debate in Chinese society. Second, although intellectuals were politically rehabilitated at the beginning of the reform, and some even moved to the center of politics prior to the Tiananmen crackdown, in the early 1990s they found themselves marginalized by rapid socioeconomic changes. Their status was "threatened once again, this time by the development of commercial culture."[10] Many of them were distracted by both the need to survive and the opportunity to profit in this commercial culture. Some were engaged in various kinds of business (*xiahai*). Third, the reform accelerated in 1992 after Deng's famous journey to the south. Not until the mid-1990s did the problems associated with this acceleration become increasingly acute.

To a certain extent, these new critics differ profoundly from one another in terms of professional and personal backgrounds, political associations, policy recommendations, and ideological outlooks. Some important characteristics, however, distinguish this new group of public intellectuals from their predecessors. A large number of them belong to the so-called Cultural Revolution generation, since they grew up or had their formative years during the Cultural Revolution. Many work in governmental or nongovernmental think tanks. They often express their views and arguments through new telecommunication channels, especially electronic magazines on the Internet. This not only helps spread their opinions very quickly but also extricates them from geographical barriers, closely linking the scholarly community in China to overseas Chinese students. A few new critics actually belong to the post–Cultural Revolution generation. Many of them are trained in the West and are very active in "online debates" about the reform. In addition, some new critics who are activists in certain social movements are more issue-oriented than ideology-driven.

Two clarifications should be made before further discussion. First, the above general observations do not describe subgroups of the new critics but rather are distinctive characteristics that the critics may or may not fully share. These characteristics are not mutually exclusive; for example, a Cultural Revolution generation critic may work for a

10. *China News Analysis*, no. 1556, March 15, 1996, p. 1.

think tank, express views online frequently, and participate in a social movement. Second, the term "critics" refers to all those who participate in the debate, whether or not they are critical of the reform per se. A large number of participants in the debate, however, are critical of certain aspects of the reform, since no one can deny its troubling side effects. Meanwhile, many Chinese public intellectuals, like their counterparts in the study of civil society in the West and elsewhere, tend to believe that government, or the state, may not necessarily be the "enemy of society" but may instead be a potential ally. Partly for this reason, most critics of the reform refuse to be identified as political dissidents or opponents of the Chinese government. This is probably best illustrated by a recent incident in which Zhang Yimou, the best-known Chinese movie director, withdrew two of his latest movies from the Cannes Film Festival because, as Zhang explained, "the West has for a long time politicized Chinese films. If they are not anti-government, they are considered just pro-government propaganda."[11]

Cultural Revolution Generation Critics

Many leading public intellectuals can be identified as members of the Cultural Revolution generation. They were in school (including elementary school, high school, and college) at the beginning of the Cultural Revolution in 1966. Many became idealistic and fanatic Red Guards who were enthusiastic about making earthshaking changes and pursuing social engineering. A majority of them were sent to the countryside and therefore experienced much hardship, both physically and mentally. They later realized the tragic nature of their generation's experience and became more or less disillusioned about Maoism and communism. After the Cultural Revolution, they managed to claw their way into colleges as Deng and reform leaders resumed the national examination for college admission in 1977. They have gotten their careers back on track during the 1980s. As a Western journalist described them, this new breed of public intellectuals "learned hard lessons about their society and its political system."[12]

Dizzying new phenomena and the once again earthshaking changes during the reform era have also made this generation of pub-

11. Maggie Farley, " 'One Less' Movie at Cannes," *Los Angeles Times*, May 7, 1999, p. F1.

12. Steven Mufson, "The Next Generation," *Washington Post*, June 14, 1998, p. A1.

lic intellectuals suspicious about the real achievements of the reform. Two of the best-known Cultural Revolution generation critics, Yang Fan and He Qinglian, were sharply critical of the pitfalls of the reform during the mid-1990s, especially regarding the rampancy of official corruption. Yang Fan lives in Beijing, where he is a senior research fellow of the Economic Institute of the Chinese Academy of Social Sciences. He Qinglian lives in Shenzhen, the frontier of capitalist development in southern China, where she is a senior correspondent of a newspaper called the *Shenzhen Legal News*. Because of their similar outrage about current sociopolitical problems and also because of their numerous writings (both academic and nonacademic), the two are often called "*bei Yang nan He*" (Yang in the North and He in the South).

Both Yang and He attended college after the Cultural Revolution. Yang went to Jilin University in 1977 and became a member of the first class of students to attend college after the reestablishment of the college entrance examination. He Qinglian was born in 1956 in Shaoyang, Hunan province, and was sent to the western part of the province to do manual labor in railway construction after middle school. She graduated from Hunan Normal University in 1985 with a degree in history and pursued graduate work in economics at Fudan University in Shanghai. Both He and Yang are very much aware of their Cultural Revolution identities. In the afterword to her book *Pitfall*, He Qinglian writes that she formed her "basic outlook on life and society" during those disturbing years. She claims that her generation of public intellectuals is a generation that is "unprecedented and unrepeatable" (*kongjian juehou*). It is "unprecedented" because the dramatic change in their lives, especially the sense of social responsibility and humanitarianism in the wake of the decade-long national madness and fanatic violence, makes this generation unique. It is "unrepeatable," she argues, because the "hardship environment that fostered her generation will never occur again in China." The majority of her peers who grew up during the Cultural Revolution lost the opportunity for a college education and a professional career, and some even lost their lives. As a lucky survivor of the Cultural Revolution, she believes that she has a "moral responsibility to pursue social justice."

In his article "Justice for the 'Third Generation,'" Yang Fan argues that the Cultural Revolution generation is the most unfortunate generation in contemporary China. He writes:

This generation not only bore the burden of the cost of the Cultural Revolution, but also has to bear the cost of the reform. They lost much during the Cultural Revolution, but did not receive any compensation during the reform era. . . . This generation has been extremely unlucky: during their childhood, they experienced "three bad years"; during the normal years of schooling, they were sent to the countryside to do manual labor; when they became adults, they lived in a time of sexual restraint; when they wanted to have children, they could have only one child. When they became experienced workers, they were unemployed, they needed to care for their elderly and paid a great deal for their children's education.[13]

Yang also rejects the argument made by some Chinese policymakers and economists that the difficulties that this generation experienced were the necessary costs of the structural transition of the country. Yang believes that the increasing "generational disparity" should be considered the fifth way in which the country is unevenly divided. The other four dichotomies include occupational differences, the east-west division, urban-rural distinctions, and the disparity between rich and poor. Tensions between these divisions challenge the positive responses to the reform. Yang argues that "the reform should not neglect one generation, and spoil another."[14]

In addition to economists such as He Qinglian and Yang Fan, the Cultural Revolution generation critics consist of many recently emerging leaders in other disciplinary studies. They include, for example, Zhu Xueqin (a professor of history at Shanghai University who teaches comparative studies of twentieth-century China and the French Revolution), Qin Hui (a professor of history at Qinghua University who specializes in peasantry and peasant movements), Li Yinhe (a sociologist and senior fellow at the Chinese Academy of Social Sciences who has written a number of pioneering works on the Chinese feminist movement, urban gay communities, and the reform's impact on family and marriage), Liang Xiaosheng (a well-known novelist who has also earned a reputation for his studies of social stratification in reform China), Xiao Gongqin (a professor of political science and history at Shanghai Normal University who has long criticized the "blind adoption of Western models to China's modernization"), and

---

13. Yang Fan, "Wei 'disandai ren' zheng gongdao" (Justice for the "third generation"), *Zhongguo yu shijie*, December 1997.

14. The "spoiled generation" refers to the one following the Cultural Revolution generation; it is largely the "one-child-per-family generation" that grew up after the Cultural Revolution. Yang Fan, "Wei 'disandai ren' zheng gongdao."

Liu Defu (who holds a doctoral degree in law and works in the General Office of the Central Committee of the CCP; he has drafted important government documents and published widely on China's political reform).

The Cultural Revolution generation critics are a diverse lot, coming from various professional backgrounds and different political spectra. But they also share several important characteristics: all of the people mentioned above were sent to the countryside during the Cultural Revolution, where they worked as farmers for about a decade. In addition to having firsthand experience of the hardship that their generation went through, they have a better understanding of the "real China." Qin Hui, for example, has devoted his professional career to studying Chinese peasantry as a result of his nine-year-long work in a poor village of Guangxi. Fan Gang and Hu Angang, two other leading economists who are actively engaged in the current intellectual discourse, also spent many years in rural China. Fan worked as a farmer, first in Heilongjiang and then in Hebei, before enrolling in Hebei University in 1977. Similarly, Hu Angang spent seven years at a collective farm in Heilongjiang. He claims that "one who has no knowledge of rural China does not know about China; one who does not understand China's poverty-stricken regions does not have a real understanding of China."[15] After becoming a well-known economist in China's capital, Hu has continued to visit frequently the rural areas in poor and remote provinces, such as Guizhou.

Most of the public intellectuals listed above received higher education after the Cultural Revolution. They were the beneficiaries of the reestablishment of the national examination for college admission initiated by Deng and reform leaders in 1977. Probably because of this factor and because of their life experience during the Mao era, the Cultural Revolution generation critics do not completely deny the benefits of the reform. Yet, their intimate knowledge of the real China makes their criticism of current problems sophisticated and objective. All these factors have echoed what He Qinglian calls the "uniqueness of the Cultural Revolution generation of scholars," making the current debate on the reform particularly lively.

---

15. Hu Angang, *Zhongguo fazhan qianjing*, p. 6.

Think-Tank Critics

Some outspoken critics are from the political and academic establishment, especially think tanks for top leaders, a trend that is not entirely new. Earlier intellectual discourse, such as that of the 1987 liberal movement and that of the 1989 Tiananmen rally prior to the crackdown, also included members of the political establishment and advisors to top leaders. For example, Fang Lizhi, Wen Yuankai, Yan Jiaqi, Su Shaozhi, Chen Yizhi, and Wang Ruoshui all had their "patrons" within the top leadership. What distinguishes the present group of critics from their predecessors is that now far more "advisors" join the debates and that many of these advisors and members of party "mouthpieces" seem to have a more independent voice. This phenomenon suggests two important trends. First, Jiang Zemin and his generation of technocratic leaders pay more attention to the role of think tanks than did their predecessors. Second, criticism from the establishment shows that there are now more people who are "at once within the system and at odds with it," as a *Washington Post* correspondent in Beijing has observed.[16]

Liu Ji, a longtime confidant of Jiang Zemin, for example, is also the "chief advisor" to China Today Press, which recently published an influential book series entitled *China's Problems* (also, *Contemporary China's Problems*). The themes included in this series are politically sensitive issues such as unemployment, crime, population pressures, rural-urban migration, and income disparity. It was Liu Ji who endorsed the publication of He Qinglian's book *Pitfall*. Another advisor to President Jiang, Wang Huning, a former professor of political science and dean of the law school at Fudan University and now a ministerial-level official, contributed to the most controversial volume in the series, *Political China: Facing the Era of Choosing a New Structure*. This volume, which discusses China's stalled political reform, contains thirty-nine recently published essays by thirty-two scholars, journalists, and government officials, including former officials who were dismissed for their democratic sympathies. In his essay, Wang suggests some specific measures for consolidating China's legal system to deal with corruption and other power abuses. He also calls for greater separation of government and industry. The editors of the series are Dong Yuyu, a senior editor of the *Guangming Daily*, and Shi Binghai, a senior editor of the *China Economic Times*.

---

16. Steven Mufson, "The Next Generation," *Washington Post*, June 18, 1998, p. A1.

That the editors of these official CCP papers would now start to sing some "unpleasant songs" is testimony to the changing contours of the debate and to the changing rules of engagement in it. At the end of 1998, for example, two senior reporters from the *People's Daily*, Ling Zhijun and Ma Licheng, wrote a book entitled *Voices (Huhan)*.[17] On the cover of the book, the authors claim that the book "combines both praises and criticisms of the reform." The authors observe that five voices coexist in post-Deng China: (1) the voice of the mainstream that follows Deng's reform policies; (2) the voice of dogmatism that advocates a return to a socialist planned economy; (3) the voice of nationalism; (4) the voice of feudalism influenced by neo-Confucianism and Asian values; and (5) the voice of democracy. The authors argue unambiguously that pluralist outlooks should be greatly appreciated, and they present the voice of democracy in a remarkably positive tone. Both of these messages would have been considered taboo during the Deng era, but interestingly, this book has been endorsed by the Chinese authorities, especially by Jiang Zemin.[18]

Some think-tank members make bold and specific suggestions. For example, Hu Angang, an economist at the Chinese Academy of Social Sciences and a consultant to Zhu Rongji at the time, proposed a "one province, one vote" system for the membership of the Politburo. In his view, this would not only give every province a voice in party policy but would also lead to a more genuine effort to ease local dissatisfaction with the central government and the increasing disparity between coastal and inland provinces.[19] He calls for political reform in China, but he believes that the priority of political reform should be technocratic decision-making in social-welfare policy, which involves more open discussion and consultation among independent think tanks, instead of adoption of the Western multiparty system. As a prominent young economist who has often been consulted by government leaders, Hu has always identified himself as an independent scholar rather than as an aide to a top leader. He has said that his role model is Paul

---

17. Ling Zhijun and Ma Licheng, *Huhan: Dangjin Zhongguo de wuzhong shengyin* (Voices: Five voices in present China) (Guangzhou: Guangzhou chubanshe, 1999).

18. *Shijie ribao* (World journal), January 16, 1999, p. A2.

19. Quoted from Wu An-chia, "Leadership Changes at the Fourth Plenum," *Issues and Studies*, vol. 30, no. 10 (October 1994), p. 134. Hu Angang also argues that the Financial Committee of the National People's Congress should consist of thirty members (each province has one representative in the committee). Hu Angang, *Zhongguo fazhan qianjing*, p. 312.

Samuelson, a U.S. economist and a Nobel laureate, who refused to serve as an advisor at the White House. During the past few years, many distinguished economists such as Hu Angang have begun working for nongovernmental research institutes, which are sponsored by the private sector in China or by foreign charitable foundations.

Public intellectuals in the establishment, of course, differ from one another in terms of their emphasis on China's problems, but they all share the conviction that the system must change in a fundamental way. Even He Xin, a longtime advisor to "conservative" leaders such as Li Peng, believes that structural economic change in China will be essential as China moves into the next century.[20]

Critics "On-Line"

An important factor distinguishing the Chinese intellectual discourse of the 1990s from previous debates is that a large number of Chinese scholars and students who work and study abroad, especially in the United States, are actively engaged in this discourse through modern telecommunications such as the Internet. Overseas Chinese magazines, including those published in Hong Kong and Taiwan, are now often on-line. For example, *Ershiyi shiji* (Twenty-first century), a scholarly journal published by the Institute of Chinese Studies at the Chinese University of Hong Kong available both in print and on-line, often contains many essays on China's reform. Some overseas dissident magazines, such as *Zhongguo zhichun* (China spring) and *Beijing zhichun* (Beijing spring), are available on-line to readers in mainland China.

Probably the leading journal attempting to analyze the pitfalls of the reform is the electronic magazine *Zhongguo yu shijie* (China and the world). This journal, which was established in 1996 by a group of Chinese students and scholars studying in the United States, focuses on social and political issues in contemporary China as well as issues of global significance. In the first issue of the journal, the editors claimed that what distinguishes this journal from dozens of other Chinese electronic journals already on the Internet is that *Zhongguo yu shijie* does not embrace mainstream ideologies when discussing social, political, and theoretical issues. As explained by the editors, this means that the journal examines the Western capitalist system with a critical eye and

---

20. Tang Dianwei, "Duoqian dongwu He Xin" (He Xin: An all-rounder), *Shijie zhoukan*, no. 792 (May 23–29, 1999), p. 26.

reviews China's experience with socialism by taking a holistic view and a historical perspective. Contributors to the journal are truly diversified in their backgrounds, including "nonmainstream" Western scholars, Chinese scholars in the United States, Chinese think-tank scholars in China, and Taiwanese left-wing intellectuals.

Zhongguo yu shijie is, of course, not ideologically neutral. A group of Chinese neo-Marxist scholars seems to dominate the journal. Cui Zhiyuan, a University of Chicago–trained political scientist who teaches at the Massachusetts Institute of Technology, is a spokesman for the Chinese "neo-left" intellectuals. Cui is a frequent contributor to the journal. Some of his articles criticize the "myth of the invisible hand" and express reservations about economic globalization and Western cultural imperialism. In an article written jointly with Robert Unger, he observed that in the West, people have the illusion or misperception that developing countries and postcommunist societies have a clear direction. The main questions are, How long will change take? and Will it involve "shock therapy" or "gradualism"? According to Cui and Unger, this view has a fatal error. It underestimates the most important consideration in forecasting the political life of states—the future of a given country can have multiple possibilities.[21]

The views presented by the Chinese scholars who live outside the PRC enliven the debate about the reform within China. In the wake of the failure of "shock therapy" (total privatization) in Russia, some Chinese public intellectuals have become increasingly suspicious about advice offered to postcommunist countries by "Harvard economic geniuses" such as Jeffrey Sachs. Cui Zhiyuan and other "neo-left" intellectuals have certainly stimulated the new thinking of public intellectuals within China. Some have wondered if Adam Smith might be as wrong as Karl Marx, although the results of their errors in philosophy have been profoundly different. For these critics, both "capitalist market economy" and "socialist public ownership" are myths. A pure form of either does not exist. A favorable view of the United States, especially of its economic and political system, was prevalent among Chinese intellectuals in the early years of the reform, but it shattered during the mid-1990s. Today, a majority of Chinese public intellectuals have "dual attitudes" toward Western ideas, as described by Xu Jilin, a seasoned Chinese scholar. While they continue to be

---

21. Robert Unger and Cui Zhiyuan, "Yi e weijian kan Zhongguo" (China in Russia's mirror), *Zhongguo yu shijie*, no. 11 (1997).

influenced and inspired by some Western values and ideas, these critics have become cynical about the moral superiority of the West and resentful of Western arrogance. Chinese public intellectuals are no longer passive recipients of Western ideologies, but have become "independent thinkers." [22]

Activists and Issue-Oriented Critics

In contrast to public intellectuals in the 1980s, new critics of the reform in the 1990s are far more interested in specific issues than in major ideological debates. Qin Hui divides intellectual discourse during the reform into two periods: during the 1980s, public intellectuals debated "isms," and during the 1990s, they have debated "issues."[23] This is largely a legacy of the 1989 Tiananmen tragedy. According to some Chinese intellectuals, the mass movement calling for democracy in the abstract was doomed to failure. Fundamental changes in both political institutions and cultural values were required. Without these changes, the subsequent crackdown on this uprising was inevitable.

Dai Qing, a well-known participant in the 1989 Tiananmen rally, believes that Chinese public intellectuals should learn a "lesson" from the tragedy. In her view, public intellectuals should be more down-to-earth. She states:

> Individually, each intellectual should first fulfill his or her professional role in society. If you are a journalist, you should seek truth; if you are a lawyer, you should fight for justice; if you are a scientist, you should oppose environmentally catastrophic projects such as the construction of the Three Gorges Dam; if you are a teacher, you should advocate freedom and democratic values to your students. As a social group, intellectuals should make efforts to study democratic procedures and structural measures, . . . and most importantly, to make progress in some specific areas.[24]

During the past decade, some public intellectuals have also played the roles of activists for various social movements. Some have super-

---

22. Xu Jilin, "Qimeng de mingyun: Ershinian lai de Zhongguo sixiang jie" (The fate of enlightenment: The Chinese intelligentsia during the past two decades), *Ershiyi shiji* (Twenty-first century), no. 50 (December 12, 1998), pp. 4–13.

23. Qin Hui, "Sishi erhuozhe zishu" (An autobiography of a forty year old), in *Zhongguo xinyidai sixiangjia zibai*, (Recollections of China's new generation of thinkers), ed. Wen Lin and Hai Tao, (Beijing: Jiuzhou tushu chubanshe, 1998) p. 494.

24. Cheng Li, *Rediscovering China: Dynamics and Dilemmas of Reform* (Lanham, MD: Rowman and Littlefield, 1997), pp. 292–93.

vised village elections; some have helped promote women's rights and have spoken out against domestic violence; some have advocated tolerance for different lifestyles and have fought for gay and lesbian rights; some have worked for the protection of migrant workers' rights; and some have been interested in academic research. Li Yinhe's published works on the Chinese feminist movement, gay communities, and changing family structure are good examples.

In a recently published book on the new generation of scholars, Yang Dongping, a senior fellow in the study of higher education at the Beijing Institute of Science and Technology, used the title "From Red to Green" for the chapter that highlights the dramatic change in political values and behavior of the Cultural Revolution generation.[25] Members of this generation were fanatic Red Guards during the Cultural Revolution. In the 1990s, some of them, including Yang Dongping, became advocates for the "green movement" of environmental protection. In the early 1990s, they established a Chinese nongovernmental organization called the "Friends of Nature," which advocates environmental protection. Yang argues that China must learn lessons both from the tragedies in PRC history and from the mistakes made by other industrialized nations. In Yang's words, China's current leadership should work to ensure that today's progress does not come at tomorrow's expense.

In addition to participating in the "green movement," Yang has also worked as a chief producer for China's first talk show, called *Shihua shishuo* (To speak honestly). More than three hundred hours have aired since the program started in April 1996. It has become one of the most popular CCTV programs in the country, similar to the feature news program *Jiaodian fantan* (Focus), which has approximately three hundred million daily viewers.[26] The talk show provides an entirely new forum for the Chinese people to learn, in Yang's words, "how to express your feelings honestly, how to be a good listener, how to care about others, and how to exchange ideas and values." The emergence of this new forum for dialogue, as Yang implies, may have profound implications for sociopolitical developments in the country.

These examples show the great dynamism and diversity of China's

25. Yang Dongping, "Conghong daolü" (From red to green), in *Zhongguo xinyidai sixiangjia zibai*, pp. 269–306.
26. Yuan Zhengming and Liang Jianzeng, *Jiaodian fangtan* (Focus) (Hebei: Zhongguo dabaike quanshu chubanshe, 1999), p. 5.

public intellectuals. A new generation of critics, thinkers, and activists with new ideas and new values has come to the fore in the late 1990s. In general, they seem to be less dogmatic and more open-minded. Yet, they differ greatly from one another in their backgrounds, interests, and outlooks. Their sharply contrasting evaluations of the reform further reflect their diversity and the lack of a fundamental consensus about the future direction for China.

Debates about the Reform: Economy, Politics, and Society

Three different but integrated debates on the economic, political, and social implications of the reform have occurred during the past few years. Before exploring each of them, two things should be kept in mind. First, these three debates certainly do not cover the full range of issues raised about the meaning and implications of the reform. Second, to explore these debates here, each of the following three sections is headed with an either/or question. This dichotomous presentation highlights the two main sides of the debate, but it should not be read to mean that there are only two views on a specific debate. Other views and more complex variations also exist, defying any attempt to organize the debates into two opposing camps.[27]

"Growing Pains" or "Deepening Pitfalls"?

When the reform started in 1978, it had a catchphrase: "Getting rich is a glorious thing." Deng Xiaoping, the architect of the reform, also offered a promise: "Let a small number of people get rich first." This implied that although wealth might first be distributed to only a small portion of the population in the early stages of the reform, sooner or later the standard of living of the entire population would be significantly improved. By the end of the twentieth century, all the people

---

27. For example, Yang Fan is very critical about policy mistakes of the Chinese government, especially the way that the government deals with economic disparity and official corruption. But he rejects the view that the reform has led to the "moral decay" in Chinese society. Yang argues that there was no morality during the Mao era. People should not be nostalgic about the "good old days" under Mao. The Mao era, especially the Cultural Revolution, was the darkest period in contemporary Chinese history, as family members, friends, and schoolmates betrayed one another and the Maoists tortured "class enemies." See Zhong Yan, *Zhongguo xinsanji xueren* (China's new scholars) (Hangzhou: Zhejiang renmin chubanshe, 1996), pp. 161–62.

in China would reach at least the level of *"xiaokang"* (a comfortable living).

This tolerance of inequality in the early stages of reform was logical, however. No one could expect over a billion people to become rich at the same time in an increasingly market-based economy. Indeed, the rural reform, especially the adoption of the household contract responsibility system and the rapid development of TVEs in the late 1970s and early 1980s, greatly improved the standard of living of millions of Chinese farmers. Some farmers were richer than others, but the income gap was not great enough to really frustrate the poor. In fact, the huge gap between rural and urban areas that had been institutionalized during the Mao era was significantly reduced during the early years of the reform.

But as the reform moved from rural to urban areas, income gaps widened enormously. This was the result of rapid changes in the price structure, the transformation of state-owned enterprises (SOEs), the establishment of stock markets, and property development (especially opening to foreign investors). The disparities take various forms— between the coast and inland, between the industrial and the agricultural sectors, between private firms and SOEs, and between managers and workers, among others. Qiao Jian, a critic of labor issues in reform China, has observed that in 1997 the average salary in Shanghai was 5,287 yuan, while in Heilongjiang it was 2,140 yuan.[28] In her recent article, He Qinglian finds that the average salary of SOE employees increased from 2,633 yuan in 1986 to 3,594 yuan in 1992 (a growth of 36.5 percent), while the average salary of workers in collective firms increased from 2,484 yuan to 5,915 yuan (a growth of 138 percent).[29] According to He Qinglian, about one hundred million retired workers receive no pension or only a partial pension. Basing their conclusions on some rough calculations, critics believe that 0.1 percent of China's population now owns one-third of the private savings in the country.

Defenders of the reform, especially those in the government, argue that income disparity is inevitable as China transforms into a market economy. The problems caused by transition should be seen as "grow-

28. Qiao Jian, "1997–1998 nian Zhongguo zhigong zhuangkuang baogao" (1997–1998 report on the condition of China's workers), *Zhongguo yu shijie*, no. 19 (May 1998).

29. He Qinglian, "Caifu yu pinkun—xian jieduan pinfu fenceng pingxi" (Wealth and poverty: An analysis of China's current polarization), *Zhongguo yu shijie*, no. 22 (August 1998).

ing pains" necessary to the process. Zhu Guanglei, the chief investigator of a recent comprehensive study of social stratification in reform China, states it succinctly: "no class differentiation, no social progress."[30] According to Zhu, the fear of polarization during the Mao era prevented the country from making any economic progress. In Zhu's view, this should provide a historical lesson for critics of the reform. But critics believe that China is now experiencing what Western economists call the "tunnel effect": two long parallel queues of cars wait to pass through a tunnel. Then the cars in one of the two lanes start to move on. The drivers of the cars in the other lane, though not entirely happy, feel hopeful because they think their lane will soon start moving as well. However, if that does not happen and they wait for a long time, they become really frustrated and angry.

The critics observe that the rural-urban income disparity grew from 1:1.71 in 1984 to 1:2.55 in 1994. In 1993 the income of urban residents was 12 percent greater than in 1992, but the income of peasants had increased only 2 percent.[31] One of the reasons for the disparity is that the government has failed to raise the prices of farm products to keep up with those of manufactured goods. In 1993, for example, the prices of fertilizer, fuel, and other farming necessities rose nearly twice as fast as those of farm commodities. As for the regional disparity, Hu Angang argues that the central government should better allocate resources to help poor regions, especially in human capital and infrastructure development. Hu proposes that the central government's favorable policies for the special economic zones be abolished.[32] Defenders, however, argue that as long as the economy continues to have an annual 10 percent growth rate, the country can absorb the shock of the reform. Distribution problems that cause the rural-urban income disparity and regional differentiation will eventually take care of themselves, as a market economy sooner or later will even out the price variations and other differences. But the Chinese economy, after over a decade of double-digit growth, has slowed during the past three years. The growth rate was 7.8 percent in 1998, and government officials hope to achieve a minimum of 7 percent growth in 1999. This growth rate may not be seen as low in many other parts of the world,

30. Zhu Guanglei et al., *Dangdai Zhongguo shehui gejieceng fenxi* (Analysis of social strata in China) (Tianjin: Renmin chubanshe, 1998), p. 41.

31. *Jiefang ribao* (Liberation Daily), November 23, 1993, p. 5.

32. Hu Angang, *Zhongguo fazhan qianjing*, pp. 334–41.

but with the workforce expanding by about eight million people each year, the Chinese government has often regarded 8 percent as the minimum growth rate needed to create enough new jobs.

The slow growth is related partly to the Asian financial crisis and partly to the decline in domestic consumer spending. Critics observe that the Chinese people are not willing to spend money because they feel insecure and uncertain about the future. One sign of this trend is that privatization of urban housing has stalled. For example, over a hundred thousand people attended a real estate sale fair in Shanghai in the summer of 1999, but only sixty housing units were sold.[33] In addition, retail sales of consumer products grew 7 percent in 1998, much lower than the 11 percent growth in 1997. Meanwhile, both state-run and privately owned factories and stores still churn out billions of dollars' worth of unwanted goods. Over two-thirds of six hundred manufactured goods are in oversupply. The government uses various methods to stimulate consumer spending; however, even though the annual bank interest rate is now about 2.5 percent, the lowest in twenty years, people still want to save for future expenses such as their children's education, their elders' medical care, the purchase of an apartment, or possible unemployment.

Meanwhile, unemployment has undoubtedly become one of the pitfalls of the reform, "a time bomb for China," as critics have described it. Based on official data from China's Statistics Bureau, the country's urban unemployment rate in 1997 was 3.1 percent; however, this number would be 7 percent if it included the 15 million "off-post" workers of SOEs. By the end of 1998, more than 17 million workers in SOEs were laid off, or more than one in five.[34] Cutting the labor force in the SOEs was a decision born of necessity. As some sinologists observe, nearly two-thirds of the 118,000 SOEs operated in the red in 1996, losing an estimated $5.4 billion in revenue and costing nearly $4.2 billion in government subsidies.[35] The unemployment pressure does not come only from SOEs. According to Lin Yongshan, vice minister of labor, China has four sources of surplus laborers: (1) 130 million surplus rural laborers, (2) about 7 to 8 million young people who join the labor force each year, (3) 5.7 million

---

33. *Xinmin wanbao* (Xinmin Evening News), June 9, 1999, p. 1.

34. *Far Eastern Economic Review*, February 18, 1999, p. 12.

35. David Shambaugh, "The CCP's Fifteenth Congress: Technocrats in Command," *Issues and Studies*, vol. 34, no. 1 (January 1998), p. 17.

unemployed people, and (4) over 20 million surplus workers in the SOEs. Altogether this is about 170 million people, which means that the real unemployment rate in the entire country may be more than 25 percent.[36]

The critics believe that the number will continue to grow because today the urban unemployed workforce not only consists of former employees of SOEs and migrant workers from rural areas but also includes three other groups: (1) about one million government officials and staff who were laid off as a result of Zhu Rongji's recent decision to downsize bureaucracy, (2) about 500,000 soldiers who will soon be demobilized as part of Jiang Zemin's plan to create a more professional defense system, and (3) over ten million former employees of TVEs who have been displaced by technology and capital-intensive development. In addition, a large number of recent college graduates cannot find jobs.

To make the situation even worse, China's high unemployment occurs at a time when the state has been withdrawing from its role in social welfare and a new unemployment-insurance or pension system is yet to be established. Based on He Qinglian's study, only 34 percent of the Chinese population is covered by any sort of social safety net.[37] Understandably, street protests and labor unrest are on the rise. According to official data, in the first three months of 1998, for example, there were 934 strikes and group petitions in the capitals of China's twenty-eight provinces.[38] The threat of unemployment will likely remain in China for the foreseeable future. Yukon Huang, director of the World Bank in Beijing, told the *Financial Times* that these days a 10 percent increase in GDP probably generates a 1 to 1.5 percent rise in jobs, down considerably from previous phases in China's development.[39] The lack of an effective social-welfare network certainly increases the chance for social unrest.

Critics see the growing inequality in Chinese society and the high unemployment as pitfalls or even the eventual doom of the reform. As He Qinglian argues, shared poverty has disappeared after two decades of the reform, but shared prosperity (*gongtong fuyu*)—the promise that

---

36. *Mingbao*, March 8, 1998; and *Nanfang zhoumo* (Southern Weekend), March 13, 1998.

37. He Qinglian, "Caifu yu pinkun."

38. Qiao Jian, "*1997–1998 nian Zhongguo zhigong zhuangkuang baogao.*"

39. James Kynge and James Harding, "Solving the Queue Problem," *Financial Times*, China Survey supplement, November 16, 1998, p. 8.

Deng Xiaoping offered at the beginning of the reform—has by no means been delivered. Instead, the economic and social consequences of the reform are devastating for the majority of people because the rich are getting richer through corruption. How can one tell an unemployed worker that life is better today than yesterday? How can one tell an elderly person who has no medical care and no pension that life will be more secure in the future? As critics argue forcefully, if the aim of the reform is to bring prosperity to China, it should be for more than just a small number of people in the most populous nation in the world.

He Qinglian is very pessimistic about China's future, but other critics such as Yang Fan believe that the reform may be able to avoid complete failure if the government uses the remaining resources (those not stolen by corrupted officials) to deal with social problems. What China currently needs the most, in Yang's view, is not rapid economic growth but social justice and fair market competition, as seen in democratic-capitalist countries.

Both He Qinglian's and Yang Fan's evaluations of the reform have been criticized by some other public intellectuals. It would be misleading, some argue, to blame everything on the reform. Many problems that China faces today are legacies of the Mao era. For example, overpopulation is partially due to Mao's policy of encouraging parents to have more children during the 1950s and the early 1960s. Unemployment is an unavoidable by-product of dismantling the inefficient SOEs. In addition, the high unemployment rate may include some who actually work in the private sector.

Defenders of the reform emphasize that the standard of living in the entire nation has improved significantly during the past two decades. While they are aware of disparities in Chinese society, defenders argue that there is no starvation, which was a serious problem in Mao's China and is still a problem in many other countries of the world. In 1998, although several major rivers in China, especially the Yangzi River, experienced their largest floods of the century, the country still had a good grain harvest. In the early 1960s, thirty million people died of starvation as a result of Mao's radical policies that were part of the Great Leap Forward. Defenders believe that both He's and Yang's assessments show hypocrisy regarding the lack of economic security in today's China. They ask what feeling of security there was during the Cultural Revolution when thousands of people, including He and Yang, could be taken suddenly from their homes and sent to the countryside or to a cadres' school (the Chinese equivalent of a labor camp) for reeducation.[40]

In commenting on Yang Fan's article "China's Crisis," the author Xin Mao criticizes Yang's notion of "fair competition" (*gongping jingzheng*). For Xin, there is no such thing as "fair competition" in the real world. Competition is not based on equality. The rules of the game are never fair because they are always made by the winners. This was true in feudalistic China, aristocratic Britain, the communist Soviet Union, and the capitalist United States. Xin challenges Yang by asking, Is it possible to have fair competition in today's world economy when the two hundred largest multinational corporations account for 28 percent of the world's GNP? Even during Adam Smith's time, there was no real fair competition. Is it possible that the landlords and farmers in Great Britain competed fairly? Did Columbus and his crew compete fairly with Native Americans? Did British opium merchants treat Chinese businesspeople fairly? Would O.J. Simpson have won his criminal case without his "dream team" of lawyers?[41] Xin's provocative remarks are intended to underscore the importance of political power in the process of economic change and the interaction between political power and economic wealth.

"Capitalization of Power" or "Toward a Pluralist System"?

The nature of the reform, many critics believe, is the transfer and redistribution of property. Yang Fan states that prior to the reform there were no market forces in China, only political power. Yang believes that there were two ways to change the situation: one was the collapse of power (often through revolutionary means), and the other was a gradual process of creating a market through use of power. China took the latter path. It is not surprising that those communist leaders who controlled resources under the planned economy took advantage of their political power and converted the wealth of the state into their own wealth during the reform. This is what He Qinglian calls the "marketization of power" (*quanli de shichanghua*) and what Yang Fan calls the

---

40. "Intellectuals: The Self and the Others," *China News Analysis*, no. 1556 (March 15, 1996), p. 7.

41. Xin Mao, "Chaoyue zuoyouyi haishi bei zuoyouyi chaoyue: Ping Yang Fan 'Zhongguo de weiji: Quanli ziben exing pengzhang' " (Transcend left-right division or be transcended by the left and right: A comment on Yang Fan), *Zhongguo yu shijie*, no. 23 (September 1998).

"capitalization of power" (*quanli ziben*). Yang believes that the growing capitalization of power in China is due to the fact that power, which
was all-embracing under the planned economy, is still unrestrained
during the reform.

Capitalization of power is not unique to China's reform. A similar
phenomenon occurred during the Industrial Revolution in Great
Britain and the Meiji Restoration in Japan. During the transition of the
former Soviet Union, some communist officials gave up their political
and legal privileges, but they became new entrepreneurs and legislators. In all these cases, the transformation of the economic structure
was accompanied by the continuation of the elite strata. What makes
China's reform unique, as He Qinglian, Yang Fan, and many others
argue, is that the capitalization of power was achieved in a very short
period of time and in a secretive manner. More important, some critics
believe that China is heading not toward a true market economy but
toward what He Qinglian calls a kind of "simulated market." A simulated market is one in which "the actual competition is political," or
even worse, one in which there is "joint rule by the government and a
mafia" in which power "determines the allocation of resources but is
not concerned with their efficient use."[42] According to He's calculation,
in recent years about 130 million yuan in public property has been
diverted annually to private use, but only about 30 million of that actually reaches the economy in the form of private capital. The larger
amount is actually spent on bribes, entertainment, and favors.

The transfer or redistribution of state property, as Yang Fan
describes it, has been achieved in four distinctive ways during different phases of the reform. First, during the late 1970s and early 1980s,
when China adopted the rural household contract responsibility system, about 2 billion yuan in collective property went to rural cadres.
Second, during the early 1980s, when more autonomy was given to
firms engaged in domestic and foreign trade, about 5,000 billion yuan
in commercial capital was transferred from the state to private enterprises. Third, the two-track pricing system allowed corrupt officials, by
issuing certificates, business permits, and quotas, to profit from the 70-
billion-yuan difference between the two tracks. The Chinese have
coined the term *guandao* (official turnaround) to refer to the process in

---

42. Quoted from Liu Bingyan and Perry Link, "A Great Leap Backward?" p. 20. For He's
detailed discussion of the loss of state property, see He Qinglian, *Xiandaihua de xianjing*,
pp. 106–16.

which officials buy raw materials or commodities at a fixed price and then "turn around" and sell them on the private market, thus reaping huge profits. It is estimated that 35 billion yuan went into officials' pockets through *guandao*. And fourth, during the late 1980s and early 1990s, when China established a stock market, mutual funds, private real estate, and leasing of land to foreigners, about 10,000 billion yuan in state assets was lost. The figures provided by Yang Fan are only calculated estimates. In some cases, the numbers may be exaggerated. Nevertheless, the loss of state assets during the reform has been enormous. According to official statistics provided by China's State Property Administration Bureau, from 1982 to 1992 the country lost a total of 500 billion yuan, which is higher than the total revenue of 1992 (418.8 billion yuan). This means that China lost 50 billion yuan annually.[43]

Both Yang and He believe that the capitalization of power was completed in the early 1990s. The completion of private capital accumulation, according to He Qinglian, is indicated by the fact that wealth is controlled by only a handful of people, mainly corrupt officials and their relatives. Not much is left in the state coffers. The nature of private capital accumulation is that elites in political and economic institutions use a *quanqian* exchange (a trade between power and money) and divide up the state assets. The means of the seizure is political power. In Yang's view, the "vicious expansion of political capital" has hurt the private economy, reduced purchasing power, and even worse, seized the bank savings of ordinary citizens, social-welfare funds, and farmers' land. Critics of the reform reject the notion that corruption is the oil of the economy. Yu Zuyao, a Chinese economist, calls corruption the "cancer of economic entities" and corrupt officials the "moths that eat" socialist public ownership.[44]

Although probably all public intellectuals participating in the debate on the reform agree that corruption is a serious problem in today's China, many disagree with Yang Fan and He Qinglian's characterization of the reform as "capitalization of power." The real question is not whether government officials have used their political power

---

43. The data in this discussion are from Yang Fan, "Zhongguo de weiji: Quanli ziben exing pengzhang" (China's crisis: The vicious expansion of political capital), *Zhongguo yu shijie* (September 1998); and He Qinglian, "Zhongguo dangdai de ziben yuanshi jilei."

44. Yu Zuyao, "Zhuanxing shiqi baofahu qunti de zhengzhi jingjixue fenxi" (A political economic analysis of new rich in the era of transition), *Jingji yanjiu* (Economic Research), no. 2 (1998).

for economic gains (they surely have), but whether the political power of officials becomes more centralized or more shared and restrained as the reform continues. Some scholars argue that critics of the reform should not forget that the planned economy created unrestrained power in the first place.

It is true that the transition to a market economy has not resulted in an equitable redistribution of state assets as was originally intended. Corrupt officials and their relatives constitute a significant part of China's nouveaux riches. But the reform has also opened the door for poor, less-educated, and underprivileged people to pursue upward social mobility. China's rural industrialization and urbanization, especially the rapid development of TVEs during the 1980s, has created, for the first time in Chinese history, a rural industrial entrepreneurial class. Some of its members might have been rural officers before, but many did not have official backgrounds or political connections.

In urban areas, many entrepreneurs were previously unemployed. Some were young people who returned to cities after the Cultural Revolution, and some were former prisoners. They became entrepreneurs not because of convenience or choice, but because it was the only way for them to make a living. These new entrepreneurs vary greatly. Some have made fortunes lawfully by applying their engineering and telecommunications skills to high-paying jobs in the information economy. Some have engaged in illicit businesses such as smuggling, swindling, embezzling, pirating, or tax evasion. Illicit business activities are often very common in a country in the early stage of capital accumulation, however. Calling these *nouveaux riches* the Chinese mafia, as He Qinglian does, is inappropriate and simplistic and may reflect the deep-rooted tradition in Chinese society to look down upon merchants. Even today, the Chinese like to use the traditional term "heartless rich" (*weifu buren*) to refer to the *nouveaux riches*.

Xin Mao argues that the bias against the entrepreneurial class reflects the anxiety of the emergent middle stratum in Chinese society in the face of the rapid rise of private entrepreneurs. Critics such as He and Yang began to talk about social justice, Xin notes, only when they began to feel threatened and eclipsed by the newly rich.[45] Reform defenders believe that the last two decades have resulted in a growing divergence between power and money, an important step toward a plu-

---

45. Xin Mao, "Chaoyue zuoyouyi haishi bei zuoyouyi chaoyue."

ralist political system. Defenders point out that under a totalitarian system, such as Mao's China, the state was the sole controller and employer. This created a truly crushing disparity of power between the rulers and the ruled. The emerging entrepreneurial class represents a new force in society, one that can restrain state power and eventually erode the legitimacy of the authoritarian regime.

Defenders also use the political experiences of China's neighbors to illustrate the positive impact of the middle class. In South Korea, government elites initially maintained their power but were forced to accommodate the business elite. Political power has been shared rather than monopolized by politicians. In Taiwan, the "main financial backer" of the emerging opposition party in the 1980s was the middle class. In China, the political role of the private sector has also become increasingly evident. For example, according to Pei Minxin, over one thousand newspapers were founded in the early 1980s, only 10 percent of which were state owned.[46] Private firms, nongovernmental organizations, and various kinds of entrepreneurs' associations have now sprung up in what Tony Saich calls "the gray area between state and society" to represent the new economic interests and, to a lesser extent, new social forces.[47]

Not all Chinese scholars in the debate believe that capitalist development and the rise of the middle class will lead to democracy. Cui Zhiyuan, for example, argues that capitalism and democracy are not compatible because they have different logics. The logic of capitalism is that the more money one possesses, the stronger voice one has; the logic of democracy is that everyone has an equal right to speak.[48] Indeed, during the market reform, some Chinese shareholding enterprises actually implemented "democratic procedures" based not on "one person, one vote" but on "one share, one vote."

With regard to official corruption, critics such as He Qinglian do not hold out much hope because they doubt that "a one party state can effectively root out its own corruption." He Qinglian recently said during an interview with a Hong Kong journalist, "even the best surgeon

---

46. Pei Minxin, *From Reform to Revolution: The Demise of Communism in China and the Soviet Union* (Cambridge: Harvard University Press, 1994), p. 161.

47. Tony Saich, "The Search for Civil Society and Democracy in China," *Current History*, September 1994, p. 260.

48. Cui Zhiyuan, "Zhongguo zhengzhi gaige de xinsilu: Feizhengdang shi jingzheng xuanju" (New ideas for China's political reform: Non-partisan competitive elections), *Zhongguo yu shijie*, no. 17 (March 1998).

cannot operate on himself."[49] Defenders of the reform, however, argue that He overlooks the historical context of the rampancy of corruption in China. For example, *guandao*, which is based on the two-track pricing system, will disappear when the two-track pricing system is no longer in use. The ruthless rush to steal from the state coffers on the part of the *taizidang* (the children of high-ranking officials) was largely a political move to force their parents to retire. In addition, there have been some genuine and effective efforts by the top leaders to restrain official corruption. For example, in 1994, Hu Angang and some other public intellectuals proposed that the Chinese government ban business activities of the military. A few years later, in 1998, Jiang Zemin ordered the People's Liberation Army, one of the most corrupt institutions, to withdraw from all commercial activities. Jiang's order has been well enforced thus far: roughly twenty thousand military-owned enterprises either have been closed or are going to be converted to civilian firms. Zhu Rongji, with his reputation as an anticorruption czar, has been very tough in cleaning up China's customs practices and major infrastructure abuses, such as those that were part of the Three Gorges Dam project.

To parallel its market reform, China has made efforts to consolidate its legal system. China has probably issued more laws and regulations during the 1990s than any other country. In the early 1980s, there were only 3,000 lawyers in a country of over one billion people. Next year China is expected to have 150,000 lawyers (the growth rate is even more rapid than in the United States, for better or for worse!).[50] This does not mean that China is currently a country ruled by law. Nevertheless, the making of laws and regulations is one important step toward that goal. Other positive political changes often cited include genuine local elections, term limits for government officials, restraints on nepotism in both central and local governments, and the growing power of the National People's Congress. Defenders such as Liu Ji argue that all these developments will provide a political environment conducive to Chinese democracy.[51] If the rise of a middle class is essential to political democracy, China is certainly going in the right direction.

---

49. Susan V. Lawrence, "Celebrity Critic."

50. The figures are based on Henry S. Rowen, "The Short March: China's Road to Democracy," *National Interest*, no. 45 (Fall 1996), p. 63.

51. Luo Ma and Xiao Bing, "Fazhi, shehui zhuyi mingzhu zhengzhi yu renquan wenti, fang Liu Ji" (The rule of law, socialist democracy and human rights, interview with Liu Ji), *Kaifang shidai* (Open time), (March/April 1999), p. 98.

"Moral Decay" or the "Renaissance of Individuality"?

A third major debate about the reform concerns cultural and moral issues. For He Qinglian and some other critics, the reform has led to "moral decay" (*daode da huapo*) or a "collapse of ethics" in society on two different levels. At the state level, state property was "peacefully" transferred from the state to the private sector (mainly to those corrupt officials). Although there was no blood or violence, the greed and immorality were as great as in capital accumulation by violent means elsewhere. The market economy has loosened the control of the state, but it has also put Chinese laborers at the "mercy of another equally merciless factor"—capitalist exploitation.

At the societal level, there is what Lu Hsiao-peng calls the "omnipresence of capital."[52] The get-rich-quick mentality has spread to all corners of society. People seem to live in "an utterly valueless condition, the goal of life is simply to make money." In the preface to a recently published volume of essays on moral issues in China entitled *Moral China*, Liu Zhifeng, the editor, lists various aspects of moral decay in today's China.[53] First of all, there is an absence, or crisis, of belief and trust in society. Crime, smuggling, prostitution, drugs, underground society, and the sale of women and children are all on the rise. Human compassion toward poor, weak, elderly, and handicapped people is not highly valued. Fake and pirate products have flooded the consumer market. Liu argues that the market reform has let China fall into the "pitfalls of secularity" (*shisuhua de xianjing*), in which people are only interested in the material pleasures of the moment and do not think much about the future. Machiavellianism and corruption, in Liu's words, have become the most prevalent social norms. A number of contributors to the volume even characterize Chinese culture during the reform era as the "culture of corruption" (*hubai wenhua*).

Wang Lixiong, a contributor to *Moral China*, argues that the absence of belief and authority in reform China is the root cause of moral decay and rampant crime. He characterizes the behavioral norms in today's Chinese society as "believe nothing, one can do anything." He believes that the most likely scenario for China's future—and the

---

52. Sheldon Hsiao-peng Lu, "Global Postmodernization: The Intellectual, the Artist, and China's Condition," *Boundary* 2, no. 24 (Fall 1997), p. 68.

53. Liu Zhifeng, ed., *Daode Zhongguo: Dangdai Zhongguo daode lünli de shenchong yousi* (Moral China: Deep concerns and thinking about ethics and morality in today's China) (Beijing: Zhongguo shehui kexue chubanshe, 1999) p. 5.

most severe crisis in the making—is not the economic and political problem but the "collapse of China's cultural structure." Wang echoes He Qinglian's argument that erosion of the moral basis of society will be the chief source of social crisis in China in the future. This is because, according to both He and Wang, during the reform era, the economic structure has been transformed very rapidly and economic ethics have altered even faster, but the change of political institutions has lagged far behind. In her essay for *Moral China*, He Qinglian cites three public opinion polls conducted in the mid-1990s that found that about 90 percent of people were not satisfied with the moral environment in today's society. Other authors in the volume cite cases to illustrate how the reform has caused ethical confusion and moral decay. For example, a criminal-turned-entrepreneur donated some money to a kindergarten and was thus seen as a philanthropist and a role model for young people.

But the moral crisis argument has been strongly criticized by other public intellectuals who see in it a glorification of the "good old days" under communism. Should the Chinese people be nostalgic, they ask, about the "socialist morality" of the Mao era? Are conformity, uniformity, and the neglect of individuality (as exemplified by Lei Feng, the Maoist hero) the needed values and norms for the Chinese people? Xu Youyu, an expert in Cultural Revolution studies, spoke for many defenders when he asked, "If there were another Cultural Revolution, what would you prefer: letting your students torture you as the idealist Red Guards did or allowing your students to be interested in their material pleasure but not political campaigns?"[54] Xu's question, and its implied answer, is not only a reminder of the moral decay of the past, typified by the betrayal and lies that pervaded the Cultural Revolution, but is also a defense of the pursuit of material self-interest.

For Xu and other defenders, there is nothing wrong with being motivated by making money. People's material needs are always a driving force for socioeconomic development. On the other hand, the reform is not just about money. As a Chinese "yuppie" said to a Western reporter in China, "It's about a better quality of life. And it moves us toward greater spiritual and political freedom."[55] A market

---

54. Xu Youyu, "Women zheyidairen de lixiang" (The ideal of our generation), in *Daode Zhongguo*, ed. Liu Zhifeng, p. 341.

55. Elisabeth Rosenthal, "China's Middle Class Savors Its New Wealth," *New York Times*, June 19, 1998, p. 1.

economy, especially China's opening to the outside world, enables Chinese consumers to encounter a world of differences, choices, and various ways of thinking.

In sharp contrast to the perception of "moral decay" and "cultural stagnation," some Chinese public intellectuals believe that the 1990s has been a period of a "renaissance of individuality" and revival of Chinese culture. Under the reform, the "public" and "private" spheres are better defined. What is emerging in China today is what Ling Zhijun and Ma Licheng call "the emancipation of mind and being" and what Tony Saich calls "a focus on the individual."[56] Every individual in Chinese society is "seeing his or her social status and personal identity redefined by the new economic system." In the cultural arena, as some sinologists observe, political and economic decentralization, transnational mobility, economic diversity, and consumerism have led to a renewed sense of locality, individuality, and diversity.[57]

During the 1990s, especially in its coastal cities and towns, China has witnessed the rapid growth of teahouses, coffee shops, Internet cafes, karaoke bars, disco clubs, private bookstores, fitness centers, private salons, and private theaters. If one accepts Habermas's argument that the pubs and coffeehouses of seventeenth-century London were the real force behind the formation of British civil society, the surge in places for informal association in reform China also signifies the emergence of Chinese civil society (*gongmin shehui*). These cultural and social changes will probably have a more profound political impact than the Tiananmen protests and other political rallies because the latter have been "movements of masses rather than of citizens."[58]

What He Qinglian and others seem to miss, according to some, is that the reform has already fundamentally altered the state-citizen relationship. During the Mao era, an identical all-purpose ideal or moral standard was imposed on everyone. Today, there exists "no all-purpose ideal that can claim to be both political and moral and be good for all,

---

56. Ling Zhijun and Ma Licheng, *Jiaofeng: Dangdai Zhongguo sanci sixiang jiefang shilu* (Confrontation: Three thought emancipations in contemporary China) (Beijing: Jinri Zhongguo chubanshe, 1998); and Tony Saich, "The Search for Civil Society and Democracy in China."

57. *Far Eastern Economic Review*, November 26, 1998, p. 50; and Arif Dirlik and Zhang Xudong, "Postmodernism and China," *Boundary 2*, no. 24 (Fall 1997), p. 8.

58. Heath B. Chamberlain, "Coming to Terms with Civil Society," *Australian Journal of Chinese Affairs*, no. 30 (January 1994), p. 116.

irrespective of individual circumstances."[59] Social and cultural diversity can be seen in all aspects of Chinese life today: fashion, music, dance, the arts, movies, advertisements, social interaction, and social tolerance. Changing norms and values, as some scholars have observed, can also be found in the vocabulary, with a rapid increase in new Chinese words. According to a recent study by China's Research Institute of Applied Linguistics, about 7,000 new terms have been added to the Chinese vocabulary since 1978.[60]

As everywhere in the world, technology serves as a powerful agent of change. In China, information and ideas flow with unprecedented speed through various channels. For instance, during the 1990s, the number of mobile phones has jumped from 50,000 to more than 13 million. In addition, 11 million new telephone lines are installed every year. The Internet, which was almost nonexistent in the early 1990s, is now expected to increase from 1 million accounts in 1998 to more than 20 million in 2000. China now has more than 2,000 newspapers and 2,100 satellite and cable television stations. Multiplicity and diversity in sources of information can have a strong effect on cultural changes.

Liu Zhifeng, however, rejects the notion of pluralism favored by some liberal scholars and writers such as Wang Meng and Wang Shuo. Wang Shuo is famous for his satiric writings and represents the so-called ruffian culture (*pizi wenhua*). Liu argues that pluralism should not only allow "unconditional acceptance of the reality" but also welcome "uncompromising criticism of the reality." During the reform era, according to Liu, people emphasize the former but ignore the latter. As a result, people care about nothing but utility. They do not have a sense of right and wrong, true and false, good and evil, beauty and ugliness. This kind of moral relativity is often favorably portrayed in Wang Shuo's literary works. Liu criticizes Wang Shuo for profaning literature and decency, and he criticizes Wang Meng, an official who was in charge of China's cultural affairs, for surrendering his "intellectual soul in the name of cultural pluralism and tolerance."[61]

To defend his position, Wang Meng argues that Liu Zhifeng and other critics forget one important historical fact: it was radicals of the

---

59. *China News Analysis*, no. 1556 (March 15, 1996), p. 8.

60. *Renmin ribao*, September 30, 1998, p. 11.

61. Liu Zhifeng, *Daode Zhongguo*, pp. 13–15.

Cultural Revolution such as Jiang Qing and Lin Biao who blasphemed humanity and human decency. The Wang Shuo phenomenon in the Chinese literature of post-Mao China was actually a critical response to hypocrisy and other ugly human behaviors of the Cultural Revolution. In Wang Meng's view, the existence of Wang Shuo's "ruffian literature" does not prevent the development of other literary schools and styles; it only reflects the diversity and pluralism of Chinese culture and moral values. The most important development in the 1990s, many defenders of the reform (and many critics as well) believe, is the effort by both the government and public intellectuals to establish a sound legal system. The burden of morality, some public intellectuals argue, should now be shifted to legality.

Some other public intellectuals believe that ongoing debate about the moral status of the reform is a healthy development. Lin Jingyao, for example, wrote a foreword for *Moral China* in which he argues that the current debate actually contributes to the establishment of the disciplinary field of modern ethics in China. If economic and technological development serves as the "engine of change," the transforming culture and the discussion of ethics in reform China, especially its pluralistic nature, may determine the "direction of change." This suggests that a truly pluralistic sociopolitical system is looming large in China at the dawn of a new century.

Conclusion

A lively debate on the pitfalls and promises of the reform has been going on among Chinese public intellectuals since the mid-1990s. Bold criticisms, striking statistics, and fascinating ideas have been openly presented. Yet, it seems premature to draw any conclusions about either the debate or the nature of China's reform. The reform has brought both remarkable progress and devastating problems, and the reform debate, like the reform itself, is an open-ended and ongoing process.

In an article commemorating the hundredth anniversary of the 1898 reform, He Qinglian identifies five major problems that held China back in 1898: population size, agricultural stagnation, inequality, corruption, and low standards in education. Her point is that all five problems are at least as severe now, suggesting the failure of reform. In pointing to the historical roots of today's dilemmas, however, and to China's century-long struggle to achieve socioeconomic development, her comparison actually undermines her criticism.[62] While some of the reform problems that she highlights are indeed caused by the market economy and the transition to capitalism, many have been caused by China's demographics and geography; some are the legacies of Mao's socialism, which did not work and could never work; and some are the side effects of rapid economic growth.

Moreover, problems such as inequality, corruption, and low standards in education are not unique to China; they exist in many countries and under many political systems. The experience of Yen Fu, a leading figure of the 1898 reform, is particularly revealing. In 1876, Yen was one of the first Chinese students sent to Britain, where he admired the West for its wealth and freedom. But later he found the Western economic and political system inadequate, for he felt that it had made little progress toward the "three criteria of an ideal society— material sufficiency enjoyed by all, moral excellence attained by many, and crimes committed by none."[63]

About a hundred years have passed since Yen Fu made this remark. One may ask, How many countries in today's world can claim that they have achieved these "three criteria of an ideal society"? The answer is not many, or even more likely, none. China's search for such a society in the twentieth century has been filled with ironies, tragedies, and paradoxes. What is truly remarkable is that despite all the pitfalls and problems of the century, the nation has not only survived but is moving dramatically ahead.

---

62. He Qinglian, "Yige jingji xuejia yanzhong de wuxu bainian" (The hundred years since 1898 as seen by an economist), *Nanfang zhoumo* (Southern Weekend), April 17, 1998; and her interview in Li Hui and Ying Hong, *Shiji zhiwen*, pp. 221–23.

63. Fred Strebeigh, "Training China's New Elite," *Atlantic Monthly*, April 1989, p. 80.

The Politics of Consumerism in Chinese Society

Yunxiang Yan

On March 15, 1999, *Beijing Youth Daily*, one of China's two most popular newspapers, published a feature article under a headline printed in unusually big characters: "The Springtime of Consumption." The author seriously advised readers that recent policy changes signaled the state's intention to stimulate mass consumption. To justify this policy shift, the author argued that "consumption used to be condemned as a kind of corrupt lifestyle and was always described with epithets such as 'hyperconsumption,' 'in-advance consumption,' and 'luxury consumption.' Some leaders even ordered banks to stop issuing personal loans for buying houses and automobiles. It is only now that consumption has been lifted to the unprecedentedly high level that it so much deserves. Consumption will be China's locomotive of economic growth."[1]

Consumption was indeed a hot topic in both official discourse and public opinion in the spring of 1999. The subject was first formally raised in a directive of the People's Bank of China, publicized in the *People's Daily* on March 4. The new directive loosened the central bank's control over loans, allowing all Chinese banks to make more personal loans, to lower the amount required for down payments, and to begin making loans for consumer durables, education, and even

This study is based on documentary data collected and interviews conducted during fieldwork in China in 1989, 1991, 1994, 1997, 1998, and 1999. The Smith Richardson Foundation, the National Science Foundation, the Wenner-Gren Foundation, and the Academic Senate of UCLA provided generous support for fieldwork in 1998 and 1999. I owe special thanks to Xiaoyan Liang and Tyrene White for their insightful and valuable comments on early drafts of this paper, and I am also grateful to Richard Gunde for his skillful editorial assistance.

1. Wu Tao, "Xiaofei de chuntian" (The springtime of consumption), *Beijing qingnian bao* (Beijing Youth Daily), March 15, 1999, p. 21.

tourism. Throughout March and April, relevant government agencies and the mass media all launched into a propaganda campaign, encouraging people to take out loans for commodities and services, a practice that was nicknamed "*jieqian yuanmeng*" (borrowing money to realize one's dream).[2] At the same time, the central bank lowered interest rates for the seventh time since 1997, hoping to reduce the extremely high rate of personal savings, which amounted to more than 60 billion yuan by early 1999. The government's purpose was obvious: to expand the domestic market by stimulating consumption and eventually to speed up the sluggish Chinese economy. However, the campaign had not been successful by the summer of 1999, and the focus of public discussion switched to the question of why the Chinese refused to take loans or spend their bank savings.[3]

This was the first time in the history of the People's Republic of China that the government openly recognized consumption as the key to economic growth and even went so far as to encourage people to consume more by taking out loans. This marked a sharp contrast to the communist ideology of the prereform period (1949–78), when "hard work and plain living" was promoted as the ideal. The officially endorsed role models during that period, such as the selfless soldier Lei Feng, barely consumed anything beyond basic subsistence needs; they all wanted to help the country by putting their modest savings in the state bank. To borrow money for consumption, many Beijing residents note, is a strange idea that they have never heard of before. Such a radical shift in economic policy obviously represents the triumph of consumerism.

The impact of mass consumption on the Chinese economy and domestic politics, however, is by no means a new phenomenon at the end of the 1990s. From the beginning of the economic reforms in the late 1970s, state policies on consumption have shifted back and forth.

2. See Men Rui, "Chong ti gaoxiaofei" (Reevaluating hyperconsumption), *Zhongguo shichang* (China Market), no. 2 (1999), pp. 37–38; and Hu Yanping, "Baixing de qianbao shui neng dakai" (Who can open the wallets of ordinary people?), *Beijing Youth Daily*, April 4, 1999, p. 13.

3. See, for example, Wen Yuan, "Xiaofei xindai: Yuanhe bulü jiannan?" (Consumption loans: Why is it so difficult to start?), *Huanqiu shichang* (Global Market), no. 6 (1999), pp. 22–24; Wang Wei, "Xiaofei xindai heyi shouzu?" (Why are consumption loans encountering difficulties?), *Zhongguo jingji xinxi* (China Economic Information), no. 9, 1999, pp. 4–8; and Zhang Xiaofei, "Jiangxi ciji bule wo xiaofei" (Reducing interest rates cannot stimulate me to consume), *Nanfang zhoumo* (Southern Weekend), July 2, 1999, p. 8.

Advocates of reform have had to fight the legacy of the anticonsumption, ascetic ideology that dominated the first three decades of socialism. During the reform era, China has been swept by three successive waves of mass consumption, each of which has led to public debates and in some cases political changes. During the late 1980s and early 1990s, consumption and possession gradually replaced political symbols as the path toward defining one's social status and drawing group boundaries. The endless pursuit of material goods also helped to reduce the role of ideology in social life and to create more social space for individual citizens. Beginning in the early 1990s, a consumer revolution exploded across urban China; along with it, consumerism became a new ideology influencing the everyday life of ordinary citizens as well as the policy-making process, so much so that the consumer market slowdown in 1998 was regarded as a dangerous signal by both Chinese economists and government leaders, which led to the official push in 1999 for the expansion of consumption.

It seems to me that consumerism carries more sociopolitical meanings in China than in free-market societies. The present study, therefore, aims to unpack these meanings by examining how consumerism arose and what it has done to Chinese society.[4] In the first part of this chapter, I review the three waves of mass consumption during the past two decades. I argue that the third wave, in the early 1990s, differed in nature from the first two, in the 1980s, in that it carried the basic features of consumerism and marked the outbreak of a consumer revolution in urban China. The second part of the chapter concerns the main consequences and implications of the consumer revolution and analyzes the initial triumph of consumerism in relation to the formation of social classes, the change of dominant ideology, the creation of social space, the awareness of individual rights, and post–1989 politics in China.

Throughout the chapter, I use the term "consumerism" in a broad sense. It refers on the one hand to the ideology and practice that

---

4. The literature on the subject is rather limited. For a good review of the economic origins of the consumer revolution in China, see Linda Chao and Ramon Myers, "China's Consumer Revolution: The 1990s and Beyond," *Journal of Contemporary China*, vol. 7, no. 18 (1998), pp. 351–68; for case studies regarding the impact of consumption on social life in Chinese cities, see Deborah Davis, ed., *Consumer Revolution in Urban China* (Berkeley: University of California Press, 2000); for a more critical analysis of the trend of mass consumption and its impact on children, see Bin Zhao, "Consumerism, Confucianism, Communism: Making Sense of China Today," *New Left*, no. 222 (March 1997), pp. 43–59; and Bin Zhao and Graham Murdock, "Young Pioneers: Children and the Making of Chinese Consumerism," *Cultural Studies*, vol. 10, no. 2 (1996), pp. 201–17.

encourage people to consume more than what they need and on the other hand to the social movement for consumer protection that seeks to augment the rights and powers of consumers in relation to those of businesses that are interested only in making profits.[5] Defined as such, consumerism arises along with the emergence of a buyer's market, with the shift of emphasis in spending from foods to nonfood commodities, the increasing importance of fashion and taste, the awareness of consumer rights, and the organized action of consumers. It is, therefore, inadequate to depict consumerism only as the expression of consumers' seemingly unlimited and excessive desires/needs for commodities, which is mass consumption instead of consumerism. The key point is to avoid reducing consumers to mindless automatons in an undifferentiated mass society; rather, people (ordinary people as well as the elite) use consumption as a critical way of defining their social positions and changing power relations.[6] This is also why the present study focuses on the politics of consumerism in Chinese society.

From Mass Consumption to Consumerism: 1978 to 1999

Anyone who visits Beijing, Shanghai, Guangzhou, or another Chinese city today cannot fail to be impressed by the dynamism and commercialism of the urban scene. The gigantic billboards along the newly constructed highways, the neon lights and skyscrapers in commercial districts, the well-dressed consumers in fancy shopping malls—all of these seem to boast to the world that at least urban China has become an affluent consumer society. The urban scene was, however, quite different two decades ago. A U.S. scholar recalled what he had observed in 1976: The streets were nearly deserted by seven in the evening; during the day a few buses moved along the streets, and tens of thousands of bicyclists dressed in blue cotton silently pedaled to and from their destinations. Vegetable and fruit stalls lined the main streets, offering

---

5. See, for example, James McIlhenny, "The New Consumerism: How Will Business Respond," *At Home with Consumers*, vol. 11, no. 2 (1990), p. 5; and Julius Onah, "Consumerism in Nigeria," in *Marketing in Nigeria: Experience in a Developing Economy*, ed. Julius Onah (London: Cassell, 1979), p. 126.

6. See Michael Featherstone, "Life Style and Consumer Culture," *Theory, Culture, and Society*, vol. 4, no. 1 (1987), pp. 55–70; and Arjun Appadurai, "Introduction: Commodities and the Politics of Value," in *The Social Life of Things: Commodities in Cultural Perspective*, ed. Arjun Appadurai (Cambridge: Cambridge University Press, 1986), pp. 3–63.

little if any variety.[7] To better understand the remarkable changes over the past two decades, we need to look first at the prehistory of consumerism in China.

The Underdevelopment of Consumption during the Prereform Era

During the Maoist period (1949–76), consumption was reduced to the minimum. Influenced by the Soviet model of development, Chinese economic planning long gave top priority to the construction of heavy industry. The state built up a highly concentrated system of planning and redistribution, monopolizing the circulation of the means of production and major items of the means of subsistence as well. In urban areas, low wages and full employment constituted the core of labor policy, and Chinese workers received a more or less fixed salary for more than twenty years. To accommodate the low income of its citizens, the state provided subsidies for basic goods, housing, and transportation. For instance, state subsidies for food supplies in urban areas alone amounted to billions of yuan each year. The result was that the more people consumed, the more the state had to provide in subsidies, which made consumption counterproductive. This, plus the lack of incentive to produce under a planned economy, led to a shortage of basic subsistence goods for many years and forced the state to limit consumption and to issue ration coupons to make sure everyone got a share, no matter how minimal, of the small pie.

Under such a distribution system, consumption bore three distinctive features. First, there were few differences in consumption patterns and lifestyles—people basically wore the same kind of clothes, ate more or less the same kind of food, and lived in similar kinds of housing. True, there were small differences in material life across different occupations and regions, but they were so minor as to hardly reflect a clear sign of social differentiation. Rather, it was the political symbols (such as class labels or party membership) that served as marks of one's social status.

Second, consumption remained at the level of basic subsistence for almost three decades. More than 55 percent of household income was spent on food, mostly grain and vegetables. It normally took years to get a new outfit or a new pair of shoes. The popular saying for basic

7. Linda Chao and Ramon Myers, "China's Consumer Revolution," p. 351.

consumption was "three years new, three years old, and another three years by mending and patching" (*xin sannian, jiu sannian, fengfeng bubu you sannian*). Expenditure on entertainment was so small that it could be ignored: people did not have much money left over for leisure activities, and besides, most leisure activities, such as movies or concerts, were organized and paid for by work units as part of employee benefits.

Third, to sustain its policy of low consumption and high accumulation (of capital for national development), the state launched consistent ideological as well as administrative attacks on the individual pursuit of luxury goods or comfortable lifestyles, condemning them as manifestations of "corrupt bourgeois culture." Shops selling jewelry, furs or other expensive clothing, and cosmetics were closed down after the mid-1950s; bars and dance halls, together with brothels, were considered corrupt and were banned. In their place grew a large number of small shops for the masses. Ideologically, the state imposed a kind of socialist asceticism in everyday life, as reflected in the leading slogan of the time, "hard work and plain living." In a well-known movie called *Must Never Forget*, a man became the captive of corrupt bourgeois thoughts when he bought himself a wool suit. This kind of thinking reached such heights that, during the radical period of the late 1960s to the early 1970s, a young girl wearing a colorful hairpin could be subject to severe criticism for having unhealthy, petty bourgeois thoughts; old, patched clothes were considered a symbol of being revolutionary, or at least politically correct.

Two Waves of Mass Consumption in the 1980s

This ascetic ideology, or communist-style puritanism, was turned upside down after Mao's death in 1976. In order to revitalize the national economy, which was, according to the reformers, on the edge of collapse, Chinese Communist Party (CCP) leaders under Deng Xiaoping decided to launch economic reforms and to break China's isolation from the world. Consumption became an important part of the political agenda underlying the government's promotion of economic reforms. A famous slogan promoted by the reformers at that time was *nengzheng huihua*, which means "able to make money and knowing how to spend it." This slogan was in direct conflict with the official ideology of Maoist socialism that emphasized "hard work and plain living."

As mentioned earlier, there have been three distinct waves of mass consumption in the reform era. The first wave (1979–82) was initiated by peasants. The quick success of rural reform doubled peasant income during the short period from 1979 to 1984, which had a profound impact on both the circulation and consumption of goods nationwide. Having been poverty-stricken for years and suddenly having cash in their pockets, peasants hurried into markets and shops for all kinds of industrial products, ranging from washbasins to small tractors. Later, urbanites, who had just received their first wage raise in twenty years, joined the consumption wave. This tidal wave of mass consumption, which peaked in 1979–80, featured massive demand in the countryside for the products of light industry and an obvious increase of expenditure on foodstuffs in urban areas. Consumer demand increased by 22 percent in 1979 and 1980, far exceeding the 15.3 percent increase in consumer supplies during the same period. The result was an inflation rate of 6 percent in 1980, China's first taste of inflation since the late 1950s.[8] This led to a three-year (1982–85) period of government-enforced economic retrenchment. As a result, although peasant income continued to grow quickly until 1985, it was the state itself that put an end to the first wave of mass consumption.

The suddenly increased purchasing power of peasants broke the psychological balance of urban residents, who had for more than two decades enjoyed a superior status, and their discontent, plus the window effect of rural reforms, pushed the CCP leaders into launching urban economic reforms in the mid-1980s. In other words, the first wave of mass consumption made an important political contribution by facilitating the urban reforms of the mid-1980s.

The second wave of mass consumption started in early 1985, shortly after the urban reform programs launched by the state in 1984, and ended suddenly in 1989. Unlike the first wave, in which peasants played a key role, urban consumers formed the major force in this second wave. An important goal of the urban reforms was to adjust the previous state redistribution structure to allocate a larger proportion of revenue to wages. As a result, the average income of urban residents almost doubled during the period from 1985 to 1988. The private sector grew quickly and vigorously, more regions opened to foreign

8. Qiu Xiaohua and Wan Donghua "Dui jinshinianlai woguo xiaofei xinshi de jiben huigu yu zhanwang" (Retrospect and prospect of China's consumption situation in the past decade), *Xiaofei jingji* (Consumer Economy), no. 2 (1990), p. 2.

investment, and rural industry also made impressive progress during this period. All these factors added up to create a strong demand for consumer goods of all kinds. During this period, the state also loosened its control of the mass media. Newspapers and popular magazines were filled with reports of the "modern lifestyle" in developed countries, which produced another window effect on ordinary consumers.

In imitation of the state's goal of "four modernizations," ordinary citizens during the 1980s worked hard to realize their own "family modernization," which meant the possession of major appliances such as refrigerators, television sets, washing machines, and tape recorders. The demand and desire for appliances and other consumer goods seemed to be unlimited in the late 1980s. As a result, the inflation rate jumped to 18.5 percent in 1988, and when the state decided to launch a new reform of consumer prices in March 1988, panic purchasing broke out nationwide. Ordinary citizens terrified by the inflation rushed to buy whatever they could get their hands on. During my fieldwork in 1989, several interviewees showed me the stored goods that they had bought in 1988, such as dozens of blankets, a hundred bars of soap, and multiple boxes of toilet paper (this actually created tremendous difficulties for these people because most Chinese families do not have extra space for storage). It was also in this period that a large number of consumer goods for daily life flowed in from abroad, and consuming imported goods quickly became a new fashion among those who had gotten ahead economically and among a whole generation of youth.

The panic purchasing in 1988 in a way contributed to the popular protest movement in 1989, and the June 4 incident ended the second wave of mass consumption. In the following two years, the real income of both urban and rural families decreased by nearly 3 percent, and the state also imposed much stricter controls on the private sector of the economy. (Strangely, standards of living did not deteriorate, owing to special consumption policies. This is discussed further below.) The 1988 panic purchasing was frequently cited to show the importance of stability and order, and "overheated consumption" was blamed for economic difficulties during this period.[9] For a short time, China's reform era seemed to have come to a dead end.

---

9. See Huang Weiting and Li Fan, *Dangdai Zhongguo de xiaofei zhi mi* (The riddle of consumption in contemporary China) (Beijing: Zhongguo shangye chubanshe, 1990). The authors offer a comprehensive analysis of conflicting consumption phenomena, such as low income with high consumption, and call for radical control of mass consumption by

Consumer Revolution in the 1990s:
The Third Wave and Its Aftermath

The economic stagnation after the end of the second wave of mass consumption (and the political repression associated with it) was ended by Deng Xiaoping's 1992 tour to the southern city of Shenzhen, where he called upon both the CCP and the nation to be bolder in carrying out the policies of openness and speeding up the market-oriented economic reforms. As if it had broken a spell, Deng's speech quickly led to a new round of rapid economic growth. This began with the unprecedented phenomenon of *xiahai* ("jumping into the sea"); in other words, a large number of government officials, professionals, and intellectuals gave up their secure positions in government to go to work in the private sector. For a year or two, it seemed that the entire Chinese population was being lured into private business, and for most people moneymaking had become the highest ideal. The fever of investment, plus the quick growth of the real estate and stock markets, not only worked an "instant miracle" (which was in reality a bubble economy) but also stirred up people's desire and demand for more and better consumer goods; this caused the third wave of mass consumption, which started in 1992 and continued until 1996. The consumer market has slowed down since 1996, in part because of the state's "soft landing" policy in 1996–97, which aimed to control the overheated economy, and in part because of the impact of the Asian financial crisis in 1997–98.

It is the third wave of mass consumption, in my opinion, that bears the essential features of consumerism, such as the emergence of a buyer's market, the shift of emphasis in expenditure from food to other goods, the awareness of individual rights, and the development of a consumer movement. More important is that through this wave of mass consumption, consumerism has become the dominant ideology in Chinese society and one of the means available to the Communist Party to maintain its legitimacy. This is why consumerism continues to play an important role in social life and politics, as shown in the beginning of this chapter, even though the high tide of the third wave of mass consumption had already passed by 1996. Therefore, for several reasons the third wave of mass consumption deserves a closer look.

First, a buyer's market has emerged. As mentioned above, the two waves of mass consumption during the 1980s arose in the context of a

---

the government in both social psychology (ideology) and spending patterns.

shortage of consumer goods, which included both regular light industrial products for rural residents and electronic appliances for urban
residents. Thanks to the previous ten-year economic reform, the tension between demand and supply began to change in the early 1990s.
According to a 1992 report by the Ministry of Commerce, among six
hundred major categories of consumer goods, 32 percent of the categories were produced in excess of market demand, 10 percent fell short
of demand, and supply and demand for the rest were in balance. The
supply-demand pattern has continued to improve. A recent report
shows that by 1998, the supply and demand of 84 percent of six hundred major consumer goods were in balance, supply exceeded demand
in only 14 percent, and in no category of consumer goods was there a
shortage of supply.[10]

Because of the abundance of supplies and the pressure on retailers
to turn a profit, consumers now have more choices as well as more bargaining power. "Customers are our god" has become a new commercial slogan, and sellers have had to resort to various techniques to promote sales, such as offering gifts or discounts, issuing discount cards,
and using sandwich men. By 1993–94, the improvement in the shopping environment had become a big issue. In just a few years (by
1998), the glut of industrial goods and the satiation of consumer
demand became a serious problem for the Chinese economy, as they
led to a severe price war that forced a large number of retailers out of
business. Clearly, for the first time since 1949, a fully developed
buyer's market has emerged in China.[11]

Second, shopping has become an increasingly important part of
everyday life for ordinary citizens, and people have begun to purchase
goods they want but do not necessarily need.[12] Strolling through fancy
shopping malls has become a popular leisure activity, especially
among young women. During my fieldwork in 1994, 1998, and 1999,
I asked my interviewees how often they went to shopping malls and
why they did so. Nearly two-thirds of the women (aged 20–35) whom
I interviewed said that they went weekly, and did so mainly "just to

---

10. Zhu Qingfang, "1998–1999: Zhongguo renmin de shenghuo zhuangkuang" (The
living conditions of the Chinese people in 1998–1999), in *1999 nian: Zhongguo shehui
xingshi fenxi yu yuce* (Analyses and predictions of social circumstances in China, 1999),
ed. Ru Xin, Lu Xueyi, and Shan Tianlun (Beijing: Shehui kexue chubanshe, 1999), p. 354.

11. See Zhu Qingfang, "The Living Conditions of the Chinese People," pp. 354–55.

12. See news reports in *Zhongguo xiaofei shibao* (China Consumption Times), February
3 and March 3, 1993.

check it out" or "to have fun." Although the frequency of regular touring of shopping malls seems to have decreased a bit among young professional women in the last two years, their overall concern with and
awareness of fashion, style, and taste has definitely increased. Several
interviewees told me that they did not "worship" the goods in shopping
malls; instead, they went there to "relax and make ourselves feel
good." Another interesting and impressive piece of evidence of this
change is that children are very knowledgeable about Beijing's new
shopping malls and the products available there. A primary school
teacher told me in 1994 that children in her class knew much more
about brand names than did many of the teachers. Every Monday, a
common topic of conversation among children was their experience in
shopping malls over the past weekend. To test children's knowledge of
commodities, I asked my two nephews, both aged nine in 1994, to
identify the cars in a newly published auto magazine. To my surprise,
they quickly named the models and manufacturers of more than half of
the cars depicted.

Third, the expenditure structure of urban households has changed
significantly in the 1990s: total spending on food, after years of steady
yet slow decrease, fell to 49.9 percent of household income in 1995. This
was the first time in the People's Republic that a significant number of
urban residents had more than half of their income available for expenditure on nonfood items. The Engle's coefficient (the percentage of
household income used for food expenditure) continued to drop,
decreasing all the way to 45 percent among urban households by 1998.[13]

Indeed, in the 1990s urban consumers began to change their consumption patterns and spending habits in many ways. According to
1994 statistics released by the China Consumers Association, the average expenditure per capita has increased 4.1 times since 1984. The
ratio of "hard consumption" (of food, clothes, and other daily necessities) to "soft consumption" (spending money on entertainment,
tourism, fashion, and socializing) has changed from 3:1 in 1984 to
1:1.2 in 1994.[14] As a result, the hot areas of mass consumption have
shifted to interior decoration, personal computers, communications
devices, air conditioners, body-building machines, and tourism.[15]

---

13. Zhu Qingfang, "The Living Conditions of the Chinese People," p. 355.

14. *Zhongguo xiaofeizhe bao* (China Consumer News), September 12, 1994.

15. See, for example, Gao Changli, "Woguo jiushi niandai chengxian duoyuanhua
xiaofei qushi" (Consumption trends have become diversified in China during the 1990s),

A good indicator of the escalating demand for consumption is the changing definition of the "three big items" (*san dajian*), referring to the three products that are the most desirable. During the 1960s and 1970s, the "three big items" were wristwatches, bicycles, and sewing machines. Families saved for years to buy these expensive items (which cost an average of two hundred yuan each). In the 1980s, color television sets, refrigerators, and washing machines, each costing at least one thousand yuan, had become the new "three big items." By the early 1990s, the "three bigs" were telephones, air conditioners, and VCRs. For the new entrepreneurial class, the stakes have become so high that the three bigs are apartments, private cars, and cellular phones.[16] By the late 1990s, communications devices and leisure activities represented the latest development of consumerism. Pagers, personal computers, cellular phones, and Internet connections took turns as symbols of social status among trendy consumers in Chinese cities. What surprised me in this regard was that, during my visit to a remote farming village in northeastern China in 1998, I was frequently questioned by villagers as to why I did not have a cell phone. Later I found out that the two village leaders and several better-off individuals all had followed the trend and purchased cell phones, which made them a necessary status symbol in the village.

Fourth, gone with the traditional patterns of consumption is "tidal-wave consumption" (*pailangshi xiaofei*), a term used by Chinese scholars to describe seemingly mindless conformity in consumer choices. During the first two waves of mass consumption, there was a ticket item each year, such as television sets or refrigerators. Consumers from all walks of life wanted the same consumer items regardless of whether those items fit the individuals' needs, economic capability, and residential circumstances. This concentrated consumer demand easily created temporary shortages of one consumer product or another, which in turn stimulated further demand (sometimes even panic demand) until the wave broke. However, because of three new factors, tidal-wave consumption did not arise in the latest trend of mass consumption.

Shangpin pingjie (Commodity Review), no. 10 (1992), p. 6; and Dong Fang, "Zhongguo chengshi xiaofei wuda redian" (The five hot points in Chinese urban consumption), *Jingji shijie* (Economic World), no. 1 (1994), p. 22.

16. Lin Ye, "Xiaofei lingyu xin sanjian" (The new three big items in consumption), *Zhongguo shichang* (China Market), no. 7 (1994), p. 28.

The first factor is that most Chinese families had basically completed their "family modernization": they had already acquired all the "essential" items, such as television sets, refrigerators, and washing machines. When they felt the need to choose from items that were more upscale and less necessary, such as air conditioners or recreational activities, they had no fixed formula to follow. Second, consumers had grown mature. Because of the rapid development of the domestic economy in the 1990s, they no longer worried about the exhaustion of supplies, and they had accepted inflation as a normal part of economic life. People remained calm even in 1994 when the inflation rate shot up above 20 percent, in contrast with the panic in 1984 when the inflation rate was 18.5 percent. The third and perhaps most important factor is that Chinese society has become rapidly differentiated economically (in a sense even polarized). People have found themselves falling into separate strata in terms of income and lifestyle. In the 1980s, the less fortunate may have resorted to the power of their kinship networks to compete with the better-off in purchasing household appliances; in the 1990s, there was no way for the majority of the Chinese people even to approach the luxurious lifestyle of the newly rich, who could easily spend 100,000 yuan for a wristwatch or 3,000 yuan for a bottle of imported wine.

The Rise of the Consumer Protection Movement

The most important aspect of consumerism in the 1990s was the rise of a consumer protection movement. In the buyer's market that existed, consumer discontent with shoddy products, bad service, and fake goods grew rapidly. Many consumers complained that even the quality of imported products, mainly household appliances, had declined. It was reported that some foreign manufacturers exploited the popularity of imported goods in the Chinese market by shipping factory seconds and rejects to China or denying customers' claims for after-sale services under warranty. Worse than shoddy products were faked goods, particularly foodstuffs. For instance, early in 1998, several peasants in Shanxi province produced fake liquor by mixing water with nine hundred times the officially permitted amount of methyl alcohol. As a result, 27 people died, and more than 200 were hospitalized.[17]

---

17. See Beverly Hooper, "From Mao to Market: Empowering the Chinese Consumer," *Howard Asian Pacific Review*, vol. 2, no. 2 (summer 1998), pp. 29–34. The rise of a con-

To fight faulty products and fake goods, a consumer protection movement gradually emerged, both in the form of a semiofficial consumer association and through individual action. The China Consumers Association was established as early as 1984, but it only gained wide support and popularity during the 1990s. Interestingly, as with the rural reforms and some other reform programs, the first push for consumer protection came from the grassroots level. In May 1983, the first local consumer association was established in Xinle County, Henan province, an area notorious for violating consumers' rights and for producing fake goods. Three months later, a similar organization appeared in Guangzhou, the most developed and open city at that time. As a response to calls from below, the China Consumers Association was established on December 26, 1984. By 1998 it had built up a nationwide network of more than 3,000 branch associations at the provincial, municipal, and county levels, plus a reported 45,000 grassroots association branches below the county level.

Although the association's constitution states that it is a mass organization, its organizational structure, budget, and personnel show that it is actually a de facto government agency. The leading positions in the association are all occupied by high-ranking officials, an indicator of both the government's support of consumer protection and the official nature of this organization. For instance, its first president was the deputy director of the State Administration for Industry and Commerce, its first honorary president was the vice-chairman of the Standing Committee of the People's Congress and the director of the Finance and Trade Committee of the State Council, and its first secretary-general was a deputy head of the Bureau of Market Administration of the State Administration for Industry and Commerce. Many staff members were transferred into the association from various government agencies concerned with commerce and market administration. This power structure has remained intact at both the national and local levels since 1984. At lower levels, the association may share the same office space and personnel with the Bureau of Administration of Industry and Commerce, a common practice called "one personnel crew with two organizational titles" (*yi ban renma, liangkuai paizi*).[18] Employees at

---

sumer movement in China has received little attention from China scholars in the West. Hooper's article is the only one that I have found thus far.

18. See Beverly Hooper, "From Mao to Market"; for more details, see China Consumer Association, ed., *Zhongguo xiaofeizhe yundong shinian* (Ten years of consumer movement

consumer associations above the county level are paid by the government, and the operating funds are provided by relevant government agencies. For instance, the consumer association in Heilongjiang province had 750 employees by 1996, all of whom were paid by government at various levels. Of its total budget of 1.5 million yuan in 1996, 600,000 yuan was provided by the Provincial Bureau of Administration of Industry and Commerce (*Gongshang guanli ju*), 100,000 yuan by the Provincial Bureau of Commodity Prices (*Wujia ju*), and the rest by the Department of Public Health, Bureau of Commodity Inspection, Bureau of Technology Supervision, and so forth.[19]

The China Consumers Association has achieved considerable success in many areas. It has sent investigation teams to visit stores and markets to inspect the quality of products and search out fake goods; it has also launched consumer-education programs through its mouthpieces—the *China Consumer Daily* (founded in 1984) and the journal *Chinese Consumer* (founded in 1995)—as well as through national and local mass media, schools, and other organizations. But its greatest achievement thus far is in representing consumers in lodging complaints against manufacturers and service providers. Because of its close links to the various government agencies mentioned above, the China Consumers Association was able to obtain compensation for consumers in nearly 90 percent of the cases. Encouraged by this high success rate and backed up by their increased awareness of consumer rights, consumers have filed a steadily increasing number of formal complaints, up from 8,000 in 1985 to over 700,000 in 1997.[20] Because of the state's support, the association's achievement has also helped to improve the government's image as the protector of consumers.

In addition to seeking help from government agencies and the semiofficial China Consumers Association, some people have begun to set up voluntary organizations to promote consumer protection. In 1996, a consulting company started accepting consumer complaints

in China) (Beijing: Zhongguo tongji chubanshe, 1994); and Zhou Rong, "Zhuanxin shiqi Zhongguo xiaofeizhe zuzhi de jiegou yu gongneng" (The structure and function of Chinese consumer organizations in the transitional period) (Master's thesis, Sociology Department, Beijing University, 1998).

19. Zhou Rong, "The Structure and Function of Chinese Consumer Organizations," p. 46.

20. See Beverly Hooper, "From Mao to Market," p. 33.

over a twenty-four-hour hot line and providing assistance such as finding good lawyers for consumers who sought compensation. Another
private foundation was established in Zhejiang province in 1995, with
the goal of detecting and fighting fake goods. By the end of 1998, several dozen voluntary organizations for consumer protection had
appeared, but they were mostly small and had very limited power and
influence.[21]

The "Wang Hai Phenomenon" and the Rule of Law in Consumption

To raise public awareness about faulty and fake products and to protect
their own interests, some individuals have taken bold and sometimes
dramatic action. Among them, Mr. Wang Hai deserves special attention
for his strategic strikes on shoddy and fake goods. According to Article
49 of the Protection of Consumer Rights and Interests Law passed by
the People's Congress in early 1995, a consumer who purchases a
faulty or fake product is entitled to be compensated by the seller in an
amount double the original price of the product. Inspired and encouraged by the new law, Wang Hai decided to attack the peril of fake
goods in his own way.

On March 25, 1995, Wang purchased two Sony earphone sets at
the state-owned Longfu Department Store in Beijing and verified that
they were fake. Unlike most other customers, who would try to return
fake products, he went back to the store and purchased the remaining
ten sets of fake earphones. He then asked the store to compensate him
with double the amount of the original price, citing the new law to support his claim. The store manager agreed to pay for the first two earphone sets that Wang had purchased but not for the other ten sets that
he had bought later with the knowledge that they were fake. The manager argued that Wang was trying to buy fake goods solely for the purpose of claiming the double compensation, and he accused Wang of
being a tricky hooligan who was cheating the store, manipulating the
law, and damaging the interests of the state (because the store is a state-
owned enterprise).

Wang went to law enforcement agencies for help but was similarly
turned down. He admitted to the media that before he purchased the

---

21. See Zhou Rong, "The Structure and Function of Chinese Consumer Organizations,"
pp. 35–36.

earphones he was already pretty familiar with the new law and planned to claim the double compensation in accordance with the law. He was therefore quite disappointed when his claim was denied both by the seller and by law enforcement agencies in Beijing. Later, in early September 1995, shortly after regulations entitled Methods of Implementing the Consumer Protection Law were issued by the Beijing municipal government, Wang returned to Beijing and resumed his adventure. He chose to buy fake goods from large department stores and shopping malls, because he felt that consumers would be angrier with these big retailers. From late September to late November 1995, he purchased fake products parading as famous brands (such as Gucci shoes and Goldlion belts) twelve times and successfully claimed double compensation in eleven cases, turning a tidy profit of more than 8,000 yuan ($1,000).[22]

The mass media responded quickly to Wang's adventures, covering his move from one city to another and rapidly turning him into a public hero. Wang's fame reached a peak when the Chinese government chose him to be among those to meet President Clinton during the latter's state visit to China in the summer of 1998. Later in the same year, he was also selected as one of twenty representative figures of the reform era to appear in the political documentary *Twenty Years, Twenty People*, aired by Chinese Central Television. However, Wang also ran into difficulties in his struggle against retailers of counterfeit goods and lost several legal battles, evidently because judges believed that Wang himself was cheating when he knowingly purchased fake goods.

The media sensation in turn transformed Mr. Wang's individual actions into a widespread "Wang Hai phenomenon." A number of individuals followed his example and purchased fake goods for the purpose of claiming double compensation. Some even set up companies to provide professional services in this respect. A man established a business for "beating fake goods" (by purchasing them and then claiming double compensation) in June 1996; by January 1997, he had spent 180,000 yuan on fake goods and had earned 140,000 yuan over that amount in compensation. He had a team of more than a dozen employees, each of whom could earn a net income of more than 1,000 yuan per month. Another consumer had gone further and set up a telephone

---

22. Liu Dong, "Mian dui Wang Hai" (Facing Wang Hai), *Zhongguo shangbao* (China Commerce Daily), December 9, 1995, p. 2.

line for free consultation, as well as a company to represent consumers in claiming the double compensation.

It is interesting that Wang Hai himself set up a firm in 1997 and worked for some large companies to investigate the forgery of the companies' products. By so doing, he shifted from representing ordinary consumers to representing big business.[23] As someone commented, "beating fake goods" itself had become a new business.[24] However, the most valuable outcome of the Wang Hai phenomenon was perhaps the awareness of consumer rights among ordinary consumers. As Wang Hai himself correctly concluded, "What I represent is a peculiar phenomenon that exists only in the era of openness and reform, that is, popularizing and raising the awareness of consumer rights."[25]

Wang's acts and the Wang Hai phenomenon led to public debates during 1995–98 that generated different opinions from retailers, consumer organizations, government agencies, lawmakers, law enforcement agencies, social scientists, and ordinary consumers. A series of interesting questions was raised: Is Wang Hai a hero fighting for consumer protection or a tricky person who just wants to turn a profit? Is it really cheating when a retailer sells fake goods? Is it also cheating when one purchases fake goods on purpose? Who should lead the fight to "beat fake goods"—individual consumers or the relevant government agencies? Should China import the notion of "punitive damages" and increase the amount of compensation? Some commentators argued that the emergence of the Wang Hai phenomenon actually revealed the impotence of government agencies and people's lack of confidence in the rule of law. It was equally urgent and important, many maintained, to perfect consumer protection laws and actually to implement those laws.[26] The consumer protection movement has therefore been part of the current reform toward a society ruled by law.

---

23. Tao Junfeng, "Wang Hai—wo wei 'diao min' zuo zongjie" (My conclusions on the tricky person Wang Hai), *Beijing Youth Daily*, January 20, 1999, p. 5.

24. Li Wanbing, "Jingcheng yongxian zhiye dajia" (The emerging profession of beating fake goods in Beijing), *Beijing Youth Daily*, January 10, 1997, p. 4. Extensive news coverage of the "Wang Hai case" in 1995 and then the "Wang Hai phenomenon" in 1996–98 can be found in issues of major newspapers and popular magazines during that period, such as *China Commerce Daily*, *China Industrial and Commercial Times*, *China Consumer*, *Beijing Youth Daily*, and *Southern Weekend*.

25. Tao Junfeng, "My Conclusions on the Tricky Person Wang Hai."

26. Some of these diversified views are nicely summarized in *Falü wenhua yanjiu zhongxin tongxun* (Newsletter of the Research Center for Legal Culture/Beijing), no. 10 (1996).

It should be noted that the media have played a double role by promoting both sides of consumerism. On one hand, both the China Consumers Association and individual consumers rely on the support of the mass media in the fight against abusive, cheating retailers and service providers. Almost all newspapers have long consumer columns; consumer hot lines on the radio publicize individual complaints and provide advice; television programs regularly air lengthy investigative reports regarding consumer protection issues; and there are a number of specialized journals on consumer protection. An interesting footnote in this respect is that, according to a high-ranking official in the China Consumers Association, the Wang Hai case was itself a dramatized event produced through cooperation between the association and the news media.[27]

Ironically, it is the same mass media that played an active role in promoting the fetishization of commodities and the endless desire for possessions in the first place, through its sensationalized coverage of fashion, modern lifestyles, and conspicuous consumption among the newly rich. A successful example is the *Purchasing Guide to Upscale Goods*, admittedly the most popular newspaper of its kind, which features special columns instructing consumers in fashion, taste, leisure activities, and interior decoration and provides up-to-date information on trendy goods. More important, the Chinese mass media have also been commercialized in the 1990s and have become an increasingly competitive business. According to a report of the Bureau of Information and Publications, there were 9,175 magazines (including 3 magazines directly imported from abroad) and more than 5,000 newspapers circulating on the market in 1998. Periodicals must fight hard to attract advertisements and readership. It is in this context that the media play the double role of promoting both sides of consumerism.

The Consequences and Implications of Consumerism: A Preliminary Assessment

It is a commonplace that consumerism is directly related to the performance of the economy in general and to the level of personal income in particular. The Chinese case is by no means an exception. The Chinese economy has been developing rapidly since 1978, with a

---

27. See the *Newsletter of the Research Center for Legal Culture*, no. 10 (1996).

double-digit growth rate on average over the past two decades. Under the impact of the Asian financial crisis in 1997, the growth rate fell to less than 8 percent for the first time in the reform era, but the economy as a whole was still considered strong. Like the economy, personal income has been increasing steadily, although it varies across different social groups in different periods. From 1978 to 1985, rural per capita income more than doubled, and as a result, rural per capita consumption also doubled. This, as mentioned above, made rural residents the major players in the first wave of mass consumption. However, the rate of income growth in rural areas slowed down after 1985 and has not recovered since. By contrast, urban per capita income increased much more rapidly between 1984 and 1988, and the trend continued in the next five-year period, albeit at a lower rate because of the economic retrenchment after 1989. It was during this period that—with a focus on household appliances and other nonfood commodities—the second wave of mass consumption swept over urban China. Beginning in 1992, urban per capita income began to rise rapidly, jumping from 1,826 yuan in 1992 to 3,830 yuan in 1995 and to 5,454 yuan in 1998. At the same time, personal savings grew to unprecedented levels: 23 billion yuan in 1992, 50 billion yuan in 1997, and more than 60 billion yuan by the spring of 1999.[28]

Although the rapid growth of the economy and the increase of personal income are obviously the main factors that made the rise of consumerism possible, a closer look from a sociopolitical perspective reveals that the rise of consumerism also involves a number of other factors. For instance, outside observers have been puzzled that so many people in China could afford to buy similar costly items at the same time, such as big-screen television sets and cellular phones in 1997–98. This contradicts the received wisdom that consumer choices are differentiated by differences in income. Here one must take into consideration that in Chinese society buying big consumer items is not just an individual matter; instead, it often involves the economic power of a larger kinship and *guanxi* network.[29] Moreover, the sign value of some status-related commodities is exploited to its maximum by people who

---

28. For a more comprehensive analysis of the link between economic growth and consumer revolution in China, see Linda Chao and Ramon Myers, "China's Consumer Revolution."

29. Bin Zhao dubs this feature "Confucian consumerism." See Zhao, "Consumerism, Confucianism, Communism."

are trying hard to reposition themselves in the transitional period. For instance, it is common to see cellular phones being loaned among good friends or relatives. In short, the booming consumerism is not merely a reflection of the booming economy; rather, it also reflects the changing social system and facilitates further changes in the system, such as redrawing the boundaries between social groups, creating social space outside state control, and forming a new ideology.

You Are What You Purchase: The Symbolism of Consumption

The most obvious change that consumerism has wrought on Chinese society is its subversion of the existing socialist hierarchy established during the prereform period. Consumerism enables some people to redefine their social status in terms of consumption and lifestyle. In this connection, a well-known case of the early 1990s is particularly noteworthy.

On November 22, 1992, a motorcade led by six black Cadillacs and followed by more than twenty Mercedes-Benzes, Audis, and other luxury cars rolled toward Tiananmen Square from the eastern end of Chang'an Avenue, the most important thoroughfare in Beijing. A policeman who was directing traffic panicked when he first saw the motorcade because he had not received any notice from above that a presidential motorcade would pass his post. He was so panic-stricken, in fact, that he could not find the right end of his walkie-talkie when he tried to contact his superiors. By that time, the motorcade had passed under his nose. It was only after talking with colleagues from other posts that he discovered it was just a wedding motorcade for Mr. Shen, a young Beijing millionaire. This event attracted a lot of public attention precisely because the policeman misidentified Mr. Shen's private wedding motorcade as a government motorcade, a strong signal that the existing hierarchy was being undermined by the emerging power of private businesspeople.[30]

It turned out that Mr. Shen used to be a poorly educated and unemployed youth who was looked down upon by his peers and neighbors. He started a small retail business in the 1980s and soon made a fortune from it—a story typical of successful so-called *getihu*, a term that lit-

---

30. Gong Wen, "Guonei gaoxiaofei daguan" (Hyperconsumption in China), *Xiaofei zhinan* (Consumption Guide), no. 2 (1993), pp. 1–12.

erally means "individual households." Like Mr. Shen, a large number of *getihu* came from humble family backgrounds, had been unemployed, lacked good education, and may even have had troubled pasts. Faced with such disadvantages, these urban youth started private retail and service businesses in the early 1980s, and they became the first group of rich people in the cities. To improve their social status and secure their positions, these *getihu* were eager to show off their wealth through conspicuous consumption of fancy clothes, luxurious banquets, leisure activities, household appliances, gambling, and various forms of senseless competition. It was reported, for example, that one man spent 188,000 yuan for a dinner in order to outdo a rival, and in another case, a rich man covered the walls of his house with 10-yuan bills.[31] Because of their conspicuous spending habits, along with their somewhat negative personal backgrounds, such people became targets of criticism by the elite strata and the focus of public envy of almost all of society. Nevertheless, they did make a strong point through their consumption, namely, that in this new era of market-oriented reforms, money speaks louder than anything else. In most cases, one can buy both comfort and respect with money—a point made conspicuously, for instance, by Mr. Shen with his wedding motorcade, and a point most people (if not all) quickly accepted as the truth.

Starting in the late 1980s, popular magazines and weekend-edition newspapers repeatedly featured and sensationalized stories of conspicuous consumption among the newly rich. The composition of the newly rich, however, changed substantially after 1992, and so did the specific manifestations of conspicuous consumption. Shortly after Deng Xiaoping's south China tour in early 1992, all across the country members of the elite rushed to get into private business. Thousands of intellectuals, scientists, artists, government officials, and even high-ranking cadres quit their jobs, which not long before had been considered symbols of their social achievement. This was called *xiahai* ("jumping into the sea"—the sea of private business and commercial activities). An important psychological push for these people was the thought, "so many *getihu* have become rich, now it's our turn." Based on their personal connections in government or their areas of expertise, plus their education and brainpower, many of these newcomers succeeded in a short time and gained a new label—"private

---

31. Cao Liang, "Jixing xiaofei yousilu" (Worrying notes on unhealthy consumption), *Xiaofei jingji* (Consumer Economy), no. 4 (1993), pp. 33–34.

entrepreneurs"—that distinguished them from the *getihu* of the 1980s.

Private entrepreneurs and leaders of state-owned enterprises or firms came to constitute the backbone of the newly rich in the 1990s. Like their *getihu* predecessors, these newly rich are notorious for conspicuous consumption. This is particularly true of those in charge of government-sponsored businesses or state-owned enterprises, because it is much safer for them to spend public money under their control than to convert it into their private property (though many have done both, as is evident from the numerous corruption cases exposed by the Chinese media). However, the newly rich of the 1990s have shown more interest in learning to be the upper class through more refined and glamorous consumption. For instance, the best a *getihu* could do in the 1980s was to spend 188,000 yuan on a banquet; by the late 1990s, one of the basic qualifications for being rich in Shenzhen is to have a golf-course membership, which can run more than $100,000.[32]

In addition to the newly rich, young professionals (or the emerging "white-collar" class) who are better educated and well paid also actively use consumption as a means of status maintenance. These young professionals emerged along with the development of the market economy, especially with the expansion of joint-venture and foreign-owned businesses during the past decade. To prove and further secure their newly obtained social status and prestige, they have taken the construction of a different lifestyle most seriously. Unlike the newly rich, the young professionals do not (and probably cannot afford to) engage in mindless conspicuous consumption; rather, they tend to follow the changing trends of fashion and taste in the outside world closely.

As mentioned above, the phenomenon of tidal-wave consumption in the 1980s disappeared in the 1990s; in its place grew a much more differentiated consumer market. A direct result of this change is that people have become even more conscious of what consumption habits and lifestyle can do to one's social status. This social construct of consumption struck me deeply on two quite different occasions during my fieldwork in the summer of 1999.

The first was in a village in Heilongjiang province, where I found that the cost of financing a son's marriage had gone up again in comparison with what I had recorded the previous year—the highest cost

---

32. Personal interview in August, 1999.

of 30,000 yuan recorded in 1998 had become a must in 1999. This heavy economic burden inevitably falls on the shoulders of parents who feel morally obligated to get their sons married in style. When asked why, all my village friends answered that they would lose face and social status, not to mention the very prospect of getting their sons married at all, if they failed to follow the trend. Two months later, I went to a dinner at a country club in the southern city of Shenzhen, where an old friend went on for hours telling me of his new life since joining the world of golf. Country-club membership has been one of the most popular gifts private entrepreneurs bestow on government officials, according to him. When I tried to remind him that bowling used to be considered a high-class activity in Shenzhen several years ago,[33] he and his friends all laughed and insisted that golf was the only true sport for high-status people with good taste. I became convinced that whether they are in a remote village or the prosperous city of Shenzhen, people are uniformly conscious of the importance of consumption in defining their social status.

Consuming properly and stylishly has become so important that consumption know-how itself has become a commodity. As indicated above, a number of magazines and newspapers are devoted solely to consumption-related issues, and one can find consumption-related news reports, columns, and discussions in almost all the popular magazines and newspapers, not to mention various advertisements. An interesting article in a specialized newspaper, for instance, offers a long list of dress codes, matching brand-name clothes, shoes, wristwatches, belts, and bags with different people at different income levels.[34] One of the most recent examples in this connection is the popularity of a translated book—Paul Fussell's *Class: A Guide through the American Status System*. Tens of thousands of copies (including pirated copies) of this book were sold in early 1999, and it was regarded as the bible of lifestyle by many readers, particularly young people. As a result, several copycat books written by Chinese authors quickly appeared on the market, all with words such as "taste," "manners," and "status" in their titles, and they also sold well.[35]

---

33. For an interesting study of bowling in Shenzhen, see Gan Wang, "Cultivating Friendship through Bowling in Shenzhen," in *Consumer Revolution in Urban China*.

34. See *Jingpin gaowu zhinan* (Purchasing guide to upscale goods), June 7, 1995, p. 7.

35. For critical comments on the book's popularity in China, see Shen Hongfei, "Yiqie cong gediao kaishi" (It all starts with "class"), *Southern Weekend*, July 2, 1999, p. 17.

Although many in the elite insist that the differentiation of the consumer market symbolizes the maturity of Chinese economic reform, the expanding income disparity between the rich and poor and the increasing social inequality are quite alarming. The rural-urban gap in consumption continued to grow in the 1990s, as the rate of rural income increase fell far behind that of urban residents. And in cities, the reform of state-owned enterprises over the past three years has led to widespread unemployment, leaving workers disadvantaged in every aspect of social life including consumption. The unpleasant side of this differentiated consumer market was demonstrated graphically in Beijing shopping malls during the hottest days of summer 1997. When the temperature climbed above one hundred degrees, a strange group of visitors arrived at shopping centers every evening; they walked into the fancy malls in family groups, wearing slippers and pajamas, waving hand fans, and sometimes even bringing little stools with them. They did not come to buy anything, not even to window-shop; instead, they just wanted to cool off in the climate-controlled malls because they could not afford home air conditioners.[36] This unexpected and unusual "invasion" of fancy shopping malls by the urban poor shows that differences in consumption capabilities and styles have become a major way of measuring people and of distinguishing them from one another both socially and spatially.

During the summer of 1999, I also witnessed a middle-aged man standing in the middle of a narrow street with his bicycle, refusing to give up the road to a red BMW that was headed in his direction. He argued angrily with the driver of the car, shouting repeatedly, "Don't think you can do whatever you want just because you have a car!" Within a few minutes, the incident drew a crowd of more than a hundred onlookers; it also caused a long line of cars to form, jammed behind the BMW. What struck me was that most of the onlookers showed their sympathy and moral support for the bicyclist, despite the fact that his angry reaction was causing a serious traffic jam. Later I was told that the explosive growth in the number of private cars in Beijing had created serious tension between those who own cars and those who don't, as they all had to fight for space on the overcrowded streets. A sociologist friend joked that if there were another land-reform-like campaign in the future, it would be a struggle by bicyclists and bus riders against car owners.

---

36. See reports in *Beijing Youth Daily*, July 15, 1999, p. 1; and *Purchasing Guide to Upscale Goods*, August 22, 1997, p. B7.

The Power of Comfort: Social Space and Individual Freedom

While it sorts consumers into different social groups (and sometimes different spaces as well), consumerism also opens up new public spaces for individuals and helps free them from the previous dominance of communist ideology and collectivism. A significant change in public life during the postreform era has been the disappearance of frequent mass rallies, voluntary work, collective parties, and other forms of what I prefer to call "organized sociality," in which the state (through its agents) plays the central role. In its place are various newly emerged forms of private gatherings in public yet commercialized venues, such as shopping malls, restaurants, cafés, bars, and clubs. Unlike the previous "organized sociality," which emphasized the centrality of the state, official ideology, and the submission of the individual to an officially endorsed collectivity, the new sociality in these commercialized venues features the celebration of individuality and private desires in unofficial social/spatial contexts. The center of public life and socializing, accordingly, has shifted from state-controlled, larger public spaces (such as city squares, auditoriums, and workers' clubs) to smaller, commercialized arenas.

As James Farrer has noted, dance halls in Shanghai during the 1990s offered places of escape where customers could explore and display their desires, aspirations, and even identities through dancing. Also conducting research in Shanghai during the same period, Kathleen Erwin discovered that radio call-in shows and counseling hot lines provided ordinary residents a new public space to talk about their problems, express their emotionality, and by implication, expand their individual freedom in public life. My own research of McDonald's outlets in Beijing shows that imported fast-food restaurants provide another such arena that meets the increasing demand for a new kind of sociality outside state control, that is, the public celebration of individual desires and life aspirations as well as personal communications in a social context. However, consuming at McDonald's also addresses a new dimension of sociality, namely, the public embrace of modernity and foreign culture (this is further discussed below).[37]

---

37. See James Farrer, "Uncivil Society: Dancing in Shanghai in the 1990s"; Kathleen Erwin, "Heart-to-Heart, Phone-to-Phone: Family Values, Sexuality, and the Politics of Shanghai Advice Hotlines"; and Yunxiang Yan, "Of Hamburger and Social Space: Consuming McDonald's in Beijing," all in *Consumer Revolution in Urban China*.

In most cases, mundane and commercialized activities of consumption provide the concrete content, the specific form, and the particular space that make this new kind of sociality possible. The power of the comfort and joy that consumption activities normally generate obviously marks a sharp contrast to the collective activities of organized sociality during the prereform era. The ideology of consumerism, which simply encourages people to indulge themselves in the pursuit of personal happiness, also effectively dilutes the influence of communist ideology, which emphasizes personal sacrifice and ascetic values. Moreover, as described in the first part of this chapter, consumerism also awakens an awareness of individual rights, which in turn has sparked the consumer protection movement. It may not be a long distance from protecting one's consumption rights to protecting other areas of individual freedom. As a U.S. reporter recently noted, lawsuits against state-owned enterprises are "multiplying across China as ordinary people learn to stand up for their legal rights in a society long accustomed to not having any."[38] Clearly, the increased purchasing power of individual consumers can, to a certain extent, erode the power and authority of the state.

Basing her analysis on case studies of consumption in the volume that she has edited, Deborah Davis concludes that Chinese consumers' enthusiastic embrace of commercial opportunities and products has accentuated the role of individual choice and diversified the venues in which individuals from a broad spectrum of urban society socialize. Through a million repetitions in cities throughout China, these seemingly innocuous, apolitical transactions create the social preconditions for realigning institutional power and authority.[39] From the party leaders' perspective, this is actually an unexpected consequence of mass consumption and consumerism. Nevertheless, the expansion of commercialized social space and of consumerism-generated individual freedom also distracts the public's attention from politically sensitive issues to material comfort, which has to a great extent helped the CCP maintain political stability and regain legitimacy in post-1989 China.

38. Henry Chu, "China: Ordinary Citizens Learn to Stand Up for Their Rights," *Los Angeles Times,* October 1, 1999, p. A24.

39. See Deborah Davis's introduction in *Consumer Revolution in Urban China,* pp. 1–22.

Consumerism and Political Stability

After the tragic ending of the pro-democracy movement in 1989, for several years many outside observers kept predicting that the CCP would not survive the simultaneous crises of economic difficulties, social discontent, and lack of legitimacy. Actual events demonstrated the contrary: the CCP leadership quickly regained political control, maintained social stability, and after 1992, restarted the engine of economic development. By the Fifteenth Party Congress in 1997, the CCP had completely reconsolidated its power and launched more aggressive market-oriented reforms. Among the many factors that contributed to the stability after 1989, consumerism, in my opinion, is an important one that has received little scholarly attention.

It is true that the post–1989 Chinese economy slowed down for a few years, and the second wave of mass consumption ended in 1989. Nevertheless, consumption became an even more important issue for leaders at all levels after 1989, because the top priority then was to alleviate social discontent and maintain stability. To achieve these goals, people's needs had to be met. It was in such a context that so-called benefits consumption (which meant the expansion of consumption in the name of employee benefits) played an active role in easing the political emergency. I observed during my fieldwork in 1991 that the living conditions of most people had improved. The improvement derived not only from wage raises but also from various bonuses and allowances distributed within the work unit. On top of these bonuses and allowances, material goods and money were distributed in the name of work benefits in three major ways.

First, consumer goods were distributed by work units to employees during holidays, especially the Chinese New Year. Although this had been practiced before 1989, it had never been so substantial in terms of the quantity and variety of goods. During the holiday seasons of 1989 to 1992, work-unit leaders did their best to purchase and distribute holiday goods such as meat, fish, fruit, and beer; workers were equally busy transporting the goods home and then worrying about how to consume so much perishable food. To secure supplies, many work units went so far as to open their own farms in the countryside. These farms were dubbed *zhigong shenghuo jidi* (employee livelihood bases). The second channel of benefits consumption involved distributing high-quality goods in the name of "labor protection." The scope of labor protection goods was expanded to include wool uniforms, overcoats, blankets, electric ovens and rice cookers, Coca-Cola, and Nestlé coffee. The third way goods were distributed was by increasing the amount of existing allowances and setting up new categories of allowances. One of the most popular categories was a vacation allowance, which was given to those who did not take a paid vacation trip.[40] To ease the existing social tension, the central government had called on leaders at various levels to do some practical things for the masses (*wei laobaixing ban shishi*); benefits consumption was obviously one of these "buying-off" efforts, which, to a certain extent, indeed helped to cure the wound of 1989. This is also why "social stability" became a consensus between the party-state and the people, as shown repeatedly in social surveys made in the years after 1989.

As mentioned above, a large number of former cadres, intellectuals, and professionals quit their jobs and moved into the private sector in 1992–93, and the third wave of mass consumption arose in the same period. The consumption patterns and lifestyles of the newly rich and the newly emerged class of white-collar professionals attracted the attention of people from all walks of life. In an earlier review of structural changes in China, I noted four important changes in people's mentality: (1) more people seemed to accept the income gap as a natural consequence of the market economy; (2) being poor had become a disgrace, and many people would rather pretend they were successful and rich; (3) people were motivated by market competition and were driven to make more money by the sense of crisis; and (4) the role of ideology and politics in everyday life had further diminished (by the end of 1993, few people whom I interviewed wanted to recall anything about 1989). I concluded that a "Chinese dream" had emerged and implanted itself in the psyches of many people, thus contributing to the sociopolitical stability of the early 1990s.[41]

Looking at these issues in retrospect, I now realize that it was the possibility of and pursuit of consumption that offered the strongest material form of the Chinese dream. For those capable individuals who had gotten ahead, consumerism provided instant rewards. It was not by accident that during the same period reports of conspicuous consump-

40. For a detailed account, see Huang Weiting and Li Fan, *The Riddle of Consumption in Contemporary China*, pp. 143–69.

41. Yunxiang Yan, "Dislocation, Reposition and Restratification: Structural Changes in Chinese Society," in *China Review 1994*, ed. Maurice Brosseau and Lo Chi Kin (Hong Kong: Chinese University Press, 1994), pp. 15.1–15.24.

tion filled the Chinese mass media. For less fortunate people, consumerism offered a whole new set of life aspirations and motivated
them to work harder. More important, when consumerism began to take
its full shape in the early 1990s, it encountered little criticism or resistance from either official or intellectual circles. Although a discussion of
the loss of humanistic spirit emerged during the high tide of commercialization,[42] it never reached beyond the small circle of elite intellectuals. The triumph of consumerism has drawn the public's attention away
from political and ideological issues, overshadowed the increased social
inequality and widespread corruption, and eased the legitimacy crisis
facing the CCP after 1989. Furthermore, the state's direct involvement
in the consumer protection movement, exemplified by its control over
and support of the China Consumers Association, has improved its
image as the ultimate judge of consumer disputes and the most powerful protector of ordinary consumers. This in turn also contributes to
political stability. It is no wonder that the party-state has shown tremendous tolerance toward consumerism since 1989 and by 1999 has begun
to recognize its importance in the economy and society openly.

Consumption and the Global Link

Finally, consumption of imported material goods and cultural products
has, on the one hand, provided the majority of ordinary people with a
direct link to the outside world and, on the other hand, raised some
nationalist concerns. During the prereform era, ordinary people rarely
saw imported goods from the West (I do remember, however, consuming brown sugar from Cuba during the late 1960s), and until the early
1980s, the state tightly controlled retail sales of foreign goods. In 1982,
for instance, the municipal government of Guangzhou officially prohibited *getihu* from selling imported goods.[43] Ordinary customers
knew little about imported goods, just as they lacked knowledge of the
outside world in general. Thus, it appeared strange to people when, on
March 10, 1980, Chinese Central Television aired the first advertise-
ment for a foreign product (a Citizen wristwatch). Many viewers called
in to protest, and some thought that broadcasting a television commercial for a Japanese company was a great shame.[44] However, within a

---

42. See articles in *Dushu* (Reading), no. 3 (1994).
43. See *Xin zhoukan* (New Weekly), no. 22 (1998), p. 27.
44. See *New Weekly*, no. 6 (1999), p. 40.

few years, Chinese customers found themselves making every effort to purchase Japanese color television sets and refrigerators; foreign goods have continued to grow in favor ever since, from household appliances, cosmetics, and soft drinks to toothpaste and laundry detergent.

Although Chinese manufacturers had taken back the domestic market for color television sets, microwave ovens, and washing machines by the early 1990s, the influence of foreign goods only increased and expanded to encompass almost all aspects of everyday consumption.[45] It was reported that imported fax machines and videotape recorders took 98 percent of the market share in China, and foreign cellular phones took 80 percent. At the same time, popular Chinese brand names were either defeated or bought out by foreign companies: Coca-Cola and Pepsi bought out seven of the eight leading Chinese soft drink brands, and more than 70 percent of the beer brewers were bought out by foreign companies. Although it caused a new round of national debate about the fate of the domestic film industry, the Chinese government finally decided to allow Kodak to purchase six Chinese film manufacturers in 1998, leaving Lekai the only domestic brand on the market. The competition between domestic and imported products was so severe that it was proclaimed "a war without gun smoke."[46]

For ordinary consumers, the influx of imported goods opened a completely new horizon of consumption and also brought in new cultural values that in turn could influence their lives. Pop music from Hong Kong and Taiwan, Hollywood movies, the NBA, and World Cup soccer games were among the "hot items" of cultural consumption sought by the majority of ordinary consumers. A *Titanic* ticket sold for 80 yuan (approximately $10) at state-owned theaters in 1998—about one-fourth of a worker's monthly wage. As in other parts of the world, Michael Jordan was the ultimate hero for Chinese sports fans, and his retirement became the cover story of many magazines and newspapers in early 1999.[47] Another interesting example came in May 1999 when

---

45. Zhao Bo, "Xingxing sese yang xiaofei" (Varieties of consumption of foreign goods), *Shichang jiage* (Market Price), no. 3 (1994), p. 9.

46. Wang Yuxian and Lin Yang, "Guohuo yu yanghuo: Meiyou xiaoyan de zhanzheng" (National products versus foreign products: A war without the smoke of gunpowder), *Shidian* (Perspectives), no. 6 (1996), pp. 16–18.

47. For instance, *Beijing Youth Daily*, one of the most popular newspapers, published reports and news on Jordan's retirement almost daily between January 13 and January 27, 1999. Other printed media also covered the event extensively.

Chinese Central Television canceled its scheduled broadcast of the NBA games as a protest against the NATO bombing of the Chinese embassy in Belgrade. A large number of viewers called in to complain, insisting that sports should have nothing to do with politics. This is in sharp contrast to the above-mentioned incident in 1980 when people called to protest the broadcast of advertisements for foreign products.

The long-term and subtle influence of these imported cultural products has yet to be explored. For example, during my 1991 field-work, I found that when the U.S. television detective series *Hunter* was aired in China, it introduced the notion of individual rights and legal knowledge to Chinese audiences. A man in the village where I was conducting fieldwork, for instance, refused to allow local policemen to search his house without a search warrant, and when his attempt failed, he filed a complaint with the county government; he told me that he had learned how to do all this from watching *Hunter*.

Consumption of imported material goods also carries social meanings. As I note elsewhere, when the fast-food giant McDonald's entered the Beijing market, local customers flooded into the restaurants to taste American cuisine. As a result of constant interaction between McDonald's management and local customers, the fast-food outlets have been transformed into middle-class establishments where consumers from different social backgrounds can, in addition to dining, linger for hours, relaxing, chatting, reading, enjoying the music, or having parties. Through these activities, Chinese customers redefine the concept of fast food and use McDonald's restaurants as a bridge to bring them the experience of consuming a Chinese version of American food culture and, in a larger sense, to link them with the outside world.[48]

The influx of foreign goods and transnational capital, however, has also generated local resistance and nationalistic reactions. Thus far, there have been a number of nationwide discussions on the "crisis of domestic products" in the mass media, all of which were triggered by the unpopularity of domestic electronic appliances, automobiles, computers, cosmetics, fast food, and soft drinks. Domestic manufacturers also appeal to consumers' nationalistic sentiment in marketing. For instance, in March 1996, Red Sorghum—a chain of noodle shops that specialized in country-style lamb noodles—opened its first outlet on

---

48. Yunxiang Yan, "McDonald's in Beijing: The Localization of Americana," in *Golden Arches East: McDonald's in East Asia*, ed. James L. Watson (Stanford: Stanford University Press, 1997), pp. 39–76.

Wangfujing Street, immediately across the street from what was then McDonald's flagship restaurant. The manager of the Red Sorghum company announced at the same time that twelve more shops would be opened in Beijing by the end of the year, all of which were to be situated beside McDonald's outlets. "We want to fight McDonald's," the manager claimed, "we want to take back the fast-food market."[49] In Shenzhen, another fast-food restaurant, Happy Chopsticks, adopted "Chinese people eat Chinese foods" as the leading slogan in its market promotion.[50]

These discussions and nationalistic commercials by local industries, however, seem to have had little effect on the actual practice of consumption. According to a 1994 Gallup survey, of the eight brand names recognized by over 50 percent of Chinese consumers, only one—Tsingtao beer—is a domestic product. The Japanese brands Hitachi, Panasonic, Toshiba, and Toyota take the lead, and the remaining three are American: Coca-Cola, Mickey Mouse, and Marlboro cigarettes.[51] A similar survey in 1997 showed the continuing popularity of foreign goods but also revealed that the influence of U.S. brands seemed to have surpassed that of Japanese brands. Among the top five brands, Coca-Cola, Jeep, and Shoulder to Shoulder all were of U.S. origin; the other two were Panasonic and Santana cars (produced by Shanghai Volkswagen).[52] To further test the degree of nationalism in patterns of consumption, a survey agency conducted a three-year-long investigation (1996–98), which found that "Beijing residents in general tend to regard the purchase of foreign goods as a personal choice and do not link it to moral judgments such as 'not being patriotic' or 'being the slaves of foreigners.'"[53]

---

49. Anonymous, "Honggaoliang yuyan zhongshi kuaican de qushi" (The Red Sorghum predicts the trend of Chinese fast food), *Zhongguo jingying bao* (Chinese Business) June 11, 1996.

50. Liu Guoyue, "Shenzhen kuancan shichang jiqi fazhan" (The fast-food market in Shenzhen and its development), *Zhongguo pengren* (Chinese Cuisine), no. 8 (1996), pp. 20–22.

51. Gallup Organization, *China: Nationwide Consumer Survey* (Princeton: Gallup Organization, 1995).

52. Zhang Qin, "Gailuopu diaocha: Zhongguo jiating xiang mai shenme?" (Gallup survey: What do Chinese families want to buy?" *Zhongguo shangjie* (Chinese Business World), no. 2 (1998), pp. 16–19.

53. Hai Ping, "Zhongguohuo da minzu pai: Shuiren hecai?" (Chinese products playing the card of nationalism: Who is cheering?), *Zhongguo qingnian bao* (China Youth Daily), April 2, 1999, p. 6.

This marks a sharp contrast to the radical movements to boycott foreign goods that swept Chinese cities in the early twentieth century, in which the masses were mobilized to save the country through consumer nationalism. It is clear that, in the 1990s, Chinese consumers tend to emphasize their own satisfaction with the goods and services they purchase more than anything else, which is yet another sign of the initial triumph of consumerism in Chinese society.

To summarize, there have been three waves of mass consumption during the past two decades, and each of them has brought further political and social consequences. By the end of the 1990s, a consumer revolution had occurred in urban China, and consumerism had replaced communist doctrine to become the paramount cultural ideology of contemporary Chinese society. Along with the flow of material goods and cultural products, consumerism had changed consumers' spending patterns, increased their awareness of individual rights, served as a new mechanism of social differentiation, linked consumers to the outside world, and played a role in promoting political stability in post–1989 China. Thus far, consumerism has overall played a more positive than negative role in China's transition toward a free-market economy and a more open society. But it has also opened a Pandora's box of new social perils, such as the fetishization of money, the commodification of personal relations, and the widespread phenomenon of corruption.

As mentioned at the beginning of this chapter, the CCP has for the first time officially recognized the crucial importance of consumption in stimulating economic growth. This may well indicate an important shift from a production-oriented to a consumption-oriented economy and lead to the further development of consumerism in Chinese society. If this is the case, the consumption-related social phenomena discussed in this chapter will continue to develop, and more questions will arise. For instance, as more and more consumers stand up to fight for their individual rights, will the consumer protection movement come to play a stronger role in domestic politics? If consumption continues to separate individuals socially and spatially, can it still help the state in maintaining social stability, or might it have the opposite effect? Is it possible that the new policy of encouraging consumption will exacerbate the widespread corruption among power holders at all levels of society, as consumption of public funds has been one of the strongest forces driving mass consumption since the early 1980s? Thus far, the consumer

consumer protection movement is confined to the cities, but what will happen when it reaches the vast majority of Chinese peasants? Whatever the answers to these questions prove to be, the politics of consumerism will surely play an important and unprecedented role in Chinese society in the twenty-first century.

Gender and Nationalism in China at the Turn of the Millennium

Susan Brownell

In the early hours of May 8 (Beijing time), 1999, three U.S. bombs ripped into the Chinese embassy in Belgrade during NATO's air strikes against Yugoslavia. Twenty people were injured, and three people, all journalists, were killed. The dead were 48-year-old female Shao Yunhuan and a young married couple, 31-year-old Xu Xinghu and his 28-year-old wife, Zhu Ying. They were quickly hailed as "revolutionary martyrs." The incident sparked mass anti-U.S. demonstrations, apparently led by university students, in cities across China, including Beijing, Shanghai, Guangzhou, Chengdu, Chongqing, Shenyang, Nanjing, Changsha, Xiamen, Lanzhou, Hefei, Jinan, and Hong Kong. The demonstrations in front of the U.S. embassy in Beijing were particularly vitriolic, with as many as 100,000 students and residents shouting slogans; holding up photos, placards, and banners; pasting up posters; throwing objects; and harassing and spitting at foreigners.

Much has already been written about these demonstrations, but very little has been said about the role played by gender symbolism in them.[1] Nor has a connection been drawn between these demonstrations and the finals of the Women's World Cup soccer tournament in Pasadena two months later, in which the United States defeated China

The research on sports in 1987–88 was supported by the Committee on Scholarly Communication with the PRC, funded by the U.S. Information Agency. The research on fashion models in the summer of 1995 and the spring of 1996 was funded by a University of Missouri-St. Louis Research Award and a University of Missouri Research Board Award. I want to express my gratitude to Tyrene White for conceiving the topic of gender and nationalism in China, inviting me to write about it, and thoughtfully working with me to develop it.

1. I wish to express my thanks to Jeff Wasserstrom for drawing my attention to the role of gender in the May demonstrations. My analysis of the anti-NATO demonstrations is very much a product of our ongoing exchange of ideas about gender and nationalism.

5–4 on penalty kicks after a hard-fought, scoreless game and overtime play. A description of the role of gender in these two events, then, will serve as the opening to this essay on gender and nationalism in China.

Why gender *and* nationalism? An initial commonsense reaction might cause a reader to wonder why gender and nationalism together form an important enough topic to warrant inclusion in a book that attempts to give a broad overview of current political, social, and economic issues in China. The central point of this essay is that gender must be taken into account in understanding popular nationalism in China, because gender issues evoke deeper, more visceral emotions than any others. A widespread, generally unstated assumption holds that "nations" are abstractions that do not have a gender, and their affairs are conducted by predominantly male heads of state, male military forces, and male businessmen who are too busy conducting important business to think about their own masculinity. In fact, as is clear in the images of President Bill Clinton discussed below, the perceived masculine potency (or lack thereof) of heads of state influences popular perceptions of their actions. This chapter argues that gender constitutes a fundamental structure in Chinese nationalism that is often ignored in academic and journalistic accounts because it is partly buried and not as immediately accessible as other aspects of nationalism that are more clearly enunciated in official ideologies and public statements (although it is present there, too, if one looks for it). If you scratch the surface of almost any relationship between self-consciously "Chinese" people and others, gender is not far below. In reality, nations are only abstract categories, and the relations between them actually consist of interactions between living people who bring their self-concepts with them to the bargaining table. Grasping these self-concepts must be the starting point for any real mutual comprehension. Thus, all those guides for Western businessmen on "how to do business with the Chinese" that emphasize "cultural differences" in negotiating style are missing the main point, since they do not start with the central point that being Chinese and being a man have certain meanings that will influence the way Chinese men view other men from other nations (the same goes for women, of course). This chapter outlines how the meanings of being a "man" and being "Chinese" have changed over the last century, and particularly in the 1990s; it also outlines how these meanings are counterposed to the meanings of being a "woman" and being "Chinese."

The May 8 Demonstrations

Two of the three journalists killed in the Belgrade bombing were women, and they died on the day before Mother's Day. Shao Yunhuan was a wife (her husband, a diplomat working in the Belgrade embassy, was seriously injured in the attack) and a mother (her son had been studying at a Yugoslavian university until the bombing began and he returned to China). Zhu Ying had been married only a year before, and while she was not yet a mother, reports portrayed her as soon to be one: fellow journalists reported that during her last talk with her husband, 15 minutes before the bombing started, she had mentioned her plan to have a baby during their vacation this year. On the whole, the major newspapers devoted much more attention to the two female deceased than to the one male.[2] This seemed to be an attempt to present the event with the strongest possible moral outrage; it thus gives us insight into the concepts of morality that influenced Chinese understanding of the event. Particular outrage was attached to the images of murdered mothers and daughters. The front-page editorial commentary in the *People's Daily* on May 10 denounced U.S. hegemonism with the words, "Because of this violent action, completely lacking in humanity, on this Mother's Day three Chinese mothers lost their children, and a Chinese child lost his mother." Popular reactions echoed this official statement. For example, the *China Daily* quoted one Web user on the large Chinese Web site netease.com who posted a note reading, "Today is mother's day, but NATO's airstrike has claimed a mother from her child, and has taken many children from their mothers." Another posting (not reported in the Chinese media) suggested, "We'll blow up their mothers, too!"

Women's organizations were particularly active in the demonstrations. On March 26, the Capital Women's Journalists Association had been the first Chinese journalists' organization to oppose the NATO

---

2. The discussion of the Chinese media coverage and popular reactions to it is based on a survey of *China Daily*, *Renmin ribao* (People's Daily, overseas edition), and *Guangming ribao* (Guangming Daily) from May 10 to May 13, 1999. The English-language *China Daily* is obviously intended to sway an Anglophone audience; the *People's Daily* is the official mouthpiece of the Communist Party; the *Guangming Daily* targets intellectuals, and was particularly significant in this case since two of the deceased were its reporters. In addition, the archives of the Web sites of H-Asia (www.h-asia.msu.edu) and of *China News Digest* (www.cnd.org), including *Huxia wenzhai*, the Chinese-language digest, were surveyed. The H-Asia archives surveyed included David Cowhig's summaries of postings from the Chinese-language Web site netease.com.

bombings. In a May 1999 letter to the editor of the *China Daily*, its vice-director called the bombing a barbaric act of "flagrant violence against women and human lives and violation of human rights."[3] She recalled Shao Yunhuan as "a filial daughter and a caring mother, but mostly a responsible journalist. . . . NATO murderously deprived her of her life, her son of his mother, her husband of his wife, her parents of their daughter. What a present they have given to a Chinese family on Mother's Day!"[4] She further observed that Chinese women journalists had learned from the West to monitor domestic violence, only to have Western hypocrisy exposed by this "relentless international violence against women." Over five hundred women gathered at the Women's Activities Center in Beijing, and the Women's Federation issued a statement containing the exhortation, "In the names of mothers, wives, and daughters, we cry out: peace-loving women of the world, mobilize! . . ."[5] These are only a few examples of the multitude of references to mothers and familial relationships that permeated media coverage of the events.

Jeffrey Wasserstrom, a historian and expert on student demonstrations who happened to be in Beijing and Shanghai at the time of the demonstrations, observed that by far the dominant television image of those days was that of Zhu Ying's father weeping over her body when he arrived in Belgrade to retrieve it.[6] He was reported to have repeatedly tried to wipe a bloodstain off her face, murmuring, "Daughter, dad is here to take you home." A vivid still photograph of this event appeared on the front page of the May 10 *China Daily* and on page four of the *People's Daily*, and a different version appeared on page three of the *Guangming Daily*. In the first photo, Zhu Ying's body lies in the foreground on a steel gurney, covered with a sheet that is pulled

---

3. Capital Women's Journalists Association, "Cowardly, Barbaric Act," letter to the editor, *China Daily*, May 10, 1999, p. 4. Interestingly, a report on the association in the May 10 *People's Daily* omits the mention of violence against women and calls the bombing simply a "trampling of human lives." The *People's Daily* did not foreground gender as much as the other two papers surveyed, which is consistent with its position as an official Party medium that is less reflective of popular sentiment than other media.

4. Xiong Lei, "NATO Killing of Innocent Feeds Silent Hypocrisy," letter to the editor, *China Daily*, May 10, 1999, p. 4.

5. "Zhongguo xinwenjie tongdao xunzhi tonghang" (Chinese journalism circles sadly mourn colleagues who died in the line of duty), *Renmin ribao* (People's Daily), May 10, 1999, p. 2.

6. Jeffrey N. Wasserstrom, "Student Protests in Fin-de-Siecle China," *New Left Review*, no. 237 (September–October 1999).

back to reveal her head. Her face, in profile, seems to have a sad, peaceful expression, but there is a large dark stain over her left eye. Zhu's father stands behind her, his face twisted in grief, his right hand stretched gently and protectively across her body. Two unidentified men, whom we might guess to be officials on the mission to Belgrade, stand behind him, one on each side. The man on his left has a firm, supportive grip on Zhu's father's forearm and looks at him with a hard, straight-lipped expression. The man on his right has eyes downcast with uncontainable emotion. The photo seems to convey the bitter grief of three men for the single fallen young woman whom they were unable to protect. To a U.S. audience, this public presentation of a father's grief and the television and photo images of the dead bodies (including in situ photos of the couple's twisted, blood-covered bodies in the debris of the embassy) might seem to be sensationalization of "private" moments. However, such emotions are not quite so "private" in China, where the familial and the national are envisioned as occupying the same space. This merging of the personal, the familial, and the national has characterized popular Chinese nationalism in the periods that I have studied, the 1980s and 1990s, and I suspect it has a long provenance, perhaps traceable to the Confucian conception of the patriarchal family as a microcosm of the state. It is also evident in the common practice of publishing diaries (such as the unfinished "War Diary" of Xu Xinghu and Zhu Ying, which was rapidly published after their deaths), letters from people involved in national events, and letters or telegrams from state leaders to individuals.

Several of these letters were published after the May 8 bombing. Shao Yunhuan's bedridden, 76-year-old father and Zhu Ying's younger sister wrote open letters, which were published in newspapers. Of particular interest are the letters written to President Clinton by Zhu Ying's father, Zhu Fulai, and Shao Yunhuan's son, Cao Lei, which were also published in whole or in part. While he was in Belgrade to retrieve the bodies, Zhu Fulai wrote to President Clinton as one father to another, recalling his own happy memories of his daughter and family, imagining that Clinton felt the same when he was with Hillary and Chelsea. "What did my daughter and her husband ever do to you?" he asked.[7] This letter was reprinted in full in the *Guangming Daily* under the title "A letter to Chelsea's father, U.S.

---

7. Bian Ji, "Journalist's Father Writes to Clinton," *China Daily*, May 11, 1999, p. 2.

president Clinton," and it was signed "Zhu Ying's and Xu Xinghu's father, Zhu Fulai."[8]

The image of Bill Clinton as a man played a key role in the protests. On the one hand, Zhu Fulai's letter appealed to Clinton's conscience as a father and a husband. In other contexts, however, Clinton's sex scandals and impeachment hearings were invoked to draw parallels between his sexual insatiability and U.S. hegemonism. Jeff Wasserstrom saw one poster at Beijing University, in English, that accused Clinton of being a "bi-raper" because first he had ravished Monica Lewinsky and then, unsatisfied, set out to rape the world. In one of the Beijing demonstrations in the embassy district, Wasserstrom saw a very large, very phallic model of a cruise missile. He was also told of a placard that appealed to Monica to "use her mouth" to distract Clinton from interfering in the Balkans. Wasserstrom notes that his observations fit the theme that will be discussed further below: In China over the last century, in times of national crisis, there has been a tendency to focus on the damage done to female Chinese bodies by foreign men, and the passivity or impotence of Chinese men.[9] In response to this feeling of impotence, one of the angry reactions on the Chinese Web site netease.com suggested having sexual relations with several generations of Clinton's family as an effective revenge.

The gender images that dominated the protests were ones that appealed to the righteous anger of the father or son whose daughter or mother has been brutally taken from him. Much more media attention was devoted to the grief of Zhu Ying's father, Zhu Fulai, and Shao Yunhuan's son, Cao Lei, than to any other relatives, including the mothers, sisters, and husband. This was symbolically reinforced by the ceremonies accompanying the return of the cremated ashes to their homeland. Zhu Fulai and Cao Lei went to Belgrade to retrieve the ashes, and when the mission returned to Capital Airport in Beijing, their exit from the plane was covered by the media. Following a special guard of two uniformed soldiers holding bayonets, Cao Lei descended first, carrying the box of his mother's ashes draped in a Chinese flag. Then Zhu Fulai followed, heavily burdened with a large box cradled in each arm, one for his daughter and one for his son-in-law, both draped in flags. The *People's Daily* carried a photo of 19-

8. "Zhi Qieerxide fuqin Meiguo zongtong Kelindunde xin," (A letter to Chelsea's father, U.S. president Clinton), *Guangming ribao*, May 11, 1999, p. 4.

9. Wasserstrom, "Student Protests in Fin-de-Siecle China."

year-old Cao Lei in the waiting room at the Belgrade airport, bent over the box of ashes in his lap, "silently weeping."[10]

Thus, the primary victims in the media coverage were women, and the primary bereaved were men: a father and a son. That the grief was portrayed from the positions of fathers and sons is not surprising if we pay attention to the composition of the protesting crowds, which appear to have been mostly male. In the photos of protesters that accompanied these reports, the ratio of clearly visible male faces to female faces is roughly 10 to 1. Such gender imbalance is typical of public gatherings in China, including sports spectatorship, and was also typical of the Chinese fans at the Women's World Cup soccer games. The appeal to fathers and sons would have resonated with this male audience.

The Third Women's Soccer World Cup

Almost exactly two months after the embassy bombing, on July 10, the Chinese and U.S. women met in the final game of the third Women's Soccer World Cup. This was the latest stage in a rivalry that went back to the first World Cup, held in China in 1991, which was won by the United States, whereas the Chinese lost in the quarterfinals. In 1996, the same country had taken Olympic gold in Atlanta; China settled for silver. In 1998, China had lost to the United States in the Goodwill Games, held in New York. In 1999, China had defeated the United States 2–1 in contests leading up to the World Cup, and entered the final game as the favorite. Seven Chinese players had been named to the tournament all-star team, but only five U.S. players were. Sun Wen had tied for the title of top scorer of the tournament. "It is very, very important that we win now, for ourselves and for China," she told Xinhua news agency.[11] Sun Wen was followed by the same kinds of mobs as Mia Hamm, the U.S. star, and Chinese fans were obvious at all of China's games. During the semifinal match with Norway, some fans held up placards reading, "Little Sisters, when it's time to kick, just kick" (*meimei ni gai chujiao shi jiu chujiao*). The night before the final game, the team had received a phone call from President Jiang Zemin, who told them, "You have demonstrated fully the aspiration to win honors for our motherland."[12] Millions of Chinese awoke in the early morning hours to watch the live

---

10. *Renmin ribao*, "Hui jia" (Coming home), May 13, 1999, p. 3.

11. *China Daily*, "Sun: A Student, Poet, Singer, Scorer," July 9, 1999, p. 10.

12. *China Daily*, "Women's Soccer Team 'Marvellous,'" July 12, 1999, p. 1.

broadcast, which started at four in the morning, Beijing time. Security around the U.S. embassy in Beijing was tightened. During the finals in the Rose Bowl, the Chinese fans unfurled a huge five-star flag in the stadium and held up placards with such slogans as "Glorious little sisters" (*meimei guangrong*). Minutes after the game, Vice-Premier Li Lanqing called to express congratulations for their efforts. Later, a team photo was taken with President Clinton. Soon after the final, Clinton sent a letter to President Jiang Zemin expressing congratulations. Jiang returned a reply on the same day and congratulated Clinton on the victory, praising the skills, sportsmanship, and friendship of the U.S. women. Upon their return to Capital Airport, the Chinese team was met in the drizzle by two hundred fans who unfurled a 60-square-meter Chinese flag. On July 13, the team members were heralded in a grand ceremony at the Great Hall of the People, attended by President Jiang, Li Peng, and other high officials (Premier Zhu Rongji sent a letter in his absence). In his address to the team, Jiang observed, "The team displayed well our nation's long-cherished virtues: unity to combat differences, independence, self-confidence, hard work and a spirit to go all-out to make ourselves strong."[13] There were no reports of riots or aggressiveness against the U.S. embassy. Although there were some Chinese complaints of unfair treatment, the Chinese team and spectators were generally resigned to the results. Sun Wen and Coach Ma Yuan'an both attributed the U.S. victory to luck.

In May, when Clinton had tried to place a direct telephone call to Jiang immediately after the embassy bombing, it had been refused—on the other hand, Boris Yeltsin's call was not only accepted but was front-page news in the May 11 *People's Daily*. That Clinton had tried to call was not even mentioned, although an article on page six conceded that he had sent a letter to Jiang on May 9. After the World Cup, however, the symbolic exchange of letters was reported in a timely and front-page fashion. The attention paid to the event by both Clinton and Jiang would seem to indicate that they recognized its deeper importance. Thus, U.S.-China relations returned to something of an equilibrium after the May 8 bombing, with an image not of Chinese women as passive victims of cruel U.S. aggression but rather of strong Chinese women nearly holding their own against a superpower that, ultimately, was just a little bit stronger and luckier—this time.

---

13. Jiang Yu, "State Accolade for Heroines," *China Daily*, July 14, 1999, p. 1.

Gender and Nationalism: An Overview

In the last decade, scholars have started to pay attention to how gender is intertwined with nationalism around the world and in China. This chapter understands gender in a broad sense as a system of cultural beliefs about manhood, manliness, and masculinity as they exist in complementary opposition to womanhood, womanliness, and femininity. Thus, it departs from the typical view of gender, which tends to concentrate more narrowly on the issue of sexual inequality in various realms of social life. Here, nationalism is also understood in the broad sense as a system of cultural beliefs about a certain kind of social grouping—the "nation-state"—and the sense of identity that emerges among those who feel that they belong to it. Nations are different from states: "state" refers to a complex form of social organization revolving around a centralized government, encompassing both agrarian empires such as Qing-dynasty China and industrialized nations such as the contemporary People's Republic of China. The modern nation-state is a relatively recent state formation that emerged in Europe and its colonies in the late eighteenth century and was introduced into China in the late nineteenth century. As it is used here, nationalism refers only to the modern nation-state and the loyalties attached to it: in this formulation, nations are cultural concepts, and it is believed that nations should be states and that they should hold formally equal status in a world order properly composed of other such states.[14]

National consciousness, or consciousness of nationhood, is often imagined in relation to other kinds of identity, such as diasporic, regional, ethnic, local, or sexual identities. Thus, mainland Chinese may conceive of themselves in opposition to categories such as "overseas Chinese," as parts of a larger region called "East Asia," or as members of a nation that embraces subnational categories, such as the Han majority and the ethnic minorities, or Northern Chinese and Southern Chinese. They may assume that all Chinese nationals are heterosexual unless they have been influenced by Western decadence. Most important, though, when they imagine themselves as a Chinese "nation," they place themselves in opposition to other nations, such as Japan and the United States. At the same time, they position their nation within a global culture that transcends national boundaries (and hence is some-

---

14. See James Townsend's definition of modern nationalism in "Chinese Nationalism," in *Chinese Nationalism*, ed. Jonathan Unger (Armonk, NY: M.E. Sharpe, 1996), p. 8.

times called "transnational culture"). Louisa Schein has labeled the latter process as "imagined cosmopolitanism," a process in which
Chinese imagine themselves as participants in a global culture through
their consumption of foreign objects and media and through their fantasies of the mobility made possible by the policies of "opening up" to
the outside world.[15] This imagined cosmopolitanism was evident in the
image, promoted in the Chinese press, of the Chinese women's soccer
team as the "eastern rose" whose rose-red-colored uniforms had won
over the hearts of the spectators in the Rose Bowl,[16] implying that they
were warmly welcomed onto the imagined world stage and that they
belonged there.

The point of this chapter is to demonstrate that notions about gender are integral to identities at whatever level they are conceived and
acted out. Thus, nations do have a gender relative to other nations,
states have a gender (usually male, although this may be expressed in
many different ways), and men (and women) conducting affairs of
state are influenced by gender in ways we are just now beginning to
understand. Moreover, notions of gender-in-the-nation permeate all
levels of social interaction, from international relationships all the way
down to the minutiae of everyday life. This chapter illustrates the fruit-
fulness of an approach that considers gender *and* nationalism for a better understanding of Chinese people and their relationships with the
rest of the world.

In writing this chapter, I have implicitly drawn on feminist and
postmodernist discussions of the difference between "subject" and
"object." A subject is a person who controls the terms of his own self-
identity; his consciousness of himself, or his subjectivity, is created
through contrasting himself with objectified "others" who are perceived to be separate and different. Feminists have used this distinction
to analyze the ways in which males create their own identity (subjectivity) by contrasting themselves with (objectifying) women. Since
men typically dominate the production of histories, mass media, and
popular cultural products, the male subject-position often predomi-
nates in public representations of gender. And to the extent that these
public representations are the dominant ones, women also accept them

15. Louisa Schein, "The Consumption of Color and the Politics of White Skin in Post-
Mao China," *Social Text*, vol. 41 (winter 1994), pp. 149, 159 n. 13.

16. Chen Shi, "Dongfang meigui fengzhong tingxiu" (Eastern rose, graceful and erect
in the wind), *Renmin huabao* (China Pictorial), September 1999, pp. 22–23.

and are influenced by them. Their own subjectivity, in other words, is strongly influenced by the way they are perceived and portrayed by men. In the discussion above, for example, it seemed that the portraits of the deceased journalists as daughters and mothers were largely drawn from the point of view of their grieving fathers and sons; in other words, they were drawn from a male subject-position (so they effectively moved the largely male audience). Somewhat surprisingly, the grieving mothers occupied a background position in these accounts and images. Even the female voices that were expressed echoed the same refrains. Likewise, the soccer fans, the majority of whom seemed to be male, characterized the players as "little sisters" and not as "older sisters," which would have given them a somewhat more superior position in the hierarchy.

This chapter pulls together the work of scholars in different disciplines who have described this process of subjectification/objectification at work in constructions of gender and nationalism in China. As will be seen, there is now a large body of postmodernist and feminist-inspired work that argues that the masculine Chinese identity has been established through using Chinese femininity as its complementary but subordinate opposite. As has been said of European nationalism, "It is as if man's subjecthood could only be attained at the cost of woman's subjection."[17] Recent scholarship has identified this structure in the relationship between gender and empire in the late Qing dynasty (1644–1911), through the period of nation-formation (the Republican era, 1912–49), continuing through the establishment of the Communist nation in 1949, and culminating with China on the eve of the new millennium. At this point, however, there is still something of a split in the field between the mostly male scholars who write about the more conventional history and political economy of nationalism and the mostly female scholars who have approached nationalism mainly through literary theory and film criticism. This has resulted in the failure of the conventional nationalist scholars to fully incorporate gender and feminist perspectives into their analyses, while the feminists have failed to fully extend their analyses outside of the realm of texts and films to include popular movements. The discussion in this chapter, then, tries to reconcile the two approaches. It ranges from official ideology to mass media to popular culture to everyday life, attempting to trace

---

17. Joan Landes, "Women and the Public Sphere: A Modern Perspective," *Social Analysis*, vol. 15 (August 1984).

some of the ways in which gender and nationalism form a thread that runs through many different levels of Chinese social life. By paying particular attention to a few key events that were not clearly controlled either by the state or by intellectuals, this chapter tries to portray the nature of a popular nationalism that is connected to official and intellectual nationalism but is not identical with them.

Gender and Empire: Filiality and Sacrifice

While the notion of the modern nation-state was emerging in eighteenth-century Europe and its colonies, the Qing empire (1644–1911) under the Qianlong emperor (r. 1736–99) was experiencing a period of relative stability, prosperity, and economic expansion. The Qing state, as embodied in the emperor, was gendered as yang, or male, in that the emperor was the most perfect example of the "body of yang power." As used by Angela Zito, the "body of yang power" refers to the (usually male) literatus who combined in one person the mastery of literacy (*wen*) and ritual (*li*), a mastery that imparted to him the authority to create the meanings (through texts) and bodily disciplines (through ritual performances) that governed the lives of the imperial subjects. This body is "yang" because, as the center of the civilizing influence and the initiator of ritual action, it occupies the active yang position in the yin-yang polarity (in which yin is the passive completer and yang the active initiator). Zito argues that, despite the metaphysical descriptions of yin and yang as perfectly balanced, imperial sacrifice tended to give precedence to yang over yin. Since yin-yang was used to model gender distinctions, these ritual practices therefore "gave concrete content to a Chinese notion of masculinity." The emperor was "a man among other men (and the perfection of yang masculinity)."[18] He provided a model for other men through two interrelated practices: filiality (*xiao*) and sacrifice. A son was obliged by the Confucian rules of filiality to honor his deceased father, grandfather, and ancestors through sacrifice. Thus, the highest ritual power resided in the role of son, through which a man received the grace of his ancestors and passed it on to the next generation. A son embodied the continuity of the lineage, and by sacrificing to his lineal ancestors he validated the authority granted to him

---

18. Angela Zito, *Of Body and Brush: Grand Sacrifice as Text/Performance in Eighteenth-Century China* (Chicago: University of Chicago Press, 1997). See especially pp. 6 and 149–50.

by his lineage. Because all men are sons, all men were in a position to perform the rituals of filiality that were largely denied to women.

In the Qing imperial court, the emperor's mother (the "empress dowager") typically possessed a great deal of power, and this was in part because the emperor expressed his filial piety in his affection and ritual respect toward his (living) mother as well as toward his (dead) father and grandfather. However, the empress dowager was not held up as an example to all women in the same way; not all women are mothers, and no other women were mothers of emperors. In this sense, like the chaste widow discussed below, she served as the yin-completer for the yang-filiality of her son, a man. In short, the role of the woman (mother) is mainly as a backdrop against which the son defines his identity (as a filial son)—a structure that, it is argued in this chapter, runs throughout Chinese nationalism in the twentieth century and was evident in the anti-NATO demonstrations in 1999. Filiality and sacrifice as both ideology and practice thus permeated social life in two ways. First, they structured gender relations in a thoroughgoing way. Second, they linked these gendered imperial subjects to the emperor and his court by portraying the emperor as the perfect example that all men should emulate.

But what about the body of yin power? Were there female ritual practices that exercised a civilizing effect owing to the strength of their moral virtue? One possible female correlate is the imperial state's practice of rewarding virtuous widows who epitomized female chastity by remaining unmarried after their husband's death or by committing suicide. It is possible to view the chastity of wives as the correlate of the filiality of sons; both were rewarded by Chinese rulers going all the way back to the turn of the first millennium A.D. The virtuous-widow cult reached its peak in the eighteenth to nineteenth centuries. The widow, or her family if she had died, received from the Ministry of Ritual a cash reward and the right to erect a memorial arch (*pailou*). That the widow's sacrifice was seen to benefit the empire is indicated by the fact that provincial governors such as Chen Hongmou (1696–1771) promoted it in frontier areas as an important measure in the "civilizing process" (*jiaohua*). Stories of widow suicides were recounted as examples of "local customs" and used by the gentry to represent their local area to the outside world.[19]

---

19. Susan Mann, "Widows in the Kinship, Class, and Community Structures of Qing Dynasty China," *Journal of Asian Studies*, vol. 46, no. 1 (1987), p. 49; Mark Elvin,"Female

If, in the imperial ideology, men were considered exemplary for carrying out the obligations of father and son, then women were rewarded for the virtue of self-sacrifice. It is possible to trace the continuance of variations on these complementary virtues throughout Chinese nationalism up to the 1990s.

Gender at the Borders of Empire

Gender played a role in the consolidation and expansion of the Qing empire—a role that was very different from that played by gender at the borders of the nations that were to follow the Qing. Intermarriage is not a strategy commonly used by nation-states in their relations with each other; much more common is protection of national female bodies against foreign incursion as if these bodies were national borders. Looking at gender thus provides a way to refine our understanding of the differences between the Qing empire and the nation-states that succeeded it.[20]

The Qing court utilized marriage as a political strategy for forming alliances. The Manchu conquerors who founded the Qing did so with the help of alliances with rival Manchu tribes, Mongols, and Chinese anti-Ming forces. While they were creating their empire, intermarriage between daughters of the paramount Aisin Goro clan and rival Manchu tribal leaders, Mongol princes, Chinese frontiersmen, and Chinese generals helped consolidate power. As the Manchu expanded into central and north Asia, daughters of emperors and princes were given to tribal leaders in marriage. The Manchu had conquered China with a system of social units called "banners": the conquering forces included eight each of Manchu, Mongol, and Chinese banners, in which less than 16 percent of the soldiers were of Manchu origin. Since the Manchu were a minority both within the conquering forces and within

---

Virtue and the State in China," *Past and Present*, vol. 104 (1984); William R. Rowe, "Women and the Family in Mid-Ch'ing Social Thought: The Case of Ch'en Hung-mou," *Late Imperial China*, vol. 13, no. 2 (December 1992), p. 18.

20. It is beyond the scope of this chapter to pursue this argument here, but there has been much debate about continuities and breaks between imperial and national ideologies in China. For two influential overviews, see James Townsend, "Chinese Nationalism," and Prasenjit Duara, "De-Constructing the Chinese Nation," both in Unger, *Chinese Nationalism*. This chapter makes the point that between empire and nation there were continuities in some of the underlying logic of gender relations, variations on themes that repeated over the century, but also some breaks in the way gender relations worked themselves out.

the Chinese empire that they now ruled, they had to protect themselves from assimilation. After 1655, all Manchu were forbidden to marry Han Chinese who were not enrolled in the Eight Banners.[21]

Nation-Formation:
Male Impotence and Female Suffering

As European ideas about nationalism were introduced into China in the late nineteenth century (often via Japan), Chinese intellectuals and statesmen began to come to terms with a new conception of the state. One of the first important schools of thought was Social Darwinism. The key figure in this development was Yan Fu, who translated Huxley's *Evolution and Ethics* and Spencer's *Principles of Sociology* into Chinese at the turn of the century. In Spencer, Yan Fu encountered the image of the nation as a biological organism struggling for survival among other like organisms. "A country is like a body," and in order to be strong, it must have citizens with strong bodies. This insight had the effect of shifting the focus on the relationship between state and subject from the more abstract ethical concerns of filiality and sacrifice toward more concrete, bodily metaphors. Thus, Yan Fu and other constitutional reformers such as Kang Youwei and Tan Sitong argued that a key reason for China's weakness lay in the physical weakness of Chinese women, who were kept bound-footed and in a condition of virtual servitude. They contrasted the Chinese woman with women from Western nations, who were said to be strong, natural-footed, and nearly equal to Western men, if not in some ways superior. Thus, physical education and sports for women became linked with nationalist ideology. However, despite the importance attached to women's sports in the early decades of the 1900s, it was clear that China must ultimately prove its worth as a nation through manly exploits on the sports field, which would erase the dread label of the "sick man of East Asia" and the effeminate image of the scholar in his robe and queue.[22] Despite the successes of China's sportswomen in the 1980s and 1990s, it might be argued that the same sentiment still exists.

---

21. Evelyn S. Rawski, "Ch'ing Imperial Marriage and Problems of Rulership," in *Marriage and Inequality in Chinese Society*, ed. Rubie S. Watson and Patricia Buckley Ebrey (Berkeley: University of California Press, 1991), pp. 171–75.

22. Andrew Morris, "Cultivating the National Body: Physical Culture in Republican China" (Ph.D. dissertation, Department of History, University of California, San Diego, 1998), p. 131.

Thus, the "oppressed Chinese woman" became a symbol of China's backwardness and weakness as a nation. From its beginning, then, Chinese nationalist ideology was intertwined with gender ideology. Tani Barlow has argued that "woman" did not exist as a unitary category until the term *nüxing* (literally "female sex") entered usage during the May Fourth Movement of 1919. In imperial China, there was no generic category of Woman; there were daughters in the family (*nü*), married wives (*fu*), and mothers (*mu*). This location of women within kinship networks, of course, resonated with the logic of gender-in-the-empire outlined above. Gender occupied a different place in the nation, and the neologism *nüxing* helped accomplish that shift: it made "woman" into a sign that could be used in the attack on Confucianism and "Chinese culture."[23]

Along with the emergence of *nüxing*/Woman, there were feelings among male intellectuals that the Chinese *nanxing*/Man was being emasculated and feminized by Western and Japanese imperialism. Clearly, the category of the backward Woman in need of modernizing emerged in tandem with the category of the modern Man who was going to lead her. However, a theme that was to recur repeatedly in Chinese nationalist ideology until the 1990s was the inability of Chinese men to take the lead. Instead, scholars have shown the prevalence of a theme of Chinese male impotence to right the wrongs done to Chinese women by Japanese and Western men. Ching-kiu Stephen Chan concludes from his survey of male May Fourth writers that woman is portrayed as an innocent scapegoat, paying for the crimes that society has committed; the real message communicated by the writers is that "the root of your suffering is to be found in my inability to right the wrongs that society has done me."[24] In short, nationalist ideology might draw upon images of the suffering, self-sacrificing Chinese woman, but it was really all about men: women suffer because men are impotent to right the injustices done to men through their women. Although most of these authors were male, female writers could not escape this logic either. Tani Barlow notes that the prominent female writer Ding Ling produced texts in the 1920s that invoked a

---

23. Tani E. Barlow, "Theorizing Woman: *Funü, Guojia, Jiating* (Chinese Woman, Chinese State, Chinese Family)," in *Body, Subject and Power in China*, ed. Angela Zito and Tani Barlow (Chicago: University of Chicago Press, 1994), pp. 254, 265.

24. Ching-kiu Stephen Chan, "The Language of Despair: Ideological Representations of the 'New Woman' (xin nüxing) by May Fourth Writers," *Modern Chinese Literature*, vol. 4, nos. 1–2, p. 27.

woman who must either die, commit suicide, or lose herself in sexual excess and mental disorder.[25]

Gender at the Borders of the Nation

The theme of the rape of Chinese women was a common one in nationalist literature, used to symbolize the rape of the Chinese nation by Japan and the West.[26] The Qing empire was envisioned as having porous borders that could be expanded through intermarriage, but the new Chinese nationalism—like the Western nationalisms that it drew upon—imagined the nation as having fixed borders that were being violated by Western imperialism. If the nation was like a body, then the occupation of the nation was like the rape of a female body. China as a nation thus became female relative to the more powerful Japanese and Western imperialist nations, which became male. Literary critic Lydia Liu concludes that, in nationalist discourse, the female body provides the pivotal point from which to view the rise and fall of the nation (and not the other way around).[27] If the early history of the Chinese nation had been one of sovereignty and expansion, then perhaps the male body would have dominated nationalist allegories. However, the suffering and violated female body seemed to be a more potent symbol for China's national humiliation at the hands of others.

In sum, whereas in the Qing the sacrifice of a woman could be lauded as the highest contribution to the morality and strength of the empire, with the advent of nationalism the sacrifice of a woman at the hands of Chinese and (more often) Western and Japanese men came to be denounced as the ultimate symbol of national shame. Yet there is a common thread: female bodily suffering is linked to the welfare of the empire/nation. The difference is that its complement in the Qing ideology is the filial son, the embodiment of male masculinity and potency; but its complement after the fall of the Qing is the unfilial and ultimately impotent son. This theme of female suffering and male impotence continued in Chinese nationalism until the 1990s.

---

25. Barlow, "Theorizing Woman," p. 267.
26. Prasenjit Duara, *Rescuing History from the Nation: Questioning Narratives of Modern China* (Chicago: University of Chicago Press, 1995), pp. 11–12.
27. Lydia Liu, "The Female Body and Nationalist Discourse: Manchuria in Xiao Hong's Field of Life and Death," in Zito and Barlow, *Body, Subject and Power in China*, p. 164.

The Maoist Period:
Emasculation and Masculinization

In nationalist ideology leading up to and following the Communist takeover, the liberation of women was always tied in with the liberation of the nation, and in a sense women's liberation was only a means to the greater end of national liberation.[28] With the founding of the People's Republic of China in 1949, the assumption was that national liberation had also liberated women. The Maoist period, and particularly the Cultural Revolution (1966–76), was for a long time said to be characterized by "socialist androgyny"; gender politics were largely replaced by class politics. Between the Yan'an period in the early 1940s and the late 1970s, clothing was essentially the same for men and women, and women wore their hair either bobbed or tied back in braids or pigtails. On the covers of women's magazines were images of women in plain working clothes engaging in manual labor; women who did difficult men's work such as oil drilling or coal mining were called "iron maidens." Women who tried to look "feminine" were criticized for their improper attitudes.[29] However, feminist scholars are now realizing that it is not accurate to say that gender was "erased" or that sex was "androgynous" during this period. Rather, on the one hand women were forced to dress and act like men, and on the other hand they were still subordinate to men in many ways.[30] Although women were encouraged to enter the workforce and take on dangerous jobs, men were not encouraged to do more housework and child care. "Equality" actually involved forcing women to conform to the male norm.

During the Cultural Revolution, for example, female Red Guards

---

28. Mayfair Mei-hui Yang, "From Gender Erasure to Gender Difference: State Feminism, Consumer Sexuality, and Women's Public Sphere in China," in *Spaces of Their Own: Women's Public Sphere in Transnational China*, ed. Yang (Minneapolis: University of Minnesota Press, 1999).

29. Harriet Evans, *Women and Sexuality in China: Female Sexuality and Gender since 1949* (New York: Continuum, 1997), pp. 137–38. There was a brief interlude in the mid-1950s, when women were urged to withdraw from the labor force to help lower the level of urban unemployment, during which femininity appeared in public images and an interest in feminine fashion was encouraged (see Evans, p. 137).

30. Yang, "Gender Erasure to Gender Difference," pp. 45–46; Dai Jinhua, "Invisible Women: Contemporary Chinese Cinema and Women's Film," *Positions*, vol. 3, no. 1 (1995); Emily Honig, "Maoist Mappings of Gender: Reassessing the Red Guards," in *Chinese Femininities/Chinese Masculinities: A Reader*, ed. Jeffrey Wasserstrom and Susan Brownell (Berkeley: University of California Press, forthcoming).

invariably dressed as male soldiers.[31] In her analysis of their violence, Emily Honig notes that observers felt compelled to explain female violence because they saw it as a departure from "ordinary" female behavior. However, in the popular culture of the early and mid-1960s, female militancy was valorized, providing heroines for schoolgirls to model themselves after. These girls also received militia training in school. The state-sponsored emphasis on military training reached its height in 1964, when the cover of *Women of China* began to portray female combatants. The model opera "Red Detachment of Women," which was made into a film (1960) and a revolutionary ballet (1970), also occupied a prominent role in popular culture. Thus, everyday life was permeated with images and practices designed to promote military effectiveness; this was a result of the highly hostile nationalism that characterized China in this period and the Cold War oppositions that set the tone of global politics as a whole.

In this atmosphere, girls recognized that in order to make a contribution to the nation, they had to follow the new models of militant women. In doing so, they were contesting old gender conventions in a way that men did not have to, so that in some ways they felt more pressure than men to demonstrate their "redness" through violence.[32] However, analysis of the treatment of female violence in popular culture also indicates a male uneasiness toward this female contestation of gender roles, with the result that female violence became increasingly contained within structures of male authority from the 1940s through the 1970s. Careful examination of the popular images of militant women shows that, at the same time that they offered women a military model, they also subjugated them to men. For example, in the historical records of the events portrayed in "Red Detachment of Women," which took place on Hainan Island in the 1920s, the peasant women were organized by a militant female commissar, and they taught themselves to use rifles. In the ballet version, however, they are led by a handsome male commissar. In the film, they are given guns by men, trained by men, and led by men into battle.[33] The discomfort with strong women is also seen in films about minority women from 1949 to 1965, in which strong but victimized female members of minorities

---

31. The following account is taken from Honig, "Maoist Mappings of Gender."
32. Thanks to Gong Xiaoxia for this insight.
33. Honig, "Maoist Mappings of Gender"; Yang, "Gender Erasure to Gender Difference," p. 43.

are saved by the arrival of Han male cadres who implement the Party's favorable policies toward women.[34]

The Transitional 1980s:
More Emasculation and Masculinization

The apparent sexual equality of the Cultural Revolution for a long time was taken at surface value, and images of strong women continued to dominate popular nationalism into the 1980s. Only recently has that sexual equality been questioned. In fact, upon closer examination, male circumscription of female warriors was still evident in the treatment of Chinese sportswomen in the mid-1980s. The 1980s were a key transitional period between the Maoist-era constructions of gender-in-the-nation and those that were to follow, but true changes did not begin to appear until the late 1980s. In 1981, the Chinese women's volleyball team won the World Cup, achieving China's first world victory in an Olympic sport and defeating China's main global rivals of Japan, the Soviet Union, and the United States along the way. Many people mark this as the turning point in the revival of Chinese nationalism after the disillusionment of the Cultural Revolution. The women became national icons, were rewarded with political positions, and were cited as inspirational examples that all Chinese could learn from. More than 30,000 letters were mailed to the team members; star spiker Lang Ping alone received over 3,000. A vast number of these were love letters and proposals of marriage from young men. Thousands of letters were written to editors of newspapers and magazines and sports departments of television and radio stations. In the letters and images surrounding the victory, it is possible to see the recurrence of the theme of female suffering linked with national salvation. In an interview in 1995, the commentator for that game, Song Shixiong, told me that he had carefully researched the image of the team that he would report on. In order to understand them more fully, he watched them practice. He described their training as "very bitter." He saw them cry, yell at the coach, sweat, fall to the floor. He saw them when they were so tired that they could not climb up stairs. The "bitterness" of their training constituted one of the enduring aspects of their story. That this resonated with the audi-

---

34. Esther Yau, "Is China the End of Hermeneutics? Or, Political and Cultural Usage of Non-Han Women in Mainland Chinese Films," *Discourse*, vol. 11, no. 2 (Spring–Summer 1989), p. 119.

ence is evident from the published letters, which often linked personal pain to the team's pain, national humiliation, and ultimately national redemption. An example is a letter written to the team by a university student who had been brought back from the depths of despair: "You have aroused again the love of country in the bottom of my heart. . . . [You] have lit the flame of my love which had already died out. . . . In ten years this was the first time I felt my heart beating—along with the strong rhythm of the pulse of the nation; in ten years this was the first time I felt the honor of being human—China's pride."[35] The role of "love" in the women's volleyball phenomenon, in the form of love letters and love of country, offers some insight into why figures of women occupy such prominent roles in Chinese nationalism. For, if the primary audience is actually a male audience, what better figure to symbolize the nation—the object of his love—than a woman? In the 1980s volleyball furor, she is a marriageable young woman; in the 1990s anti-NATO demonstrations, a daughter or a mother.

The theme of female suffering is particularly evident in a well-known feature film about the women's volleyball team, "Seagull" (*Sha Ou*), which was filmed in 1981 before the World Cup victory. Cowritten (with Li Tuo) and directed by Zhang Nuanxin, a woman and a prominent Fourth Generation director, it portrays the sacrifices of a member of the national team, Sha Ou, in her struggle to win the world championship. The film opens in 1977; the Asian Games are three months away, and she is 28 years old and nearing the end of her career. Her voice recalls, "If only we could win, I was willing to pay any price and make any sacrifice. But I didn't know that the sacrifice was that great, the price that high." Although she must retire without winning the world championship, she throws herself into coaching the next generation of champions after her fiancé is killed on the return trip following a successful ascent of Mount Everest. She does not get to see her team finally win the championship, however, because an old back injury takes its toll, and she is paralyzed. While watching the championship game from her wheelchair in a hospital room, she hears Song Shixiong's voice saying, "The people thank you. The nation (*zuguo*) thanks you." As she wipes tears from her cheeks, we hear her voice concluding, "Friends say being an athlete is too bitter. . . . Not me. . . ." The darkly tragic tone of the movie

---

35. Cao Xiangjun, *Tiyu gailun* (General theory of physical culture) (Beijing: Beijing Institute of Physical Education Press, 1985), p. 137.

offers the possibility of interpreting it as a criticism of the bitter sacrifices made by women (almost always under the guidance of men) in the cause of national honor, but the unremittingly positive nationalist rhetoric seems to condone their suffering.[36]

The women's volleyball team went on to win five consecutive World Cup and World Championship victories. Its victory in the latter tournament in 1985 occurred in the midst of a time of unrest among Beijing University students. On September 18, several thousand students from the university gathered at the school's south gate and pasted up big-character posters to protest the Party's handling of the anniversary of Japan's invasion of the Northeast in 1931. Some posters denounced Japan's "economic aggression" against China and the lack of democracy in China. Two months later, dissident students pushed pamphlets under dormitory doors calling on students to demonstrate in Tiananmen Square on November 20, the date on which the women's volleyball team would play Japan for their fourth straight world title. Only a few hundred students showed up in the Square, but a week later, several thousand gathered at the May Fourth sports field at Beijing University for a "welcoming ceremony" for the team. Seated behind a table on the rostrum in the grandstand, several of the key team members spoke briefly, with Lang Ping speaking the longest. They were clearly speaking on behalf of the state, however, as they repeatedly mentioned the hospitality shown them in Japan and the friendship between the Chinese and Japanese people. When they were finished, Yuan Weimin, the male head coach, speechified for over an hour, acting as the voice of authority. Furthermore, the high officials present were all male, most of the students who offered the letters of congratulations and gifts were male, the dissident letter writers were reportedly male, and the crowd at the "welcoming ceremony" seemed to be predominantly male. The occasion appeared to be choreographed to give the impression that these women were able to reach their full potential under the guidance of men. These women who had eaten so much bitterness for the cause of national honor were clearly subordinate to a (masculine) Party-state.[37]

---

36. The eerie parallel with the female gymnast Sang Lan, who was paralyzed from the neck down while warming up for the vault event at the 1998 Goodwill Games in New York, deserves mention here. U.S. journalists who met her and wrote about her were amazed by her willpower, optimism, and apparent view that this sacrifice for the nation had been justified (a view that was echoed by her parents).

37. For more detailed discussion and analysis of this event and the women's volleyball

Moreover, these women were not glorified as women. They were the masculinized products of a sports system with draconian rules to regulate sexuality and the expression of gender. On the state-supported sports teams, romantic contact with the opposite sex was forbidden and could result in expulsion from the team. Marriage was generally prohibited, and athletes usually had to retire before they could marry. Females were required to keep their hair short or pulled back tightly into braids or pigtails; "long hair hanging over the shoulders" (*pijianfa*) was forbidden in public. Several famous male coaches forbade their female athletes to wear face cream, makeup, or high heels. An athlete who displayed too much interest in feminizing her appearance was considered to lack the proper "serious" attitude and might be subjected to criticism meetings. This was the kind of woman who represented the Chinese nation to the rest of the world until the late 1980s.

The women volleyball players were the first of a number of women in different sports who began to achieve success internationally in the 1980s, and the theme of physical suffering was common in the other examples as well. World champion racewalker Xu Yongjiu wrote upon retirement, "It's hard to express in words the degree of pain involved in training and competing with injuries. Several times I fainted on the training grounds. I will never forget that moment so painful that one can no longer feel the pain."[38] The suffering of female athletes was portrayed in detail by the media, and it made an impression upon their audience. This was also the way in which female athletes saw themselves. They felt that the life of a state-supported athlete was "bitter" and that they had sacrificed much for it—most importantly, marriage (which they were forced to delay) and a college education (which was unattainable once they left regular school for sports boarding schools with inadequate academic programs). In discussions about why Chinese sportswomen achieved international success before the men, the reason that was most commonly given was that they were more obedient and better able than men to "eat bitterness and endure hard labor" (*chiku nailao*).

In complementary opposition to the self-sacrifice of Chinese

---

phenomenon, see Susan Brownell, *Training the Body for China: Sports in the Moral Order of the People's Republic* (Chicago: University of Chicago Press, 1995), pp. 80–87; and Susan Brownell, "Strong Women and Impotent Men: Sports, Gender, and Nationalism in Chinese Public Culture," in Yang, *Spaces of Their Own*.

38. Xu Yongjiu, "Zai jian, jingzou!" (Goodbye, racewalking!), *Tiyu bao* (Sports news), January 29,1988.

sportswomen, there was concern about the weakness of Chinese sportsmen. The relative successes of the women and men were expressed in the aphorism "the yin waxes and the yang wanes" (*yin sheng yang shuai*), which is based on classical Taoist teachings about sexual intercourse. In the 1980s, sports participants and fans were quite frustrated with the failure of men's soccer to reach the finals of the World Cup or Olympics and with the generally poor showing of men's sports in the international arena. This is the flip side of the strong sportswomen who led the resurgence of Chinese nationalism. Meng Yue argues that the images of strong women were part of the Party-state's strategy to dominate all rival forces, including the forces of sexism and patriarchy, to create a nation of subjects totally subordinate to the state. The images of strong women, then, did not arise as much out of the Party's struggle to end sexism as out of the Party's desire to create dominated men.[39] The fact that the Party succeeded to some extent is evident in that, after the end of the Maoist period, a great number of literary and film works by men began to express just how dominated men had felt. Recent reassessments of the Maoist period have suggested that many men experienced it as a period of emasculation and impotence. Scholars have noted that urban men will use the term castration (*yan'ge*) or eunuch (*taijian*) to describe the situation of men in the Maoist era.[40]

Some of the more obvious problems for sexuality included the lack of privacy and the "split family" problem. The state's low priority on providing enough private space in housing allocations meant that it was "not just that people had few opportunities to indulge individual passions; rather, they lived within a whole built world that was structured as if privacy had no uses."[41] Tens of thousands of couples were forced to live apart because they had jobs in different parts of the country, and the state gave low priority to transferring their residence permits so they could live together. I recall a conversation in 1987 with a middle-aged professor whose wife frequently lived in another part of

---

39. "Female Images and National Myth," in *Gender Politics in Modern China*, ed. Tani E. Barlow (Durham: Duke University Press, 1993), pp. 134–35.

40. Yang, "Gender Erasure to Gender Difference," p. 51; Everett Yuehong Zhang, "'Tough' or 'Soft': Entrepreneurial Masculinity in Contemporary China," paper presented at the annual meeting of the American Anthropological Association, Philadelphia, PA, December 3, 1998.

41. Judith Farquhar, "Technologies of Everyday Life: The Economy of Impotence in Reform China," *Cultural Anthropology*, vol. 14, no. 2 (May 1999), p. 168.

China, sometimes in another part of the world, for up to two years at a time while choreographing large-scale mass calisthenics displays for national events. He told me, "That's hard for you to understand, isn't it? But for us it's nothing." Because I knew this professor well, I knew that he meant what he said; but at the same time, I often felt in my conversations with him that he did have a sense of sexuality that he could not even truly feel because he had no practice in using the words to express it. He had come of age under socialism, and sexuality and gender were almost invisible for most of this period; they had been erased off the map. This was not necessarily experienced as sexual repression at the time because there was nothing to be repressed; only in retrospect did it start to feel like impotence. There were minute ways in which the state affected gender relations with repercussions for the sense of masculinity or femininity of individuals. The superior at a person's work unit had to approve a marriage before it could take place, and this control was occasionally used in malicious ways. In 1989, a friend of mine was refused permission to marry, after which he wrote an angry letter to me in the United States: "I don't even have the right to get married with my beloved. I am deprived of the human right!" In 1995, I commented to the above professor that in the United States, women are generally the cooks in the family, but in China men know how to cook. He told me, "That's because a couple is usually assigned housing by the husband's work unit, so the wife has to commute to work. Often it's a long commute, so she gets home later at night. The men have to cook dinner; there's no other way." Although feminists may not like to acknowledge it, it must be recognized that the state support of gender equality in the Maoist period may have been felt as emasculation by many Chinese men. They also felt emasculated by a power structure in which they had little say. Men who themselves feel impotent are likely to feel threatened by images of powerful women, but they may be comfortable with images of women who are more victimized than they themselves feel. Together with historical tradition, this may explain the appeal of the image of the suffering woman who sacrifices herself for the nation.

One of the pivotal popular novels in the reassessment of the Maoist period was Zhang Xianliang's *Half of Man Is Woman*. At the time of its publication, this novel sold very well and stimulated heated debate about the sexuality it depicted. The story follows the sexual history of Zhang Yonglin, a writer who is imprisoned during the anti-Rightist campaign and again at the beginning of the Cultural Revolution. The plot leads from his frustrated erotic desires to his marriage to another labor camp inmate, Huang Xiangjiu. After his years of frustration, he discovers on his wedding night that he is impotent. This impotence can be interpreted in various ways, but the reading that is relevant here revolves around the event that most clearly illustrates that he is only "half a man." Coming home one evening, he sees a party official, Cao Xueyi, entering his home to have sex with Xiangjiu. Paralyzed, he realizes that of all the humiliations he has experienced in his life, he is about to experience the ultimate one. He is unable to act to prevent the liaison; instead he engages in long dialogues with historical characters until the cadre leaves. His conversation with Karl Marx is the last. Marx begins by telling him that he has no experience with this sort of thing, but Yonglin tells him that he really needs advice on something else: "What, after all, is the future of our nation, our society, even so-called human life?"[42] Marx responds with a long discourse on the difference between East and West, but when Yonglin pins him down, he says that it all comes down to "Economics! . . . ": "Right now your [plural] forces of production have been castrated (*yan'ge*), they don't even have the ability to reproduce. . . ."[43] Thus, the author draws a parallel between economic and sexual performance, a parallel that became common in popular culture as the years went on. Yonglin's economic and sexual impotency are due to his repression by the Party-state as embodied, in this particular instant, in Cao Xueyi. Yonglin finally recovers his sexual potency with his wife after a heroic deed in a flood, but then he divorces her. As he leaves, she tells him, "Don't forget, it was me that turned you into a real man. . . ." Zhang Xianliang's authorial voice comments, "Woman will be forever unable to possess the man that she creates!"[44]

There is much that can be said about this book as representative of a key historical moment in Chinese culture. Here, I will comment only on its link with the main themes of this essay. The novel is about a suffering male, and his suffering is equated with the suffering of the nation. However, this suffering is of a different variety from the female

---

42. Zhang Xianliang, *Nanrende yiban shi nüren: Weiwulunzhe qishi lu zhi yi* (Half of man is woman: Reminiscences of the enlightenment of a materialist, volume one) (Beijing: Wenlian, 1985), pp. 144–45. Translations are my own.

43. Ibid., p. 148.

44. Ibid., p. 236.

suffering described above. It is the suffering of the junior male who is politically, economically, and ultimately sexually oppressed by a political structure controlled by a closed group of older males. Woman's body is merely the site of this power struggle; she is only there to make a half man into a whole man, and then be discarded.[45] This logic has also been remarked in the fiction of other authors of the transitional 1980s, such as the experimentalist Ge Fei.[46]

Gender on the National and Ethnic Borders in the 1980s

Another artistic work that was influential in Chinese popular culture of the 1980s was the film *Red Sorghum*, released in 1987. It was the first Chinese film to win a major international prize (Best Picture at the 1988 Berlin International Film Festival). Yeujin Wang locates the inspiration for this film in a moment in the early 1980s when Chinese intellectuals and average theatergoers became aware, on different levels, of an "excruciating lack" relative to the tough guys in Western and Japanese movies. This "masculinity anxiety" led to a search for a new kind of Chinese masculinity, and the male protagonist in *Red Sorghum* answered this need with his resemblance to the outlaws, drunkards, and rebels of Chinese legend. Wang observes that the film revolves around the kidnapping, conquering, and ravishing of women, whether successful or not. He describes the ending of the film as the birth of a masculine identity out of an all-embracing maternal power. The fact that the film is narrated by the grandson of the male protagonist harkens back to the filial triad discussed at the beginning of this chapter (with the filial son as the pivotal link between the preceding and following generations). And his grandfather is clearly a sexually potent man, who ravishes the wife of a diseased older man and impregnates her. Wang argues that this masculine potency is on the one hand an antithesis to disease and on the other hand a symbol of coming into one's own, of spiritual independence.[47] This film was quite popular in

---

45. Zhong Xueping, "Male Suffering and Male Desire: The Politics of Reading Half of Man Is Woman by Zhang Xianliang," in *Engendering China: Women, Culture, and the State*, ed. Christina K. Gilmartin, Gail Hershatter, Lisa Rofel, and Tyrene White (Cambridge: Harvard University Press, 1994), pp. 186, 188, 190.

46. Jing Wang, *High Culture Fever: Politics, Aesthetics, and Ideology in Deng's China* (Berkeley: University of California Press, 1996), p. 255.

47. Yeujin Wang, "Mixing Memory and Desire: *Red Sorghum*, A Chinese Version of Masculinity and Femininity," *Public Culture*, vol. 2, no. 1 (Fall 1989), pp. 41, 44, 50.

China and undoubtedly provided inspiration to many men in the Chinese audience. I remember watching the film in a crowded courtyard at the Beijing Institute of Physical Education in 1988, where it was projected upon a large sheet of cloth stretched over a frame, undulating in the wind. The soundtrack was a best-selling compilation of folk songs from the Northwest, sung in a hoarse, throaty masculine voice. For months and months after the film, one could hear the young male students singing at the top of their lungs, imitating the throaty voice, as they walked back to their dormitory rooms late at night. The song they sang was always the same one: "Boldly walk forward, little sister" (*meimei, ni dadande wang qian zou*). In the film, this was the song sung by "my grandpa" as he rustled along in the stalks of sorghum beside "my grandma's" wedding sedan, just before he kidnapped her, seduced her, and impregnated her.

The 1980s also saw the emergence of the "seeking roots" movement, in which ethnicity, gender, and nationalism became entwined in new ways that nevertheless followed the same logic of gender. In the preceding examples, new expressions of gender difference and sexuality allowed Han men to discover a new Han masculinity in contrast with the Han female as his "other." At the same time, Han masculinity was being defined against a minority other. It was, of course, nothing new that minority sexuality should be contrasted with that of the "civilized" Han. However, one difference from previous historical phases was that the "seeking roots" movement arose out of the feelings of impotence of Han men. It involved a disillusionment with the sterility of mainstream Chinese culture and a fear of total Westernization, resulting in a search for "authentic" culture among China's ethnic minorities, in the hope that these could revitalize Chinese culture.

Images of minorities in the Chinese popular media tended to portray eroticized females, often depicted as rural and backward in contrast with the urbanized, modernized Han. For example, in the state-sponsored pictorial *Chinese Nationalities*, only 3 of the 56 nationalities are represented by photos of males. The other 53 photos are of beautiful young women in colorful native costumes with romantic natural backgrounds. The Han, however, are represented by a middle-aged, conservatively dressed woman in an urban setting.[48] Louisa Schein and Dru Gladney argue that popular representations of minori-

---

48. Dru Gladney, "Representing Nationality in China: Refiguring Majority/Minority Identities," *Journal of Asian Studies* 53(1) (February 1994), pp. 92–123.

ties as sensual and liberated were a way in which the "margins" were appropriated to reshape the "center" of Han nationalism. When minorities are represented as exotic, colorful, and primitive, this has the effect of homogenizing the undefined majority as united, monoethnic, and modern.[49] Further, the representation of the ethnic as female establishes the majority as male. Hence, the sexualities of ethnic others serve the creation of a Han masculine nationalism.

During Schein's fieldwork in Xijiang, a mountain community in Guizhou province inhabited primarily by ethnic Miao, artists, photographers, journalists, ethnographers, and officials often visited in search of the quintessential ethnic experience. These visitors were most often urban Han Chinese. When visitors wanted to organize a photo shoot or stage an ethnic event, they usually went to the local culture station, which was staffed by a local Miao man. It was he who searched out the attractive girls that the visitors expected and demanded money for their time. Visiting officials and intellectuals were greeted by Miao maidens in ethnic dress, who offered them ritual wine out of bull horns. One Han man was so enchanted by the Miao girls who welcomed him with songs and wine offered with both hands that he was inspired to write two songs filled with romantic and sexual connotations. One contained the lines

> Xijiang, ah, Xijiang, would that I was a spring rain sprinkling upon your fertile fields
> Xijiang, ah, Xijiang, would that I could become the morning dew to kiss your smiling face.[50]

While Han men may have been infatuated with the notion of the sexually uninhibited Miao, the reality was of course not so simple. Miao themselves felt that their courtships emphasized the development and expression of a romantic love that should end in monogamous marriage and that Han men had a tendency to engage in indiscriminate sex.[51]

Schein writes that in the 1980s, the dominant Han national ideal was opposed to both the "modernized" Western woman and the "back-

---

49. Gladney, "Representing Nationality," p. 93.

50. Louisa Schein, "Gender and Internal Orientalism in China," *Modern China*, vol. 23, no.1 (1997), p. 79.

51. Louisa Schein, "The Other Goes to Market: The State, the Nation and Unruliness in Contemporary China," *Identities: Global Studies in Culture and Power*, vol. 2, no. 3 (January 1996), p. 213.

ward" minority woman. She feels that Chinese "internal orientalist" representations of minority women's sexuality contributed to the subordination of minorities, women, and peasants in Chinese society. She notes that "with the intensification of a perceived threat from the outside [in the 1980s], internal and especially non-Han others were differentiated from foreigners, and their purported sexual vitality drawn upon in an anxious consolidation of national identity."[52]

The 1990s: The Return of Patriarchy, the Sexualization of Women

With China's continued economic successes in the 1990s and increasing engagement in global networks of all kinds, Chinese nationalism came to be characterized by a greater confidence and a correspondingly reduced anxiety about gender at the national borders. The white woman became less a sign of the distant and the forbidden, and the minority woman was less prominently positioned in public culture as an erotic other. Asian women increasingly populated the eroticized domain previously reserved for foreign and ethnic others. The former fetishism of the Western woman and the ethnic woman was replaced by an "imagined cosmopolitanism," through which Chinese people perceived themselves as participants in a capitalist consumer culture that spanned the globe. As an example of this amalgamation of Western woman and modern consumerism, Schein tells the story of a Miao wedding in Guizhou in September 1993. As the bride finishes applying her makeup and thickly adorning herself with jewelry, one of the most ostentatious wedding gifts arrives, borne on shoulder poles: a yard-long, framed photograph of a blond model in a hot-pink, G-string bikini, lying in repose upon a race car. The bride poses in front of it, seemingly unfazed by any sense of sexual competition with the image.[53] Schein concludes that state control over the production of gendered national images had considerably dissipated in the 1990s and had been relinquished in large degree to the forces of commodification.[54]

The new commodification of gender, nationalism, and sexuality was evident in the debates surrounding the fourth Chinese Supermodel

52. Schein, "Gender and Internal Orientalism"; "The Other Goes to Market," pp. 204–8, 212.
53. Louisa Schein, "The Consumption of Color and the Politics of White Skin in Post-Mao China," *Social Text*, vol. 41 (winter 1994), pp. 141, 149, 156.
54. Schein, "The Other Goes to Market."

competition in Beijing in June 1995. This contest was designed to pick a model to represent China in the Elite Model Look world competition in South Korea two months later. More generally, the purpose of the competition was to promote Chinese fashion models on the international modeling scene. The models competed in swimsuit, leisure wear, and evening wear categories. They were judged on their walk, movements, agility, coordination, level of ease, aesthetic appeal, musicality, awareness of the camera lens, and harmony of appearance. Personality and English skills were also evaluated.

The nationalist rhetoric recited by the emcees during interludes, and among the Chinese audience, was very similar to the sports rhetoric of the 1980s. Chinese models were compared with foreign models, with the general consensus seeming to be that Chinese models were approaching international standards but still had a way to go. The Chinese modeling agents and journalists were preoccupied with the question of whether Chinese models had the ability to be successful on the international fashion stage. The central problem of the contest was to select a model who was suited to represent Chinese culture on the world stage but whose beauty would be appreciated and consumed by non-Chinese (who would sign her to lucrative contracts). Should she be a "traditional oriental beauty"? Or a "modern" cosmopolitan citizen of the world (which essentially meant that she was Westernized)? Or some combination of the two? The dichotomy between the "traditional oriental beauty" and the modern Western woman is one of which models and agents are quite conscious. The model who has decided to market herself as a "traditional oriental beauty" has long hair, moves slowly, and uses downcast eyes to hint at shyness. The modern, Westernized model sashays down the runway, returns the gaze of the audience, and suggests a barely restrained sexuality. Since past competitions had failed to produce international runway stars, the organizers felt that Chinese people had different conceptions of beauty from Europeans. If a Chinese model were to succeed on international runways, then she must appeal to European designers and customers. Therefore, the judges included five Westerners along with two Hong Kong Chinese, two mainland Chinese, and one Thai. This balance of five Western and five Asian judges was to ensure that the eventual winners would have pan-global appeal.

In the end, the top three places went to 19-year-old, 1.78-meter-tall Xie Dongna from Shanghai; 20-year-old, 1.83-meter-tall Luo Jinting from Xi'an; and 21-year-old, 1.82-meter-tall Guo Hua from Beijing. The winners of the first and second places had a more stereotypical "oriental" look as seen through Western eyes: oval face, arched eyebrows, long hair. All three models had a quiet, demure manner with downcast eyes. But in other respects, of course, they conformed to Western modeling standards: the second- and third-place winners were two of the tallest models in the competition, and all of them were young, pole-thin, and much taller than the average Chinese woman.

The kinds of identity problems raised by the Supermodel contest illustrate the changing nature of Chinese nationalism in the 1990s. Rather than oriented toward hostile opposed nations, this contest was directed toward the problem of enticing other nations to consume these models much as if they were commodified products "made in China." Western and Chinese ideals were sought in the proper combination, and although many people were unhappy with the hybrid results, those with a vested interest understood that they must obey the inevitable logic of the global market in fashion models. One of the Chinese judges complained that the number of foreign judges was too many and that this competition was decided according to Western standards of beauty.[55] There was also some confusion among the Chinese audience about why Xie Dongna had won. During the awards ceremony, the young woman next to me turned to her friend and said, "What's so good-looking about her?" As the designer and competition sponsor Stefano Ricci stood at Xie's side, kissed her, and looked up at her glowingly, the young woman said, "Oh, the foreigner (*laowai*) likes her."

Gender across National Borders from the 1980s to 1990s

As a female foreign student in Beijing in the 1980s, I was acutely aware, as were my classmates, of the intersections between gender and nationality. At Beijing University (Beida for short) in 1985–86, foreign and Chinese students were still segregated from each other, and Chinese students who visited the foreign-student dorms had to register at the front door. It was common that a Chinese female who visited a foreign male more than once would be warned not to do so again. However, Chinese men who visited foreign females were much more

---

55. *Zhongguo shangbao* (China Trade News), "Motuo dasai bushi xuanmei bisai" (The model competition is not a beauty contest), June 25, 1995, p. 1.

loosely controlled. As a foreign female, I walked freely into both Chinese men's and women's dormitories. The doors to the women's dormitories were watched by middle-aged women who would stop both Chinese and foreign men. The protectiveness toward the Chinese female students also extended to their relations with Chinese men outside the university. There was anger among male students toward townies who, it was rumored, were sneaking into student dances to meet Beida women. The martial arts club decided to form a patrol outside of the buildings so that they could attack any townies attempting to sneak in. Given the tight security at the university gates at that time, it seems unlikely that outsider men could have been infiltrating the dances in any numbers, even if they desired to take the risk. However, such was the paranoid protectiveness of Beida men that they were willing to believe the rumors. Outside of the university, Chinese women who visited foreign men in their hotel rooms were frequently seized by security guards and detained for self-criticism.

The possessiveness of Chinese men toward Chinese women was also evident in the attitudes toward African students studying in China. Since most of them were male, and they spent many years in China, they sometimes formed relationships with Chinese women. This was regarded with anger by Chinese men, and it contributed to an anti-African riot in Nanjing in late 1988.[56]

With the continued opening of national borders, the gendered nature of international relations became increasingly obvious. In the 1990s, an entire suburban complex nicknamed "Mistress Town" arose outside Shenzhen to house the Chinese women who were kept there as mistresses by Hong Kong businessmen. An Australian journalist who interviewed women there found that the tens of thousands of young women were from all parts of China, and most of them spoke only enough Cantonese to engage in minimal conversation with Hong Kong men. One of the few women who would talk (because, unlike most of the others, she was legally married to her Hong Kong patron) said her lover gave her 10,000 yuan per month ($1,200) to wait for him—compared with the average wage in the area of 700 yuan.[57] In 1994 and 1995, it was reported that Hong Kong men had fathered about 300,000 illegitimate babies in China, or about 5 percent of the entire Hong

---

56. Wasserstrom, "Student Protests in Fin-de-Siecle China."

57. Louise Williams, *Wives, Mistresses and Matriarchs: Asian Women Today* (Lanham, MD: Rowman and Littlefield, 1999), p. 79.

Kong population of six million. In late 1994, a group of angry wives from the colony protested to the Hong Kong government, but the resulting debate actually produced one proposal to legalize the arrangements. Taiwanese women also expressed a growing concern about the increasing numbers of mainland prostitutes and purchased brides in Taiwan and mistresses kept on the mainland by Taiwanese businessmen. One investigative report noted that the practice of keeping mainland mistresses appeared with the opening of cross-strait relations in 1988–90, at which time mainland women were relatively inexpensive. From 1990 to 1992, however, the monthly cost of a mistress had risen from $1,000 to about $2,000, in addition to the cost of a purchased apartment. This was still cheaper than keeping a mistress in Taiwan, which cost about $3,200 a month and carried greater risk of discovery by the wife.[58]

Within China, urban men could not help but be aware of the widespread desire of Chinese women to marry foreign men. Between 1982 and 1997, marriages between Chinese and foreign nationals nearly tripled, reaching 50,773 in 1997. Nearly all of those marriages were between Chinese women and foreign men.[59] In Beijing, there were certain categories of women who came into frequent contact with foreign men, and among those groups a white foreign man was considered the most desirable spouse. Two of these categories were fashion models and employees of FESCO (the Foreign Enterprise Service Corporation, which provided employees to foreign corporations). In 1995, I spent a night out at Beijing's Hard Rock Cafe with three such young women, a fashion model and two FESCO employees. They were all attractive and well dressed, and they spoke fair English by Beijing standards. One of them was already married to a white American, one was planning to marry a Chinese man who had emigrated to the United States and started his own business, and one was still trying to choose. It became clear that among these three, the one who had married the white American was considered the most fortunate, and the one who had yet to choose was encouraged to try to find a white American.

58. See Shu-mei Shih's review of the Chinese language publications in "Gender and a Geopolitics of Desire: The Seduction of Mainland Women in Taiwan and Hong Kong Media," in Yang, Spaces of Their Own, pp. 288–89. Monogamy became the sole legal form of marriage in Hong Kong only with the passage of the Marriage Reform Ordinance in 1970.

59. Zhang Kewen and Yin De An, China News Digest internet news service, "Social Changes Bring Changes in Families' Size, Value," May 27, 1999.

They did not seem to appreciate that a Chinese man who has succeeded in emigrating to the United States and establishing himself there probably has a great deal of drive and intelligence, perhaps more than the American man. Meanwhile, a Chinese man who was a mutual friend of mine and of the married woman constantly complained in private to me about her marriage to this American, whom he did not consider worthy of her because he was older and had been previously married. My friend lamented that with her intelligence and beauty, the 25-year-old fashion model was one of China's "first-class women" (*yideng nüxing*) and that China was losing her to an American man who in his own country would be considered of a lesser class but in China could outrank fine young Chinese men like himself.

In the 1990s, the impotent men were no longer the young men who had felt castrated by the state socialist system in the 1980s. The vast majority of entrepreneurs were male. Their reaction to the loss of Chinese women on the international marriage and sex markets was not so much to protest the practices of foreign men as to imitate them when they got the chance. Thus, rather than trying to control the growth of "mistress towns," it seemed that Chinese entrepreneurs were taking mistresses of their own if they had enough wealth to afford them.[60] And on the rare occasions when a Chinese man might have the chance to have sexual relations with a white foreign woman, he might seize the opportunity as a patriotic duty.[61]

While young men were discovering new forms of economic and sexual potency, reforms in the retirement system meant that cadres

---

60. A huge, related issue is the rapidly increasing trade in kidnapped wives, who are bought by men in poverty-stricken areas where it is difficult to attract wives. This trade is not self-consciously nationalistic in the way discussed here, but it does have national implications as Vietnamese women are kidnapped and smuggled across the border in ever greater numbers, with an estimated 10,000 women currently in China illegally. See Samantha Marshall, "They Don't Say 'I Do,' These Kidnap Victims Taken from Vietnam," *Wall Street Journal*, August 3, 1999, p. A8.

61. "To Screw Foreigners Is Patriotic" is the suggestive title of an essay by Geremie Barmé. He begins the essay by describing a scene in the wildly popular 1993 television miniseries "A Beijinger in New York" involving the Chinese protagonist and a buxom, blond American prostitute. Barmé borrowed the phrase from a Chinese immigrant to Australia, a prostitute by trade, who felt that Chinese mainlanders and students in Australia felt this way. One assumes that it is Chinese males who feel this way about sexual relations with foreign women, although this is not spelled out; the opposite sentiment could well be attached to Chinese women who have sexual relations with foreign men. Barmé's essay concerns the new nationalism among Chinese avant-garde intellectuals, but intellectual and popular nationalism are interconnected.

were forced to retire at 55 in order to make way for younger administrators with up-to-date technical skills. Impotence in men over 40 had
become something of a national obsession, and the most popular and
expensive tonics in the patent-medicine industry were those directed
toward aging and impotent men. Clearly, the worlds of politics, economics, and sexualities are linked.[62] It is thus not surprising that those
with an excess of economic and political power might also have an
excess of sexual power nor that those who previously possessed such
power might feel emasculated by the reforms that took it away.
Masculinity is related to state power, nationalist ideology, the free market, and the marriage/sex markets. The current situation has unleashed
an entrepreneurial masculinity that is apparently proceeding hand in
hand with the return of male privilege and female disadvantage.[63]

Chinese men are recovering their potency domestically and in the
world political/economic arena, where Chinese leaders are now flexing
their muscles on issues such as human rights, the Asian economic crisis,
and Taiwanese separatism. In the sports world, men's soccer was pro-
fessionalized in 1994 and men's basketball in 1995, so hordes of eager
male fans can now consume their favorite masculine images, while
feminine images no longer occupy center stage as they did during the
heyday of women's volleyball. Even the brief moment in the limelight
of the women's soccer team in 1999 was dimmed by the fact that no
sponsors had yet signed up for the abbreviated (compared with the
men's league) eight-team, two-month professional women's league in
China. Although the Chinese Football Association had encountered
difficulty in finding sponsors in the past and had been forced to subsi-
dize the league with one million yuan each year, this was the first year
that no sponsor had come forth at all.[64]

Fashion models are now promoted by the leaders of the textile and
garment industries, and even by top state leaders,[65] as representatives
of China to the world, even though they are commonly perceived as

---

62. Farquhar, "Technologies of Everyday Life," pp. 162, 170.

63. Everett Zhang, "'Tough' or 'Soft.'"

64. Yu Yilei, "Official Hopes World Cup Success to Ease Plight," *China Daily*, July 12,
1999, p. 10.

65. In the 1992 Supermodel contest, the medals were presented by Vice-Premier Tian
Jiyun and National People's Congress vice-chair Chen Muhua, then the highest-ranking
woman in the government. Niko Price, "That 'Dynasty' Look: China—A Nation of New
Fashion Victims" *San Francisco Chronicle, Sunday Punch* (Sunday magazine), April 5,
1992, p. 2.

sexually loose, and perhaps little better than prostitutes. And in the Chinese media, sexualized images of women are everywhere. Is a new Han female sexuality emerging in the new Chinese nationalism? Perhaps, but we cannot consider female sexuality in isolation from male sexuality, and we cannot consider either inside of China without also looking at what is happening across national borders.

So, Why Gender *and* Nationalism?

In the nationalism of the 1990s, many of the images were new, but the underlying logic was over a century old: feminine images were largely employed in the service of the production of masculinity, and both were inseparable from Chinese nationalism. For Chinese men, the image of the Chinese female body violated by foreign men carries as much emotional force as ever. The image of strong and sexy Chinese women representing China to the world also has a certain appeal. But despite the public predominance of female images, we need to investigate the masculine identities that these images are appealing to. In order to understand nationalism in China, we must take seriously the intersection of masculinity and Chinese identity and their position in global culture and politics. Approaches that ignore gender cannot grasp the full character and force of nationalistic emotions in China.

If we return to the anti-NATO demonstrations that opened this chapter, we can see how a more sensitive understanding of the popular sentiment surrounding the deaths of the three journalists might have allowed the United States to assuage Chinese anger more quickly and effectively (if such was, indeed, a policy goal). The Chinese leaders and demonstrators were adamant in demanding a proper apology. This, of course, meant an apology acted out according to Chinese rules of propriety. Since the primary sufferers in this case were perceived to be the families of the deceased, a proper apology would have been directed to them. President Clinton did, in his official apologies, express condolences to the families of the dead. However, a stronger symbolic gesture toward them might have carried more force. As was discussed, letters play an important role in Chinese political culture, and it is quite common for newspapers to publish the letters, telegrams, and texts of phone calls from top state leaders to private individuals (such as victorious athletes and the families of those who die defending the nation), but this is a channel seldom utilized by foreign leaders. The publication of a letter from President Clinton in reply to the letters from Shao

Yunhuan's son and Zhu Ying's father (if the Chinese government would allow it) might have had considerable impact. In writing such a letter, Clinton would be advised to emphasize that he wrote as "Chelsea's father" to another father and to a son who had lost his mother. In doing this, he would step into his role as a beneficent paternal man (a role that the letters invited him to step into) and help defuse his image as a sexually potent American male who is targeting Chinese mothers and daughters. If, on the other hand, the U.S. government wishes to promote an image of itself as a hypermasculine superpower, then the other side of Clinton's image will serve this purpose quite well. It may even evoke feelings of awe and respect from Chinese men—but only so long as they perceive that their mothers and daughters are safe.

Dangerous Liaisons: China, Taiwan, Hong Kong, and the United States at the Turn of the Century

Nancy Bernkopf Tucker

The last years of the twentieth century will be remembered as a difficult time in U.S.-China relations, a time of conflict, confusion, and crisis. Even as both countries grew more prosperous and the international environment after the Cold War more benign, there emerged growing fears of escalating tensions between them. Moreover, although leaders in each capital spoke of the need to work together, they proved unable or, perhaps, unwilling to make the necessary compromises, leaving areas for cooperation unduly limited. Cassandras went so far as to talk about a new Cold War that would, once again, set nuclear armed powers against each other in what would be a delicate balance of terror for the whole world.

The possibility of a new Cold War was brought closer in May 1999 when the United States, engaged in a NATO war against Yugoslavia, a war of which China disapproved, accidentally bombed the Chinese embassy in Belgrade. The violent response to this tragedy among all sectors of the Chinese population, who saw the act as intentional and provocative, suggested that anti-American sentiment had not been far beneath the surface. Frustration born of repeated confrontations between China and the United States, whether kindled by political, strategic, or economic issues, had had a more profound impact than Americans had imagined. Beguiled by the obvious Chinese enthusiasm for McDonald's hamburgers and U.S. university graduate degrees, Americans allowed themselves to hope that China might embark upon a path of liberalization in politics as well as economics, becoming a truly democratic, free-market, Americanized China. They paid little attention to the anxiety developing parallel to these rapid changes in

Chinese society, which, as in nineteenth- and early-twentieth-century outbreaks such as the Boxer movement, fueled virulent antiforeignism. The harsher reality exposed by the disaster in Belgrade demonstrated just how far from convergence the two societies remained and how large the problems could become in the new millennium.

For Taiwan and Hong Kong, U.S.-China frictions did not need to rise to the level of Cold War hostility in order to impinge directly on their security and prosperity. Given the unchangeable realities of geography and history, both remained vulnerable to collateral damage, even as their dependence on Washington and Beijing provided no options to remaining in the line of fire.

On the other hand, living in China's shadow did not necessitate passivity. Hong Kong's maneuvering room was small, but it struggled to sustain its autonomy as a special administrative region under Beijing's "one country, two systems" formula. Taiwan more explicitly and effectively sought to use U.S.-China conflict to broaden its international presence, demanding respect in its relations with both Washington and Beijing.

Political Differences

More than a decade after the massacre at Tiananmen in 1989, no assessment of U.S.-China relations can begin without reference to the events surrounding that catastrophe. Only in the context of Tiananmen are the developments of the years that followed comprehensible. In the United States, the longstanding bipartisan consensus on U.S.-China policy and popular support for the relationship declined precipitously. Americans watched on television as China's leaders brutally suppressed demonstrators whose calls for freedom of expression made them seem to be idealistic democrats. At virtually the same moment, the fall of the Berlin Wall and the end of the Cold War relieved Americans of strategic imperatives that had earlier excused repression in China. Under these circumstances, many Americans challenged continuing administration efforts to sustain and broaden cooperation with Beijing. A positive China policy, which had commanded virtual unanimity, fragmented into a multiplicity of China policies driven by interest groups, and government agencies, with disparate agendas. An era of good feeling, fueled by tentative political liberalization inside China during the 1980s, closed.

In China, similar disillusionment emerged. Chinese leaders protested foreign interference in their domestic politics at a time of chaos. In fact, they attributed much of the energy and endurance of the Beijing Spring demonstrators to outside incitement. They resented sanctions and defied human rights entreaties. Seeing the need for a unifying spirit at home to take the place of the discredited communist ideological imperative, they turned to nationalism and nurtured a nascent anti-Americanism. Meanwhile, the urban intellectuals and entrepreneurs of Tiananmen largely turned away from politics and retreated into moneymaking. They went to work for U.S. firms and pursued U.S. investment, but beneath the surface, they too were angered by relentless U.S. pressure to change.

Before any meaningful recovery in relations could take place, moreover, a new crisis erupted, this time in the Taiwan Strait. Although the confrontation was ostensibly between Taipei and Beijing, the United States played a central part in triggering the dispute and in protecting Taiwan once mounting tensions threatened to spin out of control (as discussed below). In the aftermath, U.S. perceptions of China as aggressive and hostile produced a spate of bitter denunciations of its governing principles and long-range objectives. Richard Bernstein and Ross Munro's book *The Coming Conflict with China* may have been the most infamous of these diatribes, but denunciations of China and the Clinton China policy appeared in the pages of the liberal *New Republic* as well as the conservative *Weekly Standard*.[1] Members of the Christian Coalition and the AFL-CIO mobilized to question ties to a Chinese government determined to repress Christianity and fight the trade war utilizing prison labor. Public opinion polls demonstrated that a majority of Americans had come to fear China, seeing it as an unfriendly country and perhaps as an enemy.[2] Early in 1997, there were

---

1. Richard Bernstein and Ross Munro, *The Coming Conflict with China* (New York: Knopf, 1997); Arthur Waldron, "How Not to Deal with China," *Commentary* (March 1997); editorial, *New Republic*, March 10, 1997; and *Weekly Standard* special issue (February 1997).

2. Opinion surveys are, of course, biased by how the questions are phrased and asked. Nevertheless, the negative impressions of China do stand out. A March 1996 CNN/USA Today/Gallup poll found 39 percent of respondents favorable toward China, while 51 percent were unfavorably disposed. An October 1997 poll showed a continuing of the trend, with 25 percent seeing China as friendly or an ally and 36 percent calling it unfriendly or an enemy. A *USA Today* reporter noted that in 1983, during the heyday of U.S.-China relations, some 53 percent saw China as a friend. See *Gallup Poll: Public Opinion 1996* (Wilmington, DE: Scholarly Resources, 1997), pp. 174–75; ibid. for 1997, pub. in 1998, p. 171; and Barbara Slavin, "Poll: Many Consider China an Adversary," *USA Today*, October 29, 1997.

even accusations that Beijing had funneled money into the election coffers of the Democratic Party to insure reelection of Bill Clinton.

Just at a moment, then, when strong leadership on both sides, equally determined to preserve U.S.-China ties, appeared vital, the reality proved quite different. A symbol of the drift and decline came with the February 1997 death of Deng Xiaoping. Not that Deng's passing generated much notice: he died quietly, and mourning rituals ended quickly.[3] But in earlier years, when someone was needed to put relations back on track, Deng had been there, and now he was not. Under Jiang Zemin, his heir, the government operated smoothly, but Jiang lacked the authority of his mentor. Having endured the twin embarrassments in 1995 of being snubbed on his proposal for reunification with Taiwan and being misled regarding Lee Teng-hui's trip to Cornell, he had intimidated Taiwan with missile exercises in 1995 and 1996 to prove his fortitude. Early in 1997, he reenergized a spiritual civilization campaign to demonstrate his political purity.

Bill Clinton also faced problems with purity and failure as 1997 began. He battled accusations of campaign financial irregularities, possibly including donations from China, and had been forced to dismiss his administration's representative in Taiwan because of related charges.[4] The State Department's report to Congress on human rights declared, with some exaggeration, that by the end of 1996 no dissidents remained active in China, all having been imprisoned or exiled. Clinton's 1994 decision to delink trade and human rights came under renewed attack. And, in this light, the president had no choice but to admit that his policy of "comprehensive engagement" was seriously flawed. He proved less forthcoming regarding his personal legal troubles involving sexual harassment charges by an Arkansas civil servant named Paula Jones, placing his credibility under repeated attack.

As if to illustrate administration ineptitude, Vice President Al Gore traveled to China in March 1997 and bumbled a champagne toast with Li Peng, the supposed evil genius of Tiananmen. In sharp contrast, Republican Speaker of the House Newt Gingrich, in Shanghai also in

---

3. Avery Goldstein, "China in 1997: A Year of Transitions," *Asian Survey*, vol. 38 (January 1998), p. 38.

4. This was James C. Wood, Jr., politically appointed in December 1995, who headed the American Institute in Taiwan, traditionally a nonpolitical post. Wood knew nothing about Taiwan or U.S.-China relations and allegedly used his position and connections to the White House to solicit campaign contributions from top political figures on the island. He resigned in January 1997.

March, stood up to Beijing by declaring unequivocally that the United States would defend Taiwan if China attacked.

Shocked and chagrined by the downward spiral in relations, leaders in the United States and China had concluded during 1996 that serious remedial action would have to be taken to avoid military clashes and rebuild domestic support for interaction. In the United States, the White House took control, ending the disarray produced by each agency's conducting of its own China policy that had been character- istic of the first Clinton administration. The president's constructive engagement policy, adopted in September 1993, had mandated high- level diplomatic meetings, expanded contacts between a multiplicity of agencies, and military exchanges. After the missile crisis, the pace of such visits quickened. Anthony Lake, the national security advisor, became a crucial conduit through his counterpart, Liu Huaqiu, for seeking greater understanding.[5]

But engagement had not been enough. Confrontation had soured the relationship. Beijing seemed preoccupied with an alleged U.S. policy of containment designed to keep China weak and divided. And so, for the first time in his presidency, Bill Clinton focused on Chinese affairs and moved with some alacrity toward a series of summit meet- ings with Chinese leaders. His advisors sought a new concept to her- ald a fresh start. To China's surprise, they adopted the idea of "strate- gic partnership" that Beijing had been promoting. This term appears first to have been used in a declaration by Jiang Zemin and Boris Yeltsin in March 1996 to give impetus to improving Sino-Russian relations, and until the summer of 1997 the United States had been resistant to embracing it. Now, to a White House under fire for its past mistakes in China policy and seemingly indifferent to the way the phrase would irritate allies and friends in Asia, the label "constructive strategic partnership" appeared the perfect symbol for a renewal of relations.[6]

---

5. Lake in 1993 had included China in a discussion of "backlash states" such as North Korea, Libya, Iran, and Iraq, angering Beijing. Symbolically, therefore, it was important that he reach out for the Clinton administration. Barton Gelman, "Reappraisal Led to New China Policy," *Washington Post,* June 22, 1998, p. A16; Lake speech, "From Containment to Enlargement," September 21, 1993, presented at the Nitze School of Advanced International Studies, Washington, D.C.

6. The original phrasing had included a caveat clarifying that both countries were work- ing toward a strategic partnership and that one did not already exist. As might have been expected, however, the nuance was quickly lost.

Thus Jiang Zemin came to the United States in October 1997 to rebuild relations with Washington and reveled in a long-sought ceremonial visit filled with banners, red carpets, and extravagant banquets. He saw this trip as the crowning achievement in a year of political triumphs that began with his smooth inheritance of power from Deng and progressed easily through the retrocession of Hong Kong in June to a carefully crafted and victorious performance at the Fifteenth Party Congress in September. There he sidelined rivals such as Premier Li Peng and chief of the National People's Congress Qiao Shi; brought more supporters, especially Shanghai cronies, into the Politburo; and kept the national emphasis on economic reform, including the restructuring of state-owned enterprises.

Nonetheless, just as the so-called strategic partnership was largely illusory, so too were the summits less than they appeared to be at the time. Designed to adjust images as much as to accomplish substantive goals, they proved considerably more successful in promoting temporary euphoria than in solving concrete problems. Jiang Zemin's trip to the United States in the autumn of 1997 yielded memorable "photo opportunities," as he swam in Hawaiian waters, donned a tricornered hat at Williamsburg, and smilingly debated the president at a news conference in Washington. Americans were particularly charmed by Jiang's persistent use of English phrases in speeches and news conferences.

Given all this good feeling, the paucity of results received relatively little attention. The most celebrated accomplishment was reiteration of previous promises that China would not sell more cruise missiles to Iran and would not transfer nuclear technology to unsafeguarded facilities. In exchange, the United States also pledged to fulfill an old accord, the 1985 Nuclear Cooperation Agreement, to sell China reactors and fuel, a deal worth perhaps $60 billion to U.S. companies. Boeing got a more immediate contract for aircraft yielding $3 billion. The two governments advanced communications between their naval forces, established a "hot line," and vaguely pledged joint efforts on rule-of-law initiatives, crime prevention, and environmental projects. On the other hand, no progress was made on the critical and chronic disputes over trade and human rights.

During the course of 1997, in fact, human rights problems seemed an irremediable issue, as the caustic State Department report had made clear. Madeleine Albright, upon becoming secretary of state at the start of Clinton's second term, sought to refurbish China policy, arguing that it must be "multifaceted" rather than driven by a single issue. But human rights continued to preoccupy many critics of cooperation between Washington and Beijing. Offended by Beijing's insistence that abuse of its citizens should be treated as an internal affair, members of Congress and human rights organizations asserted the universality of freedom and averred Washington's duty to assist victims of repression and hold governments accountable for their behavior.

The first battleground of 1997 became the annual meeting of the United Nations High Commissioner of Human Rights in Geneva. Given the bleak picture drawn by the State Department, there could be little question that the United States would follow its usual practice of putting forward a resolution condemning China. As in all previous years, however, China proved able to block the initiative, and in 1997, for the first time, the United States was abandoned by its European allies. Dismayed by the outcome, human rights activists pressed for increased funding to Radio Free Asia and coerced a reluctant State Department into naming a special coordinator for Tibet. Moreover, as 1997 wore on, the human rights movement received new support from unexpected quarters, such as Gary Bauer's Family Research Council, which stoked concern over Beijing's repression of Christianity. Before the end of the year, at Clinton's press conference with Jiang in Washington, the president warned the Chinese leader that China stood "on the wrong side of history" in its human rights policies.

Beijing, of course, could not easily be cowed, particularly when its leaders believed national security was under attack. As a result, they continued to arrest dissidents even as they released one of the most famous, Wei Jingsheng, on medical parole. They banned leading U.S. film studios from working in China because of controversial movies such as *Seven Years in Tibet*, and although they signed the International Covenant on Economic, Social and Cultural Rights, the National People's Congress did not move with any haste toward ratification. Nevertheless, in areas that Beijing identified as contributing to the national interest, progress had been made, as for instance in reform of the criminal and penal systems.

Reflecting U.S. concerns about human rights under Chinese rule, widespread anxiety existed at the beginning of 1997 over the impending reversion of Britain's colony of Hong Kong to China. Observers in both the United States and Beijing agreed that the retrocession in June would act as a test of China's intentions and capabilities. Deng Xiaoping's formula of "one country, two systems" had been touted as a solution to the Hong Kong, Macao, and Taiwan problems. But skeptics did not believe that Beijing had the desire or the discipline to respect Hong Kong's autonomy within the administrative system established by the Sino-British Joint Declaration of 1984 and the Basic Law of 1990.

Doubters had plenty of evidence to draw upon. Reacting to the efforts of Christopher Patten, the last British governor of the colony, to broaden democratic rights, China set about dismantling the so-called through-train even before the takeover, derailing fledgling electoral innovations and selecting a tough chief executive with strong ties to Beijing. Popular balloting for the Legislative Council was set aside, and a provisional body was created to serve until new elections could be held under restrictive regulations that sharply reduced public participation. Controversies also arose regarding representation on, and scope of, the Court of Final Appeal, at the same time that self-censorship seemed to herald a new, less open environment for Hong Kong's news media.[7]

The actual handover and the early months of China's rule, however, proceeded smoothly. None of the dire outcomes predicted by some—generalized repression, arrests of dissidents, a ubiquitous People's Liberation Army (PLA) presence, flight of capital and investors—materialized. Instead, China practiced caution and restraint. It allowed Chief Executive Tung Chee-hwa considerable maneuvering room on financial and foreign policy issues and gave scope to opposition politics, even permitting street demonstrations to continue. The U.S. business and expatriate community, which had grown far larger than the British contingent in the territory, pronounced itself well satisfied.

But Beijing's hope that the people of Taiwan would see the success of Hong Kong's "one country, two systems" experiment as an inducement toward reunification did not fare so well. Taiwan's leaders declared that Hong Kong, as a colony lacking a strong military and independent foreign relations, had no relevance to the future of a democratic people ruled by their own Republic of China government.[8]

---

7. An array of books and articles focused on the possible difficulties that reversion would bring, including Warren I. Cohen and Li Zhao, eds., *Hong Kong under Chinese Rule* (New York: Cambridge University Press, 1997). The most negative appraisal may have come from Louis Kraar, "The Death of Hong Kong," *Fortune*, June 26, 1995.

8. "Evaluation of 'One Country, Two Systems' in Hong Kong," by Mainland Affairs Council Chairman Chang King-yuh, July 18, 1997, in MAC News Briefing, August 4, 1997, p. 6.

During the handover in Hong Kong, in fact, people across the island held "Say No to China" rallies, gathering as many as fifty thousand demonstrators in Taipei.

After two tumultuous and exhausting years, 1998 began with a concerted effort by Washington and Beijing to portray U.S.-China relations in a new, positive light. Having declared the first summit meeting a great success, the White House decided to advance the date of Clinton's return trip to China from autumn to early summer in order to keep some momentum going in the allegedly buoyant recovery (although skeptics attributed the timing to the Paula Jones trial). China sought to contribute to a favorable atmosphere with a March announcement that it would sign the UN Covenant on Civil and Political Rights and with the release of Tiananmen student leader Wang Dan in April. But politics in both countries belied small gestures and rhetorical celebration.

In the United States, Bill Clinton encountered a new series of problems. His illicit affair with White House intern Monica Lewinsky erupted in the press and overshadowed domestic and foreign policy making during 1998 with humiliating months of accusations, denials, and apologies. At the same time, the president also came under scrutiny for a 1996 decision to shift authority for licensing of satellite launches from the State Department to the Commerce Department, where decisions could be made more quickly but with potential risk to national security. Accusations began to fly that the result had been Chinese acquisition of U.S. missile technology. Chinese malevolence appeared to be reflected in the crisis that materialized in South Asia on May 11, 1998, when India declared itself a nuclear power by detonating a series of explosions. Indian officials insisted that the act had been inspired not by the contentious politics of South Asia but rather by their fear of China and Chinese technology transfers to Pakistan. Clinton's congressional critics, thereupon, accused the administration of ignoring Chinese nuclear cooperation with Islamabad that had given India its justification and Pakistan its ability to respond with its own nuclear tests.

Clinton came under increasingly intense fire during 1998 for his alleged softness on China, which critics attributed to Chinese lobbying and campaign contributions. For decades, the so-called Taiwan lobby had wielded great power in Washington, particularly on Capitol Hill. Beijing had never paid much attention to lobbying, apparently convinced that Americans ought to accede to China's demands because of its size and importance. Then came the Lee Teng-hui visa debacle, and Beijing finally geared up to wage war in the realm of public relations.[9] The way the Chinese public relations effort was implemented, however, produced a crisis. As a result of either misunderstanding, folly, unscrupulous advisors, or darker motives, Beijing appeared to tamper with the U.S. political system. Intelligence monitoring of the Chinese embassy uncovered plans to promote Clinton's reelection, and a friend of the president's claimed to have gotten a large donation from a high-level PLA officer. An incipient investigation of political manipulation by Taiwan was forgotten in the flurry of accusations hurled at Beijing. Indeed, some U.S. politicians, whether from racial bias or political ignorance, blamed Beijing not just for its own alleged infractions but for those of Taiwan because they were both part of Greater China.[10]

Tensions over human rights further undermined the effort to portray a more positive picture of U.S.-China relations in 1998. The year began with stories about sales of human organs from prisoners executed in Chinese jails after two peddlers were apprehended in New York City. Then the House of Representatives advanced a popular bill designed to punish countries found culpable of persecuting their own citizens for their religious beliefs. Under this Wolf-Specter legislation, which overwhelmingly passed the House but died in the Senate, the U.S. government would have been forced to end aid, restrict exports, and oppose international loans to such a country and refuse visas to its leaders. Although the bill had a broader purview than China, many in the House and beyond saw Beijing as a prime target.

Chinese leaders, meanwhile, continued to balance human rights moderation on some fronts with harsh treatment on others. Although not indifferent to U.S. pressure, Beijing zealously guarded the govern-

---

9. On the issue of lobbying by competing interests, see Robert G. Sutter, *U.S. Policy Toward China: An Introduction to the Role of Interest Groups* (New York: Rowman and Littlefield, 1998).

10. Jim Mann, "Taiwan Gets GOP Favored Nation Status," *Los Angeles Times*, February 18, 1998, p. A7. The Cox committee report on espionage (discussed below) would do the same, suggesting that every Chinese-owned business in the United States (of which there were three thousand) was gathering intelligence for Beijing, as was each of the eighty thousand annual visitors. This was compounded by the case of Wen Ho Lee, who was accused of stealing nuclear secrets at Los Alamos. The former head of counterintelligence at the laboratory, Robert S. Vrooman, asserted that Lee had been investigated because he was Chinese American, not because of convincing evidence implicating him. Vernon Loeb, "Ex-Official: Bomb Lab Case Lacks Evidence," *Washington Post*, August 17, 1999, p. 1.

ment's security. Sometimes it allowed intellectuals to debate political reform unscathed. Publishers released a variety of controversial volumes, such as *Crossed Swords*, which detailed ideological disputes within leadership circles, and bookstores displayed them without much fear of reprisal.[11] On the other hand, it retained fairly strict control of the village elections, widely touted in Washington and Beijing as a way to bring about gradual democratization. U.S. advisors and observers found that few people understood the concept of secret ballots, and in most localities candidates continued to be chosen by party officials. The party actually used the process to recruit new members, purge corrupt officials, and provide a release for popular frustration. To government conservatives, elections were a vehicle to preserve party rule, not pave the way for multiparty politics. When a township in Sichuan province decided to extend the franchise to determine higher-level offices, the initiative was first condemned and later accepted with great hesitation. The center warned that this should not be a model followed elsewhere.[12]

Thus when Clinton planned his trip to China for the summer of 1998, pressure developed immediately for him to mount a serious human rights offensive. The announcement that he would be welcomed in Tiananmen Square stirred outrage, as did the last-minute decision by the Chinese government to prevent three Radio Free Asia staff members from joining the presidential entourage. Nevertheless, Clinton masterfully utilized television to create an atmosphere of reconciliation and progress. His famous address at Peking University made the point especially well. Although obtaining permission to broadcast live required fierce bargaining and unrelenting pressure, Chinese leaders ultimately agreed. The president conducted a veritable class in democracy, both speaking out on China's political failings and human rights abuses and engaging students critical of U.S. policy in serious dia-

---

11. Ma Licheng and Ling Zhijun, *Jiaofeng* (Crossed swords) (Beijing: Jinri chubanshe, 1998). For a brief discussion of the controversy surrounding *Jiaofeng*, see Joseph Fewsmith, "Jiang Zemin Takes Command," *Current History* (September 1998), pp. 254–56.

12. The Ministry of Civil Affairs in charge of supervising village elections assigned only five officials to the task in 1999, although China has some 930,000 villages. Anne F. Thurston, "Muddling toward Democracy: Political Change in Grassroots China," *Peaceworks*, United States Institute of Peace, 1999; "First Direct Election Conducted at Township Level," *Issue Brief*, International Republican Institute, July 1999; and Robert A. Pastor, "Elections in China: Potemkin or Jeffersonian Villages?" *Harvard Asia Quarterly* (Winter 1999), pp. 18–21.

logue. Afterward, the president's staff would proclaim this a watershed event, a new beginning for China and the United States.

But the reality had been quite different. Clinton's university audience had been carefully screened, the number watching him on television was small because the broadcast of his talk was given no publicity, and the translation of his remarks was inaccurate at several crucial points. At the same time, the government arrested dissidents in every city Clinton toured, and the White House accepted restrictions on who the President could meet during the trip. These developments undermined much of what Clinton thought he had accomplished. Indeed, almost as soon as he departed, officials tightened political controls still further. A group of dissidents who had tried to use Clinton's presence to deflect punishment for their efforts to organize a national opposition party were promptly arrested in the following weeks. Despite much talk of changes in criminal law procedures, these China Democracy Party activists lacked adequate legal counsel, were denied open trials, and were given long prison sentences. A reluctant Clinton administration felt compelled to mount the ramparts again in early 1999 to try to condemn China at the next UN human rights commission meeting.

When in 1999 the pundits and members of Congress declared the strategic partnership dead, however, that had little to do with human rights. Not only had accusations of campaign abuses accelerated, but information had begun to leak from a massive report detailing long-term espionage by Chinese agents pursuing nuclear secrets. The censure became so intense in the first months of the new year that the Clinton administration felt constrained to rebuff China in the one area where the potential for progress remained. The third of the summit meetings, this one between Clinton and China's premier Zhu Rongji convened in Washington in April 1999. Zhu bore particular responsibility for China's economic health and came to the United States in hopes of reaching agreement on entry into the WTO. To facilitate a positive outcome, he made a series of far-reaching concessions and risked opposition at home from entrenched interests to secure integration into international trade regimes. But, convinced that Congress would not accept anything less than a perfect accord, the president demanded more concessions. Then, having embarrassed Zhu by refusing to sign an agreement, the White House magnified the error by publishing Zhu's offer, ensuring political backlash in China. Finally, Clinton partly reversed course in the face of outrage from the U.S.

business community and urged that China resume talks immediately.

Zhu had known that his visit to the United States courted danger. He had come, in part, to use his forceful personality to overcome suspicion of China. As it happened, not only had Zhu encountered hostility from Congress and become ensnared in bungling by the White House, but in addition, the media largely ignored his visit. Instead, U.S. newspaper and television coverage focused on the NATO war in Yugoslavia.

From the beginning, Beijing had opposed the war and allied bombing as intervention in the internal affairs of a sovereign state, ignoring the issues that divided Serbia from the Kosovars and NATO. Chinese leaders also were angered that Clinton had not discussed with them plans to launch an air war, bypassing the "hot line" established in 1997. As diplomats tried to work with the Russian government to negotiate a settlement, questions arose as to whether China might use its Security Council veto to prevent UN action. To Beijing, the initial U.S. decision to circumvent the United Nations, where China enjoyed veto power, and make NATO a vehicle for its intervention appeared as an effort both to disenfranchise China and to dominate Europe. Chinese analysts worried about a rogue superpower determined to enforce its policies and impose its values around the world. In fact, the situation in Serbia triggered fears of future attempts to defend "splittists" in Xinjiang, Tibet, and Taiwan. Under such conditions, little flexibility existed to cope with the unsatisfactory outcome of the Zhu visit.

On May 7, 1999, the atmosphere became precipitously worse. A U.S. plane fired three missiles at the Chinese embassy in Belgrade, destroying the building and killing three people China identified as journalists. Washington insisted that the bombing had been unintended. Intelligence maps had not been updated, and targeting units did not know that the embassy had moved three years earlier. Chinese at all levels of society thought the explanation sounded ludicrous. After all, the United States used so-called smart bombs with pinpoint accuracy that had been touted by military officials since the 1991 Persian Gulf War. Given the respect that the Chinese had developed for the sophistication of U.S. technology, the immediate reaction was to assume that there had been no mistake and that the Americans had planned the attack. Even specialists on international affairs found conspiracy theory more convincing than error, concluding that either critics of China or proponents of larger intelligence budgets had purposely planted inaccurate data.

Chinese leaders battling the effects of an Asian economic crisis, failing state enterprises, bank instability, rampant corruption, and massive unemployment found it convenient to turn popular anger against an arrogant and imperious United States. The fortuitous bombing, however tragic, gave them an unparalleled opportunity to channel outrage into patriotic street demonstrations against the U.S. embassy. Further, China's leaders could use the incident to preempt antigovernment protests that might otherwise have broken out to mark the tenth anniversary of Tiananmen. Indeed, Jiang Zemin initially concealed Bill Clinton's apologies and stimulated doubts that vaunted U.S. technology and intelligence could be so deeply flawed. Military exchanges, port visits by the U.S. Navy to Hong Kong, and the human rights dialogue all were suspended. And as the anniversary of Tiananmen drew closer, Chinese officials blamed the United States for inciting the events of 1989 to plunge China into chaos. But although these tactics may have temporarily inoculated Jiang and Zhu Rongji against critics of their concessions to the United States on joining the WTO, this strategy intensified U.S. exasperation with Chinese policies and behavior.

In Washington, members of Congress hostile to Beijing capitalized on the public outcry that greeted pictures of Chinese crowds stoning the U.S. embassy in Beijing to indict executive branch leadership and denounce China policy. Distracted by more immediate problems, particularly Kosovo, the administration seemed ill prepared to confront provocative issues such as thefts from national nuclear weapons laboratories. Recognizing the danger of stimulating a Cold War, officials nevertheless found it impossible to articulate and pursue a clear policy, and, even less, to curb the destructive initiatives in Congress that further inflamed feelings on both sides. Although it appeared eminently desirable to nurture good working relations with a rising power in a region of the world that would be increasingly significant for U.S. economic well-being, that goal appeared quite distant at the turn of the century.

Taiwan Crisis

As strained as political relations were, nothing proved as dangerous and irreconcilable as the dispute over Taiwan that, having erupted in 1995, continued to roil relations at the end of the decade. Because the status of Taiwan as a self-governing entity divorced from Beijing undermined China's drive toward absolute unity, legitimacy, and sovereignty, the Taiwan issue challenged all other progress made by the People's Republic of China. Visions of a Greater China foundered upon the reality of a Taiwan able to defy Beijing and conduct unofficial relations with powerful states throughout the world, especially the United States.

The 1995 confrontation, of course, had begun with a provocative invitation to the president of Taiwan to speak at Cornell University, engineered by Lee Teng-hui himself. The Clinton administration's decision to approve the trip, after assuring Beijing that Lee would not be allowed to come, infuriated Chinese leaders. In retaliation, Beijing staged military exercises in the Taiwan Strait, suspended cross-strait talks, recalled its ambassador from Washington, and refused to receive the newly appointed U.S. ambassador to China. Finally, in 1996, as Lee campaigned to become the first directly elected president in Chinese history, Beijing hurled missiles into the seas around the island in hopes of intimidating Taiwan voters and demonstrating the impossibility of independence. Caught in the middle, the United States dispatched two aircraft carrier battle groups to keep the situation from escalating further.

In the wake of this Taiwan Strait crisis, all three parties appeared to have learned crucial lessons. Most unsettling were the conclusions drawn by Beijing. China demonstrated that it could severely disrupt the economic life of the island by applying minimal amounts of force to frighten Taiwan's people as well as foreign traders and investors. In 1996, the Taipei stock market fell, foreign-exchange reserves plummeted, and some residents of the island fled. China assumed that these indicators showed it could deal with the Taiwanese more easily than expected, preferring to forget less favorable precedents such as the failure of German rockets in World War II to force England out of the conflict. At the same time, Washington demonstrated that Taiwan might not have to stand alone. Surprised by the challenge of vastly superior U.S. military power, the Chinese leadership accelerated and targeted military modernization so as to deter or overcome interference in any future attack upon Taiwan. Among other initiatives, Beijing extended deployments of increasingly accurate ballistic missiles along the coast opposite Taiwan, with projections of increasing numbers of these in the new millennium. Further, China's rulers seemed to grow more determined and impatient to resolve the reunification issue in the short term. With Hong Kong's retrocession completed and with Macao's reversion on the calendar for December 1999, Chinese leaders felt free to focus on Taiwan, and they worried that passing time only served to erode cultural and historical ties further.

Taiwan's lessons from the 1996 crisis reflected fear and dismay. Although in the immediate wake of the missile firings a defiant Taiwan electorate gave Lee Teng-hui a landslide victory, the population evinced greater caution in subsequent elections. Lee, of course, remained popular, but his provocative behavior did not. In fact, the opposition Democratic Progressive Party (DPP), which had been instrumental in pushing Lee and the Guomindang (GMD) toward their search for greater international space, found that an independence platform limited its potential for national leadership. Success in local politics, where a record for clean and effective government won votes, did not translate easily into an islandwide mandate for political change. Thus the DPP turned in a stunning victory in November 1997 at the local level, capturing more counties than the GMD and scoring more total votes for its candidates, but then lost decisively in December 1998, when citizens elected a Legislative Yuan, where views on independence had a greater potential for disruption. Some DPP leaders, including presidential hopeful Chen Shui-bian, recognized the need to modify the party's profile and moved, as the GMD had done earlier, toward the center politically. They insisted that there would be no need for any public declaration of independence or an immediate plebiscite following a victory in the 2000 presidential campaign since Taiwan already enjoyed independence. Furthermore, the party officially adopted the designation Republic of China for the island rather than insisting on the more provocative Republic of Taiwan.

Nevertheless, Taiwan did continue its pursuit of pragmatic diplomacy throughout the period, sending its officials on trips to friendly countries around the world and awarding generous financial aid wherever it could serve political ends such as support for membership in international organizations. This opportunistic policy led Taipei to offer the United Nations $1 billion for admission, to give assistance in Southeast Asia to deal with the financial crisis in 1997, and to grant aid to Macedonia to help with the influx of Kosovar refugees in 1999. Public opinion polls demonstrated repeatedly that the effort to enhance Taiwan's international profile met with approval on the island despite the anger it generated in China.

Taiwan also reemphasized its refusal to see Hong Kong as a model for its future relationship with China. Events encouraged that posture. Although the United States paid relatively little attention to developments in Hong Kong after a year of stability diminished anxiety over the territory, Taipei remained skeptical. The main problems in the special administrative region, of course, proved to be not political but economic as Hong Kong, having survived the chicken flu epidemic in early 1998, fell victim to the broad downturn in Asia.[13] Its stock market plummeted, unemployment climbed, property values collapsed, and tourism declined precipitously. Hong Kong avoided even more serious problems when Beijing resisted the temptation to devalue its currency. As a result, Hong Kong could preserve its peg to the U.S. dollar, established in 1983, and reassure international business.

Cooperation between China and Hong Kong, however, did not always progress so smoothly. Toward the end of 1998 and in early 1999, conflict developed between Hong Kong democrats and Beijing's appointed chief executive, Tung Chee-hwa. Divergent views of legal jurisdiction and the incompatibility of civil and common law set mainland against Hong Kong courts. The most serious question focused on residency rights. The Hong Kong Court of Final Appeal decided, in a controversial ruling, that all mainlanders with a parent in the territory and even illegitimate children of illegal residents could settle in Hong Kong. Tung and Beijing, fearful of instability, turned public opinion against the decision by estimating a flood of 1.6 million refugees that would swamp already tight housing, education, and job opportunities. For Beijing, the case also touched on the sanctity of the National People's Congress, as the Court of Final Appeal asserted the right to determine whether NPC rulings were consistent with the Hong Kong Basic Law and to invalidate them if they were not. Under severe pressure, Hong Kong's courts backed down, but not without throwing autonomy and the rule of law into question. "One country, two systems" appeared to founder on the fundamental differences between the systems.

Aware of the cultural and attitudinal disparities between Hong Kong and China, Hong Kong's chief executive Tung Chee-hwa from the first had sought to resinicize the territory after retrocession on July 1, 1997. Both the government and the schools shifted to Chinese as the medium for interaction, cutting back on English-language usage

---

13. The Hong Kong government was forced to kill 1.4 million birds and bar imports from China to eradicate a deadly virus.

despite local protests. Tung also repeatedly urged Hong Kongers to identify with China's interests and follow Chinese models of patriotic behavior.

At the same time, many Americans began to worry about convergence between the former British colony and China. Members of Congress, hostile to or suspicious of China, feared sensitive goods would be smuggled across the Hong Kong border and wondered whether the time had come to eliminate distinctions in trade controls and treat Hong Kong as just another Chinese city. In April 1999, the United States government opposed export to Hong Kong of a supercomputer for weather forecasting because the equipment exceeded standards permitted to China. In May, the Cox Report asserted that Hong Kong front companies were purchasing forbidden items and that PLA trucks were passing through border checkpoints without inspections. Although the Cox Report was soon assailed as inaccurate, the possibility of harsh new strategic controls on Hong Kong remained and jeopardized its future as an information technology center for the region.

As Taipei watched Hong Kong being incorporated into China, problems such as the potential that the United States would impose high-tech trade controls were reminders of the perils that movement toward unification might bring. For Taiwan, access to cutting-edge military technology and cooperation with the United States, always important, seemed even more crucial in the wake of the strait crisis, as China's missiles made preservation of de facto independence more difficult. Thus Taiwan responded enthusiastically to the Pentagon's efforts to improve upon the military-to-military dialogue involving training, communication, and logistics, as well as to the idea of a theater missile defense (TMD) system for Asia. Aware that TMD was unproven and enormously expensive, Taiwan's defense establishment remained divided about the wisdom of such a venture. To civilian officials, however, TMD seemed less a military than a political weapon. By joining in development of the concept and its early warning network, Taiwan could reestablish close military links to the United States akin to the U.S.-Taiwan Mutual Defense Treaty relationship, abrogated in 1980. Analysts in Beijing, of course, reached the same conclusion, which made the issue of Taiwan's involvement in TMD incendiary.

The lesson Americans drew from the 1995–96 crisis was that nationalism and the commitment to the recovery of Taiwan would be more volatile than they had imagined. No longer could it be assumed that the desire for commercial ties with the United States sufficed to moderate China's behavior. Suddenly Washington understood that Beijing would use force to prevent Taiwan's independence. This disturbing realization produced contradictory impulses. The United States might in principle support the ideal of self-determination, but in practice, many officials and China specialists worried about the popularity of the DPP, with its irresponsible independence platform. An assortment of scholars and retired officials articulated formulas to freeze conditions in the strait, most advocating a fifty-year hiatus during which neither Taipei nor Beijing would disrupt the status quo.[14] Meanwhile, Washington began openly to warn Taiwan against provocative acts and privately to develop a policy designed to force Taipei to be more cautious.

In fact, in the weeks before Clinton traveled to China in 1998, Taipei worried that the United States would sign a fourth communiqué with China that would sacrifice its interests to the improvement of Washington's fragile ties with Beijing. The anxiety followed from a policy known as the "Three No's," which had originally been communicated to Jiang Zemin confidentially by President Clinton in the summer of 1995 and then had been affirmed orally in conjunction with the Jiang summit in the United States, repeated by Secretary of State Albright in China in May 1998, and reiterated by Deputy Assistant Secretary of State Susan Shirk to Congress. The "Three No's" pledged the United States not to recognize Taiwanese independence, not to support two Chinas or one China and one Taiwan, and not to endorse Taiwan's entry into any international organization for which statehood would be a requirement. Although he avoided a written statement, Clinton did subscribe to the formula orally at a highly scripted meeting on Chinese soil in July 1998, thereby jettisoning the carefully crafted two-decade-old policy designed to preserve the right of Taiwan's people to self-determination. Although members of the Clinton administration insisted that no policies had been changed, Congress made a point of voting almost unanimous support to Taiwan, believing that the

---

14. The most often quoted was Joseph Nye, "A Taiwan Deal," *Washington Post*, March 8, 1998, p. C7. Others suggested similar approaches, including Kenneth Lieberthal, who subsequently joined the staff of the National Security Council, and Chas W. Freeman, Jr., "Preventing War in the Taiwan Strait: Restraining Taiwan—and Beijing," *Foreign Affairs* (July/August 1998), pp. 6–11.

pronouncement by the president had weakened Taipei's negotiating hand.

This was of particular importance as Taiwan and China resumed their cross-strait dialogue, suspended by Beijing during the 1995 crisis. Both sides had repeatedly called for talks during 1997. Invariably these initiatives were thwarted, as each preferred the favorable publicity generated by the gesture to genuine progress on the problem. Even when Beijing finally hosted Taipei's chief negotiator Koo Chen-fu on the mainland in October 1998, there were no serious accomplishments apart from the commitment to keep meeting. Beijing continued to insist on political discussions to facilitate reunification, while Taipei wanted progress only on practical issues such as protection of Taiwan's businesspeople.[15]

The difficulty in agreeing even to an agenda for dialogue reflected the broader problem of change in the delicate balance that had kept the volatile Taiwan situation relatively quiet since the early 1960s. In the late 1990s, Beijing, Taipei, and Washington faced the reality of an unstable environment in which growing nationalism, fledgling democracy, military modernization, and economic upheaval challenged policy makers who were too focused on domestic affairs to guide their peoples effectively. Democracy in Taiwan, long nurtured by Americans, had finally come to fruition, forcing the governing authorities to take public opinion into account. But the public had also changed; it had become more prosperous and younger, increasingly emphasizing the Taiwan dialect over Mandarin Chinese, local history over that of the mainland-oriented Republic of China, and a rhetoric of de facto independence over the more traditional evocations of one China enshrined in GMD doctrine and the Shanghai Communiqué. Thus nationalism became an influential force in Taiwan just as the Beijing government decided that nationalism would be the most effective way to retain power on the mainland. As the demonstrations provoked by the Belgrade bombing of May 1999 illustrated, even the most pro-Western segments of the PRC's population could, under the right circumstances, be drawn into the streets to protect Chinese sovereignty and national integrity.

---

15. Taiwan's efforts to get China to conclude an agreement have been stymied by Beijing's arguments that (1) Taiwan businesspeople fall under Chinese domestic law; (2) since Taiwan will not legalize direct investment, there is nothing to protect; and (3) since Taiwan will not permit Chinese investment on the island, there can be no reciprocity. Leng Tse-kang, *The Taiwan–China Connection* (Boulder, CO: Westview Press, 1996), p. 114.

At the end of the 1990s, then, Beijing faced an increasingly disturbing reality. Time might not be on China's side even as it grew stronger and better able to take Taiwan by force. The diminishing interest in reunification on the island stimulated a sense of urgency that had not been felt by Mao Zedong or Deng Xiaoping. Beijing also worried about the growing constituency in the U.S. Congress that favored assistance to Taiwan. The Taiwan Security Enhancement Act proffered by Senator Jesse Helms in March 1999, which called for regular military consultations between Taipei and Washington, seemed symbolic of the disregard for China's claims.

A far greater provocation, however, arose in July 1999 when, in the midst of an interview with a German journalist, Lee Teng-hui asserted that relations between China and Taiwan ought to be conducted on a "special state-to-state" basis. Subsequent clarification of these disturbing words made matters worse, as spokesmen appeared to suggest that Taiwan wished to renounce the one-China principle. Beijing responded harshly, threatening military reprisal. During the ensuing weeks, China remained rhetorically inflexible but took no action. Taiwan continued its explanations, under U.S. pressure, trying to deflate the crisis without retracting the state-to-state formula.[16]

Lee's motives in triggering this new crisis appeared to be multiple. First might have been the frustration felt in Taipei as China worked ever harder to isolate Taiwan diplomatically, luring away countries having diplomatic relations with Taiwan and barring Taiwan from international organizations requiring statehood for membership. If Lee could draw international attention to his people's plight, the growing isolation might be breached. Next, Taipei felt considerable resentment toward U.S. policy, which seemed to be tilting toward Beijing. Not only had Clinton articulated the Three No's, but subsequently Assistant Secretary of State for East Asian and Pacific Affairs Stanley Roth had advocated that Taipei and Beijing reach interim agreements to revive the process of cross-strait negotiation. Although the Americans insisted that advocacy of interim agreements was a procedural recommendation for confidence building rather than a substantive policy prescription, to Taipei it appeared that the United States was putting pressure on Taiwan, in violation of Reagan's Six Assurances, and accepting the idea that one China

---

16. Chairman of the Mainland Affairs Council Su Chi, who spoke on July 12, 1999, had intended to distance Taipei from a "one China" that meant the PRC.

meant the PRC.[17] With the prospect of a visit by Wang Daohan, China's lead negotiator, to Taiwan to move talks forward, Lee assuredly wanted to set a precondition of parity and, perhaps, provoke cancellation of this next, perilous step in cross-strait negotiations. Finally, the president may also have been trying to secure his political legacy and circumscribe the maneuvering room of his successor.

Thus, as the United States embarked on presidential campaigning for the 2000 election, the situation in the Taiwan Strait had grown tense again. The possibility of a Chinese attack on Taiwan rapidly became a Republican issue, leading to calls upon the Clinton administration to abandon its policy of strategic ambiguity and pledge support to Taiwan should Beijing act on its threats.[18] Indeed, many observers in the United States predicted a military operation of some sort between October 1999 and the inauguration of a new Taiwan president in May 2000.

Military Challenges

Apart from the Taiwan Strait crisis, a series of other strategic issues also had the potential to array Chinese and U.S. forces against each other at the dawn of the new millennium. Many could be traced to the growing military might of the Chinese state and the problems its drive for sophistication and effectiveness caused Washington and China's Asian neighbors. At the beginning of the reform era, China's leaders had emphasized a program of four modernizations in which the military ranked the lowest. But as the economy took off and China's leaders yearned to play a larger role in the world community, strengthening the armed forces became more important.

---

17. The Six Assurances were that (1) the United States had not set a deadline for ending arms sales; (2) there would be no prior consultation with the PRC regarding the arms sales; (3) the United States would not undertake mediation between Taipei and Beijing; (4) the United States would not revise the Taiwan Relations Act; (5) the U.S. position regarding the sovereignty of Taiwan had not been altered; and (6) Washington would not pressure Taiwan to agree to negotiations. Nancy Bernkopf Tucker, *Taiwan, Hong Kong and the United States, 1945–1992: Uncertain Friendships* (New York: Twayne/Macmillan, 1994), p. 139. The Taiwan Relations Act of 1979 was passed to provide a framework for nonofficial U.S.-Taiwan relations after the United States withdrew diplomatic recognition.

18. Strategic ambiguity originated with the Eisenhower administration in the 1950s. Officials reasoned that if they said they would not defend Taiwan, China would attack. But if they said they would protect the island, then its leaders would declare independence. By not declaring definitively what the United States would do, both sides would be deterred. Nancy Bernkopf Tucker, "War or Peace in the Taiwan Strait?" *Washington Quarterly* (winter 1995).

Precisely how successful this effort had proven to be became a topic of much debate outside China. Some specialists asserted that despite foreign-arms purchases and reformulation of strategic doctrine, China continued to have a distinctly second-rate military. Others countered that although there had been no comprehensive advances, asymmetrical pockets of excellence were being created in order to target just those areas in which the United States might be vulnerable. In 1998, a Republican-controlled Congress, determined to undermine Clinton's policies, sought Pentagon assessments of China's military strength and goals as well as its threat to Taiwan and the potential for TMD in Asia. Eager to embarrass the White House by suggesting that the administration had ignored burgeoning Chinese power, Republicans also hoped to use the China threat to further the development of theater and national missile defense.

Negative images of China also grew out of startling revelations regarding alleged Chinese espionage. The first scandal broke when word leaked out that scientists from two major U.S. companies using Chinese launch facilities to put communications satellites in space had shared classified information with their Chinese counterparts. Loral Space and Communications and Hughes Electronics Corporation had hoped to improve rocket design after three satellite launches failed, destroying their costly U.S. payloads. In the process, the companies ignored prohibitions against transferring sensitive information to Chinese scientists. Subsequent revelations suggested that modifications made in civilian missile-guidance systems had quickly been adapted for military use.

Campaign finance complicated the issue. Loral's chief executive, Bernard Schwartz, had been the single largest donor to the Clinton presidential campaign in 1996. He and the head of Hughes had lobbied the administration to shift approval for satellite-launch licensing from the Department of State to the Department of Commerce, where consent would be easier and faster to secure. Clinton acceded in 1996. Furthermore, investigation of Chinese campaign contributions suggested that $300,000 had come from chief of military intelligence Major General Ji Shengde, whose responsibilities included the acquisition of foreign technology.

National security appeared even more seriously compromised by the second scandal, which hinged upon outright espionage and an ostensible willingness on the part of the administration to ignore it. In

1998 when Speaker of the House Newt Gingrich was seeking evidence to impeach Clinton, he authorized a congressional investigation of alleged technology thefts by China. The charges originated with a document revealing knowledge of U.S. nuclear warheads that was clandestinely delivered to the CIA, either by inadvertence, for intimidation, or as disinformation by a Chinese intelligence operative. The 900-page report subsequently produced by the bipartisan House Select Committee on U.S. National Security and Military/Commercial Concerns with the People's Republic of China headed by Christopher Cox (R-California) asserted that there had been serious lapses in security at the nation's nuclear laboratories and multiple instances of spying over a period of twenty years. The report insisted that although the Clinton White House had been apprised of the situation, little corrective action had been taken. The list of possible losses was formidable, including the neutron bomb, designs for every warhead in the U.S. nuclear arsenal, the electromagnetic technology needed to attack missiles and satellites in space, and scientific data for tracking submarines, which had long been the least vulnerable element in the nation's defense triad. The Cox Committee estimated, based on some of these acquisitions, that China would deploy one hundred new intercontinental ballistic missiles by 2014. Outside analysts who examined the report after its release questioned most of the findings, suggesting that the Committee had reached extreme conclusions for partisan reasons. But by then, considerable damage had been done to U.S.-China relations, already severely strained by the Belgrade bombing and its aftermath.

Chinese efforts to modernize its forces stemmed not just from concern about U.S. power, but also from longstanding fear of Japan and its ambitions in Asia. Despite the passage of time and substantial economic cooperation between Japan and China, many Chinese seemed unable to forget the past and trust Japan not to remilitarize. To them, the U.S.-Japan relationship had been troubling; barely acceptable when Washington circumscribed Japanese power, but fundamentally suspect nonetheless.[19] In 1996, at the same time that China and the United States had been caught up in the Taiwan Strait confrontation, Washington and Tokyo had been renegotiating their defense relation-

---

19. Nixon and Kissinger had, of course, presented the Japan-U.S. connections as a mechanism for controlling Tokyo during the first normalization negotiations. James Mann, *About Face: A History of America's Curious Relationship with China, from Nixon to Clinton* (New York: Knopf, 1999), pp. 43–44.

ship. The missile crisis gave impetus to a set of Defense Guidelines clarifying mutual responsibilities. China took exception to this tightening of ties both because of alarm at Japan's new activism and because of the fear that the Guidelines secretly coveted Taiwan. Disclaimers by Washington and Tokyo insisting that the agreement applied only to situations, not to particular places in the area surrounding Japan, however, did not convince skeptics in China, the United States, or Japan.

Efforts to repair strained China-Japan relations, made more urgent by consolidation of the U.S.-Japan alliance, faltered when a summit meeting between China's president and Japan's prime minister in December 1998 went awry. Jiang Zemin arrived in Japan with demands that Tokyo apologize in writing for World War II atrocities committed against the Chinese people. But whereas the Japanese had accommodated South Korean president Kim Dae-Jung just weeks earlier, they refused Jiang. Further, they rebuffed Chinese pressure to subscribe to Beijing's Taiwan policy by confirming the Three No's, as Clinton had done in Shanghai. Soon thereafter relations suffered further when the Japanese Diet voted to move ahead with implementation of the Defense Guidelines and appropriated $8 million for studying TMD. Although Tokyo decided to participate in TMD research because of North Korea's August 31, 1998, test of a three-stage missile over Japanese territory, some in Beijing as well as in Japan saw the system as a deterrent against a rising China.

The growth of Chinese power and suspicion about its possible uses troubled others in the region and beyond. In the South China Sea, transit routes vital to Japanese trade and U.S. naval operations ran through waters contested by China, Taiwan, the Philippines, Malaysia, Vietnam, and Brunei. Chinese efforts to extend influence by building facilities on various islands and their willingness to clash with the Vietnamese and Filipinos underscored the dangers that Chinese acquisition of a blue-water navy might bring. Although the United States remained on the sidelines of the multinational dispute, China's deployments and reluctance to participate in a regional solution troubled U.S. policymakers. Alarm also extended to the western hemisphere over control of the Panama Canal. With reversion of the waterway to Panama imminent and the presidential political season in Washington heating up, Senate Republicans denounced a contract to operate container terminals at each end of the canal held by the Hong Kong company

Hutchinson Whampoa. A well-established Hong Kong firm run by a widely respected billionaire became, in the eyes of China's critics, nothing more than an arm of the PLA.

Not all military exchanges with China in this period, of course, were contentious. China joined the Nuclear Nonproliferation Treaty, the Comprehensive Test Ban Treaty, the Zanger Nuclear Users Club, and the Chemical and Biological Weapons Conventions. Although not a signatory, it largely adhered to the Missile Technology Control Regime and promised to give membership serious study. Beijing denied having transferred missiles to Pakistan, although evidence of this action increased in the late 1990s, but it also noted its long and close relationship with Islamabad. As part of the effort to create good feeling surrounding the Clinton visit in 1998, China announced it would retarget its intercontinental ballistic missiles aimed at U.S. cities. Although a gesture that could be rescinded in a matter of minutes, the idea, nevertheless, was heralded as symbolic of the effort to establish better relations. In reality, according to the Cox Report, retargeting had never happened.

China also cooperated, if somewhat reluctantly, on the volatile question of Korea. Washington and Beijing agreed that stability on the contentious peninsula must be sought through diplomacy, and both participated with North and South Korea in continuing four-power talks. North Korea's dire economic and financial straits, however, compelled Beijing to give massive food aid to Pyongyang lest starvation bring down the regime and drive a flood of refugees across their common border. Moreover, Washington suspected that Beijing might not be uniformly opposed to North Korea's development of nuclear weapons and proliferation of missiles. In the early 1990s, China had not objected to North Korean missile sales to Pakistan, but it had disapproved of sanctions designed to force Pyongyang to permit international inspections of its nuclear facilities. Furthermore, Beijing and Washington differed dramatically in their hopes for a unified Korea. To Beijing, the idea of a pro-American Korean state arrayed along the Yalu border with U.S. forces helping to protect the new entity could not be less welcome.

Economic Differences

Since the end of the Cold War, trade and investment have held the greatest potential for ameliorating differences and creating strong ties between the United States and China. At a time when strategic imperatives had diminished radically and conflicting definitions of human rights challenged the patience of leaders on both sides, economic growth appeared to represent neutral ground upon which mutually beneficial relations could be conducted. The focus on the marketplace grew even stronger with the election to the U.S. presidency of Bill Clinton, whose most memorable campaign slogan had been "It's the economy, stupid." Clinton deemed his highest priority to be domestic economic renewal and saw foreign relations primarily as a mechanism for increasing exports and creating jobs at home. Although he had also spoken out on human rights abuses in China during the election, he found within the first two years of his administration that linking trade and human rights neither changed Beijing's behavior nor served the commercial goals of the White House. As a result, he discarded linkage in 1994 and focused instead on promoting U.S. business initiatives with China.

By the end of 1997, this policy would garner considerable success for U.S. enterprise. The United States exported some $13 billion worth of goods to China in that year and imported more than $62 billion, making China the nation's fourth-largest trading partner. U.S. businesses also invested roughly $5 billion inside China. The problem, however, was that although bilateral trade grew rapidly, so did the trade deficit. Americans complained about barriers to market access and the ineffectiveness of the U.S. government in eliminating them.

Meanwhile, economic threats and opportunities similarly captured the attention of China's leadership as the remarkable growth rates of previous years began to slow and the need to deal with the intertwined problems of antiquated state-owned enterprises (SOEs) and insolvent banks forced changes in domestic priorities. By 1997, roughly half of the SOEs were operating at a loss, and the banks, periodically under national government pressure to lend to them, carried so many non-performing loans that they were essentially bankrupt.[20] Although inflation fell during the year, unemployment and underemployment surged. Restructuring of the economy and government produced mounting workforce reductions, given that SOEs employed two-thirds of the industrial labor force. This led to large floating populations trying to eke out a living in China's major cities and unrest in the countryside

---

20. See Nicholas Lardy, *China's Unfinished Economic Revolution* (Washington, DC: Brookings Institution, 1998).

among those who stayed behind, idled by job losses or victimized by erratic and unequal income, as well as environmental pollution. The Fifteenth Party Congress in the fall of 1997 accelerated restructuring by sanctioning movement toward local privatization under the label of public ownership, which was designed to reduce 130,000 SOEs to 512. Foreign trade, particularly access to the U.S. market, took on greater significance in this context. By 1997, China's favorable balance of trade with the United States had risen to some $40 billion, with projections that it could surpass the Japanese deficit and reach $80 billion in the year 2000.[21]

But Americans found that the importance of their market to China gave them little leverage over Chinese practices. Officials denied entrée to the service sector, refused to lower tariffs on agricultural products (although there were significant generalized tariff cuts), abused intellectual property rights, and maintained hidden subsidies to Chinese industry as well as avoided regulatory transparency.[22] Repeated threats to sanction Chinese trade by curtailing or suspending China's most favored nation (MFN) treatment, however, did not constitute a credible threat given the inability of Congress to rally behind any measure that could surmount White House opposition.

In fact, not only China specialists and the U.S. business community but also Taiwan and Hong Kong sought to end the frantic yearly lobbying effort to preserve normal trading relations with China by granting it permanent MFN status. Their actions were not altruistic. In the 1980s, responding to high labor costs, manufacturers in Taiwan and Hong Kong had relocated factories to China, where they benefited from cheap labor, cheap land, and tax breaks. They also shifted trade surpluses to mainland quotas, thereby lessening direct pressures from the United States to reduce imbalances. As the year 2000 approached, entrepreneurs in Taiwan had established some forty thousand businesses and invested more than $40 billion on the mainland, while gov-

---

21. The Chinese calculate the trade balance with the United States differently and consider the U.S. deficit to be much lower than does Washington. According to U.S. economists Lawrence Lau of Stanford and Fung Kwok-chiu at UC Santa Barbara, the truth may lie somewhere in between. Bruce Gilley, "Perception Gap," *Far Eastern Economic Review,* April 29, 1999, pp. 62–63.

22. China announced reductions from 23 to 17 percent in average import tariffs and the intention to reduce rates again to 15 percent by 2000 just before the autumn 1997 summit. These levels would still be more than double the rates on goods charged by developed nations. Goldstein, "China in 1997," pp. 50–51.

ernment corporations were making plans for joint oil exploration. The growing trade and investments between China, Taiwan, and Hong Kong soon led to speculation on the development of a Greater China.[23]

The formation of a Greater China, however, could not be seen solely in terms of financial advantage. Taiwan's officials sought to circumscribe reliance upon mainland markets, manufacturing plants, and raw materials to protect the island's security. They feared that economic dependence on China would give Beijing exaggerated political influence. Thus Taipei instituted restrictions on the size and type of investment that could be made in China, legislated penalties for infractions, and Lee Teng-hui warned the business community to "avoid haste, be patient." Taipei refused to consider the so-called three links, encompassing direct trade, mail, and transportation, first suggested by China in the 1979 New Year's "Message to Taiwan Compatriots." In April 1997, Taiwan and China finally opened direct shipping service, but Taipei severely limited the routes and condoned only trans-shipment, stirring protests among dissatisfied Taiwan businesspeople. By 1998, the American Chamber of Commerce, Taiwan's most powerful foreign business lobby, had begun pressing the government to reconsider direct service. Indeed, Taipei's desire to create a regional operations center from which multinational corporations could conduct their business would founder without easy access to mainland China. Furthermore, Taiwan's business community rebelled at prohibitions on infrastructure investment. Formosa Plastics, barred in 1998 from putting some $3 billion into a power-plant scheme in Fujian, simply defied the authorities and moved ahead with the project using offshore resources.

China's internal economic problems made the advent of the Asian economic crisis in July 1997 a particularly unwelcome shock. Although it was initially protected from financial speculation by its nonconvertible currency, China was endangered by the crash of economies all over Asia, which made its prosperity vulnerable to competition from countries able to undersell China as they devalued their currencies. Chinese growth and stability also suffered as purchases and investments by Asians plummeted. Given the fact that as of late 1998 some 70 percent of foreign direct investment originated in Asia, such a retrenchment could not be contained or compensated for easily.

Results proved mixed. In the short term, Beijing gained stature in

---

23. See Ralph N. Clough, *Cooperation or Conflict across the Taiwan Strait?* (New York: Rowman and Littlefield, 1999) for details of cross-strait interaction.

the international community, and special praise from Bill Clinton, by resisting devaluation of the yuan (although some observers argued that it would have entailed more costs than gains for China) and offering assistance to Thailand. In the longer run, the financial crisis complicated Chinese economic modernization and made accession to the WTO a greater risk for the leadership of the country than it had been before. Necessary internal reforms that could increase unemployment and reduce Chinese competitiveness abroad and at home might be more than a weakened economic system could endure. Elements of the leadership, increasingly preoccupied with economic security, feared that the financial crisis had actually been imposed by vengeful capitalists "smothering the 'Asian miracle'" as they sought to eliminate competition in a manner "more effective, graceful, and gentle than conquest by warplanes."[24]

China had been very eager to join the WTO as a founding member when it replaced the General Agreement on Tariffs and Trade in 1994. But Beijing's entry foundered on conflicting assessments of the Chinese economy. China insisted it should be treated as a developing country, compelled to meet less stringent requirements for admission. Various industrialized nations, especially the United States, however, asserted that any country growing annually at rates fluctuating between 7 and 11 percent did not qualify for concessions. There would be little benefit to having China inside the global trade system if special terms allowed it to evade relaxation of tariffs, elimination of regulatory impediments to trade and investment, introduction of a convertible currency, and enforcement of product standards. Thus bilateral negotiations to facilitate China's entry dragged on and made little progress in 1997 and 1998.

Premier Zhu Rongji's trade concessions in the WTO negotiations in April 1999 were designed to break the impasse. The U.S. business community, increasingly alienated from the China market by new regulations restricting their opportunities, had been turning away from China. During the first two months of 1999, foreign investment dropped some 48 percent from 1998, and membership in the U.S.-China Business Council fell. But Zhu's package, particularly his

---

24. Tan Jian, "Who Will Be Responsible for Defending State Economic Security?" *Jiefangjun bao* (People's Liberation Army Daily), April 30, 1998, p. 5, as quoted in Joseph Fewsmith, "China in 1998: Tacking to Stay the Course," *Asian Survey*, vol. 39, no. 1 (January/February 1999), pp. 104–5.

unprecedented willingness to open banking, insurance, and telecommunications to foreigners, excited potential investors. Zhu had, in fact, gone so far that disgruntled elements at home condemned him for betraying China and called for his resignation. When the deal collapsed and Beijing began to back away from the most significant compromises, U.S. business brought enormous pressure to bear on the White House urging Clinton to accept the Chinese deal so that China could participate in the November 1999 WTO meeting, where the agenda would be set for a new round of trade talks.

Failure of China to enter the WTO in 1999, moreover, would mean that Taiwan's accession would almost certainly be delayed as well. China has long insisted that Taiwan must not be allowed to enter ahead of China and the world trading community has accepted that linkage. So, although Taipei has endured years of arduous negotiation and reformed its economy to qualify, its future status remained contingent. Taiwan might even be forced to reopen settled agreements should WTO requirements become more demanding while China continued to bargain.

The politicized nature of these economic relationships was similarly reflected in Taiwan's response to the Asian financial crisis. The island's industries managed to avoid the devastation wrought elsewhere in the region and the Taiwanese government saw the crisis as a chance to make loans, increase investments, and provide technical expertise to neighbors. Taipei had used its economic resources to win friends and influence diplomacy as early as the 1950s under the CIA's Vanguard agricultural-assistance program in Africa. In the 1990s, its economic involvement in Southeast Asia once again was opportunistic and triggered angry denunciations from Beijing, as well as resistance from Taiwan investors who did not want to retreat from lucrative mainland ventures.

Hong Kong suffered more from the Asian crisis than Taiwan as its currency sustained speculative onslaughts and its intermediary role in trade transactions plummeted. Hong Kong also was battered by a sharp drop in tourism and a rapid fall in property values. It had little choice but to welcome China's promise to back up Hong Kong's foreign-exchange reserves should economic decline undermine stability. At the same time, competition with Chinese business enterprises, such as the new port facilities proliferating along the southern coast, suggested that Hong Kong would have to strike out in new directions. As economic recovery slowly restored confidence, the local governing authorities aggressively courted high-tech information industries and signed an ambitious deal to build a new Disneyland amusement park.

Conclusion

What then may one conclude about the relationships between China, Taiwan, Hong Kong, and the United States in the waning days of a volatile century as fresh challenges and a new balance of forces herald an unstable beginning for the next millennium? Despite recent friction, it appears certain that Washington and Beijing appreciate the absolute necessity of maintaining a constructive dialogue. The unrealistic and rancorous ideological split that set the United States and China at odds for thirty years was a dangerous luxury from 1949 to 1979; today it would be untenable. Even Taipei, which benefited from that prolonged period of Washington's shortsightedness, would not suggest a return to an era in which Washington tried to exclude China from the world community.

There are, in fact, many bonds to build upon. The commercial relationship might be unequal, with greater access to the U.S. than the Chinese market, but it is vigorous and profitable. For the U.S. consumer, purchases of low-priced Chinese goods, especially toys and shoes, would be difficult to do without. For Chinese enterprises seeking advanced technology, no other source of knowledge and equipment would be as good as the United States. U.S. investment contributes significantly to China's rapid growth and modernization. The United States shares with and encourages China in its commitment to improving environmental controls. Both governments agree that there must be greater development of China's legal institutions and village elections, even though there may be differences over the purposes of a legal system and popular political participation. In Hong Kong, Americans have responded to the imposition of Chinese rule with tolerance and patience. Some fifty thousand Chinese students study in colleges and universities in the United States, many of whom (though not all) bring back to China a better understanding of American values and society along with their specialized training. Beijing and Washington generally cooperate on security issues regarding the Korean peninsula, and although they advocate diverging solutions, they do concur on the need for peace and stability.

Nevertheless, the disputes appear more profound and disturbing.

Chinese leaders are not convinced that the United States wants to see China become a strong and prosperous power in Asia. China's experience in the nineteenth and twentieth centuries suggests otherwise. To leaders and followers alike, the idea that Washington seeks advantages only a hegemon can claim leads directly to the conclusion that the United States plans to contain a rising China, to keep it weak and divided. This conviction produces distrust. There are also signs in 1999 that a growing belligerent nationalism could begin to endanger the United States, China, Taiwan, and the rest of Asia.

U.S. leaders are suspicious, too, and they approach the new millennium with trepidation, as do the Chinese. Clearly some Americans do wish to contain China. They see the Chinese not just as repressive and autocratic at home but as expansionist and bellicose abroad. Others, the greater number, understand that containment is not an option and that China is less likely to become a threat if it is not treated as an enemy. A China that is isolated, unstable, and unable to fulfill the rising expectations of its people would be disastrous for the region and ultimately for the United States. On the other hand, even the most sympathetic China watchers worry about Beijing's capabilities and intentions.

Nowhere are concerns about growing Chinese power more disturbing than in the context of Beijing's Taiwan policy. In the new millennium, pressures to resolve Taiwan's status and bring it into a Chinese state that has successfully unified with Hong Kong and Macao will grow. In fact, it is not clear that democratization of the Chinese political system would resolve this thorny problem or that cross-strait ties with a prosperous, confident China are necessarily safer for Taiwan, although a failing state seeking foreign adventure to solve domestic problems would surely be more dangerous.

Taiwan itself threatens to undermine peace in Asia. Its emergence as a prosperous, democratic society has produced discontent with the status quo of marginalization and disenfranchisement. Although Lee Teng-hui is more outspoken than most, it seems certain that destabilizing alterations in Taiwan's political outlook will not end when he leaves office.

At present, Washington and Beijing do agree that there are benefits to integrating China into the fabric of the world community. For China, this means a greater voice in international affairs with a chance to shape institutions and defend national interests. U.S. officials hope that integration will contribute to liberalizing China's economy and that this will inevitably also liberalize its politics. But here objectives diverge. China reserves the right to participate on its own terms, terms that do not encompass wholesale Westernization. China will change but is determined to change at its own pace and in ways of its own choosing. Bill Clinton's repeated assertions that open markets and democratization are inherently linked are not only denied by China's leaders but are also not supported by reliable evidence.[25] Nevertheless, the strains are apparent. In the nineteenth century, Confucian scholar-official Zhang Zhidong tried to allay concern about rapid modernization with an observation about limiting the convergence between East and West: "Chinese learning for the essence, Western learning for practical application." As China enters the twenty-first century, the tensions remain much the same.

China seeks to become a great power capable of defining its own place in the world as well as influencing the nature and direction of the world order. It is intent on reversing a legacy of subjugation that continues to rankle even as claims of victimization sometimes provide negotiating advantage. In achieving this goal, it will study, adapt to, and challenge existing rules, anxious to make the twenty-first century more auspicious for China's national interests. Confrontation between the United States and China is almost inevitable given the enormous part Washington has played in constructing the contemporary world. But contention can be creative and need not produce a new Cold War or a clash of civilizations. What is necessary is a sincere commitment to peace, the willingness to abandon provocative policies, and the courage to compromise.

---

25. Margaret M. Pearson, "China's Emerging Business Class: Democracy's Harbinger?" *Current History* (September 1998), p. 268.

The More Things Change, the More They Remain the Same: The World, the United States, and the People's Republic of China, 1949–1999

Bruce Cumings

Fifty years ago on October 1, Mao Zedong stood atop the Gate of Heavenly Peace (Tiananmen) and proclaimed the People's Republic of China: "China has stood up," he memorably said, but China also "leaned to one side"—the Soviet side. That event, coming only a few weeks after Moscow tested its first atomic bomb, amply justified Premier Zhao Ziyang's statement four decades later that the founding of the PRC "shook the world."[1] These two milestones detonated fundamental policy changes in Washington over the next several months, resulting in National Security Council (NSC) document 48, which brought containment to Asia and military aid to the French in Vietnam, and NSC 68, the essential U.S. blueprint for fighting the Cold War. To build the U.S. global position against communist expansion, NSC 68 called for a trebling of defense expenditures. There was, in short, an intimate relationship between this prodigious revolution and the rise to global preeminence of the United States.

In 1949, the United States accounted for 50 percent of world industrial production and had an unrivaled lead in every advanced technology; soon, it would spend more on defense than all of its potential rivals put together. Today the United States accounts for 25 percent of world industrial production and retains a lead in just about every advanced technology—and it still spends more on defense than all of its conceivable enemies put together. In 1949, China was among the

---

1. Zhao Ziyang, "Advance along the Road of Socialism with Chinese Characteristics," special supplement to the *Beijing Review*, November 1987.

poorest countries in the world, with minuscule force-projection capacity; it was poised to complete its territorial unification by invading Taiwan in June 1950, according to CIA estimates, but other observers noted China's lack of air cover for the invasion and the questionable efficacy of massive amphibious landings in what amounted to armored junks.[2] Truman mooted the point by inserting the Seventh Fleet between Taiwan and the mainland once the Korean War began.

Today China is growing rapidly, but it remains a poor country with two-thirds of its huge population still engaged in agriculture, much of it subsistence; its per capita income levels after decades of development are less than 10 percent of Western levels, and its living standards are lower than those in Iran, or Iraq and Kosovo before their recent wars. The PRC ranks fortieth in the world in total technology spending as a percentage of GDP (behind Brazil)[3] and spends little more on defense than neighbors Taiwan and South Korea put together (they spend about $30 billion, with China estimated to spend between $25 billion and $40 billion).[4] China also imports only a quarter of the weaponry that they do ($1.5 billion for China in 1988–92, for example, compared with $5.8 billion for South Korea and Taiwan in the same period). With Taiwan spending well over $20 billion in the 1990s to obtain the latest fighter jets and other means to control the air (including Patriot antimissile missiles), China still lacks the amphibious and air-cover capability to invade the island successfully.[5] Like Harry Truman before him, during the last serious fracas over Taiwan in

---

2. Bruce Cumings, *Origins of the Korean War*, vol. 2 (Princeton, NJ: Princeton University Press, 1990), p. 508, based on interviews with Robert Strong, the U.S. chargé d'affaires in Taiwan in June 1950.

3. Data from World Information Technology and Services Alliance, cited in the *New York Times*, April 3, 1999.

4. South Korea and Taiwan together spent $29 billion on defense in 1995, compared with China's official figure of about 70.2 billion yuan, or $8.4 billion. U.S. Central Intelligence Agency, *World Factbook* (Washington, DC: U.S. Central Intelligence Agency, 1997). Western estimates put China's real defense spending at somewhere between $25 billion and $40 billion. See David Shambaugh, "China's Military: Real or Paper Tiger," *Washington Quarterly* (Spring 1996); and Bates Gill and Michael O'Hanlon, "China's Military: How Good?" *The National Interest*, no. 56 (Summer 1999), p. 56. Gill and O'Hanlon cite the highest estimate, $60 billion, but discount it and point out that much of China's defense expenditure goes for maintaining a PLA that has enormous domestic responsibilities and controls a host of inefficient industries, unlike Western militaries. Some experts believe the latter expenses account for 30 percent of the budget.

5. Michael C. Gallagher, "China's Illusory Threat to the South China Sea," *International Security* (Summer 1994), pp. 169–93.

March 1996 Bill Clinton mooted the point by mobilizing two aircraft-carrier task forces to shadow the island.

In 1949, China was the most vociferous and implacable U.S. enemy; it was closely allied to the Soviet Union, and both of them were insurgent powers on the world scene determined to build a top-to-bottom, A-to-Z alternative to Western capitalism and democracy. With war scares coming almost daily, finally a major war did break out—and in spite of its manifest military inferiority, China fought the United States to a standstill in Korea. Earlier last year, it appeared that a new war might blow up in the spring of 1999—not in Kosovo, but again in Korea. The ostensible causes were Pyongyang's intransigence about opening up a mountain redoubt that U.S. intelligence officials said was a surreptitious site of continuing nuclear weapons activity, and its unwillingness to rein in its missile program. In the fall of 1998, right-wing Republicans, fueled by leaks of classified information, were screaming about Clinton's North Korea policy; soon the Pentagon leaked a new U.S. war plan that would take advantage of prevalent North Korean infirmities to wipe out the entire regime, should the North attack: to "abolish North Korea as a state and . . . 'reorganize' it under South Korean control." In other words, this was a rollback policy.[6] Predictably, Pyongyang retorted with unprecedented propaganda broadsides about taking any new war directly to U.S. territory—and erasing us instead.[7] All this came just four years after Jimmy Carter intervened to derail a crisis over the North's nuclear program that had brought the peninsula to the brink of another devastating war, yielding instead the 1994 Agreed Framework that froze North Korea's graphite nuclear reactor. In both of these crises, China provided critical diplomatic support for the United States, but should another war erupt in Korea, Beijing might again be forced to defend its ally—and it still is not clear that the United States could win another Korean war.

Fifty years ago, Dean Acheson's policy toward the PRC was to recognize China as a means of bringing it into the world economy and making it dependent on the West. Acheson and his key aide, George Kennan, thought that Moscow could not really do much to rehabilitate and industrialize China; sooner or later it would have to turn to the West for help. An Anglophile and an internationalist, Acheson wanted to work with Great Britain (which quickly recognized the PRC) to

---

6. Richard Halloran, *Far Eastern Economic Review*, December 3, 1998.
7. Korean Central News Agency, December 3, 1998.

keep China open, with the hope that this would split Beijing and Moscow and ultimately scatter China's insurgent impulses in the solvent of free trade. The way to do that was to try to stay on the good side of Chinese anti-imperial nationalism and hope to enmesh China in the world economy. The Korean War put this possibility off sufficiently long that Richard Nixon, Acheson's Red-baiting antagonist in the 1950s, could fulfill it only in the 1970s. But Nixon and every subsequent president have only deepened this enmeshment strategy, abjuring the realpolitik argument that a strong China threatened U.S. interests. Today the USSR no longer exists, and China has moved farther and faster toward economic integration with the U.S.-shaped world economy than any observer could have imagined even twenty years ago, let alone fifty; it no longer has an alternative economic model, and the Communist Party is fighting a losing battle against creeping freedom and openness.

Hindsight discloses less obvious but hardly less important moments in that pregnant year, 1949. In August of that year, the State Department released a "White Paper" arguing that whoever might have "lost China," it was not the Truman administration. Soon came the arrests of Klaus Fuchs and the Rosenbergs, amid blaring accusations that Truman had also lost the A-bomb to Moscow through lax security at Los Alamos and that his China specialists were less than sympathetic to our erstwhile Chinese ally (Chiang Kai-shek, who clearly did lose China). Instead, there were hidden spies inside the government—bringing the Chinese Communists to power by an ingenious remote control.

One of these China hands, John Paton Davies, represented the clearest case of mistaken identity: at the time, he was a State Department official immersed in a growing interagency debate over whether U.S. policy should seek merely to contain a budding communist monolith stretching from Berlin to Canton or should roll it back. (Davies preferred the latter, particularly regarding East Asia; subsequently both NSC 48 and NSC 68 stated that the U.S. strategy toward communism should be both "to contain and, where feasible, to roll it back.") Another China hand, Owen Lattimore, urged the State Department in roundtable discussions in October 1949 to pay more attention to Korea: "Korea may turn out to be a country that has more effect upon the situation than its apparent weight would indicate." Six months later, Lattimore—a professor at Johns Hopkins and a mere external advisor to the State Department—was Senator Joseph McCarthy's "chief Russian spy" in the United States, while Dean Acheson (Truman's secretary of state) was his "voice for the mind of Lattimore."[8] Three months after that, the Korean War broke out, leading first to a war for containment in South Korea and thence to a war for "a roll-back" (in the language of NSC 81) in North Korea that caused a bloody, disastrous U.S.-China collision.

When U.S. defense spending is scaled throughout the period of the Cold War, there is a curious upward blip that most Americans have never noticed. In real FY 1996 dollars, defense spending hit $500 billion—almost double what it is now—just once: during the Korean War. It never got above $400 billion during the Vietnam War, and its next crest was $425 billion, or 6.5 percent of GDP, during the Reagan build-up in 1986. Since the Cold War ended, defense spending has dropped to about $265 billion, or less than 4 percent of GDP.[9] The war in Korea was the lever ("Korea came along and saved us," in Dean Acheson's notable words) by which Washington finally found a reliable method to pay the bills for U.S. commitments at home and abroad that were without historical precedent: a huge peacetime army, a growing national-security state that quickly influenced nearly all walks of life in the United States, and a global position that soon encompassed 1.5 million U.S. troops stationed at hundreds of bases in 35 countries, with formal security commitments to 43 countries and the training and equipping of military forces in 70 countries.

Meanwhile, in the summer of 1949, an M.I.T. physicist thought by many to be the most brilliant mind of his generation settled into his new chair in Pasadena, as the Robert Goddard Professor of Jet Propulsion at Caltech. Second only to Werner von Braun as a father of U.S. rocketry, he was later credited with developing the workhorse Titan intercontinental ballistic missile—and that was just one of his many original contributions to the U.S. aerospace program. In June, he applied for U.S. citizenship. A year later, three weeks before the Korean War and with his application still pending, FBI agents knocked on his office door; that same day Caltech administrators

---

8. Lattimore in State Department, "Transcript of Round Table Discussion on American Policy toward China," October 6–8, 1949; McCarthy in the *New York Times*, March 22 and 31, 1950.

9. U.S. Defense Department numbers, cited in the *Boston Sunday Globe*, February 11, 1999, p. B4.

received a letter saying he would no longer be permitted to work on classified projects. Five years after that, with no charges against him proved but with the knowledge in his head now deemed obsolescent, Qian Xueshen was allowed to go home—where he became the unchallenged father of China's rocket program. Indeed, he cloned the Titan into the CSS-4 ICBM, still the only Chinese missile that can reach U.S. soil.[10] Today China lacks anything like a global force-projection capability, with no blue-ocean navy, an antiquated air force with no air-refueling capability, and Dr. Qian's twenty ICBMs still sitting in silos without warheads or fuel (in a crisis, the United States would be able to monitor the arming and fuel loading of each one). Meanwhile, Japan spends $50 billion on defense and boasts high-tech fighter aircraft, missiles, and satellites that would require decades of expenditure for China to match. In short, China is still a modest military power, far more like its neighbors than like the United States or the former USSR.

In 1949, we had a China lobby embedded in the right wing of the Republican Party that sought to reverse Thomas Dewey's hair-whisker election loss to Truman a year earlier by parading wild charges of treasonous activity, with all media attention going to those charges and almost none to the floods of cash with which the Chinese Nationalists and their U.S. allies lubricated Congress.[11] Today Republicans such as Caspar Weinberger charge "the Clinton-Gore administration" with "the most serious breach of national security since Julius and Ethel Rosenberg betrayed our atomic secrets to the Soviet Union,"[12] as the right wing of that party tries to find another issue on which to hang Clinton-Gore after its failed impeachment effort. Meanwhile, for three years vague charges of a shadowy Chinese conspiracy to influence the 1996 presidential election have come and gone, with the spotlight on colorful figures such as Bill Clinton's Little Rock buddy Charlie Trie but with no resolution of the allegations. All media attention goes to such charges, and none to the money that Taiwan continues to spread around in Congress and elsewhere in the United States (and still in far greater amounts than the PRC).

In 1949, we had the unfortunate and badly maligned Qian

---

10. Iris Chang, *Thread of the Silkworm* (New York: Basic Books, 1995), pp. 143–50, 188. In the foyer of the huge new library at Jiaotong University in Xi'an—funded by a Hong Kong tycoon—stands an enormous statue of Dr. Qian.

11. I document this corruption in *Origins of the Korean War*, vol. 2.

12. Caspar Weinberger, "Foreword," *The Cox Report* (Washington: Regnery Publishing, 1999).

Xueshen, pushed out of the country by the FBI's anticommunist hysteria and racial prejudice; today we have Wen Ho Lee, the Los Alamos physicist charged with giving away the entire U.S. nuclear arsenal according to the Cox Report, issued by a congressional committee in May 1999. (The purloined secrets allegedly include "classified information on seven U.S. thermonuclear warheads, including every currently deployed thermonuclear warhead in the U.S. ballistic missile arsenal").[13] Yet Dr. Lee has not been charged with any crime, and China has yet to deploy a single warhead of U.S. design—stolen, copied, or otherwise. And so, like Dr. Qian in the early 1950s, Dr. Lee putters around his yard looking like the innocuous (Japanese) gardener in the film *Chinatown*, awaiting his uncertain fate.

This 1974 classic is a useful metaphor for thinking about China and the United States. Roman Polanski's film employs artful reversals of period stereotypes about the United States' Chinatowns (inscrutable, devious, given to nefarious conspiracies and general mayhem) to examine the unchallenged dominance and massive corruption of a prewar Los Angeles political elite that would stop at nothing to aggrandize its power and line its pockets. Yet when the violent denouement comes at the end of the film, nothing happens; the private detective, who now knows everything, is simply led away from the scene by his colleagues: "Forget it Jake, it's Chinatown."

The diabolical scheme presumably exposed in the Cox Report casts suspicion not just on Dr. Lee and China but on every visitor from China, every Chinese or Chinese American professor or student in a physics Ph.D. program, and, really, on every American of Chinese extraction no matter how many generations they may have lived in this country. Yet now the Republicans have also walked away from the implications of "one of the most stunning documents ever to come from the U.S. Congress."[14] They no longer seem interested in doing much about the Cox Report—by the summer it was already forgotten, rather like the impeachment of Bill Clinton. In July 1999, the Clinton administration relaxed longstanding restrictions on the export to China of powerful U.S. computers, a measure applauded by Republican centrist and odds-on presidential candidate George W. Bush (who was touring Silicon Valley at the time, and who showed that he is as soft on China as was his father, who secretly dispatched

13. *The Cox Report*, p. 1.
14. As advertised by the Weinberger-introduced Cox Report.

274 Bruce Cumings

his national security advisor to Beijing shortly after Tiananmen in 1989).

Half a century ago, China was an abstraction to Americans, and it still is. Most Americans had no idea that the 1949 revolution culminated 150 years of decline, rebellion, and humiliation detonated by the impact of Western imperialism, just as they do not know that today in "Communist" China young people by the millions are hardwired to the World Wide Web, sport green hair, dance to hard rock, and look forward to the next hot Initial Public Offering issue. China is instead a Rorschach inkblot onto which Americans project their hopes and fears: "China" tells us much more about ourselves than it does about the real country by the same name, and this is often as true of our China experts as it is of ordinary Americans.

If the experts have been good at pointing out the nonsense in the Republican claims about the China threat, nearly all of them remain captured by the solipsistic belief that China is somehow terribly important, one-fifth of mankind, shaking the world, we ignore it at our peril, and so on. Two specialists, Andrew Nathan and Robert Ross, began their recent book as follows: "China is the largest and economically most dynamic newly emerging power in the history of the world"; two others, Orville Schell and David Shambaugh, open their *China Reader* by saying, "No nation in history has undergone as total a transformation as has China during the quarter century from 1972 to 1997."[15] (Hmmm—more so than Japan from 1960 to 1985? South Korea or Taiwan from 1970 to 1995? Germany from 1860 to 1885? America from 1900 to 1925? England from 1825 to 1850?) Elsewhere, Professor Shambaugh writes that "two continental giants," China and the United States, "are likely to be the two dominant world powers during the twenty-first century."[16] But the United States is and has been the only continental giant, formidably engaged to its east (Europe), west (Asia), south (Latin America), and north (Canada), whereas China and that other (now-defunct) "continental giant," Russia, have undeveloped frontiers and mere pockets of industrial modernity (eighty years after its revolution, Russia's GNP is smaller than those of South Korea and the Netherlands).

---

15. Andrew J. Nathan and Robert S. Ross, *The Great Wall and the Empty Fortress: China's Search for Security* (New York: W.W. Norton, 1997), p. xi; Orville Schell and David Shambaugh, eds., *The China Reader* (New York: Vintage, 1999), p. xvii.

16. David Shambaugh, "The United States and China: Cooperation or Confrontation?" *Current History* (September 1997).

Realism versus Enmeshment

Various "realists" who enjoy parlaying the China threat and chastising China watchers for their sympathetic myopia are little better: Richard Betts, for example, wrote that China is "the great power in the [East Asian] region about which U.S. strategists should worry most over the long term,"[17] somehow forgetting that Japan has the second-largest economy in the world, competes head-to-head with the United States in high technology, and is the only country in Asia to have achieved a completed modernity commensurable with that of the United States and Western Europe. The realists also seem to forget history: if China is a "rising power" akin to nineteenth-century Germany (a trope found constantly in commentary on China), why should the United States be the one to clash with it, leaving Japan or Germany to pick up the pieces? The heretical truth about the United States' rise to world power is that it entered both world wars embarrassingly late and sustained no damage to its homeland or resources, while the European powers exhausted themselves. Realists are wedded to "containment" as opposed to the enmeshers' "engagement," but wouldn't a shrewd realpolitik let someone else take up the burden of containing China?

In 1949, another realist, George F. Kennan, listened patiently to the experts declaim China's overriding significance to the world (in the same roundtable discussions that Owen Lattimore took part in) and then told them this: "China doesn't matter very much. It's not very important. It's never going to be powerful."[18] China had no integrated industrial base, which Kennan deemed essential to any serious capacity for warfare. Instead, it had merely an industrial fringe stitched along its coasts by the imperial powers, and it was unlikely to develop such a capacity anytime soon; China thus ought not to be included in his containment strategy. Japan did have such a base and was therefore the key to postwar U.S. policy in East Asia. Kennan had a strategy for that, too, which he also enunciated in these discussions: provide for Japan's defense and police the flow of resources (especially oil) to its industrial economy— thus enabling the United States a residual outer-limit veto on what Japan could do in the future. The Lattimore roundtable was thus far more pregnant with meaning than Joe McCarthy could possibly have imagined.

---

17. Richard K. Betts, "Wealth, Power and Instability: East Asia and the United States after the Cold War," *International Security*, vol. 18, no. 3 (winter 1993-94), p. 75.

18. Quoted in Cumings, *Origins*, vol. 2, p. 55.

China, of course, also has its realists and its enmeshers. To the extent that the Cox Report contains any analysis of what Chinese leaders think they are doing, it claims that a "sixteen-character policy" drives Chinese policy, one "formally codified" in 1997 (the characters themselves are deployed in large boldface, thus verifying the Cox committee's bona fide expertise and cowing the ignorati). Even given the warped translations of these phrases by the committee's researchers, the four slogans are nothing more than innocuous, post-Tiananmen bromides about uniting the people and the army.[19] Meanwhile, Deng Xiaoping's own sixteen-character policy, enunciated in 1992, remains far more important and determining of Chinese strategy. Deng stated that the PRC not only benefited from the best global and regional security environment and the longest peace since its founding but also needed such an environment for the next fifty years. It should therefore deepen cooperation and mutual trust with the United States and the West, and avoid confrontations.[20] Two years later, during one of his last strolls through one of his coastal "open cities," in this case the marvelous Chinese-European treaty port of Qingdao, Deng doubled his estimate: "the policy of taking economic construction as the key link must never be changed; the reform and open-door policy must never be altered. The party's basic line must not be shaken for 100 years. . . ."[21]

In March 1996, Beijing disregarded Deng's advice in carrying out missile tests near Taiwan but got nothing from it except the largest U.S. force deployment in the Pacific since the war in Indochina ended. In succeeding months, moreover, it was clear that the authors of that provocative strategy had egg on their faces, and the exercises have not been repeated. The Cox Report returns frequently to these intimidating missile exercises, but it might just as easily have dwelt on a programmatic statement that appeared a year later in the People's Liberation Army (PLA) newspaper, written by Liu Huaqiu and titled "Strive for a Peaceful International Environment," again touting Deng's policy of opening and peaceful engagement.[22] As do other criticisms of U.S. policy toward China, the Cox Report also ignores the truly remarkable (for a communist country) international cooperation that Beijing has

---

19. *The Cox Report,* pp. 48–50.
20. Deng's instruction can be found in Quansheng Zhao, *Interpreting Chinese Foreign Policy* (Hong Kong: Oxford University Press, 1996), p. 221.
21. Quoted in Willy Wo-lap Lam, *China after Deng Xiaoping* (New York: John Wiley & Sons, 1995).
22. *The China Reader,* pp. 459–70.

engaged in, by joining any number of global and regional organizations and making important commitments to peace and nonproliferation through the Comprehensive Test Ban Treaty, the chemical and biological weapons conventions, and the Asian Regional Federation (ARF), as well as by playing an unexpectedly responsible role on the UN Security Council. In 1994, China also agreed to various regulations governing the export of missiles under the Missile Control Regime, but Washington did not invite it to join because signatories gain access to sophisticated missile technologies.[23] The PRC also facilitated U.S. diplomacy with North Korea throughout the 1990s, joined Clinton's four-power talks to end the Korean War, provided large amounts of food aid to famine-stricken North Korea (as did Washington), and in September 1999 cooperated with Washington to bring an end to Pyongyang's long-range missile tests.

A Chinese Worldview?

Once upon a time, China projected a completely coherent worldview, or rather, a view divided into three: unite with the third world and seek revolution, connect with the second world (that is, countries such as France) in striving for independence, and gather all the world's people to oppose U.S. hegemony. Whatever the effects of this perspective were in practice, the coherence ended with the death of Mao Zedong and the arrests of the Gang of Four in 1976 and was replaced by a less articulate position at the end of 1978, when Deng Xiaoping pushed through his fundamental policy of reform and opening. Today Beijing no longer has a demonstrably different outlook on the first, second, and third worlds; it ignores the third world, and its second world is now mainly Western Europe, which it occasionally seeks to use to get something that it wants out of the United States (as by directing business to France or Germany), while making noises now and then about cozying up to its old allies, such as Russia or Serbia—an idea that instantly dissipates when the relationship with the United States warms up again, since there is so little to be had from China's ties with former Soviet bloc countries. It often appears as if the PRC is almost exclusively focused on the United States and on its relations with its near neighbors (Taiwan, Japan, and North and South Korea in particular). Ever since it joined the United Nations in 1972, however, China has

---

23. Nathan and Ross, *Great Wall and Empty Fortress*, p. 76.

been a careful and conscientious defender of the principles on which that body was founded, especially respect for the national sovereignty of its member states and the pursuit of collective security rather than letting Uncle Sam police the world.[24]

Deng Xiaoping's worldview (to the extent that this quintessential pragmatist had a vision; perhaps we should call it his praxis) coincides today not just with China's reform program but with those of top Chinese security experts and realists, who argue that the United States will be the dominant global power into the middle of the twenty-first century and therefore that China would only be foolish to challenge it militarily or strategically. The leading light of China's "enmeshment" current is Zhu Rongji—still listed as the titular dean of Tsinghua University's rapidly expanding business school—and it is his line that remains dominant in China, regardless of what U.S. hard-liners may think (or hope). Liu Huaqiu is one of China's top experts on foreign affairs, and in his 1997 essay he reiterated central themes that Deng Xiaoping clung to until he died. "The forces of peace are growing," he argued; indeed, "peace and development are the two themes of the contemporary world." China's overriding goal was to "secure a favorable, peaceful international environment and maintain good relations with our surrounding countries." In the 1990s, China moved dramatically away from Cold War diplomacy in the East Asian region, indeed much farther than Washington has; it recognized its former enemy South Korea while maintaining its longstanding relationship with North Korea, developed cross-strait trade and tourism with Taiwan, and carried on an active horizontal diplomacy with all its near neighbors under President Jiang Zemin's "good-neighbor policy."

China has been central to an East Asian pattern over the past two decades in which economic forces have systematically eroded or erased formerly impervious Cold War barriers. Its leaders believe that the world has entered a multipolar era in which several big powers interact and in which three enormous regional marketing areas (North America, Western Europe, and East Asia) "stand like the legs of a tripod." With economic factors "playing an ever more important role in international relations," Liu Huaqiu felt confident that China would stick to its program of opening and reform for the long term. One of

---

24. Over the years, Samuel Kim's work has been distinctive in drawing attention to China's behavior in the United Nations, beginning with his fine book *China, the United Nations, and World Order* (Princeton, NJ: Princeton University Press, 1978).

his few negative points was to castigate "some Western countries" for failing to respect the right of developing countries to choose "their own road of development" and instead interfering in their internal affairs under the banner of "human rights."[25]

Perhaps most representative of the current Chinese worldview, though, would be the hell-bent-for-leather capitalist upheaval obvious to any visitor; the average Chinese citizen would much prefer to catch up to Americans in consumer spending than in nuclear weapons. But that is also a program for the long term, for the long run of the twenty-first century, as the mundane plans of China's economic czars make clear. Huang Qifan, director of the powerful Shanghai Economic Commission, recently claimed that "China can grow at 5 percent or more for the next fifty years," because of its "enormous domestic market." The Chinese are just beginning to appreciate the foaming-at-the-mouth consumerism that marks more developed countries: Huang already had a car and three wide-screen televisions in his own home, but in a few years, he said, "everyone will be buying cars."[26] For two decades, China has been growing at nearly 10 percent per annum, and every year about 1 percent of the population (twelve to thirteen million people) shifts from agricultural to nonagricultural employment, with urbanization proceeding as rapidly as in any other developing country.[27]

It is often said that China is following Japan's neomercantile model of development and that U.S. planners are determined to head off precisely this outcome. This generalization is true on many levels, but it also ignores China's willingness to welcome huge amounts of direct foreign investment (DFI). Whereas Japan has long had by far the lowest levels of DFI in the industrial world, China in 1996 was the second-largest recipient of direct foreign investment—as President Clinton noted in a major address on China policy in October 1997.[28] Many scholars of political economy have drawn attention to the relatively low levels of DFI in East Asia as compared with the historically high levels in Latin America, which spawned a literature of scholarship and protest known as dependency theory; yet China does not seem to

25. Nathan and Ross, *Great Wall and Empty Fortress*, pp. 460–67.

26. Quoted in Seth Faison, "China Manages to Keep Its Economy Humming," *New York Times*, April 3, 1999.

27. Michel Oksenberg, Michael Swaine, and Daniel Lynch, "The Chinese Future," a study done for the RAND Corporation in 1998 and excerpted in *China Reader*, pp. 505–30.

28. Clinton's October 1997 speech is reprinted in *China Reader*, pp. 479–87.

fear a growing dependency as the result of its welcoming of direct foreign investment.

Throughout the 1990s, critics of the reform process inside China continued to worry about "bourgeois liberalization," perceiving a "see-saw battle" between that and "the Four Cardinal Principles," with liberalization appearing to win, in their view. In the latter category they included everything from negating Marxism and promoting basic civil and political rights to mass culture (namely, "vulgar culture"), "the 'postmodernist school,'" and imported "audio-video products" that were "immersed in a bourgeois outlook on life."[29] It is hard to argue with them: today the nightlife of Chinese cities offers something for everyone, whether they are lonely businessmen looking for female companionship; housewives seeking extra income; students sitting in computer shops exploring the Internet; teenagers hoping to find the latest heavy-metal compact discs or to score some drugs; or regime officials profiting from their personal connections or protection rackets in the criminal demimonde. Down Siping Road in Shanghai, the stroller comes upon a neon tower incongruously called "Shanghai Taiwan City," where the vulgarity for which this port city was long known has come roaring back to life: "high-slit cheongsam dresses, dimly lit karaoke bars, male and female masseuses, higher-slit cheongsams, scarlet bathtubs built for two, taxi girls, drunk girls too young to know the characters for cheongsam but available for 580 renminbi ($100) or more a night."[30]

Clearly, however, China's leaders worry much more about any hint of political liberalization than they do about the paraphernalia of mass culture, which permeates all of China's big cities; they may well be right that a combination of rapid economic growth and mass consumption of avant-garde or chic trends and fashions provides the path of least resistance to those dissatisfied with the stultifying politics of the regime. In our time there is certainly nothing strange about the intermingling of conservative free-market doctrines and an extravagant 1960s-remnant counterculture amid a general disinterest in political activity, as recent commentary about U.S. politics indicates;[31] in some ways this is the essence of the "Third Way" politics now promoted by

29. Anonymous, "The Ten-Thousand-Character Manifesto," translated in *The China Quarterly* (December 1996). Rumor had it that Marxist critic Deng Liqun wrote this essay.

30. Angelina Malhotra, "Shanghai's Dark Side," February 1994, reprinted in *China Reader*, pp. 394–401.

31. "Left and Right Make Strange Bedfellows," *New York Times*, July 11, 1999, Week in Review section, p. 1.

leaders in Washington, London, and Berlin, all of whom came of age in the 1960s.

The World and China: One Divides into Two

In 1949, realists such as Kennan and enmeshers such as Acheson worked together to place defeated industrial countries such as Japan and West Germany in a harness that would contain their military and diplomatic power while opening the path of least resistance: rapid economic development. Containers and engagers worked together on China in the 1970s and 1980s, too, because realists could justify good relations with Beijing as a counterweight to Soviet power, while enmeshers argued for the solvent effects of world trade on the Chinese revolution. Japan and Germany are still well ensconced in their harness. But China is independent, and the USSR has disappeared, leaving realists and enmeshers without a common program. That does not prevent us from saying who has been right for the past fifty years, however: the enmeshers, hands down.

The truth of the matter is that if China shook the world in 1949, it is the world that has shaken China since then—and indeed for the past two centuries, since a British emissary first sought to open trade with the Celestial Empire.[32] Since that fateful encounter, China's central leaders have swayed it in one direction or another in search of a principle for involvement with the modern West, a way to grow strong while retaining national dignity, to become modern and remain distinctively Chinese at the same time. In a requiem for Mao Zedong's legacy that Deng Xiaoping used to launch his pathbreaking reform program in December 1978, he reminded the Chinese people that Mao's principle had always been "one divides into two"—a principle he applied "toward everyone, including himself."[33] Fifty years after the revolution, China's principles for interacting with the world also divide into two, each incompatible with the other: the first, ever-increasing interaction with a world economy shaped by U.S. power, in which China inevitably trades some elements of its sovereignty for national wealth; the second, stubborn nationalism, accompanied by proclama-

---

32. See Bruce Cumings, "The World Shakes China," in *Parallax Visions: Making Sense of American–East Asian Relations at the End of the Century* (Durham, NC: Duke University Press, 1999).

33. "Communiqué of the Third Plenary Session of the Eleventh Central Committee of the Communist Party of China," *Beijing Review* (December 1978).

tions of absolute sovereignty over patches of geography that elude China's control (Taiwan, the Spratly Islands)—that is, Slobodan Milosevic's principles, which hark back to the nineteenth century on the eve of the twenty-first.

Deng's strategy has now lasted much longer than any others, however, and has brought unprecedented peace and prosperity to China. Moreover, the strategy of opening outward came only after China explored other orientations to the world that were far worse from the U.S. standpoint: alliance with the Soviets in the 1950s, followed by radical go-it-alone policies in the 1960s and early 1970s that found China embroiled in the disasters of the Cultural Revolution and dangerously at odds with Moscow and Washington at the same time. If China's vast economic opening still does not satisfy the realists (many of whom inhabit the Pentagon and the CIA, placing them at odds with the China policies of successive administrations), it is hard for them to argue that China's military history has conformed to the expectations of Western realpolitik. Before and after the revolution, China has had a singular strategy of confining its expansion to its near reaches and constraining its choice of means. When China has used force since 1949, it has done so within its historical region, and more than once it has done so judiciously and effectively. Of course, Chinese leaders still proclaim the inherent superiority of their nation and their culture, but that heritage also teaches them the ultimate weakness of a power that expresses itself only militarily. Military force cannot solve China's deepest problem, which is the continuing predominance of the West. The answer to that challenge is civilizational, not military; that is, either China will develop an alternative civilization that enables it to be distinctively Chinese and modern at the same time, or it will become merely a sinicized form of Western modernity.

A kind of consensus has emerged among most specialists who study the PLA that it is no longer the formidable force that the United States faced in the Korean War. Even today most of its equipment often dates from that era, with most of its air force dependent on aircraft built with 1950s or 1960s technologies, a navy with no blue-ocean capability whose coastal-defense vessels are also obsolete, and an army often preoccupied with domestic order, border security, and civil-construction duties. China developed a formidable second-strike capability (and therefore a technology that stabilizes nuclear rivalry) when it successfully launched its first submarine-launched ballistic missile in

1982, but it still has only one SLBM-equipped sub in service. Deng Xiaoping purposely neglected the defense budget as part of his modernization program, allowing it to decline throughout the 1980s while the PLA shrank by more than a million troops; he boosted it after the PLA again proved its loyalty in the Tiananmen crisis, and after the Persian Gulf War demonstrated the prowess of U.S. high-tech weaponry. But the increases were not great, and expenditures for the publicly announced defense budget often failed to keep up with inflation until the mid-1990s. Although it has increased in real terms since then—perhaps by as much as 50 percent—this includes a 15 percent increase in 1999 meant to compensate the military for divesting itself of business operations, after Jiang Zemin demanded that it do so in 1998. China's announced 1999 defense budget will come in at around $12 billion, which might mean a real budget of $40–50 billion, but it would require 15 percent increases for many years for PLA watchers to get alarmed. (China would have to spend annually anywhere from $20 billion to $40 billion on hardware alone for at least a decade before it would possess global power-projection capability.)[34] China did buy an aircraft carrier recently, raising fears of budding naval expansion—but then it proceeded to tether the carrier in Macao and use it as a recreation center.

Perhaps the surest sign that Americans should rest easy about Chinese military capabilities is the PLA's own entrepreneurial activity, greatly expanded in recent years. The PLA fields hundreds of firms or "front companies," often called under various rubrics (such as COST-IND, the State Commission of Science, Technology and Industry for National Defense, or CASC, the China Aerospace Corporation), to manufacture goods of all kinds for the market—or simply to make money, as with the numerous karaoke bars and brothels that the army owns and protects. John Frankenstein of Hong Kong University has estimated that this activity adds anywhere from $30 billion to $60 billion to the PLA's annual budget.[35]

The Pentagon's own studies have determined that China lacks sufficient command and control infrastructures to support any large-scale military operations "at any significant distance from the country's borders"; even landing troops in Taiwan in large numbers would be impossible, given that China's amphibious troop transport capacity of some seventy ships can move only a maximum of fifteen thousand troops. As

34. Gill and O'Hanlon, "China's Military: How Good?" pp. 56–57.
35. Cited in Malhotra, "Shanghai's Dark Side."

for the vaunted "six hundred missiles opposite Taiwan" reported in February 1999, there may be as many as two hundred now, and there might be six hundred within five years, but they are not sufficiently accurate to support an invasion by targeting airfields, ports, or bases; all would "miss their targets by several football fields."[36] Their emplacement seems designed mainly to intimidate Taiwan and reassure Chinese on the mainland.

Critics of China succeed frequently in placing stories in the press about alleged Chinese proliferation of weapons of mass destruction to countries such as Pakistan and Iran, but its help to these two countries came mainly in 1992 as a piqued reaction to President Bush's decision to sell 150 F-16s to Taiwan and has not been repeated on this scale (China transferred eleven missiles to Pakistan and agreed to help Iran build a nuclear reactor).[37] Furthermore, the critics rarely seem assuaged when China helps with nonproliferation, as it does with North Korea and as it did in canceling sales of missiles to Syria, under U.S. and Israeli pressure; ultimately it also suspended its help with Iran's nuclear program. On this neuralgic issue, China is often damned if it does and ignored if it doesn't.

None of this evidence seems to sway hard-line U.S. critics of China, however. Former defense secretary Weinberger is sure that China is making "a conscious effort to replace the Soviet Union as a superpower rival of the United States,"[38] in spite of the hundreds of billions of dollars in military expenditures required before China could do so. China's leaders frequently point to the Soviet Union's gross misallocation of resources to its military as a key reason for its collapse, but that does not stop critics from promoting a new Cold War with a China said to be "ten-feet tall," either now or in the ominously close future.

Spy versus Spy

Perhaps there is an element of similarity to the rivalry with Moscow, however, in the way that the United States and China obsessively spy on each other. If the Cox Report dwelt on alleged Chinese spying without bothering to mention that the United States surveils everything it possibly can in China by every possible means, it did produce one

---

36. Gill and O'Hanlon, p. 60.
37. Nathan and Ross, *Great Wall and Empty Fortress*, pp. 147–48, 152–54.
38. Weinberger, "Foreword," *The Cox Report*.

legitimate "spy-versus-spy" mystery worthy of a John LeCarré novel. It turns out that the counterintelligence deficiencies at Los Alamos and other nuclear weapons labs were dramatically exposed not by the FBI or by Wen Ho Lee's activities but by a PRC national who provided the CIA with unsolicited Chinese intelligence documents, including ones making clear that China had procured design information on the miniaturized W-88 thermonuclear warhead perched atop the ICBMs in the Trident submarine—the pillar of the United States' second-strike capability. This "walk-in" was later determined to have been secretly acting "under the direction of the PRC intelligence services."[39]

No one provided a plausible reason for this bizarre incident, at least in the Cox Report itself or the subsequent public discussion. What interest would be served by purposely letting the CIA know what China had managed to learn, by one means or another, about the W-88 warhead? Some observers thought it might be a sophisticated ploy to stop the brain drain of Chinese physicists to the United States,[40] but that would require any number of university physics departments to stop admitting the very Ph.D. students from China who now populate their programs—most of them unengaged with classified research. It might also have been the cheapest kind of signal that China was working toward a survivable second-strike capability, thus relieving China of actually having to deploy such weapons in the near term while deterring the United States from thinking it could intimidate or blackmail China with its nuclear arsenal in a crisis. But no one really knew the truth of this strange "walk-in," perhaps including the Chinese secret services themselves. Meanwhile, China may have tested a W-88 warhead once, according to press reports when the Cox Report appeared, but the United States tests a warhead six to ten times before having confidence that it will work properly in a crisis—and U.S. nuclear warheads outnumber China's by fifteen to one. At bottom, U.S. security alarms about China seem driven less by evidence and more by ignorance, or an unstated, often subliminal racist fear that with such a huge population the Chinese may be crazy enough to try nuclear warfare regardless of the consequences.

Part of the woodwork in the China field is the idea that U.S.-China relations seem always to oscillate from good to bad and back again, but

---

39. *The Cox Report*, pp. 5, 112–14.

40. Vernon Loeb and Walter Pincus, "Planted Documents Sow Seeds of Doubt," *Washington Post*, May 28, 1999, p. A3.

the free-for-all over China policy in recent years seems to have vastly increased the velocity of those fluctuations; one never knows what to expect anymore when opening the morning newspaper. Only days after Zhu Rongji returned from his visit to the United States in April 1999, with a fund of goodwill based on his engaging style, the war in Kosovo began, and on May 7, the Chinese embassy in Belgrade was hit during NATO's air assault on Serbia.

This errant U.S. bomb, which somehow unerringly crashed into the most sensitive rooms in the embassy, provided a case study in U.S.-China futility. Beijing declared the bombing to be intentional regardless of all evidence to the contrary (what possible benefit could Bill Clinton find in this act, with his China policy under daily fire and the outcome of the war for Kosovo still very much in doubt?) and unleashed thousands of hysterical students to parade through Tiananmen with a bestiary of crude anti-American posters and slogans, thus contriving to sink like a stone in a lake the immense goodwill that Zhu Rongji had generated during his visit. Back in Beijing, Zhu joined the line in front of the coffins of the deceased embassy employees with tears running down his face—no doubt in mourning for the temporary eclipse of *his* engagement policy. As China fumed, prominent U.S. commentators wrote that the anti-American hysteria could mean only one thing: Beijing now saw the United States as its number one enemy.[41] Meanwhile, with Clinton bashing, China hating, and secret leaking virtual pastimes among national-security professionals, it was hard for close observers to declare with certainty that the bombing was *not* intentional, given the multitude of midlevel miscreants in the intelligence community who might find profit in targeting the embassy safe rooms of their Chinese counterparts.

For several years, people in the security bureaucracies have been leaking highly classified information alleging this or that new military threat or anti-U.S. crime emanating from China, followed by polite demurrals by Clinton officials and, so far as anyone can tell, no punishment of the leakers.[42] Virtually every finding in the Cox Report had been leaked to *New York Times* reporters such as Jeff Gerth and James

41. Robert Kagan, "China's No. 1 Enemy," *New York Times*, May 11, 1999, Op-Ed page.

42. See Seth Faison's retrospective article on the difficulties Zhu had with other elements in the Chinese leadership regarding China's admission to the WTO, *New York Times*, June 8, 1999.

Risen long before the report itself appeared; running frequently as lead articles in the *Times*, their reports gave an impression of massive and highly successful Chinese spying and were rarely countered effectively by Clinton's spokesmen.[43] Around the same time, various leaks to the *Financial Times* and other papers depicted a massive Chinese missile buildup opposite Taiwan.[44] China was also said to be helping North Korea with its missile program, in spite of the role of such missiles in promoting theater-missile defense systems in Northeast Asia that China had every reason to oppose.

White House and State Department officials who see the same intelligence materials deny all of these allegations—about Wen Ho Lee giving warhead data to China, about the missiles opposite Taiwan, and about North Korea—but no one is punished and no one is fired. This, of course, leads Beijing to think that it is all part of a clever anti-China conspiracy. The truth appears to be more mundane: Clinton apparently feared taking on the CIA, either because of what he worried it might know about skeletons in his closet or because as a Democrat he cannot afford to appear soft on national security. Meanwhile, the ominous tenth anniversary of the Tiananmen uprising passed almost unnoticed, with students and young people focused instead on stoning and egging the U.S. embassy—the one clear gain Beijing's leaders got from the embassy bombing. Although Zhu's position did not seem to be directly affected by his failure to get accession to the World Trade Organization, it provided yet another opening for critics of the reform process to have their say and to aggrandize their power within the government.

"Comprehensive Engagement" and Enduring Estrangement

Under two secretaries of state, Warren Christopher and Madeleine Albright, policymakers sought to revive various contacts and exchanges that had been cut off or diminished in the 1990s, after the deep estrangement caused by the Tiananmen crisis in 1989 and the dangerous contretemps in March 1996 in which China fired missiles near Taiwan's coast, causing President Clinton to dispatch two aircraft car-

---

43. A compendium of such leaks is available in *Washington Times* reporter Bill Gertz's new potboiler, *Betrayal: How the Clinton Administration Undermined American Security*. Washington, DC: Washington Times Publications, 1999.

44. Among many examples, see Risen and Gerth, "China Stole Nuclear Secrets for Bombs, U.S. Aides Say," *New York Times*, March 6, 1999, p. 1.

rier battle groups to Taiwan's waters. "Comprehensive engagement" was the name of the policy, almost a play on Deng Xiaoping's 1992 "peaceful engagement." It was intended to overcome a fractious period in which China policy was fought over by a variety of special interests—human rights groups, business lobbies, arms manufacturers, candidates running for office, and different factions within the Clinton administration. The critics included Senator Jesse Helms, an organic conservative on everything to do with China, Congressman Ben Gilman (R-New York), a Cold Warrior who often seems equally hysterical when it comes to alleged Chinese threats to U.S. security, liberals committed to human rights agendas such as Senators Ted Kennedy and Tom Lantos and Congresswoman Nancy Pelosi (D-California), and Taiwan and Tibet supporters such as Senator Claiborne Pell, a Democrat, and Senator Alan Cranston, a Republican.

The clearest example of this fragmentation was the congressional debate every year over most favored nation (MFN) status for China, which provided an arena for anyone and everyone to have their say while never seriously threatening China's trade status. The United States granted MFN status to China in 1980, a completely appropriate and hardly unusual decision, given that nearly every country in the world enjoys the same status. But after Tiananmen dramatically changed the coloration of U.S.-China relations, debate about it seethed every spring from 1990 to 1994. When he came into office, President Clinton linked MFN status to Chinese progress on human rights, which had the virtue of pleasing both the business and human rights constituencies. However, in the succeeding year, Beijing, miffed by this linkage, did everything it could to assure that Clinton would have trouble finding any improvement in China's human rights situation. So in May 1994 he abandoned this linkage, and renewal of China's MFN status again became routine—and a routine occasion for flamboyant congressional attacks on China. The China policy cacophony reached a kind of crescendo in 1997 amid a hailstorm of criticism of Clinton's China policy, yet MFN status again passed the House, by a vote of 259 to 173. Most observers attributed the unwillingness of many congressional China critics to overturn MFN to a broad U.S. business coalition that annually mounted a concentrated lobbying effort to keep reciprocal trade going with China. China, for its part, showed increasing irritation with this debate and thus became less willing to try to solve the political problems besetting the relationship and the tenure of every U.S. president.

More important to the Clinton administration was a broad strategy of restarting day-to-day contacts with China, especially high-level communications between various government departments in the two countries. China is now a member of more than a thousand international organizations of all kinds, and Americans stepped up their dialogue with Chinese counterparts at every opportunity. Military exchanges began again, notably with Defense Minister Chi Haotian, a person implicated in the Tiananmen crackdown; he visited Washington in late 1996, meeting the secretary of defense and President Clinton and touring various military bases and facilities. The chairman of the Joint Chiefs of Staff, John Shalikashvili, also exchanged visits with his Chinese counterpart. National security advisor Anthony Lake and Liu Huaqiu (director of the State Council's Office of Foreign Affairs) held extensive discussions on mutual national security concerns in the spring of 1996.

These and many other exchanges set the stage for President Jiang Zemin's visit to the United States in October 1997 and for Bill Clinton's reciprocal and highly successful tour of China in June 1998. Clinton's well-known telegenic facility for political campaigning was put to good use as the First Family toured Xi'an, Beijing, and Hong Kong among other places; large numbers of Chinese citizens were favorably impressed, leading to a high point in recent U.S.-China relations. After more ups and downs, Premier Zhu Rongji made an equally impressive visit to the United States. For years, U.S.-China watchers touted him as the most intelligent, forward-looking, and reasonable person in the high leadership—and lo and behold, in 1997 he was promoted to prime minister. In April 1999, this clever, engaging, astute politician, such a contrast to the taciturn Deng (let alone the wooden party chairman, Jiang Zemin), made a politically brilliant whirlwind tour through the United States. It was meant to be the triumphal cap to China's entry into the World Trade Organization (WTO), after convincing his Politburo colleagues to take a set of unprecedented market-opening measures, all of them in response to U.S. pressure.[45] At a luncheon in his honor for 1,500 guests in Chicago, the CEOs of major multinationals—McDonald's, Ford, Motorola—fell all over themselves to congratulate Zhu (and themselves) on China's integration with the world economy and the wondrous opportunities of its market.

---

45. "US Fears on China Missile Build-up," *Financial Times*, February 10, 1999, p. 1.

All that remained was to dot the *i*s and cross the *t*s on the agreement, but at the last minute President Clinton pulled back, fearing congressional opposition.

The failure of the agreement on China's entry into the WTO was doubly hurtful, as it undermined support for engagement in both Washington and Beijing. For two years, U.S. officials such as former treasury secretary Robert Rubin had frequently lauded China for remaining an anchor of stability in the sea of turmoil caused by the Asian financial crisis that began with the run on the Thai baht in July 1997, especially by keeping its currency pegged firmly to the dollar while competitors like South Korea and Thailand saw the value of their currencies fall by as much as 50 percent; had China cheapened its currency at any point in 1997–99, it would have sent stock markets around the world reeling. This forbearance was all the more striking given the aggressive foreign economic policy of the Clinton administration; the successive trade representatives, Mickey Kantor and Charlene Barshefsky, became famous in Beijing (and Tokyo and Seoul) for their stubborn and tenacious pressure on trade issues, especially on opening China's market to U.S. goods, and were thought to be brash and aggressive, if not rude and crude.

The large and growing U.S. trade deficit with China ($34 billion in 1995 and around $40 billion in 1998)[46] stimulates yet more opposition, especially from labor groups worried about the loss of jobs to China and in spite of administration arguments that WTO regulations would open more markets and would better Chinese working conditions and wages. Meanwhile, congressional investigations of alleged Chinese spying make it that much more difficult to export goods that would help close the trade deficit, such as high-technology computers or large, expensive items such as nuclear reactors (which alone might account for $60 billion in sales as China's energy needs increase, according to industry estimates). Nothing is more important to "comprehensive engagement" than to enmesh China in the world economy, which has the dual effect of institutionalizing Beijing's commitment to economic opening and enhancing Washington's leverage over Chinese behavior, since the United States has a preponderant influence within the WTO (the leaders of the other advanced industrial nations all knew that the critical negotiation on China's entry was between Washington and Beijing).

---

46. *Far Eastern Economic Review*, June 17, 1999, p. 11.

Fly in the Ointment: Taiwan

In mid-July 1999, for no obvious reason, Taiwan president Lee Teng-hui did his best to put U.S.-China relations back on the roller coaster by abruptly declaring that contacts with China would now be understood as "state-to-state" relations. Somewhat cryptically, he denied that this apparent new departure represented a move toward independence for Taiwan: "Under such special nation-to-nation relationships," he said, "there is no longer any need to declare Taiwanese independence." But it was perilously close to a declaration of independence, and it caused an uproar in Beijing and Washington. Both powers backed and filled, hesitating or fearing to conclude that Lee really meant what he said. A State Department official suggested that Lee might merely be reiterating a position he had long maintained, albeit in new and dangerous language;[47] Beijing quickly condemned the statement as "a monumental disaster" but also mulled over its substantive meaning for several weeks. Official Taiwan was not helpful in trying to clarify the president's meaning: government spokesmen suggested that the "one China" idea ought to be dropped and that Taiwan's relations with China could now be captured by the slogan "one nation, two states"—which only deepened the uproar.[48] After the U.S. representative in Taipei met with President Lee in search of clarification, the State Department said that "there has been no change" in Taiwan's policy. Meanwhile, Jiang Zemin said China had "no room for retreat" on the Taiwan question.[49]

Coming just after a sportsmanlike soccer match between the United States and China in the World Cup women's final that had generated much goodwill and that many thought would help pull U.S.-China relations out of the deep freeze of the war over Kosovo, and just before Senator Jesse Helms, chairman of the Senate Foreign Relations Committee, convened hearings on new legislation known as the Taiwan Security Enhancement Act, Lee's statement appeared timed to continue stirring the hornet's nest of trouble between Washington and

---

47. Jane Perlez, "U.S. Asking Taiwan to Explain Its Policy after Uproar," *New York Times*, July 14, 1999, p. A3; and Liz Sly, "China Boasts of Neutron Bomb Prowess," *Chicago Tribune*, July 16, 1999, p. 5.

48. Seth Faison, "'What Is China?' Taiwan's New Answer Is Puzzling," *New York Times*, July 14, 1999, p. A3.

49. *South China Morning Post*, July 15, 1999, cited in Liz Sly, "China Threatens to 'Smash' Taiwan," *Chicago Tribune*, July 15, 1999, p. 12.

Beijing. On the other hand, Lee had said quite similar things to British reporters back in February, without causing a furor.[50] Some observers also thought Taiwan's domestic politics might explain the president's behavior: he is expected to step down in the spring of 2000 after twelve years in office, and he might want "to further his legacy as the father of a modern Taiwan separate from mainland China."[51]

This caused enormous problems for U.S. policy and the mutually antagonistic perspectives on China held by the White House and Congress. While politicians such as Jesse Helms continued to push the envelope toward an open, formal U.S. commitment to Taiwan's defense, President Clinton reiterated the administration's support for the consensual position of every president since Jimmy Carter, namely, a "one China" policy. This policy is the sine qua non not just of China's relations with Taiwan but also of China's estimation of whether the United States will seek to prevent its emergence as a great power. Just before Jiang Zemin's visit to Washington in late 1997, Clinton expressed "continuing support" for this policy; when he was in China in June 1998, he went out of his way to underline the importance to world peace of the one-China formula, and his aides told reporters that Taiwan was well aware of Washington's private opposition to independence for Taiwan.[52] Coming on the heels of President Clinton's decision in May to sell advanced early-warning radar equipment to Taiwan, Lee's statement had the effect of pouring gasoline on a fire.

Indeed, it prompted China belatedly to release its official response to the Cox Report. Long in coming, it appeared in the wake of Lee's departures on Taiwan's status. Beijing predictably denounced the Cox findings as a pack of lies and said it had stolen no nuclear technology from the United States. Unpredictably, however, for the first time it acknowledged that China had perfected both miniaturized warheads (such as the W-88) and the neutron bomb—but it placed these programs in the context of the nuclear arms race between Moscow and Washington in the 1970s, when both superpowers used small warheads to create independently targeted multiple reentry vehicles, or MIRVs, which put clusters of bombs atop ICBMs and thus vastly multiplied

50. President Lee "described Taiwan as an independent and separate entity of government." See the interview "The Unrepentant Leader" by Peter Monagnon and Mure Dickie in the *Financial Times*, February 15, 1999.

51. Faison, "'What Is China?' Taiwan's New Answer Is Puzzling."

52. Clinton's October 1997 address on China policy in *China Reader*, p. 481; and many newspaper accounts of Clinton's visit to China.

their destructive potential.[53] Many observers believed that the target of this remarkably candid admission was Taiwan, prompting the State Department to issue an unusual statement couched in the language of the Taiwan Relations Act: "We would . . . consider any effort to determine the future of Taiwan by other than peaceful means," department spokesman James Rubin said on July 15, "as a threat to the peace and security of the Western Pacific area and of grave concern to the United States."[54]

Beijing's response to Lee Teng-hui came in mid-August 1999, when it dramatically escalated tensions by sending large numbers of warships south from their port at Qingdao, flying large numbers of air sorties over the Taiwan Strait, and purposely poking the noses of its jets over the center line of the strait—a line that both sides had honored for decades. Taiwan did the same with its formidable armada of U.S.- and French-built and indigenous fighter jets. State Department spokesman James Rubin said the United States was "monitoring the situation closely," but he noted that the number of sorties did not come near the rates recorded in previous years during times of tension. Private analysts thought there was a high probability that some sort of incident would occur at the time, but they also drew attention to the PRC's basically defensive air force, which had far less high-tech capability than Taiwan's.[55] Chinese newspapers were full of war threats; some analysts took these seriously, while others said that Beijing was just trying to convince Washington that it would have no choice but to use force if Taiwan proceeded further toward actual independence. In early September, U.S. officials did some bluffing of their own, declaring publicly that "the use of force would be catastrophic for China as well as

---

53. "Facts Speak Louder Than Words and Lies Will Collapse on Themselves," a 36-page PRC government report cited in the *New York Times,* July 16, 1999, p. A3.

54. Quoted in Liz Sly, "China Boasts of Neutron Bomb Prowess." The Taiwan Relations Act, which was passed shortly after normalization in April 1979, stated that the United States would "consider any effort to determine the future of Taiwan by other than peaceful means . . . a threat to the peace and security of the Western Pacific area" and called for the United States to provide the defensive weaponry necessary to secure "a sufficient self-defense capability." Nathan and Ross, *Great Wall and Empty Fortress,* p. 67.

55. See, for example, Kenneth W. Allen, "Air Activity over the Taiwan Strait," August 16, 1999, a detailed paper on the sorties and the air capabilities of the two sides (posted on the Web site of the Henry L. Stimson Center in Washington, D.C., www.stimson.org). Robert Suettinger of the Brookings Institution told a reporter that he thought Beijing was "seriously considering taking action," even if it meant a confrontation with the United States. Quoted in Liz Sly, "China Raises Stakes on Taiwan," *Chicago Tribune,* August 14, 1999, pp. 1, 9.

Taiwan, and of course disastrous for U.S.-China relations, and would, no doubt, pit us in an actual war."[56]

Just at this point of apparent maximum danger, however, the tension evaporated. Chinese leaders emerged from their annual dog-days retreat along the beaches of Beidaihe with smiles on their faces, and Jiang Zemin soon flew off to New Zealand for another summit meeting with Bill Clinton (at the annual meeting of APEC). Forgotten was the embassy bombing and the war of nerves in the air over the strait, and back on track was the effort to get China into the WTO. The U.S. trade representative, Charlene Barshefsky, convened meetings with her counterpart, Foreign Trade Minister Shi Guangsheng, and although many obstacles remained (not least the developing U.S. presidential campaign, with Democratic candidates under pressure from labor groups opposed to China's admission), many analysts expected that China's thirteen-year long march into the WTO would finally be consummated.

A key turn appears to have been President Clinton's willingness to chide Lee Teng-hui publicly for having "made things more difficult for both China and the U.S."[57] Meanwhile, congressional Republicans, previously notable for their vocal denunciations of China's alleged filching of nuclear secrets, now were notable for their pregnant silence; some reports suggested that some pro–China-U.S. multinationals had weighed in to achieve this result. The Cox Report had fallen into the dustbin of history, and Senator Alan Specter announced a new investigation as to whether prejudice against scientists of Chinese extraction might have caused Wen Ho Lee to have been unfairly pilloried.

The degree to which business concerns interfere with—and often dominate—more old-fashioned realpolitik was illustrated in the plunge in the Taiwan stock market after Lee's July 9 declaration (investors withdrew about $64 billion in stocks in the succeeding month)[58] and by stark concerns in the United States' Silicon Valley during the PRC's saber rattling in August and the devastating earthquake on Taiwan in September, about even a modest (one- or two-day) disruption in the flow of electronic components out of Taiwan. That tight little island

---

56. Deputy Assistant Secretary of State for East Asian and Pacific Affairs Susan Shirk, quoted in Russell Flannery, "U.S. Issues Warning to China Not to Launch Taiwan Attack," *Wall Street Journal*, September 7, 1999.

57. David Sanger, "Clinton and Jiang Heal Rift and Set New Trade Course," *New York Times*, September 13, 1999, p. 1.

58. Liz Sly, "China Boasts of Neutron Bomb Prowess."

produces 62 percent of all computer keyboards, 61 percent of main-boards, 54 percent of monitors, and the majority of silicon chips in what have become the world's largest semiconductor foundries.[59]

One way to lessen U.S.-China conflict would be for the United States finally to shut down its Cold War security structure in the East Asian region, which still stations a hundred thousand Americans in various military bases and installations in Japan and Korea long after the Cold War ended. Although some analysts such as Chalmers Johnson have forcefully argued that it is time for the troops finally to come home, inside-the-beltway analysts have convinced themselves that this commitment should continue into the distant future because it is not only in the interest of the United States but in China's as well: "Almost as damaging to Chinese interests as heightened conflict with the United States would be American withdrawal from Asia. If the United States weakened its commitment to the region, China would have to confront security challenges without the benefit of an outside balancing power."[60] Less obvious, perhaps, is the role of U.S. forces in keeping Japan and South Korea on complex defense dependencies that inhibit their autonomy in the region. But it also is not clear how such major commitments can be maintained in the face of domestic public opinion surveys showing that few Americans would justify shedding blood if it were just a matter of keeping Japan and China at arm's length, protecting Taiwan, or defending a South Korea that towers over North Korea.[61]

Much more likely than a real change in the structure of U.S. power, however, is the perpetuation into the future (the Pentagon says two decades)[62] of the U.S. Cold War archipelago of military bases that was the consequence of the Korean War and the Chinese revolution. And more likely than comprehensive engagement, let alone the "strategic partnership" that occasionally passes the lips of Washington policy makers, is the "conditional" engagement that the Council on Foreign Relations called for in 1996, or the "constructive" engagement that the

---

59. Data in David Hale, "Will a Chinese Attack on Taiwan Devastate Silicon Valley?" Zurich Financial Services, August 25, 1999, p. 1.

60. Nathan and Ross, *Great Wall and Empty Fortress*, p. 79.

61. John E. Reilly, ed., *American Public Opinion and U.S. Foreign Policy 1999* (Chicago: Council on Foreign Relations, 1999).

62. This future is sketched most prominently in the Nye Report issued in 1995 (named after Harvard political scientist Joseph Nye, who was assistant secretary of defense at the time) and reaffirmed by the Pentagon in 1998.

Trilateral Commission favors.[63] Both programs posit several principles for U.S.-China relations that are thought (or hoped) to be mutually agreeable to both sides, and in the period 1997–99 both sides have followed them (more or less): nonproliferation, moderation in military buildups and transparency of military forces, market access, cooperation in solving international problems, and peaceful resolution of territorial disputes. It is the "less" that has caused problems: the New York Council on Foreign Relations included two additional principles involving respect for human rights, in which China has made little improvement, and refraining from the unilateral use of military force, which the Clinton administration has violated time and again (in bombing Somalia, Afghanistan, Iraq, and Serbia, to name a few, even if NATO countries joined in the Kosovo conflict). Still, the record since 1996 suggests a mutual, conscious attempt to lessen tension between Washington and Beijing, and short of major change in the security situation in East Asia, the principles are good ones. They provide the residual anchor for the most important thing: continuing enmeshment.

U.S.-China Affinities

Long inured to Atlanticist presumptions about the importance of Europe and alarmist claims about the rise to power in the Pacific of Japan or China, Americans in recent years have lived through the eclipse of any potential rival in Europe or East Asia. What is now clear is the towering ascendancy of the United States among all of them, for the foreseeable future. How can that influence be retained? One way is by thinking through our affinities with other peoples—especially the Chinese. Over the past two centuries, the United States and China essentially developed in isolation from each other; now, however, economic ties have thrown them together—and it seems safe to say that they must sink or swim together in the next century. What if we asked the heretical question, What makes China and the United States alike, rather than different?

China and the United States are both continental nations, of geographically similar size (although one is fully developed and the other

---

63. James Shinn, ed., *Weaving the Net: Conditional Engagement with China* (New York: Council on Foreign Relations, 1996); and James Steinberg (at that time head of the State Department's policy-planning staff), Address to the Trilateral Commission, in *State Department Bulletin*, May 8, 1995.

is not). Both have experienced prolonged periods of noninvolvement with the rest of the world—China through centuries in which the Han majority expanded on the continent, almost by accretion, with only a brief heyday of world trade in the eleventh century, and the United States through nearly two centuries (from the 1780s to the 1940s) of relative isolation and indifference to events abroad. Both countries thus have strong isolationist tendencies, if of different kinds.

It is striking that only ten years ago an officially sponsored and greatly popular television documentary series, *Elegy for the Yellow River*, castigated China's ingrown, navel-contemplating, sedentary, and land-bound culture and argued that China would have to join with Western civilization or risk disintegration and oblivion.[64] China's legendary self-absorption and self-sufficiency, compounded by its solipsistic (or at least Sinocentric) sense of cultural superiority and civilizational centrality as the Middle Kingdom, nonetheless led to a kind of benign neglect of its near neighbors. With a couple of exceptions such as Tibet, most neighbors lived at peace with China and to varying degrees (Korea and Vietnam a lot, Japan less so) emulated its arts and letters, philosophy, statecraft, and social institutions.

In the United States, the end of the Cold War appears to have spawned the strongest resurgence of indifference toward the rest of the world, if not necessarily isolationism, since 1941. When a major opinion poll that appeared in 1999 asked Americans to name the two or three most important foreign policy issues facing the United States, fully 21 percent of the public could not think of one (they answered "don't know"), and a mere 7 percent listed foreign policy concerns among problems that were important to the nation.[65] So, a curious isolationist affinity may be one of the deepest historical and cultural elements between the two peoples, paradoxically undergirding the chances for U.S.-China peace. If so, it is one among many other affinities.

Both China and the United States have had world-influencing revolutions, and in many ways both are or have been revolutionary societies. Both have weak military traditions and strong traditions of civil governance and civilian supremacy. Both experience profound tensions between governmental centralization and decentralization. Both have long histories of prowess in small business and petty capitalism.

---

64. Nathan and Ross, *Great Wall and Empty Fortress*, p. 33.
65. Reilly, ed., American *Public Opinion and U.S. Foreign Policy 1999*, pp. 8, 37.

Both strike foreign observers as highly egalitarian societies, just as both contain heterogeneous ethnicities, especially when compared with Japan or Germany. Both have produced large diasporas—except that the U.S. diaspora is within, through vast immigration, and the Chinese diaspora is without, through historic emigration (even if that diaspora is rapidly restitching its economic ties to China). Both have ideals of the independent, hardworking pioneer, represented in the Chinese case by the myriad Chinese families living alone for generations in small towns in the United States, running restaurants or laundries.

Isn't it interesting to imagine the many ways in which the United States and China, so often conceived as diametrically opposite in civilization, customs, values, and practices (especially political ones), are actually similar? Perhaps the Cox committee can make this its next project? Given the complex difficulties of U.S.-China relations, we need many more telling reversals of common presuppositions—something President Clinton recognized during Zhu Rongji's visit to the United States, when he asked Americans who worry about China's growing strength not to forget "the risks of a weak China, beset by internal conflicts, social dislocation and criminal activity, becoming a vast zone of instability in Asia."[66] For the century and a half following its first defeat at the hands of the West in the Opium Wars, China was exactly that—a vast zone of instability.

One day China will finally become fully modern, and it will find its way toward being the proud nation it has wanted to be through two centuries of humiliation. But that is an agenda for the Chinese people. For Americans, the route to understanding China is through self-knowledge. A wise policy begins with China's long-term humiliation at the hands of the West, and therefore Western humility: we have shaken China enough as it is, and now we should do what little we can to encourage a less dominant central government, the rule of law, and basic political rights for China's citizens, without illusions that we will make much of a difference. The main theme in our relations should still be enmeshment—a long period of economism that allows both peoples to discover a new relationship. Do we want a China shooting missiles across Taiwan's bow, or a China that polishes its application to the WTO with trade concessions to the United States? This question

66. Clinton's speech of April 7, 1999, reproduced in the NAPSNet Daily Report of April 8, 1999, on the NAPSNet on-line Web site (www.nautilus.org).

answers itself. The alternative is to bring into being the very enemy that some national security professionals appear to want (and perhaps need). If that eventuality should come to pass, in contrast with their experience with the old Soviet Union, Americans will finally have rendezvoused with a formidable adversary.

Chronology
1997–1999

Nancy R. Hearst

January 1997

5   After tainted blood products are found to have been manufactured and sold in China, China issues new rules on the handling of blood products.

10   In opposition to Guatemalan support for Taiwan, China vetoes a resolution in the UN Security Council to send a team of military observers to oversee the Guatemalan peace agreement.

15   China and Guatemala hold secret talks to repair their relationship after China vetoes a UN resolution to send military observers to Guatemala.

17   China hands over to U.S. military officials the remains of airmen whose planes crashed in Guangxi province during World War II.

19   A panel of Chinese officials and pro-China Hong Kong residents, meeting in Beijing, submit to the National People's Congress 25 measures to curtail civil liberties, including the rights to protest and to free association, in the colony after the July 1 handover to China.

20   China reverses its veto of the resolution to send UN military observers to Guatemala to monitor the ceasefire agreement.

23   Tung Chee-hwa, future chief executive of Hong Kong, defends proposed law changes, insisting that they "balance freedom against responsibility."

24   Chinese journalists are forbidden from taking money or gifts in exchange for conducting interviews or publishing news stories.

28   Speaking at a news conference, President Clinton concedes that his doctrine of "constructive engagement" with China has failed to make progress on human rights.

29   Hong Kong governor Christopher Patten warns that the recent proposal to cancel the Bill of Rights after the handover to China will cause "enormous and irrevocable damage."

U.S. trade official Charlene Barshefsky says that the United States will block China's entry into the World Trade Organization if Beijing continues to block the import of U.S. agricultural goods.

30   The U.S. State Department annual report on worldwide human rights conditions declares that by the end of 1996 there were no active dissidents left in China who had not been jailed or exiled.

February 1997

1   The Beijing Preparatory Committee overseeing the Hong Kong handover votes overwhelmingly to repeal civil liberties in Hong Kong.

2   China and the United States sign a trade agreement that extends for four years the 1994 U.S.-China textile trade pact.

Former Minister of Defense Qin Jiwei dies in Beijing at age 82.

5   During the final days of the Muslim holy month of Ramadan, Muslim separatists riot through Yining, Xinjiang province, in protest of Han rule, prompting the Chinese government to issue a curfew after at least ten people are killed.

6   China's official media strongly criticize the U.S. State Department report on human rights as "malicious attacks on and lies about China's human rights situation."

12 Senior North Korean ideologue Hwang Jang-Yop defects to the South Korean embassy in Beijing.

14 The Clinton administration announces that 53 illegal Chinese immigrants who have been held by the Immigration and Naturalization Service since 1993 when their freighter, the *Golden Venture*, ran aground will be released.

19 Deng Xiaoping dies in Beijing at the age of 92 from complications due to Parkinson's disease and a lung infection.

21 President Jiang Zemin, in his first public statement since the death of Deng, vows to continue Deng's economic reforms "unswervingly and confidently."

23 The National People's Congress approves a plan to curtail Hong Kong laws that provide for democratic elections and protect civil liberties.

25 Six days after Deng Xiaoping's death, a memorial meeting with 10,000 guests is held in the Great Hall of the People.

 Three bombs explode on buses in Urumqi, the capital of Xinjiang province, killing 5.

March 1997

1 China reaches an agreement with the International Committee of the Red Cross to reopen negotiations for unsupervised access to Chinese prisons.

2 In the annual budget speech to the Fifth Session of the Eighth National People's Congress, Finance Minister Liu Zhongli announces that Beijing will increase defense spending by 12.7 percent, to $9.73 billion.

4 A mine blast in Henan province kills 86.

5 Zhao Ziyang reportedly sends a letter to Jiang Zemin express-

ing his views on enterprise reform, political restructuring, inner-party democracy, and adhering to humanitarianism.

9   The first Taiwanese airliner to be hijacked to the mainland since 1986 is returned to Taipei; the hijacker remains in Chinese custody.

14   The National People's Congress passes revisions to the Chinese criminal code, eliminating the category of counter-revolutionary crimes.

      Forty percent of the delegates to the National People's Congress register their protest over rising crime and corruption by voting against or abstaining from approval of the work of the Supreme Court by the chief prosecutor.

21   The Information Office of the State Council issues a White Paper on the U.S.-China Trade Balance.

22   The Dalai Lama arrives in Taiwan.

23   The World Bank report shows that China attracts more than one-third of all investment in factories and manufacturing plants in developing countries, amounting to $42 billion last year.

25   In the highest-level visit of a U.S. official since 1989, Vice President Al Gore attends the signing in Beijing of two major business agreements, with Boeing and General Motors, worth almost $2 billion.

26   Vice President Al Gore, addressing students at Qinghua University, speaks of the need for change in China. After meeting with President Jiang Zemin, Vice President Gore announces that China will provide U.S. firms with more access to the Chinese market.

28   The Chinese media deny allegations of illegal contributions to the 1996 U.S. presidential campaign.

U.S. House Speaker Newt Gingrich (R-Georgia), speaking in Beijing, calls on China to end repression of religious and political freedoms.

30   Taiwan reports that a liaison office for the Tibetan government-in-exile will be opened in Taipei.

Speaking in Shanghai, U.S. House Speaker Newt Gingrich reports having warned China that the United States will intervene militarily if Taiwan is attacked.

Beijing declares that there are no political prisoners in China, describing the more than 2,000 so-called counter-revolutionaries as genuine criminals.

31   The Information Office of the State Council issues a White Paper on Progress in China's Human Rights Cause in 1996.

April 1997

8   China agrees to sign the UN International Covenant on Economic, Social, and Cultural Rights by the end of the year.

9   Tung Chee-hwa, future chief executive of Hong Kong, announces plans to limit political freedoms after the July 1 handover of Hong Kong.

At an international business conference in Shanghai, Premier Li Peng announces that China's inflation rate fell to 3 percent in the first quarter of 1997.

11   The HMS *Tanner* in Hong Kong is closed, ending the 156-year British naval presence in Asia.

14   U.S. House Speaker Newt Gingrich proposes extending most favored nation (MFN) trade status to China for only 6 months.

15   In Geneva, China blocks debate on a UN Commission on Human Rights resolution condemning its human rights record.

17   The Chinese Communist Party (CCP) issues a code of conduct prohibiting officials from personally engaging in profit-seeking activities.

18   To show U.S. support for preserving democracy in Hong Kong, President Clinton and Vice President Al Gore, in a meeting with leading Hong Kong democrat Martin Lee, discuss civil rights after the handover to the PRC on July 1.

21   Hundreds of activists march in Hong Kong to protest plans to curb civil liberties after July 1.

      An advance team of the People's Liberation Army garrison to be stationed in Hong Kong begins crossing the border from China to Hong Kong.

23   In Moscow, Russian president Boris Yeltsin and visiting Chinese president Jiang Zemin sign the Joint Declaration on the Multipolar World and a New World Order, which calls for "strategic interaction" and opposition to a "Cold War mentality."

      President Clinton "drops in" on a meeting between Vice President Al Gore and the Dalai Lama in Washington.

24   Three men are executed after being convicted of taking part in the February riots in Yining.

      The presidents of Russia, China, Kazakhstan, Tajikistan, and Kyrgyzstan agree to troop reductions along the Chinese border.

26   Former chairman of the National People's Congress and the first victim of the Cultural Revolution, Peng Zhen, dies at age 95.

30   Bao Tong, the most senior official to be jailed after the June 4, 1989, crackdown, is allowed to return to his own home outside of Beijing after seven years of imprisonment and one year of house arrest.

May 1997

1   After the Philippines protests against trespassing, China with-draws four armed vessels from near two islands that are claimed by Manila.

3   UNESCO awards its press freedom award to imprisoned Chinese journalist Gao Yu.

5   Taiwan receives the first batch of sixty Mirage 2000 fighter planes ordered from France in 1992.

6   Speaking to U.S. and British reporters, Tung Chee-hwa, future chief executive of Hong Kong, defends plans to curb civil liberties after July 1 as a means to avoid the kind of disorder that plagued the United States during the 1960s.

7   Senior Tibetan monk Chadrel Rinpoche is sentenced to six years in prison for plotting to split China and for leaking state secrets.

9   The ruling Nationalist Party in Taiwan survives a no-confidence vote initiated by legislators angry over deteriorating social order.

10   The Hong Kong provisional legislature, meeting in Shenzhen, supports Beijing's plans to limit civil liberties and rights after China assumes sovereignty over Hong Kong on July 1.

11   U.S. House Speaker Newt Gingrich, abandoning his earlier proposal to link MFN status to Beijing's treatment of Hong Kong after July 1, confirms that he favors renewal of trade privileges for one year.

13   China launches into orbit a domestic telecommunications satellite from Xichang Launch Center in Sichuan province.

     In the third bombing of the year in the capital, a bomb explodes in a public park in Beijing.

16   Tung Chee-hwa, future chief executive of Hong Kong, announces final plans to relax slightly the proposed restrictions on public demonstrations after July 1.

Visiting French president Jacques Chirac presides over the signing of a $1.5 billion contract for the purchase of thirty Airbus planes by the Chinese state aviation company.

18   The Xinhua News Agency reports that a Chinese court has sentenced four people to prison terms of three to fourteen years for smuggling AK-47 rifles into the United States.

19   The Xinhua News Agency reports that it has withdrawn a plan announced in late 1996 to impose a fee on foreign financial-news organizations.

President Clinton announces that he will renew China's MFN trading privileges despite Chinese human rights abuses.

22   The United States imposes economic sanctions on two Chinese companies and five Chinese citizens for selling chemicals and chemical-production equipment to Iran.

The U.S. Senate Appropriations Committee questions Secretary of State Madeleine K. Albright about the Iranian buildup of Chinese arms.

28   U.S. House minority leader Richard Gephardt (D-Missouri), labeling President Clinton's policy toward Beijing a failure, calls for the United States to revoke China's trading privileges.

29   Eight separatists in Xinjiang province are reported to have been executed for carrying out bombings, murders, and robberies.

June 1997

4   In the last commemoration before the handover to China, 55,000 people turn out in Hong Kong on the eighth anniversary of the Tiananmen demonstrations.

12   A Hong Kong judge throws out a lawsuit against the Beijing-appointed legislature but refuses to allow China to station troops in the colony before the July 1 return to Chinese sovereignty.

15   The provisional legislature approves new restrictions for Hong Kong, giving police broad new powers to ban peaceful demonstrations and requiring prior approval for protest marches.

19   Outgoing governor Christopher Patten makes a farewell appearance before the Hong Kong legislature.

20   President Clinton agrees, in a letter to U.S. House Speaker Newt Gingrich, to step up U.S. radio broadcasts to China in order to encourage members of Congress to support the renewal of Chinese MFN status.

Outside Zhongnanhai in Beijing, police disperse 200 protesters seeking redress for unfair housing policies.

23   Taiwan begins annual military maneuvers one week before the handover to China of Hong Kong.

Britain agrees to allow Chinese troops to enter Hong Kong in the hours before the official return to Chinese sovereignty.

24   China indicates that it will not support the creation of an international tribunal to try Khmer Rouge leader Pol Pot.

The U.S. House of Representatives, in a 259-to-173 vote, defeats the attempt to end China's MFN trading status.

27   China announces that it will send 4,000 troops into Hong Kong after sovereignty is returned to China on July 1.

28   Hong Kong's fully elected Legislative Council holds its last session before its replacement by the Beijing-appointed legislature on July 1.

29   Beijingers hold a rally in Tiananmen Square in support of the Hong Kong handover.

In efforts to reassure the people of Hong Kong and foreign governments, Tung Chee-hwa, future chief executive of Hong Kong, pledges to hold elections in Hong Kong within eleven months, and President Jiang Zemin promises that China will respect Hong Kong's rights and freedoms.

July 1997

1   China resumes control of Hong Kong, ending 156 years of British rule. The top leaders of both China and Hong Kong vow that Beijing will not interfere in ruling Hong Kong except in the areas of foreign affairs and defense.

3   The U.S. State Department warns China that the improper diversion of supercomputer technology for military uses violates U.S. agreements and international guidelines.

7   Thousands of workers protest in Mianyang, Sichuan province, demanding jobs and welfare payments, after several large state factories declare bankruptcy.

8   The Hong Kong legislature moves to establish a new electoral system that will reduce the number of pro-democracy members in future legislatures.

The U.S. Senate begins hearings on 1996 campaign finance improprieties, including accusations that the Chinese government tried to buy influence with U.S. politicians.

10   The U.S. Senate rejects a proposal to tighten control over the sale of U.S. supercomputers to China and Russia.

18   The Hong Kong legislature grants to police discretionary powers to prevent or break up demonstrations on the grounds of "national security."

The Taiwan National Assembly approves constitutional changes to end Taiwan's status as a province of China.

22   A U.S. State Department report sharply criticizes China for suppressing religious worship and persecuting Christians.

A constitutional challenge to the validity of the legal system and the appointed legislature is handed over to three senior appeal court judges in Hong Kong.

28   An article by Jiang Zemin in *Guangming ribao* outlines steps for privatization of state-owned industry.

29   U.S. secretary of state Madeleine K. Albright announces that she will name a special aide for U.S. policy toward Tibet.

The Hong Kong Court of Appeal upholds China's right to rule Hong Kong.

August 1997

7   The U.S. State Department expresses concern over reports that China has supplied ballistic missiles to Pakistan.

Beijing University professor Shang Dewen reports having written to President Jiang Zemin, openly proposing a new constitution, nationwide elections for the top leadership, a free press, a four-year presidency, and an independent judiciary in China.

9   The Hong Kong legislature passes a bill to deport hundreds of children who claim right of abode in Hong Kong.

18   Hong Kong newspapers report that Chen Xiaotong, son of former Beijing party secretary Chen Xitong, has been sentenced to 12 years in prison after being convicted on charges of bribery and diversion of public funds.

20   After a secret visit to Tibet, U.S. congressman Frank Wolf (R-

Virginia) reports on brutal repression, torture of political prisoners, and suppression of Tibetan culture.

The Hong Kong government introduces a bill to curb voter power.

21 Premier Lien Chan of Taiwan resigns after a scandal over violent crime.

26 Amnesty International reports that Chinese authorities sentenced more than 6,100 people to death in 1996 and carried out at least 4,367 executions.

28 At the conclusion of the Nationalist Party's Fifteenth National Congress, President Lee Teng-hui formally nominates Nationalist legislator Vincent Siew as premier of Taiwan.

29 Taiwan breaks official ties with the Caribbean nation of Saint Lucia.

September 1997

1 The PRC and Saint Lucia establish diplomatic relations.

6 Prime Minister Ryutaro Hashimoto of Japan ends two days of talks with Chinese leaders on security issues.

7–11 President Lee Teng-hui of Taiwan attends an international conference that is boycotted by China and the United Nations on the twentieth anniversary of the signing of the Panama Canal treaties.

10 At the end of a four-day closed-door session of the Central Committee, the Chinese Communist Party expels former Beijing party chief Chen Xitong and backs Jiang Zemin's major policy address on privatization to be presented to the party's Fifteenth National Congress.

12 At the opening session of the party's Fifteenth National Congress, General Secretary Jiang Zemin pledges the development of various forms of ownership and a shift from state ownership to a sys-

tem of shareholding. Jiang announces plans to expand direct elections from villages to townships as early as 1998.

President Clinton, meeting Chief Executive Tung Chee-hwa in Washington, expresses disappointment over the reversal of some political reforms in Hong Kong.

To ease U.S. fears of nuclear weapons proliferation, China enacts new rules requiring all sales of nuclear technology abroad to be cleared by the State Council.

Disgraced party leader Zhao Ziyang appeals to the party to review its verdict that the 1989 demonstrations were a "counterrevolutionary rebellion."

14   Wang Zhongyu, minister of the State Economic and Trade Commission, announces that China plans to reduce the number of wholly state-owned companies from 130,000 to 512.

18   At the conclusion of the party's Fifteenth National Congress, the CCP approves economic reforms, ousts Qiao Shi from his number-three position in the party hierarchy, and endorses Deng Xiaoping Theory in the party constitution.

The World Bank reports that a weak financial system, corruption, and pollution cloud China's economic boom.

22   Vice-Premier Zhu Rongji announces that China will reduce tariffs on technology imported for foreign business.

Chiang Wei-kuo, adopted son of the late president Chiang Kaishek, dies in Taiwan at the age of 80.

23   Premier Li Peng tells the World Bank that the West must stop exploiting the underdeveloped world.

China warns the United States and Japan not to infringe on its sovereignty by including Taiwan in any new regional security agreements.

28   Hong Kong's Beijing-appointed legislature approves a new election law that restricts democracy.

29   The Chinese Ministry of Radio, Film, and Television issues a memo banning cooperation with Hollywood studios that make films that "viciously attack China and hurt the Chinese people's feelings."

October 1997

8   Visiting U.S. commerce secretary William Daley warns China that the rapid growth in the trade deficit is "unacceptable."

Prominent church leader Bishop Su Zhimin is detained.

16   China formally joins the Zanger Committee, a group of nuclear-supplier nations that abide by certain export restraints.

The Information Office of the State Council issues a White Paper on Freedom of Religious Belief in China.

17   Fang Yi, former vice-premier and financial administrator, dies in Beijing at the age of 81.

In interviews with *Time* and the *Washington Post*, President Jiang Zemin defends China's human rights policies and urges Americans to tolerate China's political system and seek "common ground despite differences."

21   The Taiwan High Court acquits two Nationalist Party officials accused of spying for China after eight months' imprisonment.

22   The Clinton administration reaches an agreement with China stating that China will limit arms exports and end nuclear cooperation with Iran.

23   The Hong Kong stock market plunges 33 percent over the course of four days.

24   The United States reaches an interim agreement with the Xinhua News Agency on market access and noninterference for foreign financial information companies.

      In a speech broadcast worldwide by the Voice of America, President Clinton defends his policy of engagement.

26   In a joint letter to the White House, the chairmen of the Senate intelligence and foreign relations committees join nine other Republican senators to challenge President Clinton's assertion that China has halted assistance to the Pakistani nuclear program.

27   On the first stop of his trip to the United States, President Jiang Zemin visits Pearl Harbor.

      In New York, China signs the UN International Covenant on Economic, Social, and Cultural Rights.

28   President Jiang Zemin arrives in Washington on the first Chinese state visit in 12 years. Meeting informally in the White House, Presidents Clinton and Jiang agree to establish a hot line between Washington and Beijing.

29   At the U.S.-China summit, the United States agrees to give China access to nuclear technology in exchange for China's agreement that it will not aid Iran's nuclear program. Other agreements cover cooperation on narcotics and international crime and on economic, security, and environmental issues.

30   China releases Roman Catholic Bishop Su Zhimin.

November 1997

1   Jiang Zemin delivers a speech titled "Enhance Mutual Understanding and Build Stronger Ties of Friendship and Cooperation" at Harvard University as thousands of protesters, in one of the biggest demonstrations in Cambridge since the Vietnam War, call for democracy in China and independence for Tibet and Taiwan.

3   The World Bank predicts a surge in the AIDS epidemic in China, India, and Eastern Europe.

5   The U.S. House of Representatives considers nine bills, introduced by Republican members, that oppose President Clinton's policy toward China.

6   In an interview at the presidential palace, President Lee Teng-hui rules out concessions to China and states that Taiwan "is an independent and sovereign country."

8   At the site of the Three Gorges Dam, Premier Li Peng and President Jiang Zemin preside over a ceremony marking the diversion of the waters of the Yangzi River.

10   President Jiang Zemin and visiting Russian president Boris Yeltsin sign a declaration in Beijing on the final demarcation of the eastern sector of the 2,800-mile China–Russia border and authorize agreements on trade and on the protection of rare Manchurian tigers.

16   After spending most of the last 18 years in prison, dissident Wei Jingsheng is freed and exiled to the United States.

19   At the close of a three-day financial leadership conference held in Beijing, Vice-Premier Zhu Rongji sets a three-year timetable for reform of the nation's financial system.

20   The former deputy director of the planning commission of Fuzhou, Fujian province, Fang Jue, pens a platform of proposals entitled "China Needs a New Transformation," calling for elections at all levels of government, freedom of the press and of religion, an end to party control of the military, a reversal of the verdict on June 4, negotiations with the Dalai Lama, further opening of the economy, and a pro-American foreign policy stance.

24   President Clinton, meeting with President Jiang Zemin at the annual conference of APEC leaders in Vancouver, urges the release of more political dissidents.

29   The Hong Kong Democratic Party reports it is giving up its bid for seats in the Beijing-appointed legislature, calling the contest a "sham."

        In local elections, Taiwan's Nationalist Party suffers losses to the pro-independence opposition, winning only 8 of 23 contested municipalities.

30   The *People's Daily* quotes Vice-Premier Zhu Rongji as saying that China will not devalue its currency despite recent devaluations in several Southeast Asian countries.

December 1997

8   Wei Jingsheng, meeting with President Clinton in the White House, warns the president "not to be deceived" in his dealings with China.

13   U.S. and Chinese military officials initial an agreement to minimize the risk of naval accidents in the Pacific and to exchange information on the role of the military in relief missions.

22   In Geneva, the International Commission of Jurists urges a UN referendum on Tibet to decide its future status.

23   Hong Kong suspends chicken imports from China as the "chicken flu" in Hong Kong spreads.

30   A 25-article administrative regulation restricting the use of the Internet in China takes effect.

January 1998

1   South Africa ends relations with Taiwan and establishes diplomatic relations with China.

6   China missile expert Hua Di is detained on a visit home to Beijing from the United States.

11–20   Former secretary of defense William Perry visits Beijing and

Taipei in an attempt by the U.S. government to open a channel of communication between China and Taiwan.

11   An earthquake in Zhangbei County in Hebei province kills fifty.

12   Asia's largest investment bank outside of Japan, Peregrine Investment Holdings (Hong Kong), is forced to shut down because of the Asian economic crisis.

13   Vice-Premier Zhu Rongji appears on Chinese television, urging Chinese bankers to avert the panic that has led to the economic crisis in other Asian countries.

14   Four Chinese swimmers are suspended from the world championships in Perth for drug use.

16   China discloses new measures to overhaul its insolvent banking system, including a $6 billion fund to write off delinquent loans and reorganization of regional central bank offices on the model of the U.S. Federal Reserve system.

17   The White House rejects Secretary of Defense William Cohen's proposal to ease the ban on sales of arms to China.

        As part of a seven-nation tour, Secretary of Defense William Cohen visits Beijing to demonstrate continued U.S. engagement in East Asia.

18   China publishes a report revealing that its military factories exported $7 billion worth of goods in 1997.

19   Secretary of Defense William Cohen visits a sensitive command center in Beijing that monitors air and missile defenses.

20   Secretary of Defense William Cohen reports that he is satisfied with Beijing's assurances that it will halt missile sales to Iran.

        Foreign Ministry spokesman Shen Guofang says China is ready to begin political talks with Taiwan without any preconditions.

26   A Hong Kong judge overturns a law barring Chinese-born children of one Hong Kong parent from living in the territory.

      Four poets are arrested in Guizhou province after announcing they plan to publish a new poetry journal advocating a "literary renaissance."

28   The United States announces a plan to sell Taiwan refurbished navy ships, along with weapons and ammunition, for $300 million.

30   The U.S. State Department annual report cites modest improvements in China's human rights record.

31   Heading the Chinese delegation to the World Economic Forum in Davos, Switzerland, Vice-Premier Li Lanqing says that China will protect the value of the yuan and will invest extra money in infrastructure and environmental projects to maintain an 8 percent growth rate this year.

February 1998

2   A petition with 56 signatures is presented to President Jiang Zemin and the National People's Congress, declaring that because of his role in 1989, Premier Li Peng should not be named chairman of the congress.

6   U.S.-based dissident Wang Bingzhang, on a trip to China to set up an independent political party to challenge CCP control, is detained in Anhui province.

7   Hong Kong's six-week ban on live chicken imports from China ends.

8   Three U.S. clerics begin a three-week visit to investigate religious persecution in China and Tibet.

9   Dissident Wang Bingzhang is deported to the United States.

10   Seven prominent Chinese scientists issue a letter in support of

California physicist Peter Lee, who has been accused of passing classified secrets to the Chinese government.

12   Visiting U.S. religious leaders hold a meeting with President Jiang Zemin in Beijing to discuss freedom of religion.

14   A bomb explosion on a bus in Wuhan kills at least 16.

20   The United States and Taiwan reach an agreement to lower several Taiwanese trade barriers as part of Taiwan's bid to join the World Trade Organization.

Two men are arrested in New York on charges of conspiring to arrange transplants of kidneys and other organs taken from the bodies of executed Chinese inmates.

The Information Office of the State Council issues a White Paper on Tibet.

27   Rupert Murdoch, the owner of HarperCollins Publishers, denies trying to censor a book critical of China by former Hong Kong governor Christopher Patten.

28   China announces plans to float a $32.5 billion domestic bond in order to bail out banks.

Beijing joins 38 other Chinese cities in issuing weekly air-quality reports.

March 1998

3   Amnesty International reports that China detained 200,000 people in 1997 without charges or trials.

5   At the opening of the First Session of the Ninth National People's Congress, Premier Li Peng delivers his final work report as prime minister.

China announces that it expects to spend $1 trillion on public-works projects over the next three years to avert a financial crisis that would derail economic growth.

Taiwan announces that it will send envoys to China to restart talks on easing tensions and establishing closer communication and transportation links.

6   Finance Minister Liu Zhongli announces a modest budget plan, with only slight increases in investment.

Luo Gan, secretary-general of the State Council, announces that the bureaucracy of eight million will be cut by half, eliminating 11 of 40 government ministries and commissions.

7   At a National People's Congress news conference, Dai Xianglong, governor of the People's Bank of China, reports that because of the Asian financial crisis, exports, foreign investment, and the growth of foreign-exchange reserves may decline in 2000.

11   In New York, the organizer of the 1993 *Golden Venture* attempt to smuggle hundreds of immigrants into the United States pleads guilty on charges of manslaughter and immigrant smuggling.

12   Foreign Minister Qian Qichen declares that China is preparing to sign the UN International Covenant on Civil and Political Rights.

14   Citing progress on human rights, Clinton administration officials announce that President Clinton has decided to end the campaign to censure China for its human rights abuses at the annual meeting of the UN Commission on Human Rights in Geneva.

Officials from Sichuan province dismiss reports that the relocation of more than one million people from the site of the Three Gorges Dam project could turn into a human rights disaster.

16   Jiang Zemin is reelected (unchallenged) to a second five-year term as president of China; Li Peng is elected as chairman of the National People's Congress, with 89 percent of the vote.

17   Receiving 98 percent of the vote, Zhu Rongji is chosen as premier of China.

18   The semiofficial Straits Exchange Foundation in Taipei accepts an invitation from its Beijing counterpart to send "appropriate-ranking" personnel to Beijing for talks.

Beijing announces a new cabinet, including Tang Jiaxuan as foreign minister.

Three U.S. religious leaders who toured China in February issue a cautiously optimistic report about improvements in religious freedom over the last 20 years.

19   At a news conference at the close of the National People's Congress, Premier Zhu Rongji announces ambitious plans to overhaul state-owned industries and to restructure the banking system within three years.

25   Shanghai computer entrepreneur Lin Hai is detained for supplying a pro-democracy group in the United States with 30,000 e-mail addresses.

April 1998

1   Hundreds of retired and laid-off factory workers block traffic for hours in Shenyang, in northeastern China, protesting the government's failure to pay pensions and to compensate them for the loss of their homes.

3   Police raid activist Xu Wenli's home and hold him overnight.

7   The Hong Kong legislature exempts the Chinese state and the postcolonial Hong Kong government from some privacy and antidiscrimination laws.

13   Two hundred retired workers from a state-owned enterprise in Hubei province demonstrate, demanding payment of pensions and old-age insurance.

19   Dissident Wang Dan, coleader of the 1989 Tiananmen student demonstrations, is released from an eleven-year prison term and exiled to the United States on medical parole.

21   The Chinese government bans all forms of direct marketing and get-rich-quick schemes.

22   Straits Exchange Foundation negotiators arrive in China for two days of talks to end a three-year freeze in China-Taiwan relations.

23   China announces the resumption of diplomatic relations with the West African nation of Guinea-Bissau.

24   Taiwan breaks off diplomatic relations with Guinea Bissau.

29   Secretary of State Madeleine K. Albright begins two days of talks in Beijing to prepare for President Clinton's state visit in June.

30   In Chengdu, riot police clash with thousands of vendors whose street market was being closed down, leaving 4 dead and at least 30 injured.

May 1998

1   At least 7 Tibetans are killed and 60 wounded after Chinese authorities fire on prisoners staging a pro-independence rally that continues through May 4 at a prison in Lhasa.

4   Beijing University celebrates its one hundredth anniversary.

8   Republican leaders in Congress write to President Clinton complaining that the administration is blocking an inquiry into the 1996 case of Loral Space and Communications and the Hughes Electronics Corporation, that have been accused of giving space expertise to China.

9   The early release of Bishop Zeng Jingmu, sentenced to three years of reeducation through labor in 1995, is confirmed.

11 India sets off a nuclear device, sparking a potential nuclear arms race among India, China, and Pakistan.

China changes the English name of the Propaganda Department to the Department of Publicity "to reduce ambiguity and better reflect the nature of the department's work."

12 China condemns India's underground nuclear tests.

14 The U.S. House of Representatives votes, 375 to 41, to approve a bill to punish foreign countries that persecute people for their religious beliefs.

15 Fund-raiser Johnny Chung admits funneling $100,000 from a Chinese military officer to the U.S. Democratic Party during the summer of 1996.

19 Chinese officials deny as "groundless rumors" reported accusations that Chinese citizens contributed to the U.S. Democratic Party to influence U.S. policy.

Pakistani military leaders and diplomats leave Beijing after three days of talks focusing on India's detonation of nuclear devices.

20 U.S. House Speaker Newt Gingrich announces that he will create a special committee to investigate President Clinton's decision to waive export controls on advanced space technology to China.

The U.S. House of Representatives votes, 412 to 6, to bar exports of U.S.-made satellites and missile technology to China.

24 The people of Hong Kong elect a new legislature, in a 53 percent voter turnout, returning to office several pro-democracy politicians who had been ousted by Beijing after the July handover.

28   The Information Office of the State Council issues a White
      Paper on Development of China's Marine Programs.

      China expresses "deep regret" over Pakistan's decision to con-
      duct nuclear tests.

30   Twenty-two illegal immigrants are seized after a boat overloaded
      with illegal Chinese immigrants runs aground in New Jersey.

June 1998

2   China rules out an inquiry into the Tiananmen crackdown.

3   President Clinton announces that he will renew China's MFN
      trade status.

4   Nine years after the massacre, 40,000 people in Hong Kong
      commemorate the victims of the Tiananmen Square crackdown.

      The U.S. House of Representatives votes, 305 to 116, to
      approve a nonbinding resolution demanding that President
      Clinton avoid Tiananmen Square on his trip to China.

      Two days after openly criticizing the government, former senior
      official Bao Tong is warned that such public statements are not
      allowed.

9   President Clinton rejects appeals that he avoid an official wel-
      coming ceremony in Tiananmen Square.

11   President Clinton, in a half-hour address to the National
      Geographic Society, issues a broad defense of his decision to seek
      closer relations with China.

15   Thousands gather on the White House lawn on the National Day
      of Action for a Free Tibet.

19   The *New York Times* reports that Chinese authorities have
      detained the shipment of equipment for a performance of *The*

Peony Pavilion, a classical Chinese opera due to be performed at Lincoln Center in New York in July, and have publicly attacked the director of the opera for his portrayal of China.

The U.S. House of Representatives votes, 409 to 10, to set up a special nine-member committee to look into whether U.S. national security was undermined by the actions of the Clinton administration in allowing the launching of U.S. satellites on China's Long March rockets.

In a White House interview, President Clinton announces that he favors granting MFN status to China on a permanent basis.

23   China's central bank announces that it has closed the government-sponsored Hainan Development Bank because of a lack of funds.

24   In a letter to the Central Committee, former party general secretary Zhao Ziyang challenges Communist leaders to reassess the Tiananmen crackdown, calling it "one of the biggest human rights problems this century."

25   Members of the opposition China Democracy Party try to register their party.

President Clinton arrives in Xi'an, the first stop of his nine-day visit to China.

27   President Clinton is received by President Jiang Zemin in the west plaza of Tiananmen Square in Beijing.

In a news conference with Jiang in the Great Hall of the People, Clinton delivers a human rights lecture that is broadcast live on Chinese television. President Jiang offers dialogue and negotiation with the Dalai Lama if the Dalai Lama will acknowledge that Tibet is an "inalienable" part of China.

28   President Clinton attends a service in a Protestant church in Beijing.

29   Speaking to students at Beijing University, President Clinton calls for "freedom [which] strengthens stability and helps nations to change." He announces a plan for extensive legal cooperation and exchanges between the United States and China.

First Lady Hillary Rodham Clinton and Secretary of State Madeleine K. Albright visit a women's legal aid center on the outskirts of Beijing.

In the Great Hall of the People, China signs deals with U.S. companies worth $2 billion, including the purchase of 16 Boeing 737 passenger planes and one 747 jumbo jet.

30   President Clinton arrives in Shanghai, where he meets local leaders. Clinton reiterates the declaration of the United States' "Three Noes" policy on Taiwan: no support for the independence of Taiwan, no Taiwan entry into international organizations, and no support of a "one China, one Taiwan" policy. In an address to the U.S. Chamber of Commerce in Shanghai, Clinton cites corruption, environmental neglect, weak financial regulation, and restrictive trade practices as factors that will jeopardize China's entry into the WTO.

Foreign Minister Jason Hu of Taiwan criticizes President Clinton's announcement that he does not support independence for Taiwan.

The production of the sixteenth-century Chinese opera *The Peony Pavilion* to be performed at Lincoln Center is canceled because the Shanghai Municipal Bureau of Culture did not allow the cast to go to the United States in time for rehearsals, calling the performance "feudal trash" and "pornographic."

July 1998

1   In a change of policy effective July 1, and to be phased in by the end of the year, the government of China will no longer provide free housing to urban workers.

President Jiang Zemin visits Hong Kong to celebrate the first anniversary of the handover.

2   President Clinton meets with Chief Executive Tung Chee-hwa in Hong Kong.

3   President Clinton meets privately with democracy activist Martin Lee in Hong Kong.

In Shenzhen, 12 people are executed for murder, armed robbery, and kidnapping.

6   The new $20 billion Hong Kong Chek Lap Kok Airport opens, despite chaos in the passenger terminals and computer glitches that paralyze cargo operations.

7   U.S. Senate majority leader Trent Lott (R-Mississippi) accuses President Clinton of abandoning Taiwan.

8   Dispelling accusations of Chinese theft of sensitive technology, a Pentagon review concludes that two sensitive circuit boards that disappeared after the failed launch of a U.S. satellite by China were probably destroyed in the crash.

10   Police detain dissidents Wang Youcai and Wang Donghai, cofounders of the China Democracy Party, and several others in and around Hangzhou.

12   China releases four democracy activists, keeping four others in custody.

13   Meeting with Yasser Arafat in Beijing, President Jiang Zemin voices support for the "efforts of Palestinian people to regain their legitimate rights, including the establishment of an independent state."

14   Twelve people connected with the construction of the transportation network at the new Hong Kong airport are arrested on charges of bribery and corruption.

U.S. Senate Republicans report that their preliminary investigation found that the Clinton administration "violated U.S. policy" by providing China with sensitive satellite technology.

15   Hong Kong lawmakers reject a motion for direct popular election of the members of the legislature and the chief executive when their terms end.

16   After Chinese customs confiscates $350 million of smuggled goods in the first five months of 1998, President Jiang Zemin announces that a new antismuggling police force will be formed.

A spokesperson for the Supreme People's Procuratorate reports that former Beijing party secretary Chen Xitong has been charged with corruption and dereliction of duty, resulting in an estimated loss of $2.2 billion in municipal funds.

17   Seventy-nine dissidents from 19 provinces issue an open letter calling for the release of five men arrested for trying to register the China Democracy Party.

The Ministry of Civil Affairs reports that more than 1,000 people have died in summer floods that have destroyed nearly 3 million homes and caused economic losses of more than $10 billion.

21   In New York, Sang Lan, China's national vault champion, falls during training for the Goodwill Games, injuring her vertebrae and leaving her paralyzed.

22   For the nineteenth consecutive year, the U.S. House of Representatives votes, 264 to 166, to maintain normal trade relations with China.

The Xinhua News Agency reports that President Jiang Zemin, in an address to a meeting of top military commanders, has ordered China's military to give up its multibillion-dollar commercial empire.

24   Police detain 4 more dissidents, bringing to 21 the number arrested since President Clinton's visit to China.

27   The Information Office of the State Council issues a White Paper on National Defense, which discloses statistics about specific arms sales, including missile sales.

    Taiwan legislator Lin Ti-chuan is kidnapped and murdered in Haicheng, Liaoning province, jeopardizing the future of the next round of cross-strait talks.

28   The Ministry of Public Health reports an official total of 10,676 people with HIV by the end of June, including 301 who have developed the full-blown AIDS disease.

31   Former Beijing party head Chen Xitong is sentenced to sixteen years in prison for his role in a $2.2 billion corruption scandal; he is the highest-level Communist leader to be tried for graft.

August 1998

1   The Chinese media report that some areas of the Yangzi River have swelled to the highest level ever recorded.

2   The U.S. ships USS *Blue Ridge* and USS *John S. McCain* arrive in Qingdao for a four-day visit.

4   Floodwaters burst through a levee protecting towns along the Yangzi River; 1,000 people are reported missing.

5   The Chinese ambassador to the United States, Li Zhaoxing, backs out of a scheduled appearance before the U.S. House Subcommittee on Human Rights.

7   In the worst flooding since 1954, China evacuates more than 500,000 from Hubei province.

9   Engineers blast levees along the Yangzi River to prevent floodwaters from reaching cities and farmland in central China.

10   Hundreds of investors stage protests in Beijing, demanding that
      the government reimburse them for millions of dollars swindled
      by officials of the Xinguoda Futures Company.

11   The Political Science and Law Committee of the Central Commit-
      tee issues an emergency circular calling on police and security per-
      sonnel to maintain order in the area of the central China floods.

      Recognizing the benefits of competition in the financial sector,
      the People's Bank of China announces that it will allow foreign
      banks to start yuan operations in Shenzhen.

12   China convicts four Taiwanese businessmen of espionage, sen-
      tencing one of them to four years in prison.

      The *People's Daily* reports flooding in Heilongjiang province
      along the Nen River and its tributaries.

13   Jiang Zemin begins a visit of the flood-ravaged area along the
      Yangzi River.

14   The Xinhua News Agency reports a government decision to
      amend the controversial law permitting doctors to sterilize peo-
      ple with serious genetic conditions.

16   The state media report that three dikes along the Nen River in
      northeastern China have broken, trapping 20,000 people and
      flooding 1,217 oil wells in the Daqing oil fields.

17   Despite a government ban, student and women's groups in
      Beijing hold protests over the looting, killing, and rape of eth-
      nic Chinese during the May riots in Indonesia.

18   More than 100 demonstrators gather outside the Indonesian
      embassy in Beijing to protest the rape of ethnic Chinese women
      in Indonesia.

      The founding of the Committee for Safeguarding the Legal
      Rights of Journalists is announced.

20   Waters from the Songhua River engulf parts of China's largest oil field and farming villages in northeastern China.

22   China concedes that the recent flooding is partly the result of widespread deforestation.

23   The Yangzi River near Chongqing rises to its highest level of the year.

25   Flood-control officials evacuate areas along the upper Yangzi River.

30   Student leader Wang Youcai is released after being held in detention for more than seven weeks for attempting to register an opposition party.

31   In a two-hour interview with the *New York Times*, President Lee Teng-hui says that he is seeking ways for Taiwan to break out of the isolation imposed by China.

The Chinese release parts of a July closed-door speech by Premier Zhu Rongji outlining plans to prosecute CCP law-enforcement and military officials involved in smuggling.

September 1998

1   Citing the devastation wrought by the summer flooding, China bans any further cutting of trees in forests in western China.

5   An Amnesty International report cites an estimate of 3,000 executions in 1997, down from 4,367 in 1996.

The Hong Kong government announces a variety of measures designed to strengthen its currency's peg to the U.S. dollar.

China joins other members of the UN Security Council in condemning Iraq and ordering it to rescind its decision to stop all arms inspections.

7   An open letter from 116 dissidents appeals to Mary Robinson, the first UN human rights commissioner ever to visit China, to press the government to dismantle the "reeducation through labor" system.

Chinese scholars brief visiting UN human rights commissioner Mary Robinson on the state of freedom and civil rights in China.

9   Security agents drag the wife of dissident Liu Nianchun from the Beijing Hilton, where she had attempted to press the case of her husband with the visiting UN human rights commissioner.

11   Officials from the bureaus of civil affairs in Wuhan and in Jinan tell dissidents that they will consider their applications to establish China's first opposition party since 1949.

Because of the Asian long-horned beetle, which is blamed for ravaging trees in New York City in 1996, the United States bans imports of all Chinese goods shipped in raw wood packing material.

12   Shi Binhai, coeditor of *Political China: Facing the Era of Choosing a New Structure*, a collection of essays promoting political change, is placed under house arrest.

14   Military leader Yang Shangkun, former president of China, dies of an undisclosed illness at age 91.

15   General Zhang Wannian, vice-chairman of the Central Military Commission, meets with National Security Advisor Sandy Berger and President Clinton. The Pentagon receives assurances that China will move ahead with joint military exercises and exchanges for the next year, and the two sides sign a pact to share information on military environmental problems.

At a news conference in Beijing, visiting UN human rights commissioner Mary Robinson reports that Chinese officials are prepared to sign the UN International Covenant on Civil and Political Rights in October.

17   Dissident Ren Wanding is detained as he attempts to submit an application to register an opposition party.

18   A U.S. House-Senate conference agrees to transfer export licensing for commercial communications satellites from the Commerce Department to the State Department in order to toughen rules governing such transactions involving China.

19   Vice-Premier Qian Qichen announces that China will station troops in Macao after the territory is returned from Portugal to China on December 20, 1999.

21   In a challenge to the Communist Party, three political dissidents announce plans to run in local elections in Beijing.

22   Top Taiwan negotiator Shi Hwei-yow visits Beijing in preparation for the highest-level meeting between China and Taiwan in five years.

28   In a speech declaring a "complete victory" over the record flooding, President Jiang Zemin defends the 1989 army crackdown on demonstrators in Tiananmen Square.

29   Dissidents in China release, via the Internet and fax, copies of two manifestoes—the Declaration on Civil Rights and Freedom and the Declaration of Civil Rights and Social Justice.

Reflecting a slowdown in the shift to a market economy, the People's Bank of China announces new restrictions on foreign-exchange transactions.

In the face of lower-priced imports, the Chinese media report that the State Economic and Trade Commission will recommend prices for all major automakers.

30   In an effort to entice Taiwan into negotiations on reunification, China announces that it will grant Taiwan greater freedom than that enjoyed by Hong Kong.

October 1998

1   China bans the buying and selling of blood in an effort to stop the spread of the AIDS virus.

5   In New York, China signs the UN International Covenant on Civil and Political Rights, which guarantees freedom of expression, religion, and self-determination.

6   A reporter for *Yomiuri shimbun* returns to Japan after being expelled by Chinese state security for purported possession of state secrets.

       China plans to shut down the Guangdong International Trust and Investment Corporation because of its inability to pay its debts.

7   During the visit of Prime Minister Tony Blair, the first visit by a British prime minister in seven years, China detains dissident Xu Wenli.

14   After a three-year break, China and Taiwan resume talks on reunification as the highest-ranking member of the Nationalist Party to visit China, Koo Chen-fu, meets Chinese officials in Shanghai.

18   At the end of a four-day visit, Koo Chen-fu meets President Jiang Zemin in Beijing, and the two sides agree to continue their discussions.

19   Premier Zhu Rongji and visiting Vietnamese prime minister Phan Van Krai agree to resolve their territorial disputes by the year 2000.

20   China holds its first international conference on human rights in Beijing.

25   State Council guidelines allow the creation of private social organizations as long as they meet government approval and uphold rule by the Communist Party.

26   Forty worshipers at a house church are arrested in Wugang, Henan province.

28   Officials annul an election for village head won by dissident Yu Tielong in Wangshanding village, Zhejiang province.

        The Guangdong International Trust and Investment Corporation fails to make a scheduled interest payment of $8.75 million on a $200 million bond.

31   Timber cut in forests in western China is no longer allowed to be trucked to logging yards.

November 1998

4   The revised Adoption Law approved by the Standing Committee of the National People's Congress relaxes adoption rules for Chinese couples and imposes punishment on people who abandon or sell children.

5   The Xinhua News Agency reports that two senior anticorruption officials in the legal system, Luo Ji and Huang Lizhi, have been relieved of their posts for "not [being] suited to be prosecutors."

        More than 100 worshipers in a house church are detained in Nanyang, Henan province.

11   The Dalai Lama dismisses the possibility of reopening talks with China because of distrust between the two sides.

12   Two hundred protesters demonstrate in Beijing to pressure the government to compensate them for losses from the Xinguoda Futures Company multimillion-dollar investment scheme.

        The Guangzhou Intermediate People's Court sentences Hong Kong crime boss Cheung Tze-keung to death for arms smuggling and kidnapping.

16   President Jiang Zemin meets President Clinton in Malaysia for the annual APEC summit meeting.

18   China expels a reporter for the German magazine *Der Spiegel*, Jurgen Kremb, for possession of state secrets.

20   At the Great Hall of the People, President Jiang Zemin delivers a speech commemorating Liu Shaoqi in honor of the one hundredth anniversary of his birth.

23   At the sixth China–Russia summit, President Jiang Zemin meets ailing Boris Yeltsin in a hospital in Moscow to celebrate the completion of their border agreement and to offer relief aid for the Russian economy.

25   The city of Beijing announces that it plans to bid for the 2008 Summer Olympic Games.

26   In the first visit of a Chinese head of state to Japan, President Jiang Zemin and Prime Minister Keizo Obuchi decide not to sign a joint declaration on ties because of disagreement over Japan's apology for its actions against the Chinese during World War II.

29   As part of Premier Zhu Rongji's effort to make government smaller and more efficient, the Chinese Communist Party and state bureaucracies are ordered to end all business ties as of the beginning of next year.

30   The minister of the State Economic and Trade Commission, Sheng Huaren, acknowledges that the task of overhauling the state sector has proved more difficult than expected but says that the goal of achieving the task can still be realized within three years.

In three cities, China detains ten dissidents who have attempted to establish an opposition party, including Xu Wenli and Qin Yongmin; Wang Youcai is formally arrested after having been held in custody for one month.

December 1998

1   Taiwan confirms that it is negotiating with the United States for the purchase of four Aegis destroyers in order to improve its missile defense capability against China.

3   Xiao Yang, president of the Supreme People's Court, calls for trials to be open to the public beginning in 1999.

5   Hong Kong gangster Cheung Tze-keung and four others are executed in Guangzhou.

        In China's first Internet subversion case, Shanghai entrepreneur Lin Hai is put on trial for "inciting to overthrow state power" by selling e-mail addresses to a dissident electronic magazine in the United States.

6   In elections on Taiwan, Nationalist Party challenger Ma Ying-jeou ousts the popular mayor of Taipei, and in the national legislature, the Nationalist Party wins 123 of 225 seats.

9   China issues a $1 billion international bond offering.

10   Wang Gancheng, the designer of China's first atomic bomb, dies in Beijing of an undisclosed illness at age 90.

12   A gas explosion in a coal mine in Zhejiang province kills 32 miners.

15   The state media report that China's military has completed the handover of its commercial holdings to civilian control, one day ahead of the deadline set by the Communist Party.

17   Dissidents Wang Youcai and Qin Yongmin are tried separately in Hangzhou and Wuhan, respectively, but no verdicts are announced.

18   At the Great Hall of the People, in a speech during a ceremony marking 20 years of economic reform, President Jiang Zemin voices concern about stability and rules out Western-style democracy.

20   Former labor activist Liu Nianchun is freed after more than three years of imprisonment and put on a plane for exile in the United States.

21   After a trial that lasts less than three hours, Xu Wenli is sentenced to 13 years in prison for "inciting to overthrow state power"; Wang Youcai is sentenced to 11 years in prison.

22   Qin Yongmin is convicted and sentenced to 12 years in prison.

23   The Supreme People's Court issues new rules warning film directors, singers, and computer-software developers against attempts to "overthrow state power" or to "endanger national security."

Beijing orders the China Development Union to stop holding discussion groups on democracy and reform.

27   China sentences dissident Zhang Shanguang to ten years in prison for providing an interview about farmer protests to U.S.-financed Radio Free Asia.

30   China reports reaching economic growth of 7.8 percent in 1998, making it the fastest-growing economy in Asia.

A classified report of a U.S. House panel concludes that "national security harm did occur" after the Chinese obtained military technology, including nuclear weapons design, from the United States.

The liberal weekly *Cultural Times*, published under the auspices of the Guangzhou Academy of Social Sciences, is closed by the authorities.

31   Premier Zhu Rongji, on a tour of the construction site of the Three Gorges Dam, expresses the first public concern by a Chinese leader over potential environmental damage.

Six thousand voters in ten villages of Buyun township, Sichuan province, cast votes in a direct election for magistrate despite lack of approval from Beijing for township elections.

January 1999

4   In Wuhan, police detain more than 100 retired factory workers who are protesting that they have not received their monthly pensions.

5   Beijing announces that it is establishing a 10,000-member police force with special powers to combat smuggling.

6   Li Jizhou, a vice-minister of public security, becomes the highest-ranking security figure to be detained on charges of corruption.

8   Five thousand farmers demonstrating against local officials clash with police in Daolin township, Hunan province, leaving one dead and many injured.

10   Foreign creditors are told that the Guangdong International Trust and Investment Corporation will file for bankruptcy.

11   Seattle-based Starbucks opens its first outlet in Beijing.

     U.S. and Chinese officials resume two days of human rights talks after a hiatus of four years.

13   Four people are injured in a bomb blast near a downtown bus stop in Zhuhai.

17   A bomb causes a bus explosion that injures 37 people in the city of Changsha, Hunan province.

18   The Dalian International Trust and Investment Corporation asks Japanese banks to allow it to delay repayment on outstanding loans.

20   Taiwan agrees to hand over 9 of 16 Chinese hijackers whom it has held since a series of hijackings in 1993 and 1994.

     The Shanghai Number One Intermediate Court sentences Lin Hai to two years in prison for giving e-mail addresses to *VIP*

Reference News, a U.S.-based electronic publication that is considered hostile to Beijing.

21   The Taiwan cabinet submit their resignations to President Lee Teng-hui.

22   A Hong Kong government commission blames the bungled opening of the new airport on foreigners.

23   President Lee Teng-hui reappoints Vincent Siew as prime minister of Taiwan.

25   A pipe bomb explodes, killing 8 and injuring 65, near a farmers' market in Yizhang County, Hunan province.

27   After establishing diplomatic relations with Macedonia, Taiwan claims relations with 28 countries.

29   Challenging the legality of Chinese laws, Hong Kong's Court of Final Appeal rules that people with one Hong Kong parent have the right to live in the territory without permission from China.

31   The Xinhua News Agency reports that at a recent Central Committee meeting President Jiang Zemin has backed forthcoming amendments to the constitution that support private enterprise.

February 1999

4   A Hangzhou court sentences dissident Wang Ce to four years in prison for sneaking back into China from abroad and donating $1,000 to help launch the China Democracy Party.

Eighteen dissidents defy a ban by forming five new branches of the China Democracy Party.

8   The Xinhua News Agency reports that Chinese authorities are asking suppliers of commercial aircraft to delay deliveries due to a serious overcapacity of Chinese airlines.

9   The director of the Information Office of the State Council, Zhao Qizheng, criticizes the Hong Kong ruling that children in China of one Hong Kong parent can move to Hong Kong.

10   China suspends relations with Macedonia after the Macedonians confirm that they have established diplomatic relations with Taiwan.

Taiwan hands over five paroled Chinese hijackers to the mainland.

In Beijing, Prime Minister Hun Sen of Cambodia signs five agreements to increase China-Cambodia economic and political ties.

Military analysts cite a classified Pentagon report stating that China has stationed 150 to 200 M-9 and M-11 ballistic missiles in provinces facing Taiwan.

15   Dissident journalist Gao Yu is released from prison several months short of her six-year sentence in 1993 for revealing state secrets.

22   The Clinton administration rejects the sale of a $450 million satellite to a business group with close ties to the Chinese government.

23   Ending its ban on Disney films, China announces that it will begin showing the film *Mulan* in 100 cities.

Deputy Secretary of the Treasury Lawrence H. Summers leads a U.S. delegation in talks in Beijing with Premier Zhu Rongji to end trade disputes.

24   More than 60 people are killed in the crash of a Russian-made jet in Wenzhou.

25   In retaliation for Macedonia's decision to establish diplomatic relations with Taiwan, China vetoes a UN Security Council resolution to keep UN forces in Macedonia for another six months.

The U.S. Senate unanimously approves the introduction and passage at the UN Commission on Human Rights meeting in Geneva of a resolution condemning China's human rights abuses.

26   In a concession to China, the Hong Kong Court of Final Appeal defers to the National People's Congress in Beijing in regard to the ruling on Hong Kong residency.

The U.S. State Department annual report on human rights harshly condemns China's human rights violations.

March 1999

1   Secretary of State Madeleine K. Albright begins a two-day visit to Beijing by telling Chinese leaders that the Clinton administration "deplores" the recent crackdown on democracy activists.

5   Premier Zhu Rongji addresses the opening of the Second Session of the Ninth National People's Congress, pledging to continue with economic and social reforms.

6   Clinton administration officials announce tightened security at U.S. nuclear laboratories after reports emerge that China may have stolen nuclear secrets in the 1980s.

8   U.S. energy secretary Bill Richardson dismisses Los Alamos nuclear weapons designer Wen Ho Lee under suspicion of handing nuclear secrets to China in the late 1980s.

9   To stem the outflow of hard currency, China raises interest rates on U.S. dollar deposits.

The CCP submits constitutional amendments to the annual meeting of the National People's Congress declaring private business an "important component of the socialist market economy."

10   Thousands of demonstrators in New Delhi burn 40 Chinese flags—one for each year of Chinese rule in Tibet.

15   The CIA names retired admiral David Jeremiah to assess how much nuclear weapons technology was lost to China through leaks from the Los Alamos National Laboratory.

Speaking at a news conference after the adjournment of the National People's Congress, Premier Zhu Rongji denies allegations that China stole U.S. nuclear weapons secrets.

18   Editors of the liberal magazine *Fangfa* confirm receiving a notice from the State Press and Publications Administration that they cease publication.

The U.S. Senate rejects, by a vote of 69 to 30, a proposal to require congressional approval before the United States can support China's entry into the World Trade Organization.

22   The European Union agrees not to support a resolution condemning China's human rights record at the annual UN Commission on Human Rights meeting in Geneva.

23   China and the Philippines open two days of talks in Manila to resolve the dispute over the Spratly Islands in the South China Sea.

25   Bao Tong, former aide to party general secretary Zhao Ziyang, issues a call to the CCP and PRC leadership to "reverse the wrongful assessment of the 1989 student demonstrations."

China criticizes NATO air raids against Serbian forces in Kosovo.

26   In a speech to Swiss legislators, President Jiang Zemin complains about his reception in Switzerland by pro-Tibet demonstrators.

The U.S. State Department announces that the United States will back a resolution condemning China's human rights record at the annual UN Commission on Human Rights meeting in Geneva.

29   A Hong Kong court rules that seventeen mainland residents who have claimed the right to reside in Hong Kong must return to the mainland and then reapply to the Chinese authorities to return to the territory.

30   Exiled Chinese dissidents Wang Dan and Wu'er Kaixi begin a global petition campaign calling for a reassessment of the verdict on the Tiananmen crackdown.

April 1999

1   Despite opposition to the NATO bombing of Kosovo and U.S. attacks on Chinese human rights violations, Chinese officials confirm that Premier Zhu Rongji will visit the United States.

4   Exiled dissident Wang Xizhe attempts to return to China, but he is turned back in Seoul.

6   Premier Zhu Rongji arrives in Los Angeles for a nine-day six-city visit of the United States.

8   In a Washington press conference with Premier Zhu Rongji, President Clinton announces that China will enter the World Trade Organization by the end of the year.

The office of the U.S. trade representative releases a 17-page list of commitments China has made to open its agricultural, telecommunications, and financial-services industries.

9   At a private congressional breakfast, Premier Zhu Rongji criticizes President Clinton for not having "enough courage" to sign a World Trade Organization accord.

Lodi Gyaltsen Gyari, a special envoy of the Dalai Lama, is disinvited to a Washington private dinner hosted by several nongovernmental foreign policy organizations in honor of Premier Zhu Rongji.

Senior Communist Party member Zhu Muzhi says that the military was forced to open fire on June 4, 1989, because it lacked tear gas and rubber bullets.

UN investigator Nigel Rodley reports that China has agreed to allow him to examine allegations of torture in China.

Chinese police warn Bao Tong, the highest-ranking Communist Party official to be jailed after 1989, against making trouble in the lead-up to the tenth anniversary of the Tiananmen demonstrations.

10   China and the United States sign an agreement on agricultural trade issues, removing unfair trade barriers to U.S. agricultural products in China.

13   In the face of sharp criticism, President Clinton telephones Premier Zhu Rongji in New York and asks to resume talks in Beijing by the end of April on China's accession to the WTO. A joint U.S.-China statement issued by the White House announces that both sides have agreed to "move intensively" toward a resolution of the WTO negotiations.

14   Premier Zhu Rongji is greeted by supporters as well as protesters prior to speaking on trade and technology issues at the Massachusetts Institute of Technology.

16   The United States submits a resolution criticizing China's human rights record to the UN Commission on Human Rights in Geneva, but it is unable to get any other country to sign as a cosponsor.

20   In an open letter, 16 Chinese dissidents from within China ask ordinary Chinese to commemorate the deaths of those killed during the Tiananmen crackdown of 1989.

Amnesty International issues a report alleging Chinese use of torture to suppress anti-Muslim sentiment in northwestern China.

21   A U.S. intelligence assessment reports Chinese spying over the past 20 years not only on U.S. nuclear weapons designs but also on U.S. reentry vehicles.

23   A Beijing court rejects Marxist Duan Ruofei's copyright infringement suit against two liberal writers.

A vote for a "no-action motion" to end debate on the censure of China at the UN Commission on Human Rights meeting in Geneva succeeds, with 22 in favor, 17 opposed, and 14 abstentions.

25   More than 10,000 followers of the religious cult Falun Gong (Buddhist Law Society) demonstrate around Zhongnanhai in Beijing, protesting a recent article in an academic journal in Tianjin warning of the dangers posed by such cults.

26   In response to increased Chinese deployment of missiles along the coast, Clinton administration officials agree to sell Taiwan an early-warning radar system.

Dissident Fang Jue goes on trial on charges of fraud. The trial is adjourned with no verdict.

May 1999

7   A NATO raid hits the Chinese embassy in Belgrade, setting the building on fire, killing 3, and injuring 21.

8   Thousands of university students demonstrate in front of the U.S. and British embassies in Beijing and other cities, protesting the NATO missile attack on the Chinese embassy in Belgrade. President Clinton expresses his "regrets and profound condolences," calling the bombing "a tragic mistake."

9   Anti-American demonstrations take place in Chinese cities for a second consecutive day, as tens of thousands of Chinese attack U.S. diplomatic compounds.

10   China announces that it is breaking off talks with Washington on human rights and arms control to protest the NATO bombing of the Chinese embassy in Belgrade. Demonstrations continue in front of the U.S. embassy in Beijing for a third consecutive day, trapping the U.S. ambassador, Jim Sasser, and 13 other staff members inside the compound.

The Clinton administration notifies Congress that it has approved the export of technology to China to permit launching a communications satellite aboard a Chinese rocket.

11   The Chinese media belatedly report that President Clinton and other NATO leaders have apologized for the attack on the Chinese embassy in Belgrade, as the government-orchestrated demonstrations in major cities subside.

Democratic Party fund-raiser Johnny Chung tells a U.S. congressional committee that he received $300,000 from a Chinese general interested in influencing the 1996 U.S. presidential election.

12   The White House announces that President Clinton plans to nominate Admiral Joseph W. Prueher to replace the departing U.S. ambassador to China, Jim Sasser.

13   In a ceremony in the Great Hall of the People, China's leaders bestow the title of "revolutionary martyr" on three Chinese journalists killed in the NATO bombing of the Chinese embassy in Belgrade.

China denies government involvement in the demonstrations in front of the U.S. and British embassies protesting the NATO bombing of the Chinese embassy in Belgrade.

17   Relatives of those who died in Tiananmen Square in 1989 submit the first of two petitions to the government calling for a criminal inquiry into the "systematic and organized" killing of civilians.

18   The Hong Kong government says that it will ask China to override a Hong Kong Court of Final Appeal ruling granting residency to over one million mainland-born children of Hong Kong residents.

19   In an effort to curb dissent, at a national conference China's top prosecutor Han Zhubin calls for a crackdown on "all criminal activities that endanger state security."

21   A Foreign Ministry spokesperson announces the suspension of port visits to Hong Kong by U.S. Navy ships, signaling a further deterioration of U.S.-China relations.

24   In a *People's Daily* editorial, the Chinese Communist Party acknowledges that serious corruption and environmental and engineering problems hamper the construction of the Three Gorges Dam. Publicizing a speech given earlier by Premier Zhu Rongji at a closed conference, the paper announces a major change in the resettling of the 1.3 million people who will be driven from their homes as a result of the building of the dam.

25   A U.S. House select committee on Chinese espionage chaired by Representative Christopher Cox (R-California) releases a 700-page report detailing two decades of Chinese spying in the United States.

June 1999

2   The *People's Daily* calls on citizens to preserve "unity and sta-bility," while at least seven political dissidents are detained for publicly honoring the victims of Tiananmen Square.

3   In an attempt to improve controls over its currency flows, China curbs foreign transfers of the yuan.

4   A high-level North Korean delegation that includes political leader Kim Yong-Nam visits Beijing, thus ending an eight-year hiatus in high-level exchanges.

A lone protester in Tiananmen Square unfurls an umbrella on which there is writing urging visitors to remember the tenth anniversary of the student movement. Police confiscate the umbrella and hustle the man away. In Hong Kong, a record 70,000 residents hold a candlelight vigil in Victoria Park to commemorate June 4.

9   Following the release of the Cox Report on Chinese espionage, the U.S. House of Representatives unanimously adopts several measures to protect U.S. nuclear weapons programs.

10   The People's Bank of China cuts its interest rates by an average of three-quarters of a point in order to encourage consumer spending.

      Former government official Fang Jue, who has issued an appeal for political reform, is sentenced to four years in prison on charges of conducting illegal business activities.

11   Two leaders of a farmers' protest that took place in Daolin township, Hunan province, in January 1999 are arrested for protesting illegal taxes and CCP corruption at that time.

12   A Chinese rocket carries two U.S. satellites into orbit.

13   General Ji Shengde, the chief of Chinese military intelligence and a key figure in U.S. allegations of political donations to influence U.S. politics, is reportedly reassigned to run a military research institute.

14   A U.S. delegation led by Undersecretary of State Thomas Pickering leaves for Beijing to explain to Chinese leaders how NATO bombers accidentally destroyed the Chinese embassy in Belgrade.

      A senior Chinese official meets with representatives of the Falun Gong to dispel rumors of an imminent suppression and to warn them against disturbing social stability.

17   China publicly rejects the U.S. explanation that the attack on the Chinese embassy in Belgrade was an accident.

22   The U.S. Senate approves legislation to impose more stringent controls on the export of technology with military uses to Hong Kong and Macao.

24   The World Bank approves funding for the China Western Poverty Reduction Project, which will resettle 57,800 poor Chinese farmers from Qinghai province to the Tibetan and Mongolian autonomous prefectures.

26   The Standing Committee of the National People's Congress overturns the Hong Kong Court of Final Appeal ruling that would have allowed 1.6 million children to immigrate to Hong Kong from mainland China.

July 1999

1   President Clinton eases restrictions on the export of supercomputers to China and Russia.

6   Chinese relief officials report that 240 people have died and 60 million others are in danger following annual flooding in the Yangzi River valley.

One thousand followers of Falun Gong surround provincial offices in Jiangxi province to protest an article critical of the movement in a government newsletter.

7   China protests the decision by Papua New Guinea to establish diplomatic ties with Taiwan.

9   On his first visit to China, Prime Minister Keizo Obuchi of Japan signs a bilateral trade agreement and endorses terms for China's entry into the WTO.

In an interview with a German radio station, President Lee Teng-hui of Taiwan endorses state-to-state relations with mainland China, thus abandoning the "one-China" policy that has been the basis for China-Taiwan relations for 50 years.

13   The Xinhua News Agency warns Taiwan of "monumental disaster" in retaliation for Taiwan's retraction of the "one-China" policy.

15   The Information Office of the State Council issues a report titled "Facts Speak Louder Than Words," which announces that China has mastered the technology to build a neutron bomb on its own, not through theft of U.S. nuclear secrets.

18   In a telephone conversation with President Clinton, President

Jiang Zemin says that China will not rule out the use of force to crush the independence of Taiwan.

21   Following the police detention of some seventy leaders of the Falun Gong, demonstrations erupt in more than 30 cities.

22   The United States sends senior diplomats to Beijing and Taipei in an attempt to defuse the latest dispute between China and Taiwan.

China announces a ban on the Falun Gong organization and accuses its founder, Li Hongzhi, of plotting to overthrow the Communist Party.

23   China closes off Tiananmen Square to Falun Gong demonstrators.

Papua New Guinea reverses its earlier decision to establish diplomatic relations with Taiwan.

24   China announces that it has detained more than 4,000 Falun Gong followers in Beijing as part of a massive crackdown on the banned movement. Chinese authorities send 1,200 government officials who are followers of the Falun Gong to Communist Party school for political study.

Chinese leaders retreat to Beidaihe to discuss the spiraling deflation that has slowed economic growth.

25   In the highest-level talks since the NATO bombing of the Chinese embassy in Belgrade, U.S. secretary of state Madeleine K. Albright meets Chinese foreign minister Tang Jiaxuan in Singapore to discuss easing U.S.-China tensions.

27   U.S. undersecretary of commerce David Aaron resumes bilateral trade talks in Beijing after an interruption of two months.

The U.S. House of Representatives votes, 260 to 170, to renew China's MFN status for another year.

28   Police in more than 12 cities in China raid book dealers and destroy hundreds of thousands of Falun Gong meditation manuals.

China reports conducting mobilization exercises along its southern coast across from Taiwan.

29   China issues an international appeal for the arrest of exiled Falun Gong leader Li Hongzhi on charges of causing the deaths of over 700 followers.

30   Special envoy from Taiwan to Beijing Koo Chen-fu endorses special state-to-state relations but maintains that this does not rule out eventual reunification.

The United States and China agree that Washington will pay $4.5 million to China in compensation for the victims of the NATO bombing of the Chinese embassy in Belgrade.

31   The Chinese seize a Taiwanese freighter near Matsu Island and detain the ten crew members on board on charges of smuggling.

August 1999

2   In an attempt to intimidate Taiwan, China test-fires a new Dong Feng–31 long-range ground-to-ground ballistic missile.

3   China sentences two organizers of the China Democracy Party, Zha Jianguo and Gao Hongming, to 8 and 9 years respectively in prison for subversion of state power.

In a move toward privatization, Wang Wanbin, vice-minister of the State Economic and Trade Commission, announces a program of "debt for equity" to wipe out more than $200 billion in bad debts owed by state-owned companies.

5   China Democracy Party member She Wanbao is sentenced to 12 years for taking part in the opposition party.

6   In Sichuan province, Liu Xianbin, organizer of the China Democracy Party, is sentenced to 13 years in prison for subversion of state power.

9   China rejects a visit to Hong Kong by Pope John Paul II.

13   Hong Kong human rights groups report that nine farmers have been given sentences from 2 to 6 years for organizing a protest of 1,000 demonstrators against high taxes in Hunan province in January.

The Clinton administration warns of grave consequences if China takes military action against Taiwan.

The Xinhua News Agency reports on a major policy address by Jiang Zemin on economic reform.

15   American Daja Meston, an activist on behalf of Tibet, suffers injuries while under police detention in Qinghai province. He was detained for attempting to inspect a controversial World Bank antipoverty project.

17   China grants permission for the docking of a U.S. ship in Hong Kong in September; this is the first time such permission has been granted since the NATO bombing of the Chinese embassy in Belgrade.

18   President Lee Teng-hui of Taiwan seeks protection for the island by taking part, in cooperation with the United States, in the Theater Missile Defense, a proposed regional missile-defense shield.

25   President Jiang Zemin meets with President Boris Yeltsin of Russia for direct talks prior to a five-nation summit in Kyrgyzstan to improve stability along the China-Russia border.

26   American researcher Daja Meston is flown to Hong Kong after being detained in Qinghai province for ten days.

September 1999

2   The Chinese Foreign Ministry renounces the use of nuclear weapons in the event of a conflict with Taiwan.

Prominent Uighur businesswoman Rebiya Kadeer in Xinjiang is charged with "illegally offering state secrets across the border."

7   China announces the resumption of talks regarding entry into the World Trade Organization, ending the three-month negotiation freeze that has been in effect since the NATO bombing of the Chinese embassy in Belgrade.

8   China approves the U.S. nomination of Admiral Joseph Prueher as the new U.S. ambassador to Beijing.

In a sign of improving U.S.-China relations, during a visit to Australia President Jiang Zemin refers to President Clinton as "my good friend."

9   A U.S. National Intelligence Estimate predicts that within 15 years China will be capable of aiming nuclear warhead missiles at the United States.

11 Meeting with President Clinton at the annual APEC meeting in Auckland, New Zealand, President Jiang Zemin declares an end to the three-month freeze on U.S.-China relations that was put in place after the NATO bombing of the Chinese embassy in Belgrade.

The *People's Daily* reports that People's Liberation Army naval, air, and ground forces held large joint landing exercises this month in coastal parts of Zhejiang province and the southern part of Guangdong province.

14 Military sources report that China has executed an army general and a colonel after they were found guilty of spying for Taiwan.

U.S. intelligence sources disclose that the Chinese have transferred medium-range missiles to Pakistan.

15   The State Development Planning Commission announces that China will issue more government bonds to stimulate the economy.

16   One hundred thousand criminals are arrested "to insure social stability" in preparation for the fiftieth anniversary celebrations on October 1.

        More than 5,000 coal miners block rail traffic between Beijing and Baotou in Inner Mongolia after their coal pit is declared bankrupt.

17   The Xinhua News Agency reports that conservative leader Ding Guan'gen no longer holds his position as head of the Propaganda Department of the Chinese Communist Party, a post he has held since 1992.

20   Beijing's new $1.1 billion airport terminal opens.

21   A powerful 7.6 Richter-scale earthquake shakes Taiwan, killing over 2,000.

22   At the close of a Central Committee meeting which endorses stock issues and calls for the privatization of the state sector, Vice President Hu Jintao is appointed vice chairman of the party Central Military Commission.

23   Taiwan declines an offer of earthquake aid from mainland China.

24   Speaking at the UN, Foreign Minister Tang Jiaxuan reiterates earlier charges that the United States deliberately bombed the Chinese embassy in Belgrade.

25   Courts in Guangdong province hold public rallies to sentence 818 criminals in the lead-up to the fiftieth anniversary celebrations of the People's Republic of China.

28   In Shanghai, the Fortune Global Forum hosts more than 300 leading capitalists from throughout the world to celebrate the fiftieth anniversary of the People's Republic.

October 1999

1   Celebrations marking the fiftieth anniversary of the establishment of the People's Republic China are held in Beijing.

9   Two weeks after being elected, two local village officials in Shandong province are arrested and charged with "attacking" the local government because they challenged the corrupt Communist Party leader.

14   Li Peng, chairman of the NPC, calls for more efforts to resettle those people who will be displaced by the Three Gorges Dam.

19   On the first visit by a Chinese head of state to Britain, President Jiang meets Queen Elizabeth II in London, while demonstrators outside the palace protest China's occupation of Tibet.

19   Four leaders of the Falun Gong spiritual movement, detained since July, are charged with organizing a cult, violating state secrets, and running illegal businesses.

26   Dozens of followers of the Falun Gong movement are detained, after they stage a second day of civil disobedience in Tiananmen Square.

27   Former party leader of Guangdong province from 1991 to 1998 Xie Fei dies of an undisclosed illness in Guangzhou at the age of 66.

28   The Dalai Lama meets Pope John Paul II in the Vatican.

     Speaking at a secret news conference outside of Beijing, members of the banned Falun Gong movement promise continued defiance.

29   During hearings before the Senate Foreign Relations Committee for the next U.S. ambassador to China, Adm. Joseph Prueher receives warm bipartisan support.

Dozens of followers of the banned Falun Gong spiritual movement are detained in Tiananmen Square.

30   The Standing Committee of the National People's Congress approves, by a vote of 114-0 with two abstentions, an anti-cult law, specifying jail terms of three to seven years for cultists who "disrupt public order" and ruling that leaders of religious cults may be prosecuted for murder and endangering national security.

November 1999

2   The Hong Kong government and Walt Disney announce a deal to build the first Disney theme park in China.

5   NPC chairman Li Peng issues a sharp warning about police corruption.

The UN Human Rights Commission in Geneva calls on the Chinese authorities to strengthen democratic representation in Hong Kong.

8   State Council spokesman Li Bing announces that 111 followers of the banned Falun Gong movement have been formally arrested on criminal charges.

9   Israeli officials announce that Israel is supplying China with an advanced radar system that will allow long-range surveillance.

10   U.S. Defense Department officials announce that the United States is seeking to curb Israeli arms sales to China.

At a meeting in Beijing, American and Chinese trade officials renew talks on China's entry into the World Trade Organization.

15   U.S. and Chinese negotiators agree to terms for Beijing's entry into the World Trade Organization.

16   A Chinese government spokesman denies that China bought Israeli radar.

21   China announces its first successful launching and recovery of an unmanned spacecraft.

24   A Chinese ferry sinks in waters off the city of Yantai, in Shandong province, killing some 280 people.

25   Former visiting scholar at Stanford University Hua Di is sentenced to fifteen years in prison for leaking state secrets about China's missile program.

26   New rules are announced requiring that public gatherings of over 200 people receive approval from local public security authorities.

28   Washington National Zoo giant panda, Hsing-Hsing, dies of kidney disease.

December 1999

3   The Hong Kong Court of Final Appeal rules that the Chinese government has the right to overturn the Hong Kong court's earlier decision granting residency to more than one million people from mainland China.

9   Retired admiral Joseph Prueher arrives in Beijing as the new U.S. ambassador to China.

12   Nine hundred members of the Falun Gong spiritual movement hold a public meeting in Hong Kong, after 600 followers marched and meditated in front of the offices of the Xinhua News Agency on the preceding day.

13   Scientist Wen Ho Lee pleads not guilty to charges of endangering U.S. security, but he is ordered held without bail.

15   The Hong Kong Court of Final Appeal rules that defacing the Chinese flag is a crime.

U.S. Ambassador Joseph Prueher presents his credentials to Chinese President Jiang Zemin.

16   The United States and China reach agreement that the United States will pay China $28 million in compensation for damage to the Chinese embassy in Belgrade due to the NATO bombing. In return, China will pay the United States $2.87 million for damage to the American embassy and other diplomatic buildings in China due to anti-American demonstrations.

20   The colony of Macao is handed over to Chinese sovereignty after 450 years of Portuguese rule.

24   Jiang Hua, former president of the Supreme People's court who oversaw the 1980–81 trial of the Gang of Four, dies in Hangzhou at age 93.

        In a declaration faxed to Western news bureaus in Beijing, the banned China Democracy Party ends its long silence by demanding an end to Communist Party rule.

26   Four principal followers of the outlawed Falun Gong spiritual movement are sentenced up to 18 years in prison for spreading superstition and heresies, deceiving people, and causing deaths."

30   Vietnam and China sign a land border treaty.

31   Celebrating the New Year at the Century Altar in western Beijing, President Jiang Zemin promises a "great rejuvenation of China by reuniting with Taiwan" and building a "culturally advanced and modern socialist country."

Historical Chronology of the Twentieth Century: 1895–1996

Nancy R. Hearst

1895

The Sino-Japanese War ends, and Taiwan is ceded to Japan.

1898

The Hundred Days Reform seeks to inaugurate a modern system of government and administration but is aborted in a conservative backlash. Responding to the granting of territorial concessions to Russia and Germany in northern China, Britain presses for and receives a 99-year lease on Kowloon (the New Territories), on the southern tip of the mainland across from Hong Kong Island.

1900–1901

Eight allied powers invade China to suppress the antiforeign Boxer Rebellion. Russia invades Manchuria.

1908

Empress Dowager Cixi dies.

1911

The Republican revolution, led by Sun Yat-sen, leads to the fall of the Qing dynasty.

1912

The Nationalist Party (Guomindang) is formed in Beijing.

1914

World War I erupts in Europe.

1916

The death of President Yuan Shikai marks the beginning of the "warlord era" of political instability and regional military rule.

1917

The Russian Revolution leads to the establishment of the Union of Soviet Socialist Republics.

1919

The May Fourth Movement introduces ideas of science, democracy, and patriotism. It is sparked by May 4 protests over the failure of the Treaty of Versailles (ending World War I) to return to Chinese sovereignty territories that had been held by defeated Germany.

1921

The Chinese Communist Party (CCP) is founded in Shanghai.

1923

Soviet advisors in China help to negotiate a united front between the Nationalist and Communist forces for the purpose of organizing a campaign to reunify China.

1925

Sun Yat-sen, leader of the Chinese revolution, dies at the age of 58.

1926

The National Revolutionary Forces, under the leadership of commander-in-chief Chiang Kai-shek, launch the Northern Expedition to defeat warlord forces and reunify China.

1927

The united front between the Nationalists and Communists collapses when Nationalist forces attack and execute Communist Party members and sympathizers.

The National Government is established by the Nationalist Party, with its capital in Nanjing.

1931–32

Japan occupies Manchuria and establishes the puppet state of Manchukuo.

1934–35

The CCP makes the 6,000-mile Long March from Jiangxi province to Yan'an, which becomes the new party headquarters.

1935

At the Zunyi party conference, Mao Zedong becomes the undisputed chairman of the CCP.

1936

Chiang Kai-shek is kidnapped by one of his generals in the Xi'an incident. He is not released until the Nationalist Party agrees to unite with the Communists to fight the Japanese.

1937

Japan launches a full invasion of China, forcing the government to move west to Chongqing, in Sichuan province.

1939

World War II begins in Europe.

1941

After the Japanese attack on Pearl Harbor, the United States enters World War II and works closely with the Nationalist government in China.

1945

Japan surrenders to the Allies after atomic bombs are dropped on Hiroshima and Nagasaki in August. U.S. forces in China provide support to the Nationalist army in taking the surrender of Japanese troops. Soviet troops provide assistance to the Communist forces in Manchuria.

1946–49

Civil war rages in China as the Nationalists and Communists fight for power.

1949

The People's Republic of China (PRC) is established in Beijing on October 1. Chiang Kai-shek and his Nationalist troops flee to Taiwan.

1950

The Sino-Soviet Treaty of Friendship, Alliance, and Mutual Assistance is signed. PRC plans to invade Taiwan are thwarted by the outbreak of the Korean War and by the subsequent decision of the United States to place its Seventh Fleet in the Taiwan Strait to prevent the outbreak of hostilities.

China enters the Korean War, in which it engages United States forces. An armistice is signed in 1953.

1952

Land reform is completed in China.

1954

The First National People's Congress adopts the PRC constitution. The United States signs the Mutual Defense Treaty with Taiwan.

1956–57

Uprisings in the socialist regimes of Poland and Hungary raise fears of unrest in China. In response to these events and domestic concerns, the CCP launches the Hundred Flowers campaign inviting criticism of the party. When the level of criticism exceeds expectations, an "antirightist" campaign is launched to target and purge critics of the regime.

1958–60

The Great Leap Forward leads to widespread famine, causing thirty to forty million excess deaths. Rural people's communes are established in the countryside.

1959

The Dalai Lama flees to India after a revolt in Tibet is suppressed.

1960

As relations between Nikita Khruschchev and Mao Zedong deteriorate, the Soviet Union withdraws its experts and personnel from China.

1962

China and India fight a border war over disputed territorial boundaries.

1964

China explodes its first atomic bomb in Xinjiang province.

1966

The Great Proletarian Cultural Revolution is launched, and key senior leaders, including Liu Shaoqi and Deng Xiaoping, are purged and detained. Mao mobilizes youthful Red Guards to attack revisionists and counter-revolutionaries and rid society of feudal and bourgeois cultural tendencies. The campaign rages for three years before a semblance of central order is reimposed. Cultural Revolution policies remain in effect until Mao's death in 1976.

1968

Millions of urban young people are sent to the countryside to learn through physical labor and help in rural development. The USSR invades Czechoslovakia and issues the Brezhnev Doctrine, claiming the right to interfere in the affairs of other socialist states in order to protect the international socialist cause.

1969

Border conflicts escalate on the China-USSR border. Lin Biao is named Mao Zedong's successor at the Ninth Party Congress.

1971

Defense Minister Lin Biao dies in a plane crash while attempting to flee to the Soviet Union. China takes a seat on the United Nations Security Council as Taiwan is expelled from the body.

1972

President Nixon visits China and signs the Shanghai Communiqué, acknowledging that "there is but one China, and Taiwan is part of China." Chiang Ching-kuo, son of Chiang Kai-shek, becomes the premier of the Republic of China on Taiwan.

1975

The United States withdraws its troops from Vietnam, and South Vietnam falls to the communist forces. Chiang Kai-shek dies at the age of 87 and is succeeded as president of the Republic of China by his son Chiang Ching-kuo.

1976

Zhou Enlai dies in January, and the first Tiananmen demonstrations against the radical Cultural Revolution take place during the Qingming festival in April. The Tangshan earthquake devastates north China in July. Mao Zedong dies in September, and the Gang of Four is arrested in October.

1977

Deng Xiaoping, who had been purged by radicals after Zhou Enlai's death, returns to power. Politicians, unable to form an opposition under the martial-law regime, begin to organize in large numbers as *dangwai* ("outside the party") candidates for elections in Taiwan.

1978

The Third Plenum of the Eleventh Central Committee endorses modernization and agricultural reforms.

1979

Diplomatic relations are established between the United States and China; new, informal offices are established to handle U.S.-Taiwan affairs. China sends forces into Vietnam for three weeks to "punish" Vietnam for border incursions and for its treatment of ethnic Chinese in its territory. The Democracy Wall in the Xidan district of Beijing is closed down. The U.S. security treaty with Taiwan expires at the end of the year.

1980–84

Rural reforms lead to progressive decollectivization and household farming and to the abolition of the people's communes. Town and township governments are established in their place.

1982

Prime Minister Margaret Thatcher of Great Britain visits Beijing to discuss the future status of Hong Kong.

1984

The Sino-British Joint Declaration on Hong Kong is signed, inaugurating a fifteen-year process of preparing for Hong Kong's return to Chinese rule.

The Third Plenum of the Twelfth Central Committee endorses urban reforms.

1985

Mikhail Gorbachev comes to power in the Soviet Union.

1986

Student demonstrations in Hefei spread to Shanghai, Beijing, and other cities. The Democratic Progressive Party of Taiwan holds its first party congress, defying the martial-law ban on organized political opposition to the Nationalist Party.

1987

Chinese Communist Party general secretary Hu Yaobang is blamed for the student demonstrations and forced to step down. An antibourgeois liberalization campaign is launched to dampen pressures for political reform and warn against further protests.

After Taiwan's legislature passes a new national security law, President Chiang Ching-kuo announces the lifting of the four-decades-long regime of martial law. The Democratic Progressive Party organizes large demonstrations to protest the new national security law.

1988

Lee Teng-hui, a native Taiwanese, becomes the president of the Republic of China after the death of Chiang Ching-kuo.

1989

The death of Hu Yaobang leads to massive demonstrations, martial law in Beijing, and the June 4 Tiananmen massacre. General Secretary Zhao Ziyang is dismissed from office and replaced by Jiang Zemin of Shanghai. In the wake of Gorbachev's reforms and his loosening of control over the Warsaw Pact countries, popular mobilizations lead to the collapse of communist regimes in Eastern Europe.

1990

Lee Teng-hui is elected to the presidency of the Republic of China on Taiwan by a vote of the members of the National Assembly.

1991

Mikhail Gorbachev survives a conservative coup in August only to be forced to resign by his liberal rival, Boris Yeltsin, in December. The USSR disintegrates as republics declare independence from the union.

1992

Deng Xiaoping travels to southern China to reinvigorate the economic reforms; the Fourteenth Party Congress endorses the concept of a socialist market economy.

1995–96

China test-fires missiles off the coast of Taiwan in the lead-up to the first democratic election for president of Taiwan.

1996

Taiwan holds its first direct election for president. Lee Teng-hui wins with 54 percent of the vote.

Glossary

Asset Management Corporation. A corporation established to purchase nonperforming loans from state banks, take control of and restructure the debtor companies, and sell them off. Similar to the Resolution Trust Company established to clean up insolvent savings and loan institutions in the United States during the 1980s.

China Consumer Association. A national organization for consumer protection. Established in 1984, it grew by the late 1990s into a nationwide, semiofficial organization with more than 3,000 branch associations at the provincial, municipal, and county levels. Although it is registered as a mass organization, the association is actually a de facto government agency, as its leaders are government officials and its funding derives from government sources.

Containment. The essential strategic policy of the United States during the Cold War, usually linked to George Kennan, who was head of the State Department's Policy Planning Staff in the late 1940s.

Cox Report. The common name for the report of a major congressional investigation of Chinese spying in U.S. nuclear laboratories, released in April 1999. The report is named for Congressman Christopher Cox, who oversaw the Select Committee investigation.

Critical methodologies. This term is used broadly here to encompass a number of schools of thought that have grown up in the West and have been taken up recently by many well-known Chinese intellectuals. These schools of thought include postmodernism, deconstructionist interpretations, postcolonialism, and orientalism, among others, all of which seek in one way or another to "unmask" the power relations that exist behind seemingly benign facades, including capitalist relations, the relations between Western nations and the colonial and postcolonial world, and so forth.

Cultural Revolution generation. This generation includes those who grew up or had their formative years during the decade of the Cultural Revolution (1966–76). Most of them were in school (including elementary school, high school, and college) at the beginning of the Cultural Revolution in 1966. Many became idealistic and fanatic Red Guards who were enthusiastic about making earthshaking changes and pursuing social engineering. A majority of them were sent to the countryside and therefore experienced much hardship, both physically and mentally.

Democratic Progressive Party (DPP). Taiwan's major opposition party. The DPP was established in 1986, defying a martial-law ban on such political associations that had been in place for thirty-five years. With the lifting of martial law in July 1987, the DPP gradually grew into a serious political competitor for the Guomindang. The DPP has been a strong advocate of Taiwanese independence.

Dependency ratio. Dependency ratios are calculated in several different ways. A population's overall dependency ratio is expressed as the number of elderly dependents and children (under working age) per 100 working-age adults. Separate ratios may also be calculated for old-age dependency (the number of elderly per 100 working-age adults) and for child dependency (the number of children under working age per 100 adults).

Dual-track system. The reform system dominant in China during the 1980s, under which public enterprises operated both under the plan and on the market. After fulfilling their plan and selling that output at government-set prices, state-owned and collective enterprises were allowed to sell additional output at market prices, which were usually higher.

Emancipation of the mind. A slogan raised by Deng Xiaoping when he introduced his reform program in 1978. In general, it has implied the need to break away from the overly rigid, hierarchical, and bureaucratic ways of doing things associated with the prereform era (although the Cultural Revolution of 1966–76 was also intended to break with conventions, albeit in a very different way). In general, "emancipating the mind" has stood in tension with other values, such as "upholding the four cardinal principles" (Marxism-Leninism-Mao Zedong Thought, the Socialist Road, the People's Democratic Dictatorship, and the Chinese Communist Party).

Enlightenment tradition. During the New Culture Movement (1915–20), Chinese intellectuals called for a remaking of China's tradition, particularly an emancipation from restrictive ways of thought rooted in the Confucian tradition and restrictive modes of behavior exemplified in family relations and political hierarchy. Drawing inspiration from the European example, Chinese intellectuals called for introducing "Mr. Science" and "Mr. Democracy" into China to reconstruct their culture. Since that period, this enlightenment tradition, which is often conflated with the May 4 Movement of 1919, has set an agenda and provided inspiration for the liberal intelligentsia.

Enmeshment. The essential world economic strategy of the United States in the post-World War II period, with roots in the open door policy enunciated in 1899–1900 and in Woodrow Wilson's policies during and after World War I. The current policy of "engagement" is an elaboration of the enmeshment strategy.

Entrepreneurial class. Entrepreneurs in a market economy are characteristically engaged in risk-taking businesses. In the Chinese context, an entrepreneur is defined as a manager and/or owner of private property—a person who has managed to come to possess property either through capitalization of personal income or through the private operation of a collective, public, or joint-venture enterprise. The rapid development of rural industries, urban private enterprises, and foreign trade has produced this new social class in the PRC.

Falun Gong. The Buddhist Law Society, led by spiritual leader Li Hong Zhi (who resides in New York). This society, which combines traditional *qigong* exercises with spiritual beliefs, was banned in July 1999 after thousands of followers engaged in peaceful protests in Beijing and other cities.

Family modernization. Following the national slogan of achieving the "four modernizations" by the year 2000 (in agriculture, industry, science and technology, and national defense), this term refers to a type of family-level modernization based on the possession of household appliances and other valuable consumer goods by a given household. It is not uncommon that, in order to achieve the goal of family modernization, the members of a household make contributions to a common budget pool and use the fund to purchase big consumer items, which are not affordable otherwise.

Floating population. The portion of China's population that migrates temporarily in search of work, which currently numbers 100 million or more. Most (although not all) in the floating population move from rural to urban areas. They are also known as "transients" or "migrants."

Gender. A system of cultural beliefs about manhood, manliness, and and about womanhood, womanliness, and femininity.

Getihu. Literally meaning "individual household," this term is used to label those individuals who started small-scale private businesses during the 1980s, such as vendors, repairpersons, and traveling merchants. As many of the *getihu* were marginalized people during the prereform period, their instant success in private business caused social critique and public envy.

Guandao. This reform-era term, which literally means "official turnaround," was coined to refer to the process by which officials take advantage of China's two-track pricing system in order to reap huge profits.

Guomindang (Nationalist Party). The governing party in Taiwan. Organized in 1912 by Sun Yat-sen, the Guomindang became a major political force in China during the first half of the twentieth century. In 1928, Chiang Kai-shek became chairman of the Guomindang and head of the Republican government in Nanjing, and he remained the leader throughout the civil war. In 1949, the Nationalist government on the mainland collapsed; Chiang and his followers retreated to Taiwan.

Imagined cosmopolitanism. Coined by anthropologist Louisa Schein, this term denotes a process in which people imagine themselves as participants in a global culture through their consumption of foreign objects and media and through their fantasies of the mobility made possible by embracing transnational culture.

Jiang Zemin. The former mayor and party secretary of Shanghai who replaced Zhao Ziyang as general secretary of the Chinese Communist Party in June 1989 in the aftermath of Tiananmen. Later that year, he took over from Deng Xiaoping as chairman of the party's Central Military Commission, and in March 1993, he became the president of the People's Republic of China. Deng designated Jiang as his choice to lead the party and nation after his death.

Lee Teng-hui. The first Taiwanese president of the Republic of China as well as the first directly elected president in Chinese history. Lee was selected by President Chiang Ching-kuo of Taiwan as vice president in 1984. When Chiang died in 1988, Lee assumed the presidency and pushed ahead with cross-strait contacts as well as with democratizing reforms begun under Chiang. Although as head of the Guomindang he publicly advocates reunification with China someday, he has worked hard to broaden Taiwan's international presence and has co-opted much of the Democratic Progressive Party's political platform.

Little emperors. The epithet given to only children who are doted on by their parents and grandparents. The first generation of "little emperors," born since the one-child policy was inaugurated in 1979, is now coming into adulthood.

Marketization of power. A term used by some critics of China's reform to refer to a phenomenon that has occurred during the reform era. Government officials who controlled resources under the planned economy took advantage of their political power and converted state money into personal wealth. Therefore, the benefits of the so-called market reform have been allocated not by "impersonal market forces" but by corruption and favoritism. Critics argue that the post-Communist economic transition has led not to expansion of the middle class and prosperity in society but to income disparity and the rise of a kind of mafia.

Nationalism. A system of cultural beliefs about a certain kind of social grouping—the "nation-state"—and the sense of identity that emerges among those who feel that they belong to it. Nationalism is a cultural concept in which it is believed that nations are and should be the fundamental political units in global politics.

Neo-Malthusianism. A modernized version of the late eighteenth- and early nineteenth-century arguments of Thomas Robert Malthus. Those who subscribe to this view are very pessimistic about the impact of population growth on poverty and development, and they advocate strong private and governmental efforts to slow population growth.

One country, two systems. The formula introduced by Deng Xiaoping in 1983 to deal with the issue of Taiwan's reunification with China.

Deng suggested that Taiwan accept the status of a special administrative region under the authority of the central government in Beijing. Beijing would retain control of foreign relations and military affairs but would otherwise grant Taiwan autonomy. As the retrocession of Hong Kong approached, Deng decided to apply "one country, two systems" to the British colony, hoping that a smooth transition would expedite agreement with Taipei. However, the formula was rejected by Taiwan even though Beijing offered to enhance the package of rights granted to Hong Kong.

Public intellectuals. Scholars and educated people who participate in public affairs and social movements. They often express their views on government policies and present intellectual opinions on social, political, economic, and philosophical issues.

Qigong. A form of physical and mental exercise that is supposed to enhance the flow of *qi* (inner energy or spirit) in a person, thereby enhancing health and longevity. It may or may not be combined with various spiritual messages.

Sex ratio. The sex ratio of a given population is expressed as the number of males for each 100 females. A sex ratio may be calculated for the entire population of a territory or for a particular age cohort within that population (for example, children under age four). The sex ratio at birth refers to the number of infant males for each 100 infant females. In a normal population, the sex ratio at birth is usually about 105 males for every 100 females.

Shock therapy. A term referring to the process of rapid and total privatization of state-owned assets, along with the creation of market institutions to replace the institutions of the socialist planned economy. Critics of shock therapy advocate a more gradual approach to institutional change.

State-owned enterprises (SOEs). State-owned enterprises are owned by the government at any level, including national, provincial, and county. There are over 100,00 SOEs in China, many of which are inefficient and run budgetary deficits.

Subject. A person who controls the terms of his own self-identity. His consciousness of himself, or his subjectivity, is created through contrasting himself with objectified "others" who are perceived to be separate and different. Feminists have used this distinction to ana-

lyze the ways in which males create their own identity (subjectivity) by contrasting themselves with (objectifying) women.

Subjectivity/subject-position. The point of view of a person who is in
a position to define himself against objectified "others" (who do not
control the representations of themselves to the same degree). The
male subject-position is one in which events and people are perceived through the eyes of, for example, a father, a son, a husband,
or some other typically male status.

Taiwan Relations Act. After President Jimmy Carter severed diplomatic relations with the Republic of China government on Taiwan,
his administration submitted a bill to Congress designed to facilitate
continued economic, legal, and cultural relations. Members of
Congress, however, believed the bill to be too weak and transformed
it into the Taiwan Relations Act, which was passed in April 1979.
The most important changes included pledges to sell defensive arms
to Taiwan and to take any PRC threat to Taiwan's security as a matter of "grave concern."

Tidal wave of consumption. A term used frequently by Chinese
scholars in the 1980s and early 1990s to refer to a repeated pattern
of brief, intense surges in consumer demand for particular goods,
such as color television sets, refrigerators, and washing machines.
With the emergence of a buyer's market in the mid-1990s, consumption has become more stratified, and the tidal-wave effect has
subsided.

Township and village enterprises (TVEs). TVEs are generally collectively owned enterprises at the lowest levels of government administration, the township and village. Although they are collectively
owned, many have close ties, including ownership ties, with their
respective governments. In recent years, an increasing number are
only nominally collectively owned, being privately owned in reality.

Transnational. A term for the global culture that transcends national
boundaries, carried by flows of people, capital, and information that
have rapidly accelerated since the end of the Cold War.

Tung Chee-hwa. The chief executive of the Hong Kong Special
Administrative Region. Tung was chosen by Beijing officials to lead
Hong Kong as it prepared for the 1997 transition from British to
Chinese rule.

World Trade Organization (WTO). Established on January 1, 1995, as the successor to the General Agreement on Tariffs and Trade (GATT), a multilateral agreement based on the principles of free trade and the market economy formed at the 1944 Bretton Woods conference. The WTO is somewhat more expansive in scope than its predecessor, but like the GATT, its basic purpose is to promote nondiscriminatory trade by reducing import tariffs and other barriers to global commerce. It also provides a forum for the resolution of trade disputes. To join the WTO, a country must agree to abide by its free-trade and free-market principles, be certified as doing so by the WTO, and be approved by two-thirds of the existing members.

Xiagang. A Chinese euphemism that literally means "off post" and refers to people who have lost their jobs (posts) as a result of structural changes in the Chinese economy (particularly the closing of inefficient state-owned enterprises). These "off post" workers may continue to receive some portion of their salaries, but they are actually part of China's huge unemployed labor force.

Xiahai. A new Chinese term that literally means "jumping into the sea" and refers to those state employees and intellectuals who quit secure jobs in order to engage in private and risk-taking business ventures with the hope of earning more money.

Zhao Ziyang. The premier of the State Council from 1980 until his appointment in 1987 as general secretary of the Chinese Communist Party. A trusted colleague and protégé of Deng Xiaoping, Zhao built a reputation at home and abroad as a capable technocratic leader and a chief architect of the post-Mao reform program. He fell from power during the democracy demonstrations in the spring of 1989 for being too sympathetic to the students and opposing the use of force to suppress the protests.

Zhu Rongji. A member of the Chinese Communist Party Politburo Standing Committee and the premier of the PRC. An electrical engineer and former mayor of Shanghai, Zhu has earned a reputation as a strong proponent of market reforms and a skillful statesman.

Suggestions for Further Reading

Historical Echoes and Chinese Politics: Can China Leave the Twentieth Century Behind?

Gilley, Bruce. *Tiger on the Brink: Jiang Zemin and China's New Elite.* Berkeley: University of California Press, 1998.

Oi, Jean. *Rural China Takes Off: Institutional Foundations of Economic Reform.* Berkeley: University of California Press, 1999.

Steinfeld, Edward S. *Forging Reform in China: The Fate of State-Owned Industry.* Cambridge: Cambridge University Press, 1998.

Wank, David L. *Commodifying Communism: Business, Trust, and Politics in a Chinese City.* Cambridge: Cambridge University Press, 1999.

Zheng Yongnian. *Discovering Chinese Nationalism in China: Modernization, Identity, and International Relations.* Cambridge: Cambridge University Press, 1999.

The Chinese Economy: Fifty Years into the Transformation

Chen Baizhu, Kim Dietrich, and Yi Feng, eds. *China's Financial Market Reform: Problems, Progress and Perspective.* Boulder, CO: Westview Press, 1999.

Lardy, Nicholas. *China's Unfinished Economic Revolution.* Washington, DC: Brookings Institution, 1998.

Lu Xiaobo and Elizabeth Perry, eds. *Danwei: The Changing Chinese Workplace in Historical and Comparative Perspective.* Armonk, NY: M.E. Sharpe, 1997.

Rosen, Daniel. *Behind the Open Door: Foreign Enterprises in the Chinese Marketplace.* Washington, DC: Institute for International Relations, 1999.

Solinger, Dorothy. *Contesting Citizenship in Urban China: Peasant Migrants, the State, and the Logic of the Market.* Berkeley: University of California Press, 1999.

Power, Patronage, and Protest in Rural China

Chan, Anita, Richard Madsen, and Jonathan Unger. *Chen Village under Mao and Deng.* Berkeley: University of California Press, 1992.

Gao Mobo. *Gao Village: Rural Life in Modern China.* Honolulu: University of Hawaii Press, 1999.

Goldman, Merle, and Roderick MacFarquhar, eds. *The Paradox of China's Post-Mao Reforms*, pp. 129–45, 197–219. Cambridge: Harvard University Press, 1999.

O'Brien, Kevin J., and Lianjiang Li. "Selective Policy Implementation in Rural China." *Comparative Politics*, vol. 31, no. 2 (January 1999).

Oi, Jean. "Economic Development, Stability and Democratic Village Self-governance." In *China Review 1996*, ed. Maurice Brosseau, Suzanne Pepper, and Tsang Shu-ki. Hong Kong: Chinese University Press, 1996.

Ruf, Gregory. *Cadres and Kin: Making a Socialist Village in West China, 1921–1991.* Stanford: Stanford University Press, 1998.

Unger, Jonathan, and Anita Chan. "Inheritors of the Boom: Private Enterprise and the Role of Local Government in a Rural South China Township." *The China Journal*, no. 42 (July 1999).

Promises and Pitfalls of Reform:
New Thinking in Post-Deng China

Chen Feng. "An Unfinished Battle in China: The Leftist Criticism of the Reform and the Third Thought Emancipation." *The China Quarterly*, no. 158 (June 1999).

He Qinglian. *Zhongguo de xianjing* (China's pitfall). Hong Kong: Mingjing chubanshe, 1998. The edition published in mainland China is entitled *Xiandaihua de xianjing: Dangdai Zhongguo de jingji shehui wenti* (Pitfalls of modernization: Economic and social problems of contemporary China). Beijing: Jinri Zhongguo chubanshe, 1998.

Hu Angang. *Zhongguo fazhan qianjing* (Prospects for China's development). Hangzhou: Zhejiang renmin chubanshe, 1999.

Li Cheng. *Rediscovering China: Dynamics and Dilemmas of Reform.* Lanham, MD: Rowman and Littlefield, 1997.

Liu Binyan and Perry Link. "A Great Leap Backward?" *New York Review of Books*, vol. 45, no. 15 (October 8, 1998).

The Shape of Society: The Changing Demography of Development

Banister, Judith. *China's Changing Population.* Stanford: Stanford University Press, 1987.

Davin, Delia. *Internal Migration in Contemporary China.* New York: St. Martin's Press, 1999.

Eberstadt, Nicholas. "Asia Tomorrow, Gray and Male." *The National Interest*, 53 (Fall 1998).

Goldstein, Alice, and Wang Feng. *China: The Many Facets of Demographic Change.* Boulder, CO: Westview Press, 1996.

Johnson, Kay, Huang Banghan, and Wang Liyao. "Infant Abandonment and Adoption in China." *Population and Development Review*, 24 (September 1998).

Solinger, Dorothy. "China's Floating Population." In *The Paradox of China's Post-Mao Reforms*, ed. Merle Goldman and Roderick MacFarquhar. Cambridge: Harvard University Press, 1999.

Consumerism: A Revolutionary Change in Chinese Society

Chao, Linda, and Ramon Myers. "China's Consumer Revolution: The 1990s and Beyond." *Journal of Contemporary China*, vol. 7, no. 18 (1998).

Davis, Deborah, ed. *Consumer Revolution in Urban China.* Berkeley: University of California Press, 2000.

Edgel, Stephen, Kevin Hetherington, and Alan Warde, eds. *Consumption Matters: The Production and Experience of Consumption.* Oxford: Blackwell Publishers, 1996.

Hooper, Beverly. "From Mao to Market: Empowering the Chinese Consumer." *Howard Asian Pacific Review*, vol. 2, no. 2 (1998).

Watson, James L., ed. *Golden Arches East: McDonald's in East Asia.* Stanford: Stanford University Press, 1997.

Zhao Bin. "Consumerism, Confucianism, Communism: Making Sense of China Today." *The New Left*, no. 222 (1997).

Gender and Nationalism in China at the Turn of the Millennium

Brownell, Susan. *Training the Body for China: Sports in the Moral Order of the People's Republic.* Chicago: University of Chicago Press, 1995.

Schein, Louisa. *Minority Rules: The Miao and the Feminine in China's Cultural Politics.* Durham, NC: Duke University Press, 2000.

Unger, Jonathan, ed. *Chinese Nationalism.* Armonk, NY: M.E. Sharpe, 1996.

Wasserstrom, Jeffrey N. "Student Protests in Fin-de-Siecle China." *New Left Review,* no. 237 (September–October 1999).

Yang, Mayfair Mei-hui. "From Gender Erasure to Gender Difference: State Feminism, Consumer Sexuality, and Women's Public Sphere in China." In *Spaces of Their Own: Women's Public Sphere in Transnational China*, ed. Mayfair Mei-hui Yang. Minneapolis: University of Minnesota Press, 1999.

Zito, Angela, and Tani Barlow, eds. *Body, Subject and Power in China.* Chicago: University of Chicago Press, 1994.

Dangerous Liaisons: China, Taiwan, Hong Kong, and the United States at the Turn of the Century

Clough, Ralph N. *Cooperation or Conflict in the Taiwan Strait?* New York: Rowman and Littlefield, 1999.

———. *Reaching across the Taiwan Strait.* Boulder, CO: Westview Press, 1993.

Cohen, Warren I. *America's Response to China*, 4th ed. New York: Columbia University Press, 2000.

Mann, James. *About Face: A History of America's Curious Relationship with China, from Nixon to Clinton.* New York: Knopf, 1999.

Roy, Denny. *China's Foreign Relations.* New York: Rowman and Littlefield, 1998.

Tucker, Nancy Bernkopf. *Taiwan, Hong Kong and the United States, 1945–1992: Uncertain Friendships.* New York: Twayne/Macmillan, 1994.

The More Things Change, the More They Remain the Same: The World, the United States, and the People's Republic of China, 1949–1999

Chang, Iris. *Thread of the Silkworm.* New York: Basic Books, 1995.

Cumings, Bruce. *Parallax Visions: Making Sense of American-East Asian Relations at the End of the Century.* Durham, NC: Duke University Press, 1999.

Kim, Samuel. *China, the United Nations, and World Order.* Princeton: Princeton University Press, 1978.

Nathan, Andrew J., and Robert S. Ross. *The Great Wall and the Empty Fortress: China's Search for Security.* New York: W.W. Norton, 1997.

Schell, Orville, and David Shambaugh, eds. *The China Reader: The Reform Era.* New York: Vintage Books, 1999.

Shinn, James, ed. *Weaving the Net: Conditional Engagement with China.* New York: Council on Foreign Relations, 1996.

Selected Chinese Language Readings

Cui Zhiyuan, *Di'erci sixiang jiefang* (The second thought liberation). Hong Kong: Oxford University Press, 1997.

Huang Weiting and Li Fan, *Dangdai Zhongguo de xiaofei zhi mi* (The riddle of consumption in contemporary China). Beijing: Zhongguo shangye chubanshe, 1990.

Ling Zhijun and Ma Licheng, *Huhan: Dangjin Zhongguo de wuzhong shengyin* (Voices: Five voices in present China). Guangzhou: Guangzhou chubanshe, 1999.

Ling Zhijun and Ma Licheng, *Jiaofeng: Dangdai Zhongguo disanci sixiang jiefang shilu* (Crossed Swords: The third thought liberation campaign in contemporary China). Beijing: Jinri Zhongguo chubanshe, 1998.

Liu Zhifeng, ed., *Daode Zhongguo: Dangdai Zhongguo daode lunli de shenchong yousi* (Moral China: Deep concerns and thinking about ethics and morality in today's China). Beijing: Zhongguo shehui kexue chubanshe, 1999.

Luo yi ning ge'er (pseud.), *Disanzhi yanjing kan Zhongguo* (Looking at China through a third eye), trans. Wang Shan. Taiyuan: Shanxi Publishing House, 1994.

Song Qiang, Zhang Zangzang, and Qiao Bian, *Zhongguo keyi shuobu* (China can say no). Beijing: Zhonghua gongshang lianhe chubanshe, 1996.

Wang Hui and Yu Guoliang, eds., *90 niandai de 'houxue' lunzheng* (Post-ism in the nineties). Hong Kong: Chinese University Press, 1998.

Wen Lin, and Hai Tao, eds. *Zhongguo xinyidai sixiangjia zibai* (Recollections of China's new generation of thinkers). Beijing: Jiuzhou tushu chubanshe, 1998.

Xu Jilin. "Qimeng de mingyun: Ershinian lai de Zhongguo sixiang jie" (The fate of enlightenment: The Chinese intelligentsia during the past two decades). *Ershiyi shiji* (Twenty-First Century), no. 50 (December 12, 1998).

About the Contributors

Susan Brownell is associate professor of Anthropology at the University of Missouri, St. Louis. She studied sport theory at the Beijing University of Physical Education (1987–88), and based on these experiences wrote *Training the Body for China: Sports in the Moral Order of the People's Republic* (1995). She has acted as an expert and consultant for numerous television and print reports on Chinese sports. Her current research focuses on cosmetic surgery, fashion models, and the changing politics of appearance in China.

Bruce Cumings is the Norman and Edna Freehling Professor of International History and East Asian Political Economy, University of Chicago. He is the author or coauthor of eight books, including a 2-volume study, *The Origins of the Korean War* (1981, 1990); *War and Television* (1992); *Korea's Place in the Sun: A Modern History* (1997); and most recently, *Parallax Visions: Making Sense of American-East Asian Relations at the End of the Century* (1999). He also served as the Principal Historical Consultant for the Thames Television/PBS 6-hour documentary, *Korea: The Unknown War*.

Joseph Fewsmith is associate professor of Internaional Relations at Boston University. He is the author of *Party, State and Local Elite in Republican China: Merchant Organizations and Politics in Shanghai, 1890–1930* (1985) and *The Dilemmas of Reform in China: Political Conflict and Economic Debate* (1994). He is currently working on a book about Chinese politics since 1989.

Nancy R. Hearst is librarian at the Fairbank Center for East Asian Research, Harvard University.

Cheng Li, a native of Shanghai, is professor of Government at Hamilton College. He is the author of *Rediscovering China: Dynamics and Dilemmas of Reform* (1997), which was based on two years of research in Shanghai as a fellow of the U.S.-based Institute of Current

World Affairs. His forthcoming volume, *China's Leaders: The New Generation*, focuses on China's technocratic leaders and their domestic and foreign policies. Li's academic writings have appeared in numerous journals and edited volumes, and he is a frequent television and radio commentator on Chinese affairs.

Barry Naughton, an economist who specializes in China's transitional economy, is the So Kuanlok Professor of Chinese and International Affairs at the Graduate School of International Relations and Pacific Studies of the University of California at San Diego. His study of Chinese economic reform, *Growing Out of the Plan: Chinese Economic Reform, 1978–1993* (1995) won the Masayoshi Ohira Memorial Prize. His most recent book is the edited volume *The China Circle: Economics and Technology in the PRC, Taiwan, and Hong Kong* (1997). Naughton is currently engaged in a study of provincial economic growth in the People's Republic of China.

Nancy Bernkopf Tucker is professor of History at Georgetown University and the Georgetown School of Foreign Service. She is the author of *Patterns in the Dust: Chinese-American Relations and the Recognition Controversy, 1949–1950* (1983) and *Taiwan, Hong Kong and the United States, 1945–1992: Uncertain Friendships* (1994); the author and editor of the forthcoming *China Confidential* (2000); and coeditor of *Lyndon Johnson Confronts the World* (1994). She has contributed articles to numerous journals and many edited volumes.

Jonathan Unger is a sociologist who has published a dozen books about China. He is director of the Contemporary China Centre at the Australian National University and coeditor of *The China Journal*. His writings on China range broadly, examining China's education system and student attitudes, rural social change, urban family structures, the Chinese bureaucracy, social stratification, ethnic minorities, nationalism, and the politics of economic development. He is in the midst of writing a book about China's countryside. His previous work in this subject area includes, as coauthor, *Chen Village Under Mao and Deng* (1992).

Tyrene White is associate professor of Political Science at Swarthmore College, and coeditor, with Christina Gilmartin, Gail Hershatter, and Lisa Rofel, of *Engendering China: Women, Culture,* *and the State* (1994). Her articles on population policy, rural reform, and village democracy in China have appeared in a variety of journals and edited volumes.

Yunxiang Yan is Associate Professor of Anthropology at the University of California, Los Angeles. He is the author of *The Flow of Gifts: Reciprocity and Social Networks in a Chinese Village* (1996) and has published articles on family and kinship, the political economy of rural reforms, and urban consumption. He is currently writing a book on the transformation of private life in rural north China during the past five decades.

Index